901.92082

St.9   v. 3   72070

DATE DUE			

GAYLORD M-2   PRINTED IN U.S.A.

WITHDRAWN

STUDIES IN MEDIEVAL AND RENAISSANCE HISTORY

Volume V

STUDIES IN
Medieval and Renaissance
History

Volume V

Edited by
W<small>ILLIAM</small> M. B<small>OWSKY</small>
University of California, Davis

UNIVERSITY OF NEBRASKA PRESS · LINCOLN
1968

Publishers on the Plains

UNP

Copyright © 1968 by the University of Nebraska Press

First printing: July, 1968
Second printing: July, 1969

Library of Congress Catalog Card Number 63–22098

Manufactured in the United States of America

CONTENTS

INTRODUCTION

Studies in Medieval and Renaissance History is a series of annual volumes designed for original major articles and short monographs in all fields of medieval and renaissance history.

The first impetus for the creation of this series came from a belief that there is a need for a scholarly publication to accommodate the longer study whose compass is too large for it to be included regularly in existing media but too small for it to appear in book form. The editors will consider articles in all areas of history from approximately the fourth through the sixteenth centuries—economic, social and demographic, political, intellectual and cultural, and studies that do not fit neatly into a single traditional category of historical investigation.

The editorial board hopes that the *Studies* creates another link between the work of medieval and renaissance scholarship; for many articles pertinent to both disciplines appear in publications consulted almost exclusively by either medieval or renaissance scholars.

While this series is devoted primarily to the publication of major studies it contains occasional bibliographic essays and briefer articles dealing with unpublished archival or manuscript resources. The *Studies* also makes available in translation original articles by scholars who do not write in English.

Studies in Medieval and Renaissance History is not the official organ of any association or institution. Publication in the series is open to all historians whose research falls within its scope and fields of interest.

A STUDY OF MEDIEVAL QUEENSHIP: CAPETIAN FRANCE 987–1237

Marion F. Facinger

The City College
of
The City University of New York

ABBREVIATIONS

BEHE	Bibliotèque de l'école des hautes études
CTEH	Collection des textes pour servir à l'étude et l'enseignment de l'histoire
Mansi	Giovanni D. Mansi (ed.), *Sacrorum conciliorum nova et amplissima collectio*
Migne, *PL*	J. P. Migne (ed.), *Patrologiae cursus completus. Series latina*
MGH SS	*Monumenta Germaniae Historica Scriptorum*
RHGF	*Recueil des historiens des Gaules et de la France*
RS	Chronicles and Memorials of Great Britain and Ireland during the Middle Ages. Rolls Series

A STUDY OF MEDIEVAL QUEENSHIP:
CAPETIAN FRANCE
987–1237

INTRODUCTION

Queens have received but casual and sporadic attention from students of the middle ages. Surely an investigation of this member of the royal dyad has something to contribute to our general knowledge about medieval life, and hopefully, some specific information about the development of the crown in the country chosen for study—France. Although there exist a few scattered articles and biographies of some of the more colorful French queens, there is no unified study of queens over any period of time, nor has there been any attempt to analyze queenship as an office. The present essay addresses itself to this lacuna. For the formative years of the Capetian monarchy, from Hugh Capet's ascent in 987 to the death of Philip Augustus in 1223, information as complete as the sources permitted was assembled for each queen who at some time shared the throne. The resulting thirteen miniature biographies were then searched for the public aspects of the queens' lives which would indicate an official position in the government. The assumption was that somewhere behind the transitory, behind the multiple roles played by the individual personalities, there lay an office with prerogatives, norms, limits within which each incumbent functioned.

The queen of France always occupied a dependent position, for by definition she was either wife, mother, or widow of a king. She became a queen at the imposition of a crown followed by a special benediction, and she kept the quality of royalty imparted by this ceremony until her death. During the years when her husband was alive she bore children, managed the royal household, traveled with the court from castle to castle within the domain, appeared beside the king on ceremonial occasions, and engaged in a wide range of charitable activities. Her years of widowhood were usually spent upon her dower lands although she was found upon occasion at court assisting her son, or even as regent of the kingdom; in addition she might sometimes remarry or go to the opposite extreme and retire into a convent. In both phases of her career—queen regnant or

3

dowager queen—she could and usually did play a part in the public affairs of the realm. The difficulty has been discriminating what was private and what was public during a period when such distinctions were not clearly made by the government itself.

The principle sources used for assessing the public functions of the queen have been the royal acts collected for each reign. In the absence of any financial records or more detailed administrative minutes for these years, I have assumed that royal charters are most representative of how the Capetian monarchy functioned and that they give the most reliable indication of the queen's participation in the business of governing. Other source materials—annals, letters, chronicles, cartularies, biographies, histories, obituaries—have also been utilized; but the attempt to glean information about women in an age that belonged to men and from works written by men, usually clerics whose antifeminism was highly developed, was frequently disappointing. Such sources were, of course, indispensable for the vital statistics of each queen, but it was the rare medieval reporter who made notes of the queen's day to day activities in the affairs of government. All too often, if her actions created no scandal or outraged no monkish mores, they were unrecorded leaving both her life and role shrouded in silence.

Despite the paucity and opacity of the evidence, it has been possible to create a generalized profile of the career of the queen for the early Capetian period and evaluate its significance as one of the royal institutions which facilitated the rise to power of the monarchy which welded a congeries of feudal states into territorial France. The attempt has been made to avoid a static concept of queenship, as throughout the period under consideration changes occurred in the role as well as the office. The dimensions of the office have been traced from the tenth century, when the queen was the king's "partner" in governing, to the fullest expansion of the office in the early twelfth century; and then its gradual diminution has been followed to the beginning of the thirteenth century, when the queen vanished from the political arena. The changes have been related to the institutional developments and the changing social milieu of the period, for as the power and prestige of the crown increased and as the business and structure of the government expanded, the queen's position within this complex was weakened. The intent has been to show that this process was a logical development due principally to impersonal forces, political and social, rather than to individual actions and caprices.

The analysis of the office opens with a consideration of factors influencing the king's choice of a wife and a discussion of the ritual which transformed her into a queen. It then proceeds to an examination of the two public roles which each incumbent played—queen regnant (the years when she shared the throne with her husband) and dowager queen (her years of widowhood). The changes observed over time in the queen's public actions are then used to define and evaluate the office itself. Before proceeding, however, with this anatomy of queenship, a brief discussion of the queens themselves is appropriate.

THE EARLY CAPETIAN QUEENS

Most of the queens of the early Capetian dynasty are but shadowy personalities, for there exists no contemporary *vita reginae* for any of these thirteen women. There is no description of their physical characteristics in the extant sources—if described at all, they are always called beautiful, at best an ambiguous term when applied so automatically. Any attempt to give flesh to the stereotype must necessarily rest on accidental and indirect evidence. Of the four queens who span the reigns of Hugh and Robert II—Adelaide, Susanna, Bertha, and Constance—only Robert's third wife, Constance of Arles, assumes individuality within the royal frieze.

The portrait of Constance (1005–1032) which can be constructed from incidental references to her by men who were writing about Robert[1] is that of a vivid and forceful personality. Coming north to the Capetian domain from Arles she brought novelty in manners, mores, fashions—duly noted and castigated. Thrust unwittingly into a domestic triangle—for Robert had reluctantly separated from Constance's predecessor, Bertha of Chartres—Constance soon revealed the violent passions of which she was capable. Inflamed by jealousy and hatred of her rival, Constance contrived the murder of the leader of the Chartrian faction at court, Hugh of Beauvais, although it was her cousin Fulk Nerra of Anjou who executed the deed. Hugh's assassination was double revenge for Constance because he was also Robert's closest confidant at court. Other intimate glimpses of this queen depict a highly volatile personality given to outbursts of rage—against her husband, against unfortunate clerics befriended by Robert,

---

1. The principle sources for information about Constance are: Rodulfus Glaber, *Historiarum Sui Temporis Libri Quinque, RHGF*, X (Paris, 1874); *Chroniques des Comtes d'Anjou*, ed. F. Marchegay and É. Salmon, Société de l'histoire de France (Paris, 1856–71); Aimon and André de Fleury in *Miracula Sancti Benedicti*, ed. M. de Certain, Société de l'histoire de France (Paris, 1858); and Helgaud de Fleury, *Vie de Robert le Pieux*, ed. and trans. R. H. Bautier and G. Labory, Sources d'histoire medievale, I (Paris, 1965).

against thieves, rogues, and heretics—she seems either to be threatening to or actually scratching out the eyes of all those who displeased her.[2] Nor did her need to dominate her husband stop at the merely verbal. She was instrumental in stirring up three brief rebellions; two pitted her sons against the king and the last proved to be nearly a civil war of son against son. The responsibility for the loss of the one large acquisition of the crown during this era, Burgundy, can be partially laid to Constance. Her son King Henry I was forced to cede Burgundy to his younger brother Robert, who was also Constance's favorite, before the civil war could be satisfactorily ended.[3] Headstrong, aggressive, domineering—Constance was certainly all these, but living with the saintly Robert the Pious must have been trying. To cite just one instance, Helgaud, monk of Fleury and the king's biographer, eulogizing Robert's charity, relates how Robert in order to give alms to a beggar pried out the silver inlays of a sword expressly commissioned for the king by Constance. Few women would have contained their rage at such an affront, for as told by Helgaud, Robert decided to give away the silver first and then went looking for an indigent.[4]

After Constance's death in 1032, sixty years pass before it is again possible to observe a personality behind the presence of a queen—neither Anne of Russia nor Bertha of Holland emerge as more than conventionally pious queens and dutiful wives. Although seen darkly and with much of the evidence inferential, Bertrada of Montfort (1092–1108), Philip I's second wife, leaves an image of a strong and intriguing personality.[5] A woman who could maintain her position and her personal hold over the king for some sixteen years in the face of hostility and threatened and real anathema from the church because of the illegality of her marriage must have possessed that elusive thing called charm. Although Ordericus Vitalis called this quality of Bertrada's "female cunning,"[6] the quality is nevertheless acknowledged by another of Bertrada's critics, Suger of

2. Helgaud, *Vie de Robert, passim*; Council of Orleans, Mansi, XIX (Venice, 1774), col. 380.

3. *Chroniques des Comtes d'Anjou*, p. 112.

4. Helgaud, *Vie de Robert*, p. 72.

5. The most important sources for Bertrada's affairs are: Ordericus Vitalis, *Ecclesiasticae Historia*, ed. A. Le Prevost, Société de l'histoire de France, 5 vols. (Paris, 1838–52), III; Suger, *Vie de Louis VI le Gros*, ed. and trans. H. Waquet (Paris, 1929); Yves of Chartres, *Correspondance*, ed. and trans. Jean Leclerq (Paris, 1949). The long struggle between the royal couple and the church is recorded in the accounts of the Councils of Autun, of Clermont, of Nîmes, of Poitiers, and of Paris in Mansi, XX (Venice, 1774). Rome never legitimated the marriage of Bertrada and Philip, and yet it was accepted within France, and Bertrada was acknowledged as queen.

6. Ordericus Vitalis, III, 388.

Saint-Denis. He has described the spell she was able to cast over her former husband, the man she had deserted in order to elope with Philip, in the following words: "[Fulk of Anjou] . . . respected her as though she were [still] his wife; seated at her feet as if enchanted, he bowed to all her wishes." [7] Rather than the nagging, domineering woman who fought the king every inch of the way for what she wanted as Queen Constance seems to have been, we glimpse in Bertrada a clever woman who used her beauty, her femininity, her charm, and her personal influence over the king to further her ambitions. She was accused of extravagances, simony, nepotism, and even of plotting against the legitimate heir to the throne— all seemingly well-founded charges. She failed, however, to displace the heir presumptive with one of her own sons. When Philip I died and her personal influence within the royal complex became of little account, she retired completely from the political arena and died within a convent, presumably as a religious.

Although the next queen, Adelaide of Maurienne (1115–1155), was a most competent and effective queen, the evidence is so neutral that it is impossible to attribute significant individuality to this woman. [8] She reigned for twenty-two years, she bore at least seven children, traveled with the itinerant court on its ceaseless rounds, and participated with Louis VI in affairs of state. She survived her husband for seventeen years, married a minor noble of the realm, and is recorded energetically administering her dower holdings still under the title of queen. This certainly bespeaks a great vitality, even toughness of character; but while we know much of what Adelaide did, we can only guess at the kind of person she was.

For the middle decades of the twelfth century we must consider Louis VII's three queens. The first is Eleanor of Aquitaine (1137–1152), whose long and dramatic life as wife and mother of kings has exercised an appeal over the centuries to literator and historian. [9] And, because her later career

---

7. Suger, *Vie de Louis VI*, p. 122.

8. Although the principal evidence for assessing Adelaide's active life is found in A. Luchaire, *Louis VI le Gros, annales de sa vie et de son règne* (Paris, 1890), scattered data indicating her influence on Louis VI and within the *curia* will be found in Ordericus Vitalis, IV; Suger, *Vie de Louis VI*; *La Chronique de Morigny*, ed. L. Mirot, CTEH, XLI (Paris, 1909); Galbert of Bruges, *The Murder of Charles the Good, Count of Flanders*, trans. J. B. Ross, Columbia University Records of Civilization, LXI (New York, 1960); Walter of Therouanne, *Vita Karoli Comitis Flandriae*, ed. R. Kopke, *MGH SS*, XII (Hanover, 1856).

9. Of special note are the two recent biographies: A. Kelly, *Eleanor of Aquitaine and the Four Kings* (Cambridge, Mass., 1950), and C. H. Walker, *Eleanor of Aquitaine* (Richmond,

was extraordinary, there has been a tendency to fabricate an early queen consonant with the later one. A dispassionate examination of the documentation for the first ten years of Eleanor's career as queen of France, however, reveals almost no information about either her activities or influence. Her presence in the royal *curia* is unnoted, her name rarely appears on Louis' charters, and no sources support the historical view of Eleanor as bold, precocious, and responsible for Louis VII's behavior. It is not until Eleanor's participation in 1147 in the Second Crusade[10] that we have some direct information concerning her behavior. There is little doubt that it was during this adventure, probably in Antioch, that the initial estrangement occurred between Eleanor and Louis. As reported, the dissension focused around a real or pretended impediment of consanguinity to the marriage. The couple were not reconciled until their return to Italy. Eleanor and Louis were reunited at a special audience with Pope Eugenius III and he forbade any further mention of consanguinity between them. Despite this injunction, they were divorced in 1152 on the grounds of consanguinity[11]—France lost Aquitaine, and England soon gained an extraordinary queen.

Much scholarship has been expended in discovering the real reasons for this divorce. While the element of marital discord certainly was present, a further motive, at least on the part of the king, was the absence of a male heir after fifteen years of marriage. Louis VII married Constance of Castille (1154–1160) two years later and was again presented with two daughters—the second being responsible for Constance's death. Beyond this we know little of Louis' second queen.

Adele of Champagne (1160–1206), Louis's last wife, finally bore the much desired male heir to the throne. The king's marriage with Adele had been part of a triple wedding alliance of Capetians with members of the house of Champagne (two of Louis' daughters had been married to brothers of Adele) in an effort to ally this family and the rich county of

---

Va., 1950). Less complete but not less valuable is A. Richard's study in Vol. II of his *Histoire des Comtes de Poitou* (Paris, 1903). To this list should be added the very judicious study of Edmond-René Labande, "Pour une image véridique d'Aliénor d'Aquitaine," *Bulletin de la Société des Antiquaires de l'Ouest*, II, Ser. 4 (1952).

10. The most relevant sources are: John of Salisbury, *Historia Pontificalis*, ed. R. L. Poole (Oxford, 1927) and William of Tyre, "Historia Rerum in Partem Transmarinis Gestarum," *Recueil des Historiens des Croisades, Historiens Occidentaux*, I, Part I (Paris, 1844).

11. The divorce is recorded in: Council of Beaugency, Mansi, XXI (Venice, 1776), cols. 751–754, and Suger, *Vie de Louis le Gros suivi de l'histoire du roi Louis VII*, ed. A. Molinier, CTEH, IV (Paris, 1887), p. 163.

Champagne to the crown. It was a successful venture; and, in addition, Adele appears to have been a capable and energetic queen for the twenty years of her reign and the twenty-six of her dowagerhood. But as with so many of her predecessors, it is impossible to find the personal Adele behind the official queen. Whether it was her ambition or that of her family which prompted her attempt to seize control of the government after Louis' death cannot be determined.[12] In any case, neither she nor her brothers were a match for Philip Augustus who effectively and quickly established himself as master.

The next queen of France is a poignant instance of a political marriage. Isabel of Hainaut (1180–1190) was crowned when but ten years old and died in childbirth a decade later.[13] She had been married for the territory she would bring the crown and for the support her uncle, the count of Flanders, would give Philip II in his struggle against his mother and his Champagnois uncles. During her brief reign her youth and vulnerability were exploited by Philip in his machinations against both her father and her uncle. Surrounded by the hostility of her in-laws, brutally treated by her husband, Isabel can have regretted little leaving the honor of her position.

Ingeburge of Denmark (1193–1237), Philip's second wife, is the one queen of our series who has aroused nearly as much historical curiosity as Eleanor of Aquitaine; but despite the research and the relatively fulsome source material, the enigma of her story persists while hypotheses remain but hypotheses.[14] Ingeburge's marriage was negotiated by Philip for money and Danish assistance to France in his war with England. After the coronation ceremony on the day following the wedding, Philip packed Ingeburge off to a distant corner of the kingdom while he began legal

12. Rigord, "Gesta Philippi Augusti," *Oeuvres de Rigord et de Guillaume le Breton*, ed. H. F. Delaborde, Société de l'histoire de France, 2 vols. (Paris, 1882), I, 15 f.; Roger of Hovedon, *Chronica*, ed. William Stubbs, RS, No. 51; 4 vols. (London, 1868–71), II, 193.

13. The few details we have of Isabel's short life are in Gilbert of Mons, *Chronica Hanoniae*, ed. and trans. G. Ménilglaise, Memoires de la société historique et littéraire de Tournai, XIV–XV; 2 vols. (Tournai, 1874), I.

14. Some of the more interesting studies of this queen and her marital difficulties are: R. Davidsohn, *Philipp II August von Frankreich und Ingeborg* (Stuttgart, 1888); A. Cartellieri, *Philipp II August, Koenig von Frankreich*, 5 vols. (Leipzig, 1899–1922) III; H. Géraud, "Ingeburge de Danemark, reine de France (1193–1236)," *Bibliotèque de l'école des chartes*, VI (1894); A. Luchaire, *Innocent III, les royautés de Saint-Siége* (Paris, 1908), chap. v; C. E. Smith, *Papal Enforcement of Some Medieval Marriage Laws* (Baton Rouge, 1951), chap. vi. The most comprehensive account of Ingeburge's tribulations during these years is to be found in papal correspondence especially Innocent III, *Opera Omnia*, Migne, *PL*, CCXIV, cols. 4, 149 f., 321, 348, 882 ff., 887, 892 ff., 1014 ff., 1193 f., CCXV, cols. 86 ff., 198 f., 680, 1135 f., 1266, 1403, 1493 f., 1496 ff.; CCXVI, cols. 258, 617 ff.

procedures to be rid of her as wife and queen. For twenty years he refused to acknowledge the legitimacy of her position—he swore solemnly that the marriage had never been consummated, while Ingeburge gave papal investigators equally solemn depositions that it had been.

The social conditions of early Capetian France no longer obtained—in 991 Robert II had repudiated Susanna with no formalities and had remarried twice; one hundred years later Philip I had dismissed Bertha of Holland with only the sanction of his Gallican clergy and had then remarried and maintained the alliance in the teeth of papal fulminations. By the end of the twelfth century, however, the authority of Rome was not to be trifled with; and while Philip II was adamant in his determination to be rid of Ingeburge, his overriding efforts were directed toward securing papal legitimation of the separation. During the many years that he sought new hearings of his case, he directed his anger and frustration against the hapless Ingeburge. After an unsuccessful attempt to send her back to her brother, the king of Denmark, she was held prisoner in various convents. Humiliated and insulted, Ingeburge was deprived of her Danish intimates, given inadequate maintenance, and isolated from all solace except that of her religion. With a determination equal to that of the king, the Danish princess, leaning on the support of a sympathetic clergy and the powerful Pope Innocent III, resisted Philip's frantic efforts to secure an annulment. And she won the battle. Ingeburge was publicly acknowledged as queen of France by Philip Augustus twenty years after her coronation. At the conclusion of the affair there is infrequent mention of her name in the surviving records although she outlived Philip by fourteen years. The truth about the motives of the antagonists in this struggle must always remain a mystery. It is easy to call Philip a bully and a brute, but what was Ingeburge?

Brief as the above sketches of the French queens are, they do give some indication of the variation in role of the incumbents of the office for a period spanning more than two centuries. Although there were always limits to *what* any queen might do, it is apparent that, dependent upon circumstance and personality, *how* each played her royal part differed dramatically. When we turn to an analysis of the office, we find less fluctuation and a much more consistent pattern.

THE MAKING OF A QUEEN

There need be no argument over the relative weight to be given the elective as against the hereditary principle which has engaged historians discussing Capetian kingship, because neither principle applies to the queen. A queen was always selected, nor was it primarily a matter of a government or kingdom choosing a queen, rather it was the ruler who chose a wife. The institution of marriage was fundamental to that of queenship. The church, controlling the bestowal of marriage sacraments, forbade bigamous and consanguineous marriages—injunctions which, although resisted, evaded, or ignored at times, were nevertheless acknowledged as among the canons of marriage.

The choice of the future queen could be made at various stages of the king's career: when he was either heir presumptive, king-elect, or reigning king. The choice was never solely that of the individual bridegroom but rested upon the advice and assistance of members of the royal family, councilors of the king (whether it was the king or his son who was to be married), and the *curia regis*. Beyond the determination of impedimenta to the proposed marriage (affinity, consanguinity, a living spouse, or previous betrothal of either partner) for which the responsibility rested largely with the clergy, there remained another assessment to be made which was of equal if not greater importance to the monarch and his court—that of the lineal suitability of the bride.

From its inception the Capetian dynasty had insisted that the intended bride be "worthy" of the dignity to be conferred upon her. Although the church might talk endlessly of such moral virtues demanded of a woman as piety, chastity, charity, and the like,[15] "worthy" as applied to a possible queen specifically denoted nobility of birth. The subtleties of the gradations in rank of medieval French society may be difficult to trace, but an examination of the families of the Capetian queens supports two contentions: noble birth was a salient requirement, and the hunting grounds for such a candidate existed only among the *higher* nobility and the royalty of the areas comprising western civilization. Of the thirteen queens who reigned between 987 and 1223, four were the daughters of kings and one of a grand duke, two were fathered by dukes and six by counts; territorially they came from as far away as Kiev and as close as Montfort. Protest was voiced against only one of these queens on grounds of birth—Isabel of Hainaut. The objection, however, was specious since what was really being protested was a young king's choice of wife while

---

15. Vincent of Beauvais, *De Eruditione Filiorum Nobilium*, ed. Arpad Steiner, The Medieval Academy of America, XXXII (Cambridge, Mass., 1938), pp. 172, 178, 181, 190, 192. Although a thirteenth-century treatise, the ideas expressed about the proper rearing and education of young ladies certainly represent opinions current in previous centuries about the preparation of women for their place in society.

under the influence of a powerful kinsman of the bride, rather than a selection made in accordance with the wishes of his mother and the currently predominant faction at court.

Another factor considered in the selection of a queen was whether the alliance would bring and was intended to bring political advantages and territorial aggrandizement to the Capetian monarchy. Until 1137 no marriage was contracted which brought any landed property into the royal domain; of the first eight queens, none was a sole heiress to her father's fief, and none was given a *dot* comprising land. The modest extension of the domain occurring between 987–1137 was achieved through other means than marital alliances. But while the early Capetian marriages were not "unions of fiefs," they did bring advantages of a more intangible, but not less valuable, kind to the dynasty. During these years the crown was faced with two crucial needs—the maintenance and extension of the principle of monarchy, and the preservation of the territorial integrity of the domain in the face of its more powerful and sometimes predatory vassal states. The first need both dictated and was served by the insistence that the queens of France be of high birth. Even when the dynasty and the monarchical principle had been firmly established, two queens were still specifically lauded in the late twelfth century for their Carolingian ancestry—Adele of Champagne and Isabel of Hainaut— through whom the line of the great Charlemagne was felt to have been returned to France.[16]

Similarly, the second need was met in part by the choice of queens in most instances before 1137, when wedding alliances helped bring into the Capetian sphere of interest vassals who might otherwise have allied against the less powerful kingdom of France. Among the most notable was the count of Flanders, first brought into alliance when Hugh Capet married his son Robert to the dowager countess Susanna in 988, an alignment continued by Philip I who married a stepdaughter of the count of Flanders (Bertha of Holland in 1072), and reinforced later by Louis VI's union with a niece of the dowager Flemish countess (Adelaide of Maurienne in 1115). No less important were the bonds between the county of Anjou and France, strengthened by Robert II's marriage to a niece of the Angevin count

16. F. Lot, *Les derniers Carolingiens*, BEHE, LXXXVII (Paris, 1891), p. 285, states that Isabel was not positively a descendant of Charles of Lorraine and that the contention was probably a fabrication. It is significant that the Carolingian ancestry ascribed to the Capetian dynasty in the late twelfth century is coincidental with the revival of monarchial power in France. See J.-M. Lemarignier, *Le gouvernement royal aux premiers temps capétiens (987–1108)* (Paris, 1965), chap. 3.

(Constance of Arles in 1005); and, irregular as the arrangement was, Philip I's marriage to the undivorced wife of the count of Anjou (Bertrada of Montfort in 1092) did not interrupt the former close relations between the two polities but continued them as before.

Whether the politically advantageous unions of the early Capetians were also economically profitable cannot be determined. In only one instance is there specific reference to a *dot*[17]—a rather casual mention of Constance of Arles' use of money brought in *dot* for purchase of lands to donate to the monastery in which her son Hugh was buried.[18] It is probable that moveables (specie, jewels, and *objets d'art*) were the usual *dots* arriving with these queens—Anne of Russia is said to have been sent to France to marry Henry I with *pluribus donis*[19]—but the bride's gift does not seem to have been an important element in the marriage negotiations for the period up to 1137.

The seeming indifference to bride's property on the part of the French crown was dramatically reversed in 1137 when Louis le Jeune was married to Eleanor of Aquitaine. Although it was fortuitous that William X of Aquitaine died without a male heir, leaving only a female minor to inherit his fief, Louis VI's immediate marriage of his heir to Eleanor was a calculated act whose significance and desirability was apparent to the French monarch and which set a precedent followed by later kings. The union with Eleanor satisfied the criterion of high birth, facilitated the strengthening of the political ties binding Aquitaine to France, and obtained the largest *dot* yet carried by a bride to a French king. Although Aquitaine could not become a part of the domain at the time of the wedding, there was the expectation that it would become so for the first-born male heir to the throne. That the plan did not succeed must again be laid partially to chance in that no sons were born to Eleanor and Louis. After their divorce, the desire for a male heir, although paramount for the crown,

17. In this paper *dot* will be used to designate the marriage settlement given to a girl by her family at the time of the marriage. Dower will be used to specify that portion of her husband's property the usufruct of which she could claim for the duration of her life should her husband predecease her. See Émile Chénon, *Histoire générale du droit français public et privé*, 2 vols. (Paris, 1926), II, 102 ff.; Jean Brissaud, *Manuel d'histoire de droit privé*, 2d ed. (Paris, 1908), pp. 716 ff. 731, 741.

18. W. M. Newman, *Catalogue des actes de Robert II roi de France* (Paris, 1937), No. 81; *Diplomata Roberti Regis*, RHGF, X (Paris, 1874), No. XLIX. ". . . quod de auro ex patris sui dono asportato. . . ."

19. *Chronicum S. Petri Vivi Senonensis*, RHGF, XI (Paris, 1876), 197; see also mention of the hyacinth, which had belonged to his Kievan grandmother, donated by Louis VI to the abbey of Saint-Denis in Suger, *Vie de Louis VI*, p. 276.

still did not preclude the calculation of other advantages in the choice of a new queen.

Despite the emphasis on the noble birth and illustrious virtues of Adele of Champagne, the primary factor in the selection of her as Louis VII's third queen rests on the political benefits which the alliance would bring the crown. For over a century, perhaps because of its contiguity, the house of Champagne (Blois, Chartres, Meaux, Troyes) had consistently been the most threatening and the most fractious of all the crown's vassals. The ancient enmities were finally resolved through negotiation and marital alliances culminating in 1160 with Louis VII's marriage to Adele.[20] Although the county of Champagne was not united formally to the crown until 1361,[21] it was a dependably loyal ally to the kingdom of France from the mid-twelfth century.

Under the last king in our study, Philip II Augustus, the policy of selecting a queen for the real and concrete advantages she could bring to the crown reached full fruition. Although the principle of noble birth for the future incumbent still held, it was peripheral to Philip's negotiations. His marriage with Isabel of Hainaut was contracted because of the promised *dot* and the allies he could obtain in Flanders and Hainaut to be used in his struggle against the controlling faction at court—his mother and her Champagnois relatives. And even though the possession of the marriage settlement by the crown had been hedged about in 1180 with clauses restricting its transfer to "an heir of Isabel's heir" to placate the count of Hainaut who was to inherit the county of Flanders,[22] Philip II succeeded in obtaining Isabel's *dot*, which comprised most of southwest Flanders,[23] but a year after her death. King Philip II's second marriage was negotiated in a similar but even more blatant manner. He was preparing to invade England and needed money and men; after a deal of haggling with the king of Denmark for both, Philip obtained 10,000 marks of silver from the Danish monarch as *dot* for his sister, the Princess Ingeburge.[24]

On the whole the factors underlying the choice of a queen form a consistent pattern. The prime requisite of high birth, articulated at the beginning of the dynasty, was augmented whenever possible by calculated political advantages to be gained by the monarchy from the union. As the

20. F. Lot, *Fidéles ou vassaux?* (Paris, 1904), pp. 140, 172 f.

21. F. Lot and R. Fawtier, *Histoire des institutions françaises au moyen age*, Vol. I: *Institutions seigneuriales* (Paris, 1957), p. 126.

22. Gilbert of Mons, *Chronica*, I, 204 f.

23. Lot and Fawtier, *Institutions seigneuriales*, p. 352.

24. Cartellieri, *Philipp II August*, III, 52, 61, 63; Roger of Hovedon, *Chronica*, II, 224; Rigord, "Gesta Philippi," I, 124.

polity was strengthened and the prestige of the king increased, a third requisite entered the negotiations—the economic gains to be obtained from the alliance. The territorial acquisitions by marital contract aimed at by the French crown from 1137 on were surely not solely economic in value, but the *dot*, whether land or money, assumed and continued to retain greater prominence in marriage arrangements from this date.[25] Quite obviously the women in question did not take part in the marriage negotiations; the honor to be conferred upon them was sufficient to secure the "consent" insisted upon by the church as necessary for a valid marriage.

Before leaving the discussion of factors influencing the choice of queens, there is one additional problem to be dealt with—the claims made in the late twelfth century of Carolingian blood for two queens, Adele of Champagne and Isabel of Hainaut. It is an interesting problem, but seemingly its significance lies in the intensification of royal absolutism, the heightened image of royalty constructed around the French king, which had begun under Suger of Saint-Denis in the mid-twelfth century. As we have seen, Philip Augustus' marriage to Isabel of Hainaut had been contracted precipitantly and without sanction from his mother Adele and her relatives. It was undoubtedly this court faction who used the accusation of "unworthy" birth against Isabel to protest a marriage alliance they mistrusted. The fabrication of Isabel's descent from Charles of Lorraine must then have been made as an answer to this calumny, whether at the instance of Philip or his in-laws is immaterial.[26] But the claim has to have been made posterior to the attempt to denigrate Isabel's lineage. Especially pertinent for interpreting later claims to be made for Philip is the fact that at this time, 1180, Carolingian lineage is ascribed only to Philip's wife, not to his mother. Is this incident the fount for the subsequent adulation of Philip Augustus as a *Karolide*? In the 1160s no mention was made of such distinguished ancestry for Adele when she married Louis VII; nor was the shade of Charlemagne evoked in the recorded jubilation at the birth of Philip.[27] Even more singular is the absence of Carolingian ancestry for Philip II in the panegyric written

25. Cf. the letter from Hugh Capet in the tenth century seeking a princess from the Byzantine Empire as bride for Robert II with its sole emphasis on birth (*Epistolae Gerberti*, ed. J. Havet, CTEH, VI [Paris, 1889], p. 101) with the accounts of Philip II's protracted bargaining over Ingeburge's marriage settlement with the Danish king in the twelfth century. It should be added that this was undoubtedly a policy dictated by necessity and not an ideology, because until the kings of France had a position of power from which to negotiate, the most they dared bargain for were wives.

26. See discussion in F. Lot, *Les derniers Carolingiens*, p. 285.

27. *Suger, Histoire de Louis VII*, pp. 166 ff.; Rigord, "Gesta Philippi," I, 7.

about him by Rigord,[28] and continued to the king's death by Philip's chaplain, William le Breton. However, around 1218 William "versified" his account of the deeds of Philip, and in this later version Philip is celebrated as a Carolingian.[29] Quite obviously such a claim necessitated ascribing a source, which could only be his mother Adele. Sometime after 1180 a kind of Carolingian contagion seems to have been released. Perhaps the example of Isabel, or even confusion over whom these claims were first made—whether Isabel or Philip in 1180—may have been the source of the infection. The times were certainly ripe for such extravagances about Capetian kingship, but what should be clear from this digression is that late twelfth-century imputation of Carolingian blood to two queens does not demonstrate that Carolingian ancestry was a factor in their choice as brides. In both cases the claims were subsequent to the coronation ceremony—for Isabel they clearly seem a defense against her calumniators, while in the case of Adele they were necessitated by adjectives applied to her son Philip some forty years after her marriage. The lineage of future queens was certainly of importance to the Capetian dynasts, but choice was usually made on more practical calculations; for, as we have seen, it was possible to embellish lineage *post matrimonium* should the occasion so demand.

At the conclusion of the contractual arrangements, preparations would be made to send the future bride, suitably accoutered, to the French court where the wedding would take place; after which at least part of the entourage which arrived with the lady would remain with her.[30] During the eleventh century neither the place of the wedding, the officiating clergy, nor the form of the ceremony seems to have developed a tradition. This may seem so partly because the chroniclers have simply neglected to add such data to their jejune accounts of the installation of a new queen. Frequently all that has been recorded is a bald statement of the marriage

28. Rigord was a monk of Saint-Denis and wrote his "Gesta" between 1185–1206. It is to him that the epithet *Augustus* is due; surely if the Carolingian magic were in the air, this was an opportune time to include it in Philip's biography. See the editor's introductory comments on Rigord in *Oeuvres de Rigord et de Guillaume le Breton*, I.

29. *Ibid.*, I, xxv, xlvi, lxx, for editor's discussion and *ibid.*, Vol. II, for the "Philippide." See also E. Kantorowicz, *The King's Two Bodies* (Princeton, 1957), p. 333 n. 65, who states that the earliest instance of this claim for Philip was made in 1196, but that it became widely current only through Vincent of Beauvais' *Speculum* after the middle of the thirteenth century.

30. As early as Bertha of Chartres (996) we are told of Chartrian partisans at court, while her successor, Constance of Arles, was thoroughly taken to task for the immoral customs and costumes introduced by her followers. Although the queen's native retainers were not always mentioned by the chroniclers, it seems certain that they were present.

presented in one of two general formulas: "*Rex duxit in uxorem Bertam,*" or "*Rex in matrimonium Bertam accepit.*" Although the earlier queens in all likelihood had received some kind of formal investiture into office after marriage, it is not until 1050 that such a ceremony is actually mentioned, and then the statement is neither descriptive nor that of an eyewitness.

A chronicler states that at the convocation at which Saint Lietbert was to be consecrated bishop of Cambrai by the archbishop of Rheims, King Henry I had requested that his bride should at the same occasion receive benediction and royal consecration. The account concludes with, "Our Lord Bishop of Cambrai presided at this royal consecration." [31] In all probability the ceremony mentioned by the anonymous biographer of Saint Lietbert included the celebration of the nuptials of Anne and Henry, the imposition of the crown, and the special benediction given the queen who would be the mother of the future successor to the throne. [32]

Marriage vows, coronation, [33] special benediction—such was the protocol for the making of a Capetian queen until the middle of the twelfth century when an elaboration of the ceremony occurred, or at least was first described. The continuator of Suger states that in 1154 Archbishop Hugh of Sens united Louis VII in marriage to Constance of Castille and then "anointed her queen and crowned both Louis and Constance," and he uses the same language to describe Louis' marriage to Adele of Champagne six years later. [34] The two new elements in the queening ritual—

31. *Vita S. Lietberti, RHGF,* XI (Paris, 1876), 480 f. ". . . sponsa . . . benediceretur regalique consecratione pariter insigneretur. Huic regiae consecrationi Dominus noster Lietbertus Cameracensis Episcopus interfuit et praefuit."

32. C. A. Bouman, *Sacring and Crowning* (Groningen, Netherlands, 1957), pp. 16, 151 f. The author states that the *ordo ad ordinandam reginam* became a permanent feature of accession liturgies in France from the late ninth century on, but warns that such formularies do not represent liturgical practice in detail.

33. That consecration of the queen always occurred even though not described by the chroniclers is further affirmed by a letter, dated 1089, to the archbishop of Rheims from Pope Urban II, who confirmed the ancient claims of the See of Rheims to alone possess the privilege of consecrating the kings and queens of France. ". . . ungendi Reges et ordinandi, sive Reginae, prima potestate fungamini." *Epistola Urbani II Papae ad Rainoldum Remensium, RHGF,* XIV (Paris, 1877); P. Jaffe and W. Wattenbach, *Regesta Pontificum Romanorum,* I (Leipzig, 1895), No. 5415.

34. Suger, *Histoire du Louis VII:* "[Louis] . . . Constantiam, filiam imperatoris Hispanie, conjugio sibi junxit, et Hugo, Senonensis archiepiscopus . . . eam in reginam inunxit et cum ipsa regem coronavit" (p. 164). "[Adele] . . . regi Ludovici maritali lege sollempniter sociata fuit, et Hugo . . . eam inunxit regemque cum ipsa coronavit, missam etiam eodem die ibidem celebravit" (p. 166). Both excerpts are from the *Historia Gloriosi Regis Ludovici VII,* of which the editor (A. Molinier) states that the first part was certainly

unction of the queen and *coronamento*[35] of the king—are uncorroborated by other French writers of the period with the exception of the chronicler of Saint-Pierre-le-Vif, who includes a similar description of Louis' marriage to Adele.[36] The ritual recrowning of the king at the time of the queen's coronation was repeated by Philip II for both of his wives, while there is also evidence suggesting that unction of the queen continued. Gilbert of Mons, undoubtedly present at the ceremony, says that Philip had Isabel anointed and crowned, then to honor his new bride at the celebration himself wore his own crown.[37] Thirteen years later, when Philip had his second wife made a queen, only Robert of Auxerre states that Ingeburge was anointed.[38] Rigord, an indispensable source for Philip II's reign, does not mention unction in connection with either of Philip's queens, using instead the phrase *"Philippus reginam Isemb. coronari fecit."*[39]

The ambiguities surrounding the question of anointment for queens center about the kind of unction which the queen received, the significance to be attributed to the act, and the probable date when the rite was introduced into the ceremony. There does not exist evidence for concluding that all the Capetian queens were anointed at their consecration to office,[40] but some of them certainly were. It seems well established that

---

written by Suger and continued after 1151 by a monk from Saint-Germain-des-Prés who probably wrote the *Historia* between 1171–1173 (p. xxxi).

35. *Coronamento* is indirectly indicated for Philip I at the time of his marriage to Bertrada of Montfort. See A. Fliche, *Le règne de Philip Ier roi de France* (Paris, 1912), pp. 48 f.; P. E. Schramm, *Der Koenig von Frankreich*; 2 vols.; 2d ed. (Weimar, 1960), I, 122 f.

36. *Chronicum S. Petri Vivi Senonensis, RHGF,* XII (Paris, 1877), 284: "[Adele] . . . Hugo Senonensis archiepiscopus Parisius in Reginam unxit, ipsamque cum domino suo Rege, ipsa die . . . in Ecclesia B. Mariae coronavit . . . et in eodem Ecclesia missae officium solemniter celebravit."

37. Gilbert of Mons, *Chronica*, I, 206: "[Isabel] Rex . . . apud S. Dionysium in Francia inungi et regia corona insigniri qua decuit veneratione fecit; ubi ipse, ad suae nuptae novaeque Reginae honorem, regalem cum ea gestavit coronam. . . ." Cf. Robert of Torigny, *Chronica*, ed. R. Howlett, *RS*, No. 82 (London, 1889), IV, 290: "1180 [Philip] fecit consecrari in reginam uxorem suam et coronati sunt ipse et ipsa ab archiepiscopi Senonensi."

38. Robert of Auxerre, *Chronologia, RHGF,* XVIII (Paris, 1879), 259. "[Ingeburge] . . . uncta est in Reginam."

39. Rigord, "Gesta Philippi," I, 21, 124.

40. Cf. A. Luchaire, *Histoire des institutions monarchiques de la France sous le premiers Capétiens,* 2d ed. (Paris, 1891), and Luchaire, *Manuel des institutions françaises* (Paris, 1892), p. 477: "A la bénédiction nuptial s'ajoutaient pour la reine la sacre et la couronnement." Much of the author's discussion of the *royalty* of the queens of Capetian France rests on the explicitly stated conviction that each queen had been anointed at her coronation, but he cites only the twelfth-century notice of Constance of Castille's unction. See Luchaire, *Histoire des institutions monarchiques,* p. 145 n. 2.

the unction given the queen was not of the same kind as that given the king. That is, while the king was anointed with the Holy Chrism supposedly brought from heaven for the baptism of Clovis and kept at Saint-Remy of Rheims,[41] the queen was anointed with only the simple consecrated oil used for baptism.[42] For this reason the rite did not impart to the queen the quasi-sacerdotal quality assumed by the Capetian kings; but the introduction of even this "simple" form of unction into the procedure for sacring a queen was not without significance. It was undoubtedly intended to increase the solemnity of the consecration ceremony and to exalt the idea of royalty. The relevance of this latter point, the embellishment of the image which was being created of the French monarchy, suggests the probable period when anointing of the queens was begun.

If it is remembered that the twelfth century was a period of innovation and change, of growth and extension of royal prestige, of conscious effort to fix the essence of kingship in artifact and ritual, if Suger's success in fostering the affinity between the crown and the abbey of Saint-Denis which nourished the cult of the king and enhanced the image of royalty[43] is borne in mind, then the idea that the unction of the queen was introduced in mid-twelfth century under the aegis of Saint-Denis seems credible. It is plausible to accept the *in reginam inunxit* of 1154 for Constance and 1160 for Adele as a preservation of the actual protocol. It is also noteworthy that both consecrations were performed by the same man, Archbishop Hugh of Sens, the metropolitan of the see within which lay Saint-Denis and that neither took place at Rheims.[44] Louis VII's brother,

41. M. Bloch, *Les rois thaumaturges* (Strasbourg, 1924), pp. 487 f., states that queens were never anointed with the Holy Chrism, which he then cites as a prime reason for the exclusion of women from the French throne when the Capetian dynasty failed to produce a male heir in the early fourteenth century, but he does not explicitly deny unction of the queens. Fawtier, in effect, avoids that problem by taking no position, stating only that "la reine de France est couronnée comme son époux." Lot and Fawtier, *Histoire des institutions . . .*, Vol. II: *Institutions royales* (Paris, 1958), p. 49.

42. See Schramm, *Der Koenig von Frankreich*, I, 124 ff., 202; Jean Pange, *Le roi très chrétien* (Paris, 1949), pp. 377 f. Both authors state that queens were anointed but *not* with the Holy Chrism from Saint-Remy which was used on the kings only. The statements are based on *ordines* of the ninth and tenth centuries quoted in Schramm, *op. cit.*, II, 97 n. 3: "Westfrankish Ordo—*in oleato capite*: Fulrad Ordo—*tunc debet caput eius ungui oleo*"; and the thirteenth century "Ordo of Rheims—*regina . . . ingunitur . . . non inunctione regis celitus misso, sed oleo sanctificato simplici.*" Neither author cites any evidence, however, which would demonstrate the use of unction on queens prior to the mid-twelfth century. Cf. Bouman's caution that formularies do not necessarily represent liturgical practice (Bouman, *Sacring and Crowning*, pp. 16, 151 f.)

43. R. Giesey, *The Royal Funeral Ceremony in Renaissance France*, Travaux d'Humanisme et Renaissance, XXXVII (Geneva, 1960), 30 f.

44. Suger, *Histoire du Louis VII*, pp. 164, 166.

Archbishop Henry of Rheims, was reportedly very displeased because he had not officiated at Louis' third wedding.[45] One likely reason for the choice of Hugh was that Louis should have preferred that the same man officiate who had consecrated his previous queen so that a similar protocol might be followed—that is, that Adele recieve unction as had Constance.[46]

To summarize: the early Capetian queens were consecrated to their office in a relatively simple ceremony comprising three elements—nuptial vows, imposition of the crown, and a special blessing. By the middle of the twelfth century the rite had been elaborated to include unction of the queen and recrowning of the king[47] at the point when the queen received her crown. One further change took place during the last decades of the twelfth century when the marriage ceremony was separated temporally from the sacring of the queen. Whether the lapse in time between nuptials and coronation was purely a matter of circumstance or an effort to solemnize the regal rite by making it more distinct from the wedding ceremony is indeterminable; but at the conclusion of the festivities following the culminating act of the drama, a new queen of France had been created.

THE DOWER SETTLEMENT

One other matter which may be presumed to have been settled at the time of the royal wedding was the queen's dower. Although the first extant royal act specifying a dower dates from so late as 1193, a similar procedure had undoubtedly been followed by Philip II's predecessors.[48] After the nuptials, whether in charter or by pledge before witnesses, the king enumerated the lands and rights within the domain which should provide for his wife and queen should he die before her.

45. *Chronicum S. Petri Vivi Senonensis, RHGF,* XII (Paris, 1877), 284.

46. See discussion in Bouman, *Sacring and Crowning,* pp. 85, 87 f., on the possibility of change occurring in ritual from coronation to coronation because of the lapse of time between ceremonies. Bishops were ordained fairly often and regularly so that protocol was more easily established and maintained, while stabilization was less easily achieved for the more infrequent royal rite.

47. The king was not reanointed at these *coronamenta.* See E. Kantorowicz, *Laudes Regiae,* University of California Publications in History, XXX (Berkeley, 1946), 92 f. It is most probable that recrowning of the king had occurred before 1150, but the ritual is described by no chronicler prior to Louis VII's marriage to Constance of Castille.

48. H. F. Delaborde, *Recueil des actes de Philippe-Auguste (1179–1206),* Chartes et diplômes relatifs à l'histoire de France; 2 vols. (Paris, 1916–43), II, No. 456. "[Philip] . . . Notum . . . quod nos Engenbergi . . . donamus in dotalicium quicquid pertinet ad preposituram Aurelianensem . . . etc."

Dower, with its roots in Germanic customary law—"*Morgangabe*" and the bride's purchase price [49]—had gradually developed so that "legal dower" [50] in the late twelfth century comprised one third to one half of the husband's holdings at the time of the marriage. There was also a "conventional dower" or dower by agreement [51] which permitted the husband to fix the dower, and it was this latter system which was followed by the Capetian kings. Since dower granted usufruct only, the property could not be alienated by the widow and was to be returned undiminished at her death to the heirs. So, although only one charter of endowment is extant, because of the necessity of obtaining the heirs' sanction for property transfers and the like, or because of fortuitous references to *dotalicium* holdings, it has been possible to suggest, however incompletely, most of the dower settlements arranged for the different queens of this study.

Four queens must be excluded from the discussion because they never entered upon the usufruct of their dowries, and, since no account of the settlement has survived, there is no way of determining where, within the domain, dower might have been assigned. They are Bertha of Chartres and Eleanor of Aquitaine, who were divorced by their husbands, and Constance of Castille and Isabel of Hainaut, who predeceased their husbands. All but two of the remaining nine queens received dowers which may be specifically located even though their extent is indeterminable. The first exception is Hugh Capet's queen Adelaide. As the founder of Notre-Dame of Argenteuil, she later endowed the abbey with extensive holdings in the area of Argenteuil, which donation was confirmed by her son Robert II in a charter in which the lands were specified as having belonged to Hugh.[52] Although never called *dotalicium*, the procedure for the transfer of the Argenteuil holdings makes them fit the definition of a dowry and would suggest that Queen Adelaide held the usufruct of this area in dower. The second exception is Constance of Arles, who died only a year after her husband King Robert II. While no part of the domain is ever named as her *dotalicium*, it is a likely possibility that she had been endowed with property in the environs east of Paris because it is from the Sens, Melun, Senlis area (and Poissy northwest) that she drew the principal support for her military rebellions against her husband and son.

49. Brissaud, *Manuel d'histoire de droit privé*, pp. 716–720.

50. Dower fixed by custom. See *ibid.*, p. 731; Chénon, *Histoire du droit*, II, 102 ff.; L. Delisle, *Catalogue des actes de Philippe-Auguste* (Paris, 1856), pp. 338 f.; P. Beaumanoir, *Coutumes de Beauvaisis*, ed. A. Salmon, CTEH, XXIV–XXV (Paris, 1899), p. 208.

51. Brissaud, *Manuel d'histoire de droit privé*, p. 731; Chénon, *Histoire du droit*, II, 102 ff.

52. Newman, *Catalogue*, No. 19.

It is difficult to find consistency or pattern in the assignment of dowries to the other seven Capetian queens. To the above possible settlements in the vicinity of Paris must be added positive endowments of property on the fringe of the kingdom. The seaport of Montreuil-sur-mer was given in dower first to Susanna, countess of Flanders,[53] and nearly a century later to Bertha of Holland.[54] Both of these queens were later repudiated by their husbands and more or less "banished" from the center of the French kingdom to their dowers at its periphery.[55] But since dowers were assigned at the time of marriage and since the union in both cases had been a Flemish-Capetian alliance, Montreuil had more likely been selected because of its "border" location between the two states than because of any anticipation of repudiation.[56] Whether Philip I (after his repudiation of Bertha of Holland) was being consistent in assigning dowers on the periphery of the domain, or merely ironic, he followed a similar policy for his second wife Bertrada of Montfort. She was given dower in Touraine on holdings ceded the king earlier in his reign by Fulk le Rechin, Bertrada's first husband.[57]

In contrast with the merely speculative knowledge of the marriage settlements given Adelaide and Constance at the beginning of the dynasty, specific documentation indicates that several later queens were assigned dower on the more ancient holdings of the crown in the vicinity of Paris. They are Anne of Russia with properties near Senlis,[58] and Adelaide of Maurienne established as dowager in Compiègne[59]—both northeast of Paris—while to the southeast, Adele of Champagne received holdings in Melun and Corbeil.[60] The one dower fully known, the prèvôté of Orleans

53. Richer, *Histoire de France*, ed. and trans. R. Latouche, 2 vols. (Paris, 1937), II, 286.

54. *Continuatio Aimoin, RHGF*, XII (Paris, 1877), 122.

55. Actually Robert would not let Susanna take possession of Montreuil, and after unsuccessfully trying to acquire its usufruct, the queen retired into Flanders. See Richer, II, 292.

56. Montreuil had been seized from Flanders by Hugh Capet in 980 while Susanna's first husband, Count Arnold II, was still alive. See Lot and Fawtier, *Institutions seign-euriales*, p. 347 n. 1.

57. See Fliche, *Philippe Ier*, pp. 142 f., for Fulk's transfer of the Gatinais to Philip in 1067. See also Luchaire, *Louis VI le Gros*, Nos. 205, 278, for a list of Bertrada's dower holdings which were ceded to Saint-Martin of Tours (1119) and the Abbey of Marmoutier (1115); discussed in M. Prou, *Recueil des actes de Philippe Ier roi de France (1059–1108)*, Chartes et diplômes relatifs à l'histoire de France, I (Paris, 1908), xi.

58. *Ibid.*, No. CXXX.

59. Suger, *Histoire du Louis VII*, p. 150; Luchaire, *Louis VI le Gros*, No. 495.

60. Delaborde, *Recueil*, I, No. 133; II, No. 562.

assigned to Ingeburge of Denmark in 1193, although at a greater distance from Paris, had the distinction of having once been the center of Capetian government.

As is obvious from the preceding catalogue, the Capetian kings from Hugh Capet to Philip Augustus followed neither formal policy nor established tradition in the assignment of dower. By definition endowment had to involve crown lands, but within the domain few locations were assigned twice, and, although documentary evidence indicates that in the majority of cases the dowager enjoyed usufruct of holdings in the environs of Paris, there were sufficient departures from this practice to make it a vagary not a policy. Nor is it possible to compare with any accuracy the extent of the holdings of the earlier queens with the later. Territorially the prévôté of Orleans was probably larger than any previous dower, which in the enlarged domain of the late twelfth century was to be expected, but in the absence of all relevant financial records for the period under consideration, no comparison, either relative or absolute, can be attempted of the revenues received by each queen from her dower. One can only assume that for each epoch *dotalicium* had been arranged which should be appropriate for the status and dignity of a dowager queen.[61]

EXERCISE OF OFFICE

After the queening rites had been performed and the bride had risen from the conjugal bed as *Regina Francorum*, she entered into that phase of her career which has most engaged our curiosity—the exercise of the office to which she had been ordained.

A significant fact in western kingship is that the king's wife became a queen—a title which refers to more than a wife inasmuch as it also designates a political office. It was not necessary that a king's wife be given official recognition; she could as well have remained spouse and mother in a private capacity. But once having been granted recognition by title and ceremony, a public role had been created from which evolved the office of queen. It was, however, an office with its roots in the institution of marriage because without the husband-king the *raison d'être* of a queen largely disappeared and with it her functions; so it is only in conjunction

61. Brissaud, *Manuel d'histoire de droit privé*, p. 785, notes that as the post-medieval European system of "joint-ownership" between spouses developed and extended to all classes, it did not obtain in the royal family where "the queen never lived in a community of possessions with the king" but was always assigned specific dower—"a remarkable example of the survival of the early system."

with a king and in her capacity to share the royal province that the queen's office may be understood. The problem here shall be to determine the extent of her partnership and its changes over time.

Luchaire's metaphor, "the Capetian Trinity,"[62] implying the oneness of royal power shared by the king, queen, and heir presumptive is an appropriately ambiguous manner of attempting to define the exercise of royal power, at least for the eleventh century when all else was so ill defined. It should be borne in mind that a kingdom of France scarcely existed for these years: there was no fixed capital, the domain was without form and magnitude, and few regalian rights remained to the crown except in theory.[63] But within these circumscriptions a Capetian monarchy did exist and was acknowledged by the church, the feudal baronage, the Empire, and other monarchies; and reduced as the functions of governing might be, those remaining were shared by the king with the queen.

In assessing the part of the queen in the government, it is necessary to note the two modes open to the queen for making her influence felt in affairs of state. First, she had personal influence over the king as his wife, for although there was little of present-day privacy in the lives of medieval persons,[64] conjugal intimacy allowed opportunity for a queen to make known wishes and exert pressures and fulfill them away from the eyes of the court. And second, her status as consort[65] found the queen a member of the *curia regis* free to express herself publicly and to share in the decisions and strategies of governing. The first two reigns of the Capetian dynasty exemplify the queen's unequivocable right to share in government and the manner in which she operated.

From 987 to 1032 two queens play conspicuous roles in the French court—Adelaide, Hugh Capet's wife, and Constance of Arles, Robert II's third spouse. The nine years of Hugh's reign are poorly documented so that little is known of either the king's or queen's activities,[66] but crucial

62. Luchaire, *Histoire des institutions monarchiques*, p. 133; W. M. Newman, *The Kings, the Court, and the Royal Power in France in the Eleventh Century* (Toulouse, 1929), pp. 50 f., 55.

63. W. M. Newman, *Le domaine royal sous les premiers Capétiens (987–1180)* (Paris, 1937), *passim*; Auguste Longnon, *Atlas historique de la France*, 2 vols. (Paris, 1882–89); Lot and Fawtier, *Institutions royales*, Bk. II; and J.-M. Lemarignier, *Le gouvernement royale*, *passim*.

64. L. F. Salzman, *English Life in the Middle Ages* (London, 1950), pp. 90, 92 f., 104, 106 f.

65. See discussion of *Mitherrschaft* in T. Vogelsang, *Die Frau als Herrscherin in hohen Mittelalter* (Gottingen, 1954), pp. 3–7, 44 f., 68.

66. F. Lot, *Études sur le règne de Hugues Capet et la fin du X⁰ Siecle*, BEHE, CXLVII (Paris, 1903), *passim*.

for the argument is Hugh's designation of Adelaide as his partner in governing.[67] And while Adelaide's right of sharing in government is poorly illustrated during her husband's reign, the fact that she was active during her son's early tenure implies that she had been accustomed to participating in affairs of state, such as they were. Robert II was no minor when he succeeded his father in 996; crowned co-king in 987 at seventeen years of age, he had shared the monarchy with his father and mother for nine years. It is unnecessary to make any assumptions about Robert during the years when the dowager Adelaide dominated the court[68] since habits tend to persist—Robert was accustomed to his mother's participation in governing, and Adelaide was used to sharing the duties and prerogatives of a monarch. Furthermore, in the absence of any organized administrative apparatus, the seasoned and experienced dowager queen Adelaide provided a desirable continuity between the two regimes. Her guidance also gave a needed stability to Robert's reign during the years when his energies were at least partially deployed in defending his anathematized marriage to Bertha of Chartres. Some indication of Adelaide's dominant position in the French court during these years is found in royal charters wherein Adelaide is called queen while Bertha is referred to merely as Robert's wife.[69] However, Gerbert, archbishop of Rheims and the future Pope Sylvester II, is the principal source emphasizing Adelaide's authority, for his letters specifically charge her, not the king, with threatening him and ordering him back to France, with supporting his (Gerbert's) enemies, with interfering in church appointments, with making France unsafe for him, and with aiding and abetting Robert in his proscribed marriage—the implication of all these charges being that Adelaide was responsible for the court policy of the time.[70] Queen Adelaide's death in 1006 and Robert's third marriage brought no changes in queenship because Constance of Arles continued to function and to dominate the court and the king in the same manner as had Robert's mother.

Poorly illuminated as it is by the infrequent royal charter and the rare mention of activity made by a chronicler, the routine life of the queen in the eleventh century can be dimly apprehended, the seasonal rhythms

---

67. Gerbert, *Epistolae*, No. 120.

68. Lot, *Études sur Hugues Capet*, p. 118: "Il semble que, apres la mort de Hugues Capet, la royaume ait été quelque temps dirigé par sa veuve, Adelaide."

69. Newman, *Catalogue*, Nos. 9, 13, 19. Of the eight authentic acts issued in Robert's name between 996–1006, these three specifically state Queen Adelaide's intervention.

70. Gerbert, *Epistolae*, Nos. 181, 208.

which probably changed little over the decades dimly grasped. First, there were always the relentless peregrinations with the king from one royal "palace" to another, with hospitality claimed along the way from various royal monasteries and bishoprics.[71] From place to place the *curia regis* remained fluid, some few persons remaining permanently in the entourage, other vassals staying behind while new ones from the freshly entered territory augmented the court. For at whatever *palatio* the court settled, there was the seat of government whose authority was primarily local in extent, administrative and judicial in nature. Settled temporarily in one locality, the court was accessible to the inhabitants of the environs. From the king *and queen* monasteries sought and received charters confirming donations, bishops sought and received confirmation of ancient privileges, religious houses appealed to the royal justice against depredations of their own vicars, or asked for settlement of disputed inheritances.[72] In the charters mirroring these court activities, the queen's name appears fairly regularly as assenting or intervening or assisting; less frequently her *signum* appears along with the other witnesses listed. The queen was undoubtedly also present when the provosts accounted to the crown for the administrative and financial responsibilities entrusted to them.[73] Regrettably, there are no financial records extant before the thirteenth century to indicate either the extent of receipts or how they were handled. Although it has been suggested that the Capetian queen quite likely had some share in the administration of the treasury because the Carolingian queens had,[74] there is no evidence direct or indirect which would support such a hypothesis.

In addition to sharing in the routine discussions and decisions of the more intimate *curia*, the queen was also a public part of the ritual and ceremonial aspects of the monarchy: she appeared with the king at grand

71. See Newman, *Le domaine royal*, p. 103. Royal palaces listed for the eleventh century were located in Compiègne, Orleans, Étampes, Paris, Saint-Denis, Senlis, and Verberle. See pp. 202 ff., for royal bishoprics and monasteries. Cf. Lot, *Études sur Hugues Capet*, pp. 222 f., and Longnon, *Atlas historique*. For a discussion of the divergent accounts of the domain and its growth see R. Fawtier, *The Capetian Kings of France*, trans. L. Butler and R. J. Adam (London, 1959), chap. vi.

72. Based on the collections of royal charters made by Newman, Soehnée, and Prou for the reigns of Robert II, Henry I, and Philip I. (F. Soehnée, *Catalogue des actes d'Henri Ier roi de France*, BEHE, CLXI [Paris, 1907]). See Lemarignier, *Le gouvernement royal*, pp. 164 ff. for a discussion of the circumscribed nature of "royal justice" in the eleventh century.

73. Lot and Fawtier, *Institutions royales*, pp. 141 f.

74. Luchaire, *Histoire des institutions monarchiques*, p. 743.

assemblies,[75] she was present at the coronation of a son,[76] she and the king welcomed foreign dignitaries to the court,[77] in conjunction with the king she received homage from the vassals of the crown.[78] Except for elaboration and embellishment, this public and ceremonial role of the queen was to change little over the centuries. It was rather the more politically significant role of the queen in the *curia* which was to undergo greatest change.

The intimacy of court life in the early eleventh century cannot be too strongly emphasized—where the king was, there too was the queen; his every act and decision was approved or assisted or contended by the queen *because she was there*, and because custom and tradition allowed that the queen was an ally and partner in governing. So long as the court was small and itinerant, so long as functions were undifferentiated, so long as the physical locus of administration was the hall or "common room" where the king and court ate, slept, and governed, so could the queen share every aspect of her husband's suzerainty except the military campaign.[79] Such were the conditions which obtained from 987 through the first quarter of the twelfth century.

Although the careers of the eleventh-century queens seem to vary dramatically, the office remained in essence the same, reaching its culmination during the reign of Adelaide of Maurienne (1115–1137), whose tenure marks the apogee of Capetian queenship for the years 987–1236. The structure, organization, and function of the court changed so minutely during the eleventh century that a sixty-year hiatus in queenship[80] left the office undiminished and unimpaired. When a dominant personality again shared the throne, Bertrada of Montfort with Philip I (1092–1108),

75. Luchaire, *Louis VI le Gros*, No. 514; A. Luchaire, *Études sur les actes de Louis VII* (Paris, 1885), p. 37.

76. Glaber, *RHGF*, X, pp. 28, 39; Luchaire, *Louis VI le Gros*, Nos. 264, 476.

77. Richer, II, 212 ff.; Luchaire, *Louis VI le Gros*, No. 466; Suger, *Vie de Louis VI*, p. 260.

78. Richer, II, 105 f.; *The Letters of Saint Bernard of Clairvaux*, trans. B. S. James (London, 1953), No. 122.

79. Although Constance of Arles was the instigator of the armed rebellions against Robert II and her son Henry I, the sources do not suggest that she ever took the field herself.

80. After Constance's death in 1032, twenty years passed with no queen; then came Anne of Russia's short reign (1051–1060) and self-effacing dowagerhood (until 1075), concluding with Bertha of Holland's almost unnoted tenure of twenty years (1072–1092). For Anne see A. Caix de Saint-Aymour, *Anne de Russie, reine de France et comtesse de Vallois au XIe siecle*, 2d. ed. (Paris, 1896)—a valiant effort to construct a biography out of cobwebs.

the new queen's mode of operating, her conception of the office and the role permitted her differs in no respect from that of her predecessors, Adelaide and Constance, at the beginning of the century. Bertrada has left a trail of scandal behind her, and her critics have been harsh, but it was her morals, personality, and the impropriety of her marital status which were criticized. It was not her activities per se as queen which outraged them, but the fact that a woman whom they considered Philip's concubine dared call herself queen and act as queen which drew their principal censure. Bertrada on the other hand, having been crowned queen of France, considered her status legitimate and acted accordingly— that is, she shared the throne with Philip I and participated vigorously in the administrative activities of the government of the day.[81]

But it is the reign of her successor Adelaide of Maurienne which marks the high and the turning point of this early concept of queenship—of free sharing in the royal power as a matter of right. Her reign represents in a way the codification of all the previous ideas, variously expressed and never regularized, about the office; still, before it had run its course, the necessary conditions were laid which would change the office and gradually eclipse the "consort idea." But in 1115 when Louis VI married Adelaide, he made her his royal partner and elaborated her role as had no previous Capetian king. Although there is little demonstrable difference in the office and its role enactment between the two queens, Adelaide, perhaps because of her unassailable marital status, has been accorded far greater official recognition in the documentary sources than has Bertrada. For the first time royal acts include the queen's regnal year[82] along with that of the king. Although only twice the number of royal charters are extant for Louis VI's reign as for Philip I's,[83] Adelaide's name in the

81. That Bertrada even dared to scheme against the rightful heir to the throne in favor of her own sons by Philip differs little from Constance of Arles' effort against Robert II and Henry I to establish her younger son (Robert) on the throne. These acts have more significance than merely underscoring the audacious and ambitious personalities of the two queens, for they also suggest a persistence of the idea that the office was still elective. See Lot and Fawtier, *Institutions royales*, pp. 16, 547. In addition these actions may be indicative of the queens' conceptions of their own prerogatives. In other words, since no law existed providing for succession to the throne, the queen, sharing the royal power, may have considered it equally her privilege to co-opt for the next king. Most certainly if her husband predeceased her, her position as dowager would be significantly determined by which son or heir occupied the throne.

82. Initiated in 1115, never found on all charters, disappearing in 1124 as suddenly as begun, but totaling fifty-five. Luchaire, *Louis VI le Gros, passim*.

83. Fawtier, *The Capetian Kings of France*, p. 8, gives the length of kings' reigns and number of extant charters listed for each.

charters signifying her participation in the decision appears forty-five times and her *signum* six times,[84] while there exist only four *signa* for Bertrada and no acknowledgment of her queenship in the charters.[85]

Whatever the formula used in the royal charters to indicate the position of the queen as a partner in government,[86] whether by inclusion of her regnal year or specification of her consent to the act or her *signum* (all three might occur in one charter), the idea that the queen shared in government spanned all of Adelaide's reign both in theory and practice. The court, although growing and tending toward a division of functions, was still itinerant and compact enough to allow the queen full comprehension of all its activities. Court business was growing in extent and variety as Louis VI consolidated the domain, and through it all Adelaide kept apace with the king; as long as Louis VI lived, she was not excluded from any aspect of the government. In addition to doing the things her predecessors had done as the kings' consorts—sharing in benefactions to *ecclesiae*, confirmations of donations made by other parties to religious establishments, ecclesiastical appointments, settlements made of cases brought before the king's justice, and the like—Adelaide shared also in new extensions of the royal authority. Her name appears with Louis VI on charters granting "royal protection" to monasteries and churches;[87] on charters granting communal privileges to towns in the realm;[88] on charters dealing with serfs—privilege to witness and combat injustice against free persons,[89] freedom to enter a monastery;[90] on charters granting special privileges—to hold a fair,[91] free use of royal mills,[92] freedom of a city.[93]

84. Luchaire, *Louis VI le Gros, passim.*

85. Prou, *Actes de Philippe Ier, passim.*

86. In the first ten years of Adelaide's reign when charters frequently included her regnal year as a matter of course, she was seldom designated *in* the charter as having consented to or urged or advised the act, and her *signum* appears but once. However, after 1124 her participation in the decision is noted thirty-seven times while the other five *signa* are scattered over the remaining twelve years of her tenure.

87. Luchaire, *Louis VI le Gros*, Nos. 585, 569, 570, 310.

88. *Ibid.*, Nos. 419, 435.

89. *Ibid.*, No. 408.

90. *Ibid.*, Nos. 212, 472.

91. *Ibid.*, No. 451.

92. *Ibid.*, No. 499.

93. *Ibid.*, No. 434. In all these charters the usual formula is "King Louis *with the consent* (sometimes *assent*) of Queen Adelaide" grants, etc. Nos. 419 and 212 are Louis' acting upon *Adelaide's intercession or plea*, and No. 434 "assures to so and so freedom in the name of the king *and the queen*."

In addition to Adelaide's participation in the more formal administrative activities of the government as illustrated in the royal charters, she also shared in the executive and policy-making functions of the crown. She issued safe conducts in her own name; she joined Louis in his oath of allegiance to Innocent II against the antipope Anacletus; she was instrumental in the elevation of William Clito as the count of Flanders; and she bears the onus for the disgrace of the chancellor Stephen of Garland.[94]

At this point it is appropriate to discuss one further increment to the queen's prerogatives—the possession and use of a personal seal.[95] It would seem that both signature and seal should have been employed to validate the safe conducts first recorded for a queen during Adelaide's tenure, but there is no mention of the use of a seal by this queen until later in her dowager years. In 1153 when Adelaide established a new town, the charter confirming the privilege specifically mentions the presence of the queen's seal.[96] Subsequent to Adelaide of Maurienne, the later Capetian queens continued each to possess her own seal,[97] but it is difficult to assess the significance of this innovation, how often and for what purposes it was used.

During the queen's regnant years there was small opportunity for the employment of the queen's seal in matters of any consequence since royal charters were issued only under the king's seal. The probable use of a queen's seal during these years would be on the more informal and hence less permanent letter whose traces have not been preserved—the safe conduct, the mandate or letter of instruction for the more domestic administrative matters in which the queen may have been involved.[98] There are no data which would suggest that the seal of the queen possessed the symbolic value attached to the king's, representing the authority of the state. A seal was no doubt a necessary convenience for the queen, especially during her widowhood when she was administering that part of the domain which she held in dower; but it should not be construed as an extension of her official status. It is also significant that the mention of the usage of a seal by a queen occurred during Adelaide of Maurienne's career when the office received its most careful articulation. That this innovation persisted,

94. *Chronique de Morigny*, pp. 16, 29, 43, 27; Suger, *Vie de Louis VI*, p. 260; Ordericus Vitalis, IV, 476; Walter of Therouanne, *MGH SS*, XII, 537–561.
95. See Luchaire, *Manuel*, p. 477.
96. J. Mabillon, *De Re Diplomatica*, 3d. ed. (Naples, 1789), p. 622.
97. See description in Natalis de Wailly, "Notice sur une Collection de sceaux des rois et reines de France," *Bibliotèque de l'école des chartes*, IV (1842–43), 479.
98. See Luchaire, *Études sur Louis VII*, chap. i, for a discussion of the diplomatics of the period.

however, while the queen's regnal year on charters did not, would further emphasize the limitations of its employment to private and domestic matters, a usage which would in no way conflict with the growing concentration of power in the person of the king.

In the face of the abundant evidence demonstrating that for approximately the first 150 years of the Capetian dynasty the queen regnant shared the royal power, influenced events not only by her private hold upon the king but also as his acknowledged ally and partner, intervened in affairs of state as a matter of right, was a power on the throne by privilege of office; in the face of such evidence and more indicating the accumulative growth, extension, and definition of the office, how does one explain the paradox that after the clearest exposition of the office in the person of Adelaide of Maurienne a noticeable transformation occurred as early as Adelaide's dowager years?

It is hazardous to pick a particular date and call that the dividing line between the old and the new because changes in the institutions of society occur slowly and subtly, the transformations often less a result of conscious innovation than of adaptation to the exigencies of the moment. Customary law was still the rule of the land in the kingdom of France whose governance in the early twelfth century was grounded in tradition.[99] The development of the apparatus of government which took place during Louis VI's reign was a necessary condition for a reformulation of the status of the queen, but the persistence of anachronistic ideas and the vigorous role played by Adelaide while she reigned with Louis VI may have served to conceal for the time the fundamental revision of the norms of her office which would become apparent only during the tenures of succeeding queens.

A most significant development in the monarchy under Louis VI was the consolidation and growth of a permanent group of persons around the king—the "palatines." The organization of the palace and the stabilization of the advisers around the king, which were in effect the initial steps leading to a bureaucratization of the government, had already taken root in the court under Louis VI's father, Philip I.[100] In the continuation of

99. See P. Vinogradoff, *Roman Law in Medieval Europe* (London, 1909), pp. 62–71; Lot and Fawtier, *Institutions royales*, pp. 189 f.

100. See Fliche, *Philippe Ier*, p. 105, on the change of the *curia* after 1085 under Philip into the *palatio*—"a permanent bureau of non-high-ranking families"; *ibid.*, p. 113, on the growth within the "palatines" of a certain number of specialized officers—*dapifer*, etc.; *ibid.*, pp. 120 f., on the development of the four grand officers of the crown who were "simple chevaliers" into "veritable councillers of the king." Also Lemarignier, *Le gouvernement royal*, pp. 151 ff.

his father's policies,[101] Louis' main concern at the beginning of his rule had been the royal domain—in which subjugation of the petty feudality, enforcement of rights of justice, and the exercise of real power on a restricted scale were gradually achieved. The reconstituted domain would be the basis for future extensions of royal power and the nucleus of later territorial growth. The process of organizing and consolidating the domain accomplished by Louis VI, predicated initially on military force, had by its success increased the royal prestige and succeeded in turning and keeping the loyalties of the domainal feudality to the crown. The extension and maintenance of the royal authority demanded and obtained a corps of officials loyal to the king. This group of persons comprising Louis' "palatines" were drawn from the petty feudality—simple chevaliers and clerics whose advantages were grounded in a devotion to the principle of monarchy. Administrative needs naturally increased with the extension of royal power so that the personnel around the king both increased and became more permanent. At the end of Louis VI's reign he was able to leave his son a relatively stable court, already partially bureaucratized and under the guidance of two capable men who had long been his closest confidants—Suger, abbot of Saint-Denis, and Ralph, count of Vermandois. That the *curia* was still small, however, and government still largely personal, is testified to by the part which Queen Adelaide had been able to play in affairs of state during Louis VI's lifetime. But while the king and queen still theoretically shared the royal power and authority, the composition and structure of the court had reached a stage where so ill-defined a status as queen—with no specified duties nor regularized privileges, and characterized only as a partnership—was extremely vulnerable to the forces of change rampant in the twelfth century.

Before proceeding, it is well to examine the concept of the queen's office as a partnership with her husband-king. That the queen had the right to share in royal power is an implicit assumption of scribes of the tenth and eleventh centuries. By the twelfth century this assumption, still unquestioned, has become explicit. Perhaps because it was never questioned, the need did not arise for developing a formal elaboration of the queen's regal rights; therefore the shape of the office always remained ambiguous. Quite obviously the queen shared the royal dignity and prestige, while socially hers was the highest position a woman could hold. But her royalty went beyond the merely decorative and ceremonial, the conjugal and material; it possessed political significance by reason of the official part the queen played in the governance of the realm. Although

101. Luchaire, *Louis VI le Gros*, pp. xlii–lxxxiv.

the Capetian kings through Louis VI considered their queens as partners in the government, this should not obscure the fact that it was a very unequal partnership, with the king-husband always the dominant member of the dyad. Still the fact remains that the queen did share the royal power even into its most important function of this period—the dispensation of justice.[102] As early as Constance of Arles, the queen had been present as a participating member of the *curia regis*[103] when it acted as a court of justice, and the prerogative was maintained by succeeding queens. However, the king was the final authority. Restricted as was the office, the very idea that the queen did legitimately share in the royal power gave great flexibility to the public role which any particular queen might play. The clever, the ambitious, the energetic had sufficient scope for her activities and could and did play a meaningful official role in the affairs of state. And so long as the French monarchy remained a small and impotent entity, and the enforcement of regalian rights a matter more of theory than practice, no questions or qualifications of the queen's right to share seem to have arisen.

In the middle of the twelfth century changes occur in the way the queen functioned which can only be understood as a reflection of concurrent modifications of the office itself. It is difficult to hold particular persons or events solely responsible for changes occurring slowly and insidiously, and certainly never articulated as modification; but beginning with Eleanor of Aquitaine, the queen's position suffers a diminution in its official status. This is not to say that the queen did not continue to influence governmental policy and to be a power in the government through her control over her husband, the reigning king, but she ceases to be called the king's partner, and her name gradually disappears from the royal *diplomata.* Eleanor's name appears as assenting to an act on only three royal charters dealing with matters outside Aquitaine for the fifteen years of her tenure[104] which is in startling contrast to the records documenting

102. Lot and Fawtier, *Institutions royales*, p. 162: "Le premier devoir du pouvoir royale, c'est la distribution de la justice. Celle-ci est la caracteristique, l'essence de la monarchie . . . ."

103. See discussion in G. Langmuir, "Counsel and Capetian Assemblies," *Studies Presented to the International Commission for the History of Representative and Parliamentary Institutions*, XVIII (Louvain, 1958), 24, on the gradual use of the term *curia regis* to specifically designate the court of justice. Constance's participation in such courts is specified in three acts—Newman, *Catalogue*, Nos. 78, 85, 91. She was also present at The Council of Orleans, called in 1022 to investigate charges of heresy against a number of French clerics. See Mansi, XIX, cols. 373–380.

104. Luchaire, *Études sur Louis VII*, Nos. 18, 119, 137.

the reign of her immediate predecessor, Adelaide of Maurienne with ninety-two acts in twenty-two years containing either assent, *signum*, or regnant year, or a combination thereof. Since such a profound difference cannot be due solely to accident, it is not inappropriate to take it as a kind of barometric measurement recording, however crudely, a change in attitude toward the office of the queen, a different understanding of its norms, whether on the part of the incumbent and the court or just the court must remain moot. Since the change must have occurred almost at the beginning of Eleanor's tenure, it is desirable to review briefly the persons and circumstances of the new regime.

Two factors seem especially important for understanding the later developments—the youth of the new king and queen, and the structure of the government. Louis VII had already been crowned in 1131 while only eleven and associated in the administrative affairs of the kingdom which were increasingly dominated by Abbot Suger of Saint-Denis. When Louis made his trip south to marry Eleanor, he was accompanied by the abbot and by Ralph of Vermandois, the seneschal of France. These two men—devoted to Louis VI, long in his service, and experienced in government—were retained by the new king in the fall of 1137 when he ascended the throne at the age of seventeen while Eleanor was but fifteen. There is every indication that Suger was as devoted to Louis VII as to the old king and that the young king fully respected the abbot's abilities. Government continued as before with no break in continuity—the same grand officers and household functionaries, Suger and Ralph as the king's chief advisers, even the queen mother were all a part of the court at the beginning of Louis VII's reign. Adelaide's retirement, forced or not, from the court in 1138 at the same time that Ralph of Vermandois also withdrew, removed the two most experienced persons who could be expected to rival Suger in claims to influence and control the young king. The evidence is much too vague to indict Suger for the removal of potential rivals to his dominant position, but their retirement was to his advantage, and until his death in 1151 the abbot of Saint-Denis, without holding any office, was the most influential member of the king's court.[105]

The exclusion of the dowager queen from an active part in government

---

105. Suger, *Vie de Louis VI*, p. 282; Suger, *Histoire du Louis VII*, p. 150; Luchaire, *Études sur Louis VII*, p. 46, and *ibid.*, p. 182, for another conflict in 1150 between the dowager queen and Suger in which the latter was the victor. Note too that Suger and Ralph were appointed regents of the kingdom in 1147, not Queen Adelaide. (*Chronique de Morigny*, pp. 83 f.; Odo of Deuil, *De profectione Ludovici VII in Orientem*, ed. and trans. V. G. Berry, Columbia Records of Civilization, XLII (New York, 1948), 20.

was not inconsistent with past policy of the Capetian dynasty, but the failure to accord the new queen regnant the recognition and functions possessed by her predecessor is singular. Louis VII may possibly have considered Queen Eleanor his partner since he had grown up in the shadow of his mother's partnership with Louis VI, but he made no effort, successful at least, to foster the concept in his administration, and the "consort idea," if not deliberately subverted by his court under Suger's guidance, was allowed to slide into abeyance.

Furthermore, the youthful queen of France was also the duchess of Aquitaine. It is very likely that her first loyalty lay with her inheritance, the duchy of Aquitaine, a large and politically important entity in itself and traditionally having very loose feudal ties to France. So the situation in the late 1130s and early forties entailed not only a court which was structurally inhospitable to a queen's sharing in routine affairs of state, the ascendancy of Suger over the king, and the youth of the royal couple; but also a queen whose commitment to her office was tempered by her involvement as the suzerain of another polity.

Whether the particular conjunction of persons and events as described above for the mid-twelfth century fully accounts for the subsequent developments of the queen's office may be debatable, but that the transformation began here, and not at the end of the century as usually maintained,[106] seems undeniable. From the inception of Louis VII's reign, the automatic and casual acceptance of the queen as the king's partner begins to disappear, to be replaced by a seemingly more self-conscious and manipulative attitude toward the holder of the title as one who should also produce, in addition to the male heir, political and material advantage for the crown.

Queens were still publicly conspicuous, sharing in the growing prestige accorded royalty, and they were still able to exert influence on the course of events. But the dissipation of the former intimacy of court life had certainly lessened their opportunities for intervention and participation which led inevitably to a decreased expectation that queens should share in the government. One clear sign of the dissolution of the previous close intimacy of the royal household appears in the charters of Louis VII which witness the beginning of the separation of the queen's *hôtel* from that of the king. As early as the time of Constance of Arles in the eleventh century, there had been factionalism in the court—members who supported the repudiated queen, Bertha of Chartres, against Constance who,

106. See W. Walker, *On the Increase of Royal Power in France under Philip Augustus* (Leipzig, 1888), pp. 14 f.; Lot and Fawtier, *Institutions royales*, p. 49; Luchaire, *Manuel*, pp. 500 ff.

accompanied by retainers from the Midi, was also supported by Angevin partisans because of her consanguinity with the count of Anjou. Anne of Russia must also have been accompanied by some retainers alien to the rest of the court even though her seneschal for her dowager years, the first "queen's officer" in the records, bears a French name—Amaury (L. Amalricus).[107] Bertrada of Montfort too had her followers at court with whom she was able to intrigue against her stepson, and there is one charter containing the *signa* of two men identified as Queen Bertrada's chamberlains.[108] But despite factionalism and the increase in the size of the royal household and the occasional reference to a functionary designated as a "queen's man," there had been no real division within the royal entourage between the king and the queen—they had lived, traveled, and functioned together in one household with one court.

While there are data to indicate that this state of affairs also continued under Eleanor and Louis VII, for the king traveled with Eleanor on itinerary through Aquitaine, and she was present on numerous occasions with Louis in France—to say nothing of their mutual crusading adventure —there is also information to show that Eleanor had probably a larger personal retinue and certainly a more formally organized group of functionaries than previous queens. This situation is accounted for by the fact that the queen of France was also the duchess of Aquitaine and required a more structured retinue for the administration and maintenance of liaison with her own holdings. Still the very increase in the size of the court lessened the immediacy of personal relations, and the task of administering two different polities—the domain and the duchy—was divisive to the common interests of king and queen. In such a way was the stage prepared for a complete separation between the royal couples and their retainers, interests, goals, and functions. As the queen was slowly excluded from her former right to share the royal power and to participate in governing, as she came to be separated in function from the king and the more specialized *curia*, so similarly did she and her household tend to coalesce and to separate spatially at times from the royal household. This process would result in the well-documented *hôtel du roi* and *hôtel du reine*[109] of later centuries, but which were already nascent as early as Louis VII's second wife, Constance of Castille. From 1154 on, royal charters document provisions for separate tables for the king and queen and testify that the royal

---

107. Prou, *Actes de Philippe Ier*, Nos. XXXVI, XIX.
108. *Ibid.*, No. CXXXII.
109. Lot and Fawtier, *Institutions royales*, pp. 234 f.

couple were no longer together all the time.[110] A reasonable assumption
would be that the queen, no longer a necessary part of the machinery of
governing, became largely sedentary, presumably at Paris, while the king
and court continued to be peripatetic.

Nevertheless, although the queen's official status in government had
suffered eclipse, she was still the king's wife and mother of his children—
both roles which would give her ample latitude for influencing policy
contingent upon her personal hold over husband or son. But it should be
noted that the development of separate households was a potential source
of greater factionalism and court intrigue than had previously obtained, a
situation which certainly occurred during the tenure of Louis VII's third
queen, Adele of Champagne.

Capetian-Champagnois rapport had been assiduously cultivated by
Louis VII from as early as 1154 when he had married two of his daughters
into the family and made Theobald of Blois his seneschal. Six years later
when Louis himself married the sister of his sons-in-law, the already close
ties with this house were strengthened and the nucleus formed for the pre-
eminence of the Champagnois faction at the French court. Queen Adele's
triumph in bearing Louis his first son in 1165 further assured her position
at court and her hold over the king. In addition to the queen and the
seneschal, another member of the house of Champagne successfully
paralleled their careers in France. He was William of the White Hands,
who became bishop of Chartres in 1165, archbishop of Sens in 1168, and
of Rheims in 1176—all royal bishoprics and closely controlled by Louis
VII.[111] For the twenty years of Adele's tenure as the reigning queen of
France, although granted no more official recognition [112] as a partner of
the king than her two predecessors in Louis' bed, her influence and the
interests of the faction from Champagne increasingly pervaded the court.
Near the end of his life Louis may have come to fear the dominance of this
feudal house as exercised through Queen Adele, especially in relation to
their young son Philip II, who might possibly ascend the throne still a
minor. At any rate when he arranged his son's coronation and association
to the throne in 1179, he introduced counterpoise into the court by selecting Count Philip of Flanders as sword-bearer to the king-designate and by

110. Luchaire, *Études sur Louis VII*, Nos. 377, 378, 421, 440, 450, 455, 568, 614, 638,
652, 718, 738, 777.

111. See M. Pacaut, *Louis VII et les élections épiscopales dans le royaume de France* (Paris,
1957), pp. 53, 61, 138.

112. Her name appears on only five royal charters during these years.

encouraging his son's close association with his new mentor. Early in 1180 when Louis VII's final illness had rendered him incapable, Queen Adele and her brothers attempted to seize control of the government by reason of Louis' incapacity and Philip's minority. It was an abortive attempt subdued principally by Philip II's energetic attack upon his mother in which he was aided by Philip of Flanders.

With Philip II's assumption of the crown in 1180, the transformation, long in process, of the queen's office was accelerated. He continued to employ his mother on occasion as an ancillary to the throne—to hear a few lawsuits,[113] to share control of a carefully regulated regency in 1190 [114] —but the major portion of Adele's twenty-six years of widowhood were spent in quiet care of her dower holdings in retirement from court activities. At the same time neither of Philip's two queens was granted any role in the government on what could be considered an official basis. Isabel and Ingeburge make no appearances in court records in either advisory, administrative, or judicial functions. A trend, long apparent, was consummated with the complete disappearance of the queen's name from the royal *diplomata*, with the dropping of any pretense that she shared in the governance of the realm.

Each of Philip's marriages was flagrantly contracted for the political and material advantages it should bring the crown and the kingdom. His first queen, Isabel of Hainaut, in addition to the *dot* she brought in marriage and the heir she bore the throne, was also expected to keep her father in line for the political game which the king was playing with Flanders—a matter for private manipulation and exertion of influence. Ingeburge of Denmark was brought to France as Philip's second wife with a *dot* of 10,000 marks of silver and an understanding between the two governments, France and Denmark, that they should bear each other mutual aid. While Philip kept the *dot*, he was willing to forswear the Danish alliance in his efforts to be rid of Ingeburge. Nothing more sharply defines the position of the queen in late twelfth-century France than the anomalous condition of Ingeburge from 1193 to 1213. Although constituted the queen of France, her status was completely without authority because Philip refused to accept her as his wife. For twenty years the king sought a legitimate decree of divorcement from Ingeburge who, from whatever prison she was held in at the time, sought through agency of

113. Delaborde, *Recueil*, I, No. 390; M. Guérard, *Collection des Cartulaires de France*, Collection de documents inédits; 4 vols. (Paris, 1840–50), I, No. XXXIII; L. Merlet and E. Lepinois (eds.), *Cartulaire de Notre-Dame de Chartres*, 2 vols. (Chartres, 1865), I, 229 ff.
114. Rigord, "Gesta Philippi," I, 99.

family and church to force Philip to acknowledge her as his wife, because only if the king held her as spouse could Ingeburge occupy the office whose title she claimed. Because Philip already had an heir and because the office of queen had lost its essence as a part of the machinery of government, the king could with fair impunity ignore the primarily ecclesiastical censure of his treatment of Ingeburge. When Philip finally publicly received her as his wife and queen, again a political expedient to placate the Danes, and Ingeburge's claims were at last vindicated, the office she entered, while surrounded with the dignity of royalty, was devoid of power and authority, and her official role in the monarchy had been reduced to the decorative and ceremonious.

It is plausible to argue that Philip treated both his wives so cavalierly precisely because the office of queen was so unimportant to the government of the time. The process of eliminating the queen as an instrument of royal power had begun before the middle of the twelfth century—its movement slow, its reality often unrecognized—and Philip was not an innovator in this respect. Bureaucratic processes, relentless, cumulative, and impersonal, had brought about changes in the queen's status even before Philip II's birth. It was the social reality of the queen as *ancilla* not *consocia*, as a private power (perhaps intriguer) not an official figure, which had conditioned and educated Philip in the person of his mother Queen Adele. With a lack of cant, it is this reality which he recognized and completed when he eliminated the fiction of the queen's sharing officially in any of the business of government, and thus made both conspicuous and absolute the demise of the partnership idea which had been basic to the dynasty at its inception.

The change in the office and role of the queen over these two centuries was at one with the transformation occurring in the polity itself. From an amorphous cluster of independent feudal territories acknowledging theoretical supremacy to the first Capetian dynast, there took place a steady growth and organization of the royal domain which enabled the monarchy to extend and enforce its regalian claims ever wider. As the kingdom was consolidated and its organization became more complex, as royal authority was fortified and extended, so political power came to be centered more and more in the person of the king. The advice of the great nobles of the realm was decreasingly sought, the functions of the grand officers were taken over by bureaucrats (clerics or minor feudality) who could be completely controlled by the king, and feudal ties were consistently undermined as the ties to royalty were strengthened. The greater the growth of royal power, the more firmly was it concentrated in the hands of one person—the king. And just as other rivals to the prime authority of the king had been skillfully atrophied by bureaucratic manipulation—duplication of office, institution of assistants, division of function and the like,[115] so too had the office of the queen been allowed to decline from its earlier definition as a partnership into a status which was largely honorific. The queen shared in the pomp and pageantry of court life, partook of the dignity of royalty; but she had no official place in the structure of the government, no part in the regulation of the kingdom. As the king's wife and the mother of his children, the queen was of course in a position to affect the direction of policy dependent upon her personal influence over the king. But private influence is always difficult to assess and almost impossible to weigh, while at the same time the lack of official prerogatives and rights made the queen that much more vulnerable to manipulation and pressures from ambitious factions within or without her family. In many ways the loss of the earlier status—when social necessity had dictated her public role beside the king as an instrument of royal authority— brought no real diminution in the queen's potential for exercising power. It did, however, reformulate the mode in which she would have to act, for without official authority, the queen could make her will felt only through behind-the-scene machination. Queenship had become by the thirteenth century a career embracing a public office clothed in honor and dignity, but shorn of all functions except the decorative and symbolic; privately the office was limited only by the role the queen chose and was able to play as the wife of the king.

DOWAGERHOOD

Since queens did not lose their queen-ness upon the deaths of their husbands and since many kings did predecease their wives, there remains a final phase of the queen's career to be discussed—her years of widowhood. The status of the queen mother was ill-defined in the early eleventh century. In addition there is insufficient evidence concerning dower holdings and dowager activities to permit more than an outline of the position and functions of a widowed queen for early Capetian France.

At the inception of the dynasty it is evident that Queen Adelaide, widowed in 996, remained at court and participated beside her son King Robert in the governing of the realm for the ten years of her dowagerhood. Similarly, Robert's third wife Constance of Arles gave every proof of

115. Lot and Fawtier, *Institutions royales*, pp. 35–39, 52–59, 108–112, 179.

feeling herself entitled to an active role in the government after her husband's demise, and quite possibly only her premature death, one year after Robert's, prevented recurrences of the initial conflicts between her and her eldest son King Henry I. Adelaide and Constance were queens during the period when the Capetian dynasty was struggling to establish its legitimacy, when the kingdom of France was at its nadir, and the apparatus of government nearly nonexistent. Under these circumstances, when government was personal and functions undifferentiated, the queen had played an active role during her regnant years because she was needed, and it was in the nature of things that she should continue to function as queen during widowhood. An experienced queen mother was so valuable an adjunct to the primitive government of early eleventh century France that this period no more questioned its duplication of queens than it did its dual kings.[116] But the long hiatus between Constance's death in 1032 and the appearance of the next dowager in 1060 had begun changes in the fabric of government which would make themselves felt in the cloak of queenship.

The reign of King Henry I, orphaned and long a bachelor, had necessitated a nonfamilial and more organized, although still intimate and nonbureaucratized, machinery of government. His late and short marriage to the alien Anne of Russia had not adequately prepared the new queen for a significant role in government nor produced an heir old enough to rule at Henry's death, so for the first time in the Capetian dynasty a regent was appointed as guardian to Philip I and as keeper of the kingdom.[117] Although Baldwin of Flanders' designation as regent did not exclude Anne from her natural rights as guardian of her seven-year-old son nor from her consecrated status as queen of France, it had at least the oblique effect of declaring her incapable. Whether as a consequence of Baldwin's appointment or whether he had been named regent because of her anticipated performance, Anne's career as dowager queen was singularly uneventful in respect to affairs of state. She remarried shortly after Henry's death and during the seven years of her son's minority made but infrequent appearances at court. Her known activities—mostly charitable and church-oriented—were centered around her dower holdings in Senlis, while there are no data to suggest that as *Regina Francorum* she intervened in administrative matters or attempted to influence policy.

116. Kings Hugh and Robert II, 987–996; Robert II and Henry I, 1027–1032. Queen Adelaide with Susanna of Flanders and Bertha of Chartres, 996–1004.

117. See discussion in F. Olivier-Martin, *Les régences et la majorité des rois* (Paris, 1931), pp. 12 f., 24.

The last queen of the eleventh century, Bertrada of Montfort, spent her eleven years of widowhood in even more total retirement from the social scene than had Anne, for it seems very probable that she ended her career as a religious. Because of her anomalous position—she was step-mother to the heir apparent and not a queen mother—and because of her intrigues against the legitimate heir, it must have appeared expedient to Louis VI when he became king to have Bertrada as far as possible from the center of government. After her attempted coup against Louis VI had failed, it was perhaps her sense of self-preservation together with the realization that her career as queen of France had ended with Philip I's death which prompted her withdrawal to a cloister upon her dower lands in Touraine; but it is equally possible that she was coerced into retirement by her stepson. Nor, given the irregularity of her marriage to Philip I, does it seem entirely accidental that she had been endowed with properties quite isolated from the rest of the domain.

But as is obvious, there is really very little known about the activities of the eleventh-century dowagers, and hence few generalizations can be made about the role of the widowed queen until the following century. During the course of the 1100s, as a result of more copious documentation and the coincidence of three queens with long tenures of dowagerhood (Adelaide of Maurienne—eighteen years, Adele of Champagne—twenty-six years, and Ingeburge of Denmark—fourteen years), the structure of this phase of the queen's career assumes greater clarity.

The first and most striking quality of the queen's dowager role as it appears in the twelfth century is its duality. Following her husband's death, the widowed queen left court and took up residence, more or less permanently, on her dower lands functioning as "lord" of a fief, while at the same time retaining her public identity as *Regina Francorum*. She administered her holdings in her own name, but under her royal title; she did not serve as a deputy of the king although she was evidently in frequent consultation with her son about the disposition of the fraction of the domain to which she held title. Her activities in the management of her holdings are distinguishable from those of any other landed baron only by her title and the fact that any alienation of her property had to be made with the approval and charter of her son, the king. Her vassals paid homage to her as overlord of their fiefs and sought favors from her which were granted in the name of the queen of France.

On the other hand, the dowager's continued use of her title was sup-ported by public activities significant for the whole kingdom when she responded to a son's request for service. She might be appointed arbitrator in judicial disputes,[118] guardian of wards of the crown,[119] even regent in the king's absence.[120] Her presence in the royal court on ordinary and festive occasions is attested, an attendance which would in itself tend to keep the image of her royalty unimpaired for the kingdom at large. Royalty had always been surrounded in Capetian France with majesty and an aura of quasi-sacredness, and it had not been lightly conferred upon its queens. Something of regal awesomeness had surely touched her. So even when she became a widow and her *raison d'être* disappeared, the queen was still royal and her royalty honored and provided for. Medieval France did not develop a drastically restrictive policy as solution to its supernumerary queens. Rather a practical compromise seems to have evolved which allowed the retention of a status while most of its functions were removed. The dowager would carry her queen-ness until her death, but she would not reign; her royalty would be acknowledged publicly by continued use of her title and occasional employment of her assistance, while her energies would be consumed in the administration of a dower— the compensatory substitution of a fief for a kingdom.

It is during the years after the queen mother had assumed the responsibility of administering her endowed properties that the majority of charters issued in a queen's name make their appearance.[121] But acts which have been issued during a queen's widowhood, chartering a new town or whatever, cannot be construed as part of the queen's royal prerogatives in the governing of the realm. It is in this respect that the title *Regina Francorum* misleads, for the acts are essentially not royal but seigneurial and must be evaluated accordingly. The chief significance of these widowhood charters is that they were promulgated in the name of *a* queen who, although no longer *the* queen, was still suffused with a royalty undiminished by a second marriage, retirement from court, or curtailment of function.[122]

118. Merlet and Lepinois (eds.), *Cart. de Notre-Dame de Chartres*, I, 229 ff.

119. Delaborde, *Recueil*, II, No. 678.

120. Rigord, "Gesta Philippi," I, 99.

121. This statement rests on an appraisal of thirty-one acts (printed reproductions from a number of collections) which have been issued *in the name of the queen* (not upon her advice or urging, in her presence, or with her consent, etc.). They begin in the twelfth century, and all but two bear dates which indicate that they were promulgated during dowagerhood: Adelaide of Maurienne, dowager—one; Ingeburge of Denmark, dowager —twelve, regnant—one (a testament); Adele of Champagne, dowager—fifteen, regent— one, regnant—one. Although undoubtedly not a complete record, it is an improvement over the eleventh century for which there are no extant charters issued in the queen's name.

122. Cf. early twentieth-century stereotypes of royal personages who, although exiled

It does not seem fortuitous that control of fortifications and military obligations were withdrawn from the dowager queen, further rendering her position innocuous.[123] Since power rested ultimately on force, the abridgement of these potentially dangerous resources by the new king was politic—certainly no other interpretation of Philip II's treatment of his mother Adele of Champagne seems possible. During the power struggle which erupted between mother and son shortly before Louis VII's death (September, 1180), Philip had seized the queen's dower lands and, after a settlement was finally mediated between the two, had specified that the *dotalicium* should be returned in full to his mother with the exception of *castellis et munitionibus* which should pertain to him.[124] If the young king had not feared the possible uses against himself of Queen Adele's military potential, it is unlikely that he would have considered it necessary to remove these instruments of power from her control. In 1223 a similarly prudent arrangement was made by Philip's son Louis VIII, concerning Queen Ingeburge's dower holdings when he confirmed them in full, but reserved military service and liege homage to himself.[125] No such qualification of tenure is reported for the first twelfth-century dowager queen, Adelaide of Maurienne, who, although several times in conflict with her son Louis VII, was never overtly rebellious. In 1139 she had married the constable of France, Matthew of Montmorency, whose loyalties as one of the crown's four grand officers would lie with Louis VII.[126] Matthew, as the dowager queen's representative, was probably responsible for host duties from Adelaide's holdings although no explicit information supports this supposition, while the evidence does indicate that she, not Matthew,

---

from homeland and driving taxicabs or running nightclubs, had not lost their royalty. This situation contrasts provocatively with the case of the President of the United States, who while in office wields great power but who at the conclusion of his term loses both function and title.

123. See Chénon, *Histoire générale du droit français public et privé*, II, 175 f. As early as the tenth century women were inheriting and assuming the full administration of fiefs. They were usually "represented" to their lords for duties of host and court; but some women had themselves led their own military contingents, so it was always a possibility. Also see Brissaud, *Manuel d'histoire de droit privé*, pp. 151, 155, 593 ff.

124. Roger of Hoveden, *Chronica*, II, 197. The qualifying clause strongly suggests that endowment had originally included control of fortifications and probably duty of host.

125. *RHGF*, XIX, 324.

126. Fawtier, *The Capetian Kings of France*, p. 171: "The constable was usually a Chaumont, a Montmorency, or a Clermont ...." Luchaire, *Louis VI le Gros*, p. lxiv: "The grand officers were in the hands of families whose fidelity could not be doubted ...." See also Lot and Fawtier, *Institutions royales*, p. 52, on the constable.

managed her dower lands and that under the title *Regina Francorum* she administered a portion of the royal domain.

The increasingly delimited and circumscribed role which was developed for the dowager queen in the twelfth century is in sharp contrast to the ambiguity of the queen mother's position in the early eleventh century. The changes in the norms surrounding widowhood proceeded in a direc-- tion reflecting both adaptation to a changing social and political structure and response to unique circumstances. The informality and vagueness of the first two regimes, when there was no appreciable change in roles between a queen regnant and a dowager queen, were replaced in the latter third of the eleventh century with the first directive (Baldwin's regency in 1060) which should in some respect regulate the dowager queen's prerogatives. Early in the twelfth century it was recognized that an ambitious dowager queen could be not only an annoyance but a positive danger to the throne. The solution adopted of enforced sequestration (Bertrada in 1108) was not repeated, but for the remainder of the century queen mothers are found firmly engaged in administering more carefully specified dower holdings which kept them busy and away from court. The final delimitation of role occurred in the last quarter of the twelfth century when control of fortifications and military forces within the dower was removed from the dowager's hands and made to pertain immediately to the king.

While never clearly articulated and always receptive to improvisation, the dowager's role had become fairly well stabilized by the early thirteenth century. Although her royalty and her right to appropriate dower had remained invariant over nearly two and a half centuries, her functions had been sheared to ancillary dimensions which were best fulfilled by the efficient administration of a small portion of a growing domain, sporadic attendance at court for ceremonial occasions, and infrequent employment as a special emissary of the king. The gradual diminution of royal function to which the dowager was subjected from 987 to 1236 reflects more or less precisely and much more explicitly the changes which the office underwent during the queen's regnant years during this same period.

Quo Regina

By the close of the twelfth century the office of the queen had assumed its ultimate shape. Her official position, which at the beginning of the dynasty was clearly a partnership with the king in governing, and which had continued as such throughout the eleventh century reaching its greatest elaboration of function in the first third of the twelfth, changed abruptly in the middle 1100s. By the close of the twelfth century all pretense of partnership had been abandoned, and the queen was no longer granted any official status in the governance of the kingdom. The delimitation of the rights and prerogatives of her office had first begun in the dowager phase of the queen's career. In the last third of the eleventh century, curtailment of her role and derogation of her office had taken place with the appointment of a special regent to assist the dowager queen with the administration of the realm during a son's minority. Because the office of queen was founded in the institution of marriage and because of the conventional system of dower, the widowhood period of a queen's tenure was the most vulnerable to abridgement of regal function. Deprived at once of her dual roles of wife and partner in governing by the death of her husband-king, the dowager queen had no official status. Although her advice and assistance might be sought by her son, the queen mother's regal rights had dissolved into a title honorably supported by allowance and *dotalicium* (whose military potential was, however, controlled by the king) and a position which was devoid of royal function.

While the process spanned nearly a century, the transformation of office which had begun with the dowager role eventually caught up with the queen regnant. The means of the change are neither so precise nor so neatly articulated as for the dowager, but beginning in the 1140s evidence indicating the reigning queen's official participation in the decisions and strategies of governing becomes increasingly scarce, and finally disappears entirely during the 1180s. The idea that the queen was the king's partner in government was permitted to fall into oblivion because it was irrelevant to the social and political realities of Capetian France in the late twelfth century. In the expanding and increasingly complex government of the period, royal power and authority were being concentrated in the person of the king and not divided with either wife or son.[127]

The loss to the queen of formal political function did not mean, however, the loss of all function significant for the monarchy. As the queen was displaced more and more from any share in the government on an official basis, her prestige was at the same time elevated and extended through symbol and ritual. A more elaborate coronation ceremony, an increasingly autonomous *maison*, the possession of a seal—all added to the dignity of

127. Note also that it is at this point in time, under Philip Augustus, that sons cease to be crowned during the king's lifetime. This is usually cited as an indication of the stability of the dynasty, but it equally well illustrates the focusing of the aura of royalty upon one sole figure—the reigning king in whom alone power resides.

the office without increasing its power and at the same instance enhanced the image of royalty fabricated during the twelfth century for the Capetian monarchy. To the public eye of the thirteenth century the queen was the wife of the ruler, the social companion of the king in the ritual performance of regal rites, and a part of the splendid facade built around royalty itself.

In the following centuries, although the queen could participate in government on an informal basis as she was able to effect policy through her influence over the king, her main role would be enacted in the social not the political sphere. And although upon occasion she might be designated regent for a minor or absentee king, the great extensions of power possible to the queen in this capacity would not be a part of the norms of her office but merely the result of extraordinary circumstances. However, in spite of the faet that her office was deprived of power, there existed avenues through which the queen would be able to exert considerable influence significant for the crown and the kingdom. Perhaps one of the most enduring monuments of the later monarchy was the development over the centuries of the royal court at Paris into the artistic and intellectual center of the kingdom [128]—an achievement in which the queen as the arbiter of court life and patroness of arts and letters would play a large role. Even though the queen was without official status in the government, she would continue to function both as an agent and as a symbol of royalty in a process which would culminate in the cult of divine kingship.

128. In the twelfth century the Capetian court was still largely untouched by the intellectual and literary ferment of the period which was making itself felt in, for example, Champagne, see John F. Benton, "The Court of Champagne as a Literary Center," *Speculum*, XXVI (1961), 551–591; for Anjou, see C. H. Haskins, "Henry II as a Patron of Literature," *Essays in Medieval History Presented to Thomas Frederick Tout* (Manchester, 1925), pp. 71–77; or even the episcopal court of Rheims, see J. R. Williams, "William of the White Hands and Men of Letters," *Haskins Anniversary Essays*, ed. C. H. Taylor and John La Monte (Boston, 1929), pp. 380–381. See Achille Luchaire, *Social France at the Time of Philip Augustus*, trans. from the 2d. ed. by Edward B. Krehbiel (New York, 1929), pp. 354–357, on the general rudeness of the age despite the literary evidence from Champagne and the Midi.

LIST OF QUEENS

Hugh Capet
  Adelaide (987–996; Dowager, d. 1006)

Robert II
  Susanna (988–991; Repudiated, d. 1003)
  Bertha of Chartres (996–1004; Divorced, d. 1020)
  Constance of Arles (1005–1031; Dowager, d. 1032)

Henry I
  Anne of Russia (1051–1060; Dowager, d. 1075)

Philip I
  Bertha of Holland (1072–1092; Repudiated, d. 1094)
  Bertrada of Montfort (1092–1108; Dowager, d. 1119)

Louis VI
  Adelaide of Maurienne (1115–1137; Dowager, d. 1155)

Louis VII
  Eleanor of Aquitaine (1137–1152; Divorced, d. 1204)
  Constance of Castille (1154–1160)
  Adele of Champagne (1160–1180; Dowager, d. 1206)

Philip II
  Isabel of Hainaut (1180–1190)
  Ingeburge of Denmark (1193–1223; Dowager, d. 1237)

LEONARDO BRUNI AND HIS PUBLIC: A STATISTICAL AND INTERPRETATIVE STUDY OF HIS ANNOTATED LATIN VERSION OF THE (PSEUDO-)ARISTOTELIAN *ECONOMICS*

Josef Soudek

*Queens College of the
City University of New York*

LEONARDO BRUNI AND HIS PUBLIC:
A STATISTICAL AND INTERPRETATIVE STUDY OF HIS ANNOTATED LATIN VERSION OF THE (PSEUDO-)ARISTOTELIAN *ECONOMICS**

INTRODUCTION

Leonardo Bruni's annotated Latin version of the (pseudo-)Aristotelian *Economics* was the first and most widely read renaissance translation of this ancient Greek work on moral philosophy. For the greater part of the fifteenth century Bruni's translation was well known through an impressively large number of handwritten copies, and within a short time it largely replaced the medieval Latin version of Durand d'Auvergne, which was still acclaimed in countries not so exposed to the humanistic movement as Italy. For this reason alone a survey of the extant manuscripts of the Bruni version would be justified.[1]

The present study is primarily intended to establish how extensively Bruni's version of the *Economics* circulated. Such knowledge is particularly valuable as we know so little about the public appeal of literary works in the renaissance. A review of the scribes and owners of the extant copies of Bruni's work or, lacking such data, of the places where they originated, where they circulated, and where they finally were deposited is likely to afford some glimpses of its audience in the first century after its publication (1420–1520). What exactly constituted its attraction is not easy to ascertain. The *Economics*—and more specifically the two of its three books which Bruni translated—was considered an integral part of Aristotelian moral philosophy in the middle ages as well as in the renaissance, and it had already held the interest of scholars and educated laymen alike for about 150 years before Bruni's annotated version appeared. The humanistic

* I wish to thank Professor Hans Baron for his valuable suggestions and constructive criticism and Professor Albert D. Menut for his generous assistance in preparing this study for publication.

1. The present bibliography was prepared in connection with an annotated list of the handwritten copies and printed editions of Latin translations of the *Economics* planned for the project entitled *Mediaeval and Renaissance Latin Translations and Commentaries* (Catalogus Translationum et Commentariorum), sponsored by the Union Académique Internationale, Editor-in-Chief, P. O. Kristeller. Volume I was published by the Catholic University of America Press (Washington, 1960).

character of his Latin rendition and of his commentary also made Bruni's work a document of humanistic critical scholarship. Its dissemination was therefore intimately connected with the spread of that renaissance movement. This dual appeal may leave us in some doubt about the reason for the success of Bruni's work, but the figures themselves leave no uncertainty as to its popularity with identifiable groups in certain areas at specified times. The list (Appendix II) at the end of this paper comprises 223 extant and 6 lost or not-located copies, penned in the course of the fifteenth and early sixteenth centuries.

Bruni's work consists of five parts: a Preface (dedicatory epistle), a Latin translation from the Greek of Book I, a humanistic adaptation of the medieval Latin text of Book III (the *liber secundus* as counted by Durand and Bruni in their respective versions), a commentary on Book I as translated by Bruni, and a commentary on Book II as adapted by him. A sketch of this compound of writings will be found in Appendix I. Only 34 per cent of the extant and known copies contain all five parts of the work (groups N and O in the index of the manuscripts, Appendix II, p. 129). Another 43 per cent of the copies (group D) have the first three parts of it: the Preface, Books I and II, but no commentaries. The remaining 23 per cent have either three parts—not those mentioned, but for example, the Preface, Book I and the commentary on Book I, two parts such as the Preface and Book I, or even only one part such as the Preface or Book II alone.

The authors of catalogues of manuscript collections containing Bruni's work have observed that copies in their collections were incomplete without being fragmentary.[2] I too consider as fragmentary only those copies in which *portions of any single part* of the text are missing, be it because the text was not completely copied, or because portions of the text were lost in the process of binding the leaves of a codex, or because leaves were evidently torn out of the codex. Fragments in the sense so defined are infrequent; altogether they amount to thirteen items or about 6 per cent of the total number of extant copies. To the fragmentary copies may be added those in which *one entire part* is known to be missing for similar reasons. In three

---

2. Thus, e.g., H. O. Coxe in his description of the MS Cod. 19701 [MS Canon. Lat. Misc. 225], fols. 69v–71, of the Bodleian Library (24)* containing the Preface and Book I only. *Catalogi codicum manuscriptorum Bibliothecae Bodleianae.* III (1854), col. 604. Also E. Narducci in his description of MS Cod. 234 [C.3.15], fols. 44v–61v, 63v–65, of the Biblioteca Angelica (126) in his catalogue of this collection (below, p. 55), pp. 134–135.

[* NB. The numbers in the text and notes placed within parentheses, when not otherwise identified, refer to the numbers of manuscripts as listed in Appendix II, below.]

instances (68, 126, and 166) the arrangement of the text indicates that provisions had been made for the inclusion of the wanting part but that the scribe failed to pen it. In one case (146) there is evidence that the leaves of the codex that contained the missing part are lost. I have listed these four copies (groups G, L, M, and one item in group H in Appendix II) in both their actual and their supposedly complete form.

Essentially different from the fragmentary are the incomplete copies which comprise one or more parts of the annotated version by Bruni but not all five parts of it, such as the Preface alone or the Preface together with Books I and II in the translation by Bruni without the commentaries, or the commentaries without his version of the two books. Such omissions may have been motivated by clearly discernible intentions or they may derive from the manuscript models that were copied. Therefore, I am distinguishing between intentionally and customarily incomplete copies. *Intentionally* incomplete are copies where one or more parts are left out because the scribe did not see fit to copy the entire work, although it was known to him (such as 90, Books I and II only, penned by Marsilio Ficino). Included in this category are copies of Bruni's annotations to the two books without his version of the pseudo-Aristotelian text, as well as copies of one or both books of the version which were to serve as basis for commentaries by other authors. As *customarily* incomplete I would regard copies evidently based on earlier ones that contained only two or three parts—e.g., the Preface together with Book I or the Preface with Book I and the commentary on it—probably presumed by the scribe to be the entire work of either Aristotle or Bruni (such as 5 and 114). Intentionally or probably intentionally and customarily incomplete copies (groups A, B, C, E, F, H, I, and P in Appendix II) add up to forty-two items or approximately 19 per cent of the total number of the extant and known manuscripts. Finally, one group (K in Appendix II) represents a hybrid type in that the Bruni version of the two books together with the Preface, which can be considered a complete copy of one sort, is combined with the commentary on Book I only.

Among the intentionally and customarily incomplete copies a goodly number yield interesting clues as to the genesis as well as the peculiar transmission of Bruni's work. The primary objective of setting aside these descriptive groups arranged according to their textual content as special categories was to differentiate these copies. However, the dividing line between intentionally and customarily incomplete copies is not always clear cut. It is not unreasonable to presume that the Preface of Bruni's version of the *Economics*, as any preface authored by a humanist of Bruni's reputation, would sometimes be copied solely for the sake of style and content. Of one copy (63) of the Preface we know that it was penned to honor the memory of Cosimo de' Medici, to whom the annotated version had been dedicated. But we cannot be sure that each of the other four manuscripts of the Preface only (group A in Appendix II) was intended to be a copy of the preface alone. It is not impossible that an extant manuscript of the Preface is the only preserved part of a copy of the entire work.

I. TRANSMISSION OF THE TEXT

The observation that an uncommonly large number of incomplete copies of this work by Bruni exists does not come as a surprise. A number of years ago, Hans Baron drew attention to the fact that Bruni in the Preface talks of only *one* book translated from the Greek and accompanied by a commentary—an indication that Bruni's Book II (the third book of the Greek original of the *Economics*) and the commentary on it did not yet exist when the Preface was written.[1] This observation of Baron put an end to the old riddle why Bruni, in his Preface, should have talked of having *translated* the *Economics*, although his Latin text of the second book is not a *translation* but merely an adaptation to humanistic taste of one or perhaps two medieval Latin translations. When Bruni did his work on the *Economics*, the Greek text of what he called the *liber secundus* was already lost. Recently scholars have doubted whether even Durand d'Auvergne had seen the Greek original when he rendered the same text in Latin in 1295.[2] Since

1. Hans Baron, *Humanistic and Political Literature in Florence and Venice at the Beginning of the Quattrocento* (Cambridge, Mass., 1955), pp. 166–172.
2. Among those who doubt that Durand d'Auvergne translated the third book of the Greek original are Father Lacombe and his collaborators in the inventory of the manuscripts of medieval Latin translations of Arisotelian works (*Aristoteles Latinus*, I, 75–77; for a detailed citation of this inventory see below p. 64, n. 4). They hold that Durand merely revised the Latin text of Books I and III of the older anonymous Latin translation (*translatio vetus*) of the three books that have come down to us as the Aristotelian *Economics*. They, therefore, refer to Durand's version as the *recensio Durandi*. In the older translation—preceded by a still more ancient one which exists only in fragmentary form—all three books are supposed to have been rendered from the Greek. The numbering of the first two books in the older medieval Latin translation corresponds to that of the two books of the Greek text in the extant medieval manuscripts, in late fifteenth and sixteenth centuries prints of the Greek original and in the Bekker edition (for a detailed description of it see below p. 79, n. 32). On the extant handwritten copies of the Greek text of Books I and II penned from the thirteenth to the sixteenth centuries, see André Wartelle, *Inventaire des Manuscrits Grecs d'Aristote et de ses Commentateurs* (Paris, 1963), p. 179, where twenty-eight copies are listed. No trace of a Greek text of Book III, Durand's and Bruni's *liber secundus*, has shown up thus far. On the relation of Bruni's translation to the Durand

Bruni's Preface was accompanied by the first book and the commentary on it alone, he could, at that time, truthfully speak of a *translation*.

If Baron's conclusions are correct, we would expect to find a number of copies that represent, or descend from, manuscripts of the phase when the adaptation of the second book and its commentary were not yet in existence. Baron himself knew merely one such manuscript (69), the transcription made by Antonio di Mario, now Cod. Laur. 79 c. 19, which has at the end of the commentary to Book I a note by the scribe: "Finis Commentarii super primo Libro Oeconomicorum. Leonardus Arretinus edidit. Antonius Marius Florentinus scripsit V. Non. Martii MCCCCXIX. Valeas qui legis." Reading the date in the Florentine style of chronology—the year 1419 denoting the twelve months from March 25, 1419 to March 24, 1420—Antonio completed writing this segment of the Bruni work on March 3, 1420. With this manuscript Baron compared another, Cod. Conv. Soppr.C.7.2677 of the Biblioteca Nazionale Centrale at Florence, which includes all of Bruni's translations of Aristotle—both books of the *Economics* (86) in addition to the *Ethics* and *Politics*—with the correct dates for the two latter translations. At the end of the *liber secundus* of the *Economics* (fol. 70v) one reads: "... Leonardus Aretinus traduxit e Greco MCCCCXX." This note would indicate that the whole work—the prefaced translation of Book I with the commentary on it and the adaptation of Book II with the commentary—was completed by March 24, 1421. Leaving aside the scribe's ignorance of the fact that the second book is really only a humanistic adaptation of a medieval Latin version and not a "translation," his listing of a later date for Book II confirms the thesis of a successive publication of the two books, each accompanied by its respective commentary. The date for the completion of Bruni's work on the *Economics* as given in the Florence manuscript is also found at the end of Book II (fol. 7v) in another copy (127) of the entire annotated version, Cod. 1023 (R.7.4), fols. 2–17, of the Biblioteca Angelica at Rome.[3] The evidence thus provided by the Preface and these three manuscripts will be complemented below by a systematic examination of the manuscript tradition that shows that there exists a whole group of copies which correspond to the one-book pattern found in Antonio di Mario's transcript.

As early as 1958, I knew and described three manuscripts containing

version see Eugenio Garin, "Noterelle sulla filosofia del rinascimento," *Rinascimento*, II (1951), 326 n. 3.

3. E. Narducci, *Catalogus codicum manuscriptorum praeter graecos et orientales in Bibliotheca Angelica olim Coenobii Sancti Augustini de Urbe*, I (Rome, 1893), 424.

only the Preface with the first book and its commentary.[4] I now know of nine, written at various times in the course of the fifteenth century (group I in Appendix II). The most important copy, next to Antonio di Mario's transcript, is Cod. VIII.G.45, fols. 1–31, of the Biblioteca Nazionale at Naples (114).[5] At the end of the commentary on Book I the scribe has noted: "Leonardus Aretinus edidit. Scriptus per me Andream de Arnoldis de Florentia in mense Junii 1421." This otherwise unknown scribe, therefore, must have based his copy of the manuscript from Antonio di Mario's hand and must have penned it fifteen months after the latter was completed. A second dated copy (62) is Cod. A.VII.1, fols. 96–117, of the Biblioteca Queriniana at Brescia,[6] written by Bartolomeus de Ganasonibus, a member of an old noble family of Brescia, who completed his copy on September 18, 1439. A third copy (9), penned in Italy about 1459, is Cod. DB.V.6, fols. 13–36, in the library of the former Strahov monastery at Prague.[7] The fourth (38), the manuscript Cod. lat. 11 138, fols. 49–65v, of the Bibliothèque Nationale at Paris,[8] was written in a fine humanistic script by a Bartholomaeus Cersolus in 1471. Among the manuscripts from unknown hands two are notable. The one (53) is the Cod. Perizonianus Q 18, of the Bibliotheek der Rijksuniversiteit at Leiden,[9] a parchment

4. "The Genesis and Tradition of Leonardo Bruni's Annotated Latin Version of the (Pseudo-)Aristotelian *Economics*," *Scriptorium*, XII (1958), 260–268. On pp. 262–263, I cited MSS 38, 53, and 62 in support of Hans Baron's conclusion as to the two-stage genesis of Bruni's version.

5. This manuscript is listed in P. O. Kristeller's *Iter Italicum*: Vol. I (London–Leiden, 1963), 428. Dott. ssa Guerriera Guerrieri, director of the Biblioteca Nazionale at Naples, provided me with microfilm of the manuscript and a description of the parchment codex which at one time belonged to the Farnese collection.

6. A. Beltrami, "Index codicum classicorum latinorum qui in bybliotheca Queriniana Brixiensi adservantur," *Studi Italiani di Filologia Classica*, XIV (1906), 49 n. 15. Dott. Ugo Baroncelli, director of the Biblioteca Civica Queriniana, furnished me with microfilm of the manuscript and added to Beltrami's description valuable information about the codex and the scribe.

7. The codex and the copy of the *Economics* contained in it are described in great detail by Ludwig Bertalot, "Uno zibaldone poetico umanistico del Quattrocento a Praga," *La Bibliofilia*, XXVI (1925), 59–66, 134–144, esp. 65–66. Mr. Vladimír Závodský of the Strahov Library (Památník národního písemnictví, Strahovska Knihovna) provided me with microfilm of the manuscript.

8. L. Delisle, "Inventaire des manuscrits conservés à la Bibliothèque Impériale sous les Nos. 8823–11503 du fonds latin," *Bibliothèque de l'École des Chartes*, XXIV (1863), 221. Mlle Jeanne Vielliard, the former director of the Institut de Recherche et d'Histoire des Textes, supplied me with a detailed description of this codex.

9. *Bibliotheca Universitatis Leidensis. Codices manuscripti*: Vol. IV (comp. by T. P. Sevensma, Leiden, 1946), 71–72. The librarians of the Bibliotheek der Rijksuniversiteit Leiden helped me in studying this manuscript by lending me a microfilm copy of it and by searching for all available data on the history of this codex.

copy which was circulating in Holland in the late seventeenth and early eighteenth centuries and was acquired in auction by the university for its Perizonianus collection from the library of a classicist at the Leiden University. The script appears to be that of a professional scribe and the initial with rich ornamentation in the margin on the first page would point to Florence as the place of origin. The other manuscript (99) is Cod. A.IV.16, fols. 65–87, of the Biblioteca Comunale at Mantova,[10] written on paper in the late fifteenth century and by the middle of the eighteenth century still circulating among Italian collectors.

A variant of "one-book" copies contains the Preface and Book I only, but not the commentary on Book I. There are nine such copies known (group B in Appendix II).[11] It is not unlikely that they derive from copies that included the commentary on the first book. In any case, we shall see later that among the "two-book" copies the earlier ones contain (besides the preface) the two books and the commentaries on them, while the later ones have the Preface and the text of the two books only. The same may have happened with the one-book manuscripts. In the case of two-book manuscripts lacking commentaries, one would conjecture that the scribes were exclusively intent on acquainting themselves or those who had them pen the copy with the "new" translation of the pseudo-Aristotelian work and the preface of its author. But why should scribes have copied the first book alone? If we were to presume that the copyist had a one-book manuscript in front of him, then we might have a plausible explanation of these copies and of the fact that scribes failed to include the second book of the text.

Only two copies of this variant of one-book manuscripts are dated. The older one (20) is a very beautiful copy in a codex which is a celebrated English collectors' item. The codex was until 1957 part of the collection of C. W. Dyson Perrins and came at that time through public auction into the possession of an unknown private owner. While still in the Perrins collection, the manuscript was Cod. 64, fols. 199–205.[12] It was written by

10. G. Benelli, "Cenno storico della R. Biblioteca di Mantova," *Giornale delle Biblioteche*, III (1869), 31 n. 110. Kristeller verified the text and Dott. Ubaldo Meroni, director of the Biblioteca Comunale at Mantova, supplied me with a description and a partial microfilm of the codex.

11. In *Scriptorium*, (cited above, p. 56, n. 4), 262–63, I listed five manuscripts (2, 3, 5, 61, 223) of this variant of one-book copies. Since at that time I did not yet distinguish one-book copies containing the Preface, Book I, and the commentary on it (group I in Appendix II, below p. 129) and copies comprising the Preface and Book I only, I erroneously grouped them together.

12. G. Warner, *Descriptive Catalogue of Illuminated Manuscripts in the Library of C. W. Dyson Perrins*, 2 vols. (Oxford, 1920), I, 164–165, and II, 67 with plate.

a Gaspar Garimbertus at Milan, a professional scribe, for Giovanni
Amerino, auditor of Francesco Sforza, and completed on May 26, 1451.
About thirteen years later, in or before 1464, the scholarly Bohemian
nobleman Johannes von (de) Rabenstein, a friend of Enea Silvio Piccolomini, copied the same two parts of Bruni's work (the Preface and the
translation of Book I without its commentary) at Pavia where he had
temporarily retired to escape the religious and political tribulations in his
native country. The manuscript (2) is now Cod. 143 (Cpl. [454.b] 59),
fols. 62–63v, of the Stiftsbibliothek Schlaegl in Upper Austria.[13]

Three other copies of the same type from unknown hands are noteworthy on account of the titles or notes at the end of the text. One (5) is
the manuscript Cod. Vindob. 3420 [Philos. 240], fols. 124–125v, of the
Oesterreichische Nationalbibliothek at Vienna.[14] It was probably penned
after 1460 in central Italy, possibly in Siena. At the end of the text the
scribe observed: "Explicit oeconomicorum liber Aristotelis primus Latini-
tati redditus et perfectus est, non enim plures quam unum scripsit."
Presumably the scribe was unaware of any other translation of the *Economics* and had happened accidentally on a one-book manuscript of Bruni's
version. Otherwise this remark might mean that some scholars in the
middle of the fifteenth century had their doubts about the ascription to
Aristotle of Book III (the *liber secundus* of Bruni). A copy of the same one-
book variant (187) in the MS 78.1, fols. 72v–79, of the Newberry Library
at Chicago,[15] written in Italy in the fifteenth century, bears the laconic
superscription: "Leonardi Arhetini interpretatio Aristotelis opusculi de
re familiari ad Cosmum de medicis florentinum." At the end of the manuscript Cod. 2 828 [lat. 1512], fols. 147v–158v, of the Biblioteca Universitaria at Bologna (61),[16] in which Book I is superscribed with "Incipit
tractatus," is this note: "L.A. ICHONOMICE. ARISTOTELIS. TRANSLATIO FINIT.

13. G. Vielhaber and G. Indra, *Catalogus codicum Plagensium (Cpl.) manuscriptorum*
(Linz, 1918), p. 249; on Johannes von Rabenstein cf., Bachmann in *Allgemeine Deutsche
Biographie*, XXVII (Leipzig, 1888), 93–94.

14. *Tabulae codicum manuscriptorum praeter graecos et orientales in Bibliotheca Palatina
Vindobonensi Asservatorum*, II (Vienna, 1868), 284–287; Dr. Franz Unterkircher, director
of the Manuscript Division of the Oesterreichische Nationalbibliothek, gave me important
information on the history of the codex and of the *Economics* copy and drew my attention
to the interesting note at the end of the manuscript.

15. I owe the detailed description of the codex and of the copy of the *Economics*
contained in it to Professor Hans Baron.

16. L. Frati, "Indice del codici latini conservati nella R. Biblioteca Universitaria di
Bologna," *Studi Italiani di Filologia Classica*, XVII (1909), 114, No. 1512; Professor L.
Rickels inspected the text in that library for me and pointed out some of its peculiarities
as compared with other copies of Bruni's version of the *Economics* in the same collection.

FELICITER." Would the last two cases not suggest that the scribes were unaware that another book of Bruni's version existed?

In summation, the one-book manuscripts embrace two groups of copies. The one consists of manuscripts containing the full first segment of Bruni's work—the Preface, Book I, and the commentary on Book I—and these manuscripts appear to be copies of that portion which Antonio di Mario penned and which he completed on March 3, 1420. The other group is made up of manuscripts containing the Preface and the translation of Book I only. They are probably based on copies of the former type. The significance of copies containing merely the translation of Book I and of Bruni's adaptation of Book II (group E in Appendix II), or of Book II alone (group F), or, finally, of excerpts from both books (group Q) will be taken up in other contexts (Parts III and IV).

The two quantitatively predominant types of fifteenth-century copies are those of either all five parts—the Preface, Books I and II, and the commentaries on them—or of the Preface and Books I and II. Of the first type the earliest known manuscript is the copy made by Antonio di Mario (Laur. 79 c. 19) to which Book II with its commentary was added after Antonio had indicated the date of March 3, 1420, at the end of the commentary on Book I. As Baron has pointed out,[17] it is unlikely that this manuscript served as the presentation copy. Although it was in the library of Piero de' Medici, the son of Cosimo to whom the version was dedicated, and presumably has come from Cosimo's library, we observe corrections in the margins from a hand yet unidentified. But since there is no more authentic copy, the study of the transmission of the text must start with the arrangement of this first two-book copy. Taking the arrangement in MS Laur. 79 c. 19 (Preface, Book I, commentary on Book I, Book II, commentary on Book II) as the first form of the extant two-book manuscripts, a survey of all two-book manuscripts must, in addition to this pattern (*a*) still consider two other patterns: (*b*) Preface, Books I and II, and, following them, the commentaries on both books, and (*c*) Preface and Books I and II without their commentaries. These three patterns are represented in the groups N, O, and D in Appendix II and, as will presently be shown, originated in a sequence of time.

Of manuscripts of form (*a*)—the Antonio di Mario transcript excluded —eleven copies are known, two of which date from the year 1425. It should be noted that there is a slight but interesting difference between these two dated manuscripts, in that in the one each book is *followed* by the commentary on it, while in the other the commentaries, in common

17. Baron, *Humanistic and Political Literature*, p. 167, n. 4.

medieval fashion, are marginal. The first (198) is the manuscript Cod. Vat.lat. 3 347, fols. 38*v*–56*v*,[18] penned by a certain Franciscus Beninus de Redolfinis, who completed it on May 25, 1425. He sold it, bound together with a copy from his hand of Plato's *Gorgias* in Bruni's translation, to the Sicilian scholar Nicolaus Scyllacius. The other manuscript of the same year (26) is Cod. 29 438 [MS Add.C.264], fols. 107–119, of the Bodleian Library,[19] written by one Ioannes de Manasseis de Interamna at Florence. We find the arrangement of the text in the Franciscus Beninus de Redolfinis copy in five other manuscripts from various times in the fifteenth century and the arrangement of the text in the Ioannes de Manasseis copy in three other fifteenth-century manuscripts. A printed edition of the entire annotated version of the *Economics*, which appeared at Siena in 1508, was based on a copy of the latter kind.[20] The editor, Bartholomaeus de Lombardia, persuaded the well-known printer-publisher Simon Nardi to put out this edition so as "to preserve the work by Bruni for posterity." Editor and printer pretended to be unaware or perhaps really were not cognizant of the fact that by this time Bruni's version had been printed two dozen times, half a dozen times with the commentary, mostly in widely circulating editions of Aristotle's collected works in Latin translations. Possibly they meant to preserve the text in this rare, indeed unique, printed layout.

18. H. Baron (ed.). *Leonardo Bruni Aretino. Humanistisch-Philosophische Schriften*, Mit einer Chronologie seiner Werke and Briefe (Leipzig, 1928), pp. 228–229. Monsignor José Ruysschaert, vice prefect of the Vatican Library, generously described this manuscript for me as well as many others in the Vatican Library. The note at the end of the manuscript enabled me to understand the history of this important early copy of Bruni's version of the *Economics*.

19. F. Madan, H. H. E. Craster, and N. Denholm-Young, *A Summary Catalogue of Western Manuscripts in the Bodleian Library at Oxford* . . ., V (1905), 623. Dr. R. W. Hunt, keeper of the Western manuscripts of the Bodleian Library, made a microfilm copy available to me.

20. This printed edition, completed February 1, 1509, may be found in the British Museum; one copy is listed in the *Gesamtkatalog der Deutschen Bibliotheken* (14 vols. [Berlin, 1931–1939]; hereafter cited as DK with serial number of the cited item. VI [1934], col. 685, No. 6882), and there is a copy in the Columbia University Library and another in the Library of the University of Pennsylvania (Lyman W. Riley, *Aristotle Texts and Commentaries to 1700 in the University of Pennsylvania Library* [Philadelphia, 1961], hereafter referred to as "Riley," No. 136). The edition is a faithful copy of the entire work by Bruni in an arrangement resembling the one in the copy penned by Ioannes de Manasseis. Besides this edition there are about half a dozen others based on manuscripts. Among them is the first known print of the Bruni version without the commentary, done by Johann Mentelin at Strasbourg and completed before April 10, 1469 (GW 2367), and the first edition of the version with the commentary, published about 1470 by Christophorus Valdarfer at Venice (GW 2435).

The other two copy arrangements—forms (*b*) and (*c*)—are probably the latest variants. The dates of the manuscripts do not allow definitive conclusions as to the time when either pattern was first composed. It seems very likely that both arrangements appeared sometime between 1438 and 1442. One of the oldest manuscripts of Bruni's whole work, where the prefaced text of the two books precedes the commentaries on them, is the already mentioned manuscript Cod. Conv. Soppr.C.7.2677, fols. 66*v*–70*v* (Preface, Books I and II) and fols. 147–156*v* (the commentaries on both books) of the Biblioteca Nazionale Centrale at Florence. It comes from the Benedictine abbey at Florence and was penned after 1438. As to the other copy, the previously cited manuscript Cod. 1023 [R.7.4], fols. 2–17, of the Biblioteca Angelica at Rome, which is arranged in the same way as the Florence manuscript and which has the identical note concerning the date of completion of Bruni's entire work at the end of Book II, we have no information as to the time at which it was written. 1447 is the earliest available date of a manuscript like the one in the Biblioteca Angelica, except for the note at the end of Book II. The copy (133) which is now manuscript Cod. Vittorio Emanuele 238, fols. 116–127*v*, of the Biblioteca Nazionale Centrale Vittorio Emanuele II at Rome dates from this year.[21]

We are a bit better off with copies of the other pattern (*c*), consisting of the Preface and the two books of the Bruni version alone. The oldest (208) of the dated manuscripts is Cod. Ottob.lat. 1 353, fols. 272*v*–285*v*, in the Vatican Library,[22] written by Giovanni Pietro Paolo of Ancona. He finished copying the various texts in this codex on March 7, 1442, but he may have penned Bruni's version of the *Economics* some years earlier. Although a man of learning, he superscribed the text with "De ingenuis moribus," the title of a treatise by Pier Paolo Vergerio. The next manuscript and one with a definite date (163) is Cod. 13 521, fols. 122–129*v*, of the Biblioteca Nacional at Madrid,[23] written at Siena in August, 1443.

21. Baron, *Leonardo Bruni Aretino*, p. 232, describes this codex; the *Economics* text was verified by Dott. ssa Olga Pinto, director of the Centro Nazionale di Informazioni Bibliografiche at the Biblioteca Nazionale Centrale at Rome.

22. A. Campana, "Giannozzo Manetti, Ciriaco e l'arco di Traiana ad Ancona," *Italia medioevale e umanistica*, II (1959), 490–491, holds that the texts in this manuscript were written between 1436 and 1442. I received detailed descriptions of the codex from Kristeller, and of the *Economics* copy from Monsignor Ruysschaert. On the erroneous title cf., Baron, *Leonardo Bruni Aretino*, p. 185.

23. L. Bertalot, "Zur Bibliographie der Uebersetzungen des Leonardus Brunus Aretinus," *Quellen und Forschungen aus italienischen Archiven und Bibliotheken*, XXVII (1937), 186. Rev. Dr. J. López de Toro, former assistant director of the Biblioteca Nacional at Madrid, verified the content of the *Economics* copy.

Thus, among the dated or approximately datable copies of Bruni's prefaced version followed by the commentaries, the earliest was completed some time after 1438; among the copies with the prefaced version only the earliest originated perhaps some years before 1442. This is as close as we can come to dating these two manuscripts, but we cannot be certain that no other manuscripts of these two patterns could have been written earlier. However, it is worth noting that the oldest copies of the entire work, modeled after the one by Antonio di Mario, should date back to 1425, while none of the copies with the texts in the arrangement of the manuscript from the Benedictine abbey in Florence or in the arrangement of the copy by Giovanni Pietro Paolo of Ancona—i.e., patterns (*b*) and (*c*)— bears a date before 1438. To assume that the arrangements of the text most widely known were the latest does not therefore appear to be unreasonable.

II. STATISTICAL COMPARISONS

The 219 extant handwritten copies and the 15 printed editions of Bruni's annotated Latin version of the *Economics* which were penned and printed in the fifteenth century testify that it must have been a fairly well-known work in that century. But how much of a success was it?

To measure the degree of its popularity one must compare the number of its manuscripts with the numbers of the handwritten copies of other literary products from about the same period. Two examples cited by scholars interested in the development of the handwritten and printed book may serve as guides for measuring the dissemination of popular writings in the later middle ages. The one is the extraordinary voyage by the fourteenth-century English traveler Sir John Mandeville, who composed in Norman-French his fanciful story of marvelous experiences in the East and completed his narrative in 1356. Thus far about 250 handwritten copies are known, 200 of the more widely circulated ones are extant in five languages—German and Dutch, seventy-three; Latin, about fifty; English, about forty in at least three different translations; French, thirty-seven—and the rest in Spanish, Italian, Czech, and the Old Irish.[1] The other very popular work is the English chronicle *Brut* [=Brutus, the

---

1. Josephine Waters Bennett, *The Rediscovery of Sir John Mandeville* (New York, 1954), p. 219; the handwritten copies are listed and briefly described in Appendix I (pp. 265– 334). Lucien Febvre and Henri-Jean Martin, *L'apparition du livre* (Paris, 1958), p. 23, present the data on the manuscripts of the *Travels* from the book by Bennett; but in n. 24 they erroneously refer to the study by H. S. Bennett mentioned p. 63 n. 2, below.

mythical great-grandson of Aeneas of Troy, the founder of New Troy, i.e. London] by the early thirteenth-century cleric Layamon. The tradition of the text is somewhat involved, but not so much as that of Bruni's version of the *Economics*, insofar as two different texts are known, a text A from 1205 and a text B (in fact a paraphrase of text A) from 1275. The chronicle was also translated into Latin. An incomplete listing of the manuscripts of the two English texts copied prior to 1480, i.e., for almost three centuries, comprises 121 copies. "The wide diffusion of the *Brut* in manuscript," wrote an English scholar, "and the numerous printed editions which appeared between 1480 and 1530 would alone make it important." [2]

A third set of statistical figures brings us closer to our area. It is a recently compiled catalogue of the extant copies of Ovid's *Metamorphoses*, penned from the tenth to the seventeenth centuries. [3] Altogether 390 items from these seven centuries are there listed. I counted 133 manuscripts written in the fifteenth century and another 4 from the sixteenth century. The total number of copies from the fifteenth century of the 3 then circulating Latin versions of the *Economics*—2 medieval ones and the Bruni translation—amount to 260. Of Bruni's version alone we know 219 extant copies from the fifteenth century and 4 from the early sixteenth century. Thus the spurious work by Aristotle stands up well in comparison with the work by Ovid in its appeal to a partly identical public. Had we complete figures for the English chronicle *Brut*, I presume that in comparison Bruni's version of the *Economics* may still come out ahead of the chronicle, but it does not outdo the popularity of the travelogue by Sir John Mandeville.

Finally, we may compare the diffusion of Bruni's humanistic version of the *Economics* with that of the medieval Latin translations. As to the latter, we will confine ourselves to the two translations which actually circulated in the thirteenth and fourteenth centuries and were still being copied in the fifteenth century: the older translation (*translatio vetus*) of the three books by an anonymous author, done about 1280, and the later translation or revision of the first and third books of the older one by Durand d'Auvergne (*recensio Durandi*), completed in 1295. Of the two medieval translations the one by Durand was the more popular; the authors

2. H. S. Bennett, "The Author and his Public in the Fourteenth and Fifteenth Centuries," *Essays and Studies by Members of the English Association*, XXIII (Oxford, 1938), 22. The list referred to by Bennett was compiled by a Dr. Brie; the quotation comes from an unidentified publication by C. E. Kingsford.

3. Franco Munari, *Catalogue of the MSS of Ovid's Metamorphoses*, University of London, Institute of Classical Studies, in conjunction with the *Warburg Institute. Bulletin*, Supplement 4 (London, 1957).

of the *Aristoteles Latinus* and its Supplements[4] list altogether seventy-six copies of it. The total number of the copies of the *translatio vetus* listed there amounts to only seventeen. Further research will turn up copies undetected so far, determine the nature of the texts not yet identified, and eliminate others that are in fact the Bruni version or derived from it.[5]

4. G. Lacombe in cooperation with A. Birkenmajer, M. Dulong, and E. Franceschini (ed.), *Aristoteles Latinus*, 2 vols.; I (Rome, 1939), II (Cambridge, England, 1955). The Index to both volumes was prepared by L. Minio-Paluello. In the Index (II, 1306) we find reference to twenty-two copies of the *translatio vetus* and seventy-five copies of the *recensio Durandi*. These figures include "contaminated" texts (i.e., copies in which the text of the older translation of Books I and III is combined with that by Durand), listed among both versions, and also dubious texts. To arrive at more representative figures, the "contaminated" texts were, following the analysis of the authors of the *Aristoteles Latinus*, assigned to the older translation or to the Durand version depending on which of the two versions was prevalent in the conflated copies. Dubious texts were eliminated as far as is possible in our present state of knowledge. Thus, I counted fifteen copies of the *translatio vetus* and seventy-two copies of the *recensio Durandi*. In the second supplement to *Aristoteles Latinus*, prepared by L. Minio-Paluello (*Aristoteles Latinus Codices. Supplementa Altera* [Bruges-Paris, 1961]), several entries in the two volumes published in 1939 and 1955 were corrected and some new items, located after 1955, were added. According to the Supplement, there are now seventeen known copies of the *translatio vetus*—thirteen of them containing the pure text and four the conflated text—and seventy-six copies of the *recensio Durandi*, including one still not fully identified, two fragmentary copies and four manuscripts of the Durand version conflated with the older translation. Of the seventeen copies of the older translation two were possibly written in the thirteenth century, ten in the fourteenth century and five in the fifteenth century. Of the seventy-six copies of the Durand version two were penned in the thirteenth century, thirty-eight in the fourteenth century (three of them possibly earlier), and thirty-six in the fifteenth century (three of them possibly at the end of the fourteenth century). While most copies of the older translation originated in Italy, the Durand version was copied mainly in Germany, France, and Italy in that order. A few manuscripts of the Durand version can be traced to other countries such as England (two), Austria (one), Spain (perhaps one), and Switzerland (one). Finally, it should be noted that, in his Supplement, Minio-Paluello refers to the Durand version as the *translatio Durandi* rather than to the *recensio Durandi* as Father Lacombe has done, and thus he assigns to the work by Durand d'Auvergne and his collaborators the status of a translation independent from the older one.

5. Professor Kristeller added one copy of the *translatio vetus* to those listed in the two volumes of the *Aristoteles Latinus*: MS Cod. 5, 3 D 30, fols. 106v–119, of the Biblioteca Comunale at Macerata, interesting from many points of view and notable for its owner, Coluccio Salutati. I gave a detailed description of it in *Scriptorium* (cited above, p. 56, n. 4), 266. In the second supplement to the *Aristoteles Latinus* it is now listed on p. 143 as No. 2158; it is one of the two additional manuscripts of this version mentioned in the preceding note. A manuscript of only Book III (according to the numeration in the Greek original), the *liber secundus* of Durand's and Bruni's Latin *Economics* translations—MS Cod. IV. F. 67, fols. 52–55v of the Biblioteka Uniwersytecka at Wrocław—was listed in *Aristoteles Latinus*, I, 761, No. 1117, as unidentified; Kristeller recognized it as a copy of the *liber secundus* of Bruni's version (150).

If we further break down the totals into the numbers of manuscripts penned before and after 1399, we may catch a glimpse of the rivalry between the medieval translations and Bruni's version of the *Economics*. In the course of the fifteenth century thirty-six copies were made of the Durand version in addition to the five copies of the older one just mentioned. We do know the dates of merely nine copies of Durand's version of the *Economics*. One was penned while Bruni's work was still little known (1429) and the eight others after the translation by Bruni had gained wide circulation (1441, 1459, 1461, 1468 twice, 1472, 1474, 1488). Furthermore, it is worth noting that three or possibly four copies of Durand's version from the fifteenth century were written in Germany, two others possibly in Bohemia, one certainly in Switzerland (Basel), and another certainly in Italy. We have no precise information as to the provenance of the remaining twenty-eight copies of Durand's version penned in the fifteenth century but circumstantial evidence suggests that they originated in Germany, France, Italy, or Spain. Thus Bruni's version of the *Economics* first circulated and replaced Durand's version in Italy and became gradually known in Spain and in the Northern countries in the late 1460s or later by way of handwritten copies and printed editions as well.

While the two medieval Latin translations of the *Economics* were less frequently copied in the fifteenth century than in the fourteenth century, the total number of manuscripts of the Latin versions of the *Economics* from the fifteenth century was four times as large as the number penned in the previous century. About five-sixths of the fifteenth-century copies were those of Bruni's version. It was quite a success for a work by Bruni, but by no means spectacular as far as dissemination of his translations and writings goes. Since there are no statistical figures available for any of his other works, I can only summarize impressions gathered in leafing through a vast mass of catalogues of manuscript collections and Kristeller's *Iter Italicum*. I would differentiate between three groups of works by Bruni according to the number of handwritten copies: (*a*) those of which more than three hundred copies are extant, mainly translations from the Greek such as Xenophon's *Tyrannus* or St. Basil's *De studiis saecularibus*;[6] (*b*) those

6. Ludwig Bertalot, after scanning major Italian, Spanish, and German manuscript collections and catalogues of collections in other countries for copies of Bruni's writings, came to the conclusion that in the fifteenth century Bruni's early translations of St. Basil's *De studiis saecularibus* and of Xenophon's *Hiero* [= *Tyrannus*] were the most widely read works from Bruni's pen. As he put it: "Es sollte ausgesprochen werden, dass die . . . Uebersetzungen des Basilius und Xenophon die gelesensten Produkte der philologischen Muse und Schriftstellerei Brunis überhaupt waren . . . ." "Forschungen über Leonardo Bruni Aretino," *Archivum Romanicum*, X (1931), 302.

of which two or three hundred copies are preserved such as his translations of the *Ethics*, *Economics*, and *Politics* by Aristotle; (*c*) those of which less than a hundred copies are known to exist such as most or all of Bruni's own, original works. I should not be surprised, however, if the numbers of copies of his translations of writings by Plato and Plutarch would far exceed the three hundred mark. The *Economics* version would be in the lowest third of group (*b*) while his *Ethics* and *Politics* translations would figure in the second or first third of this group with numbers of manuscripts exceeding by a good margin the number of copies of the annotated version of the *Economics*.

III. THE CIRCULATION OF MANUSCRIPTS AMONG VARIOUS SOCIAL GROUPS

"For as health is the aim of the art of medicine, so is wealth the aim of the art of household management. Wealth is useful indeed as it provides those who possess it with distinction as well as the ability to practice virtue...."[1] These are the objectives of that part of practical philosophy that concerns itself with *Economics* (*res familiaris* or *oeconomica*), explains Bruni in his dedicatory epistle to Cosimo de' Medici in reply to the rhetorical question he had before directed to him. "For on the leadership of an army to whom else can advice be given on its better conduct but to one who has an army? And on the administration of the household again, to whom else can advice more appropriately be given than to one who owns ample means and who desires to preserve them with praise and to increase them with dignity?"[2]

This is the way in which Bruni, a scholar and man of public affairs, looked at that "little book" (*libellus*) by Aristotle, whose translation he

1. "Ut enim medicinae finis est sanitas, ita rei familiaris divitias finem esse constat. Sunt vero utiles divitiae, cum et ornamento sint possidentibus et ad virtutem exercendam suppeditent facultatem...." The text is cited from the edition of the preface by Baron (ed.), *Leonardo Bruni Aretino*, p. 120, ll. 25–28. The comparison of medicine with household management is a reference to *Nicomachean Ethics*, Book I, chapter 1: "the end of the medical art is health, ... that of economics wealth" (translated by W. D. Ross, *The Works of Aristotle*, IX [Oxford, 1925], p. 1094ᵃ, ll. 8–9). Bruni paraphrased this passage from his own *Ethics* version which he had completed in 1417.

2. "Cui enim rectius de gubernatione exercitus praecipi potest, quam illi, qui exercitum habeat? Cui rursus de rei familiaris administratione, quam ei, qui rem amplam possidet et tueri illam cum laude gliscit et augere cum dignitate?..." Baron (ed.), *Leonardo Bruni Aretino*, p. 120, ll. 18–21. The first sentence is evidently an allusion to *Nicomachean Ethics*, Book X, chapter 9: "and so it seems that those who aim at knowing about the art of politics need experience as well" (as translated by Ross, *The Works of Aristotle*, IX, p. 1181ᵃ, ll. 11–12).

dedicated to a man of wealth and culture who could afford to practice virtue and, as Bruni assured him, manage his riches in a praiseworthy fashion and enlarge them with honesty. To make the reading of the book easier for Cosimo, Bruni also added to his version "an explanation of the more obscure passages."[3]

There is more truthfulness and less conventional rhetorical praise than was customary in such dedicatory epistles in this assertion in the dedication as to why the translation was addressed to Cosimo. Aristotle had composed his treatises on *Ethics* and *Politics* for readers who possessed as much property and education as he considered to be prerequisite for practicing civic virtue and who were also inclined to be active in public affairs.[4] The references to the *Ethics* and *Politics* in the above-mentioned passages from the epistle are obvious. Like Aristotle did before him, Bruni put his version of the *Economics* in the hands of a man who, in the Aristotelian sense, was eminently qualified to practice the virtues of an exemplary citizen. Bruni's "commentary," which he characterized as "an explanation of obscure passages," consisted in fact of no more than annotations of the text. It was tailored to the taste of a person who was not in the habit of studying the traditional kind of commentary, i.e., the scholastic exegesis of the writings of "the philosopher." Hence, Bruni's annotations were not devoted to such academic topics as one would find in the scholastic commentaries on works by Aristotle—for instance, lengthy disquisitions on the difference between the sciences of economics and politics—but almost exclusively to the practical issues treated in the work and to the many references in the text to history and to classical literature.

When Bruni's work was finally copied for readers other than Cosimo himself, the annotated version of the *Economics* quite as much as the Preface turned out to be attractive to a broad audience for a variety of reasons. Some readers were in a position similar to that of Cosimo; they were men of means and education and they may have sensed that Bruni's

3. "... verum etiam explanationem quamdam obscurorum verborum adiunxi, quo tibi legenti dilucidior esset" [Baron (ed.), *Leonardo Bruni Aretino*, p. 121, ll. 8–10]. In his copy of Bruni's *Economics* version (69) Antonio di Mario names Bruni's annotations to Book I "Commentarium," although Bruni himself called them an "explanation of obscure passages" in the cited quotation from his Preface. The distinction of annotations and commentaries as made in the fifteenth and early sixteenth centuries and the significance of this distinction will be discussed at length below in Part IV.

4. *Politics* iii. 12. 1283^a 16–17: "There is thus good ground for the claims to honour and office which are made by persons of good descent, free birth, or wealth" (translated by Ernest Barker, *The Politics of Aristotle* [Oxford, 1948], p. 131), and also *Politics* iv. 12. 1296^b 17–19: "By 'quality' [of citizens] we mean free birth, wealth, culture, and nobility of descent" (*ibid.*, p. 185). To these qualities must be added the experience of which Aristotle spoke in the *Nicomachean Ethics* (see above p. 66, n. 2).

appeal to Cosimo to read this guide to virtuous management of domestic affairs would apply to them as well. Others, not as amply endowed with riches as Cosimo but quite as sensitive to cultural values as the Florentine banker, shared with Bruni and Cosimo a keen sense for reflections on the virtuous conduct of mundane affairs. The emphasis on the ethical aspects in matters of household management made this work of Aristotle interesting to those who, by profession and vocation, were concerned about virtue in all actions, private and public. Finally, the new Latin garb of an Aristotelian work, which had been studied in less eloquent Latin for more than two centuries before Bruni's translation appeared, appealed to all groups and in particular to men engaged in the *studia humanitatis* and others sympathetic to their aspirations for reviving ancient Greek literature.

Among the owners and readers of the handwritten copies of Bruni's version of the *Economics*, we shall indeed meet several men in elevated public positions and professionals, besides scholars and clerics of all sorts and ranks. University teachers of moral philosophy were the last ones to join the public audience and only after a long period of hesitation.[5] But before we turn to these various groups, something should be said about the scribes of the manuscripts. Ordinarily, they would be considered intermediaries between the author and his public, somewhat like printers and publishers in the age of the printed book. In our case, however, they may have been both—intermediaries and final consumers—if they copied the text for their own use, be it for the mere study of the text or for preparing the basis for their own commentaries on Bruni's translation.

Only a few copyists were professional scribes or scholarly scribes of fame. This is not to say that the number of copies expertly written and lavishly ornamented with beautifully colored initials is very small. On the contrary, a surprisingly large percentage of the manuscripts were written by expert hands and illuminated by artists specializing in painting initials; some worked on direct orders by prospective owners and some in the service of booksellers. Since their copies were merchandise, no matter how highly priced, they did not sign their names.[6] The only exception is the

5. On the public audience of humanistic literature see P. O. Kristeller, "Der Gelehrte und sein Publikum im spaeten Mittelalter und in der Renaissance," *Medium Aevum Vivum; Festschrift für Walther Bulst*, ed. H. R. Jauss and D. Schaller (Heidelberg, 1960), pp. 212–230, esp. 218–223, 226–228.

6. Curt F. Bühler, *The Fifteenth-Century Book: The Scribes, the Printers, the Decorators* (Philadelphia, 1960), pp. 25–27, on scribes in the second half of the fifteenth century; also Kristeller, "Der Gelehrte und sein Publikum," p. 227.

famous pioneer in the development of humanistic script, Antonio di Mario.[7] The other copyists, whether Italian or foreigners working in Italy, are today merely names. They were Andreas de Arnoldis from Florence (114:1421), Andreas de Montelupono, who claimed to be a "velocissimus scriptor" (31), Bartholomeus Cersolus (38:1471), Dominicus Carrolus (7:1458), Gaspar Garimbertus in Milan (20:1451), Iacobinus Sangallius from Bergamo (144), A. Ludovici (179), Ioannes de Manasseis de Interamna in Florence (26:1425–1426), Panigallius Jacobus (10), Johannes Pottere de Ziricsee in Rome (22:1456) and Franciscus Beninus de Redolfinis (198:1425).

Marsilio Ficino is the most famous of the Italian scholars who did copying. We do have two copies from his hand, one of the Preface, Books I and II, written before 1454 and probably closer to 1452 (41). The other is a copy of Books I and II, penned in May, 1455, and owned by him (90). It is one of a group of copies (group E in Appendix II) from the hands of scholars who were not only interested in the content of the spurious Aristotelian work but also in the style of Bruni's translation. The Brescian nobleman Bartholomeus de Ganasonibus, who penned a one-book copy (62:1439), was probably a scholar; so was certainly Pietro Paolo of Ancona, the disciple of Ciriaco of Ancona who rendered a Latin version of the pseudo-Aristotelian *De Virtutibus*.[8] The Bohemian nobleman Johannes von (de) Rabenstein, who copied for himself the Preface and Book I at Pavia in or before 1464 (2), was both a scholar and courtier. Two of the finest copies were penned by Spanish scholars and professional scribes: the one (167: 1461) by the famous humanist Antonio de Lebrija (Antonius de Lebrixa) and the other (153: 1464) by Antonio de Morales. Some copies by otherwise unknown non-Italian clerics and scholars will be discussed in other contexts as significant for peculiarities in the transmission of Bruni's version.

With a few exceptions, all handwritten copies are of Italian provenance. The few exceptions—thus far amounting to fifteen, but a few more may be established as such—are manuscripts originating in Spain, Switzerland, Belgium, France, Germany, and Poland. They are of interest because they give us an inkling of how and when Bruni's version became known outside his native country in the wake of the spreading humanistic

7. B. L. Ullman, *The Origin and Development of Humanistic Script* (Rome, 1960), pp. 98–109.

8. Eugenio Garin, "Le traduzioni umanistiche di Aristotele nel secolo XV," *Atti dell' Accademia Fiorentina di Scienze Morali "La Colombaria,"* VIII (Florence, 1950), 14–15.

movement. Four of the better items were copied in Spain by professional scribes; in addition to the two just mentioned there is one by a Gundisalvus de Oviedo (169). The earliest was the work by Antonio de Lebrija who did it in 1461. The printing press in Spain took over from the scribes in *ca.* 1475–1477, when Lambert Palmart in Valencia brought an exquisite print (GW 2370) on the market. Next in time is a copy written in 1465 at Bruges, Belgium, by an unknown scribe who signed F. M. B., possibly a cleric (*F* may stand for "Frater"; in another manuscript, preceding this one in Cod. 1373 [T.5.11] of the Biblioteca Angelica, he signed M. B.). Here also may be mentioned a manuscript (162), written in Italy, which Brother Michael bought at Louvain in the middle of the fifteenth century. He brought it to the monastery at Poblet (Spain) which he later headed as abbot. The copy penned at Bruges and the Italian manuscript acquired by the Spanish Cistercian monk at Louvain indicate that Bruni's version was known in Belgium at about the same time as in Spain.

In Switzerland it may have been known even earlier, to judge from information that appears to be reliable. According to an inventory from 1432, there was among the books in the Benedictine monastery at Wiblingen (southwest Germany) a manuscript (220), now lost, with an explicit at the end of the commentaries on both books, noting that it was copied at Basel.[9] A copy in Zurich (186) of the entire version with the commentary was penned in 1464 by an unknown but apparently clerical hand. From 1469 on and until 1515 six manuscripts originated in Germany. The oldest, dated 1469, containing the Preface and both books, was done by a minor cleric in the bishopric of Constance (51); another, completed by a German hand before 1477, belonged to the Dominican convent at Regensburg (49). The remaining four manuscripts are much later and they will be described below (Part IV). In the same year in which the Constance copy was penned, Bruni's version was printed for the first time in the history of its printed editions by Johann Mentelin at Strasbourg (GW 2367). The Cod. 570 of the University of Paris has various copies of works by Bruni, among them one of his version of the *Economics* with the Preface. They were written, probably at Paris, for

9. *Mittelalterliche Bibliothekskataloge Deutschlands und der Schweiz*, Vol. I: *Die Bistuemer Konstanz und Chur*, ed. P. Lehmann (Munich, 1918), 435. On humanistic tendencies in the fifteenth- and early sixteenth-centuries intellectual life of the city of Constance and of the Swabian Benedictine convents at Ottobeuren and Wiblingen where manuscripts of Bruni's version of the *Economics* originated or were deposited, see the instructive study by Friedrich Zoepfl, "Kloster Ottobeuren und der Humanismus," in *Ottobeuren: Festschrift zur 1200-Jahrfeier der Abtei*, ed. Aegidius Kolb O.S.B. and Hermann Tüchle (Augsburg, 1964), pp. 187–267.

Odon Charlier (Carlier), a professor at the Collège de Laon, in 1486.[10] The first Paris print of the same text, prepared by an unknown editor in scholastic fashion, was done by George Wolff for the publisher Durand Gerlier in 1489/90 (GW 2447).

There are two dated manuscripts from the early sixteenth century in Poland. Christopher Koszucki, a nobleman from Poznań, copied in 1518 the two books of the *Economics* in the translation by Bruni (149) and earlier, in 1505, a scholar by name of Bernard from Lublin (Bernardus Lublinius), a disciple of Filippo Buonaccorsi di S.Gemignano (called Callimachus, 1437–1496), excerpted both books (148); the significance of these copies will be the subject of a later discussion (Part IV). Both manuscripts may have been based on printed editions of the Bruni version which by that time had appeared in various countries and were widely circulating. The Poznań manuscript may even have been copied from an edition printed in Poland. In 1512 the Cracow printer-publisher Floryan Ungler turned out what is probably the earliest Polish print of the Bruni version. The manuscripts penned outside Italy suggest, therefore, that Bruni's version of the *Economics* was received, from the early 1460s on, first in Spain, Belgium, and Switzerland, then in Germany and France, and finally in Poland.

Turning to the persons who acquired copies of Bruni's annotated version of the *Economics* by having them made on order or through purchase of extant manuscripts in the open market we may now consider the public reached by Bruni. Already in the middle ages educated laymen as well as academic teachers and clerics were attracted to the Aristotelian writings on moral philosophy. King Charles V of France, a patron of the sciences, had Nicole Oresme translate in 1371–1374 the *Ethics*, *Economics*, and *Politics* into French so that he and his courtiers might be better acquainted with these works. Oresme made his French version of the *Economics* from the Latin translation by Durand d'Auvergne and added to his translation a commentary in the form of glosses, in some respects resembling the annotations by Bruni on his own version. Oresme completed his annotated version of the *Economics* probably in 1374. Two years later Charles

10. *Catalogue Général des Manuscrits des Bibliothèques Publiques de France. Université de Paris et Universités des Départements* (Paris, 1918), pp. 139–140; Comité Internationale de Paléographie, *Catalogue des manuscrits en écriture latine portant des indications de date, de lieu ou de copiste*, ed. Ch. Samaran and R. Marichal; I: *Musée Condé et Bibliothèques Parisiennes*, comp. by M. Garand, J. Metman, and M. Th. Vernet (Paris, 1959), 434, No. 283; Augustin Renaudet, *Préréforme et humanisme à Paris pendant les premières guerres d'Italie (1494–1517)*, 2d ed. (Paris, 1953), p. 126 and n. 6. Renaudet believes them to be copies by Charlier for his own use.

V had it copied, together with the *Ethics* and *Politics* translations by Oresme, by his favorite scribe and beautifully illuminated.[11] While still at work, Oresme received a letter from his royal patron in which he said: "Nous faisons translater à nostre bien aimé le doyen de Rouen, maistre Nicolle Oresme, deux livres, lesquieux sont très necessaires et pour cause, c'est assavoir Polithiques et Yconomiques . . . ."[12] For this task he detailed the needed financial support.

More than two centuries later King Henry IV of France acquired for his private collection a copy of Bruni's Latin version which, through various intermediaries, came from the library of King Ferrante of Aragon in Naples. This was indeed a copy worthy of royalty. It is now the manuscript Cod. lat. 6 310, fols. 111–117, of the Bibliothèque Nationale (29).[13] We have no way of ascertaining how much attention Henry IV paid to the Aristotelian *Economics* in the translation by Bruni, but we do know that Ferrante of Aragon treasured it as a piece of great personal concern. His father Alfonso "the Magnificent" was as much intrigued by this supposed treatise by Aristotle as by the version of it by Bruni. In fact, Bruni sent a copy of his translation to Alfonso with a personal letter[14] and Alfonso expressed his appreciation of this gift and his sentiments about the Aristotelian *Politics* and *Economics* in two extant letters.[15] The interest of Alfonso in Aristotelian philosophy was not confined to the moral branch of it. He sponsored, it is true, the translation of the *Eudemian Ethics* by Giannozzo Manetti, but it must also be remembered that Cardinal Bessarion dedicated to him his *Metaphysics* translation.[16] There were four

11. Albert D. Menut (ed.), "Maistre Nicole Oresme: Le Livre de Yconomique d'Aristote," *Transactions of the American Philosophical Society*, N.S., XLVII, Part 5 (1957), 791; the copy of the *Politiques* and *Yconomique* which Charles V carried with him while traveling is MS 2904 of the Bibliothèque Royale at Brussels.

12. L. Delisle, *Le Cabinet des Manuscrits de la Bibliothèque Impériale*, I (Paris, 1868), 41–42.

13. G. Mazzatinti, *La biblioteca dei Re d'Aragona in Napoli* (Rocca S. Casciano, 1897), pp. 36–37, No. 56; T. De Marinis, *La Biblioteca Napoletana dei Re d'Aragona*, II (Milan, 1947), 16–17.

14. L. Mehus (ed.), *Leonardi Bruni Arretini Epistolarum libri VIII*, 2 vols. (Florence, 1741), II, 130–134.

15. The letters are from August 12, 1440, and March 12, 1441. In Cod. 828 of the Biblioteca Universitaria at Valencia which Ferrante bought in Florence in 1470 (see below p. 73, n. 17), on fol. 91 there is one of the two letters from Bruni to King Alfonso. The two letters of Alfonso are now to be found in A. Giménez Solar, *Itinerario del rey Alonso de Aragon y Napoles* [Zaragoza, 1909], pp. 179 and 185.

16. Garin, *op. cit.*, pp. 17–19.

copies of Bruni's version of the *Economics* in the Neapolitan library of the kings of Aragon. Besides the one already mentioned there was the entire annotated version although distributed over two codices—the one containing the Preface, Books I and II and the other the commentaries on both books (177)—one copy of the two books with the Preface (176), and finally a copy of the two books and their respective commentaries but without the Preface (178) in a codex comprising the three Aristotle translations by Bruni, the *Isagogicon*, and the correspondence between Alfonso and Bruni. Ferrante purchased this codex in 1470 in Florence through the banker Filippo Strozzi, a political exile from that city.[17] In the next century the Spanish statesman and humanist Don Diego Hurtado de Mendoza, Emperor Charles V's ambassador to Venice, carefully studied the version by Bruni. Over many years, mainly in the 1540s while residing at Venice, Don Diego built up an impressive collection of handwritten books, primarily Greek. In 1573–1574 he sold his collection to Philip II for the El Escorial palace. Among the books owned by Don Diego was one containing a copy of Bruni's version of the *Economics* with marginal notes in the hand of Don Diego (155); it is still in El Escorial with two other copies (154, 156) of the Bruni translation.[18] No copy has thus far turned up from the library of King Matthias Corvinus where Bruni writings were otherwise well represented.

Copies of Bruni's version, some expressly written for their owners, were in the collections of the Italian high nobility. Three manuscripts belonged to the library of Federico da Montefeltro, duke of Urbino; they are now in the Vatican Library (215, 216, 217). The last mentioned (217),

17. These manuscripts, now in the Biblioteca Universitaria at Valencia, are described by M. Gutiérrez del Caño, *Catálogo de los Manuscritos Existentes en la Biblioteca Universitaria de Valencia*, I (1914), 45–46 and 140, and by De Marinis, *op. cit.*, II, 14–15, with the documented history of Cod. 828 purchased by King Ferrante, pp. 17 and 27. Both Gutiérrez and De Marinis overlooked the *Economics* copy in Cod. 389, fols. 145–153, although they quoted the ending words of the *liber secundus* in the Bruni version; I verified this copy with the help of a microfilm. King Ferrante was in a close political alliance with Lorenzo de' Medici against the kings of France who claimed the Italian realm of the kings of Aragon. But Ferrante kept out of Lorenzo's domestic strife, even granting exile to Lorenzo's domestic foes. On the interest of Ferrante in the cultural life of Florence and on his relation to Ficino, see Kristeller, *Studies in Renaissance Thought and Letters* (Rome, 1956), pp. 411–413, and 114–115.

18. Charles Henri Graux, "Essai sur les Origines du Fonds Grec de l'Escourial; Épisode de l'Histoire de la Renaissance des Lettres en Espagne," *Bibliothèque de l'École des Hautes Etudes . . .*, *Sciences Philologiques et Historiques*, fasc. 46 (Paris, 1880), pp. 163–273 [Le Fonds Mendoza].

containing the entire annotated version, was bound separately.[19] Three copies (112, 113, 114) are traceable to the collection of the Farnese family, the dukes of Parma; they are now deposited in the Biblioteca Nazionale at Naples.[20] We do not know when they were acquired, but it is not unlikely that the one or the other may have been purchased by the scholarly Cardinal Alessandro Farnese, later Pope Paul III (1468–1549), whose passion for collecting manuscripts and whose interest in Aristotelian studies are well known. It was particularly Aristotle's moral philosophy which attracted him. As pope he patronized the Jewish scholar Jacob Mantino from Tortosa, his personal physician, whom he had translate in 1539 Averroës' paraphrase of Plato's *Republic*. (Averroës composed this paraphrase in lieu of a commentary on the Aristotelian *Politics*, whose text was unknown to Averroës; the paraphrase was considered to belong to the commentaries on the Aristotelian corpus and as such it was included in two editions of Latin translations of and commentaries on the works of Aristotle, printed in Venice in 1550–1552 and 1560.) The Marquis Gian Ludovico Pallavicini (1425–1488), lord of Cortemaggiore near Milan and then a dependent of the Sforzas, had a copyist pen the Aristotle translations by Bruni with the *Economics* (107) placed at the end. This paper codex is now in the Biblioteca Ambrosiana in Milan.

A good number of copies were in the book collections of the renaissance Italian merchant princes. In the library of Piero de' Medici there were two, the celebrated transcript by Antonio di Mario (69) and a copy of the entire annotated version (71) in the arrangement which became so popular after the late 1430s or in the early 1440s. The family library contained also a very beautifully written and richly adorned manuscript of the version with the Preface (72), combined with Bruni's translation of the *Politics*. A fourth manuscript is particularly interesting; it is a copy of the Preface (63). As a rule, we do not know whether the extant manuscript is part of a once complete or of an unfinished copy. Here we do have

19. C. Stornaiolo, *Codices Urbinates Latini*, III (Rome, 1921), 267 and 273–275. In the inventories of the various collections which belonged to the d'Este family, the dukes of Ferrara, no copy of Bruni's translation of the *Economics* is listed; the two manuscripts in the Fondo Estense (108, 109) of the Biblioteca Estense at Modena were no part of the fifteenth or early sixteenth century d'Este Libraries.

20. Dott. ssa Guerriera Guerrieri, director of the Naples Biblioteca Nazionale and an expert on the Farnese collection, provided me with descriptions and microfilm of these copies and identified them as being from the Farnese library. They are not listed in her study "Il Fondo Farnesiano," *I Quaderni della R. Biblioteca Nazionale Vittorio Emanuele III—Napoli*, Series II, No. 2 (Naples, 1941).

evidence that no more than the Preface was intended to be reproduced. It is a neatly written copy in the famous manuscript known as the *Collectiones Cosmianae*. Bartolommeo Scala, for many years chancellor of Florence, humanist and member of the Ficino circle (he lived in the Medici house until the death of Cosimo), compiled sometime between 1464 and 1469 documents honoring the memory of the deceased Cosimo. Besides letters of sympathy upon the death of Cosimo, the collection includes honorary decrees and poems on Cosimo and also letters, poems, and prefaces addressed to him. The compilation was dedicated to Lorenzo.[21] Wealthy friends and business associates of the Medicis and their rivals too, and patrician families in and outside Florence, possessed, among other manuscripts of Bruni's writings, copies of the *Economics* translation. Francesco Sassetti, a partner of the Medici bank and an ardent book collector,[22] had in his library an exquisitely written and richly ornamented copy (66) in a volume which contained besides this work by Bruni, the *Isagogicon* and the *Ethics* translation by Argyropulos. In the collection of the influential Florentine Pucci family there was a copy (84), but it is not certain whether the codex containing it may not have been purchased after the fifteenth century. A nicely done copy (144), illuminated with initials and combined with the Bruni translation of the *Ethics*, was owned by the Venetian patrician family Loredan; the statesman and military commander Pietro Loredano was the father-in-law of Francesco Barbaro.

Professional men with academic training in law and medicine—

21. A. M. Bandinius, *Catalogus codicum latinorum Bibliothecae Mediceae Laurentianae*. II (1775), 643–651. A thorough study of the *Collectiones Cosmianae* was made by Alison M. Brown in her essay "The Humanist Portrait of Cosimo de' Medici, Pater Patriae," *Journal of the Warburg and Courtald Institute*, XXIV (1961), 186–221. In reference to Bruni's preface to his version of the *Economics*, "the earliest writing in his [Cosimo's] praise," Miss Brown observes (p. 188) that Bruni pictures Cosimo there "as head of a prosperous merchant family" and emphasizes the significance of his wealth, while seven years later, in his dedication to Cosimo of the translation of Plato's *Letters*, Bruni extols the virtues of the mind. The terms of praise and the shift of emphasis in it "were, of course, largely imposed on him [Bruni] by the subject of the translation he was sending to Cosimo" (p. 188).

22. Francesco Sassetti, the son of a money-changer in Mercato Nuovo, entered the Medici Bank around 1440 as a factor in the Geneva branch and rose to the position of branch manager. Called to Florence in 1459 to relieve his friend, the overburdened Giovanni di Cosimo, he amassed a sizable fortune in the ensuing five years, part of this he invested in the Medici company. Included in this fortune was "a fine library of books, in both Latin and the vernacular. His *ex libris* displayed the significant motto, in French: A mon pouvoir." Raymond de Roover, *The Rise and Decline of the Medici Bank, 1397–1494*, Harvard Studies in Business History, XXI (Cambridge, Mass., 1963), 362.

administrators, notaries, lawyers, physicians—were important and significant partisans of the humanistic movement and of nonacademic studies of Aristotelian moral philosophy including, of course, the pseudo-Aristotelian treatise on *Economics* in the annotated version by Bruni. Some of these men could afford to purchase handwritten books, but not to form a collection of such books which would be handed down from one generation to the next. Ordinarily, their books would be sold by their heirs or would be donated to a convent in the hope that this good deed would be rewarded in the hereafter. Only a man of means like the auditor of Francesco Sforza, a Giovanni Amerino, doctor of civil and canon law, was in a position to enrich his library with as splendid a copy as the manuscript (20) of the Preface and Book I, penned for him on parchment by a professional scribe and profusely illuminated. A man of similar background and in a comparable position, Nicolaus Arcimboldi, doctor of civil and canon law and auditor (*ducalium exactor*) for the dukes of Parma possessed a parchment codex with Bruni's translations of the *Ethics* and *Economics* (105) copied for him. A paper codex containing a large number of works by Bruni, among them his version of the *Economics* with the commentary (32), was sold by the Florentine notary Grisus for five papal ducats and was subsequently in the possession of various owners in Ferrara. A volume of humanistic texts, one a fragment of Bruni's dedicatory epistle to Cosimo de' Medici (202), belonged at one time to a Ioannes Franciscus, *annualis advocatus*, at Venice. It was a Bolognese physician by name of Gregorio Malisardi who owned and eventually gave to a Father Cannetti a codex with Bruni's versions of the *Ethics* and *Economics*, the latter with the commentary (123). Two Swiss copies of the annotated version of the *Economics* and an Italian transcript only of the translation are particularly helpful in answering the question as to the fate of copies owned by educated laymen and professionals. The older (186) of the two Swiss copies was part of a manuscript penned in 1464, containing the three Aristotle translations by Bruni. It belonged to a magister Johann Gaudenhemer, a man engaged in a profession unknown to us; he presented it to the Carmelite monastery on the Zurichberg. The entry by a monk on the bottom of the first page, recording this gift, closes with the notation "oretur pro eo." The later copy (182) was bought for one florin in Basel by a Berchthold Kirsseman from Horw who was matriculated at the University of Basel in 1471. Subsequently, it was acquired by a Ludwig Moser from Zurich, a "prothonotarius" in Rheinfelden and later a Carthusian monk; he donated it to the Carthusian monastery at Basel. Its prior, recording that the codex was given to the Carthusian monks by their Brother, ends his note with the words "pro suisque oretur in caritate."[23] In Italy, an unknown person donated a fine parchment codex of mainly humanistic writings, some of them by Bruni and among these his version of the *Economics* (15 b), to an unidentified convent "pro remedio animae suae." The codex belonged at one time to Niccolo di Cocco di Donato, the head of an influential Florentine family, who had extensive business relations with Cosimo.[24]

Scholars of humanistic orientation were naturally one another's most attentive and appreciative audience.[25] As we have seen, Ficino penned two copies of Bruni's version but apparently retained only one copy (90). Angelo Poliziano too, possessed a copy (79) with his notes in the margins. It is now combined with a copy of the *Ethics* translation by Bruni with corrections and notes, based on lectures given by Poliziano in 1491 and 1492, added in the margins by a certain Augustinus Terriculus.[26] Poliziano lectured on the *Ethics* in the Florentine studio at that time and had earlier written an introductory lecture to the *Ethics* under the title "Panepistemon" which was first printed *ca.* 1485 at Rome (Reichling 290). Giannozzo Manetti, who was distinguished by great though recent wealth and by scholarship—he rendered new Latin translations of the three Aristotelian

23. The codex of the Carmelite monastery on the Zurichberg and its former owners are extensively described by Cunibert Mohlberg in the *Katalog der Handschriften der Zentralbibliothek Zürich*, I (Zurich, 1932), 112–113, No. 267. The data about the previous owners of Cod. AN. IV. 14 [F. IV. 1] of the Oeffentliche Bibliothek der Universität Basel were kindly furnished by Dr. Max Burckhardt, conservator of the manuscripts of the Basel University Library.

24. It is now MS Harley 3651 of the British Museum. *A Catalogue of the Harleian Manuscripts in the British Museum*, III (1808), 40. Bruni's version of the *Economics* is in the folios 34–41. Since the text is not identified in a title or in an explicit, the otherwise detailed Index of the catalogue fails to list it as this work by Bruni. Professor Kristeller identified the text when inspecting the codex. A note on the flyleaf of the codex states that it belonged at one time to Niccolò di Cocco di Donato (Nicolaus Chochus de Donatis, cives Florentinus); a later unidentified possessor of the codex may have given it to the monastery. On Niccolò and his newly rich family, called after 1434 the Cocchi-Donati, and on the political connections of the family with the Medici, see Lauro Martines, *The Social World of the Florentine Humanists* (Princeton, 1963), pp. 71–72.

25. The financial circumstances and social positions of the cited Florentine humanists who owned copies of Bruni's work were as varied as the esthetic qualities and costliness of their copies and of the codices containing them. On the social and financial situations of Ficino, Poliziano, and Manetti, see Martines, *op. cit.*, pp. 5–8, 131–138, 178–191.

26. Bandini Catalogue, Supplement, II, 392–393. At the end of the *Ethics* version: "Augustinus Terriculus ex lectura Politiani viri doctissimi anno 1491 and 1492." Augustinus Nettuccius and friends and (fol. 1) Senatore Carlo di Tommaso Strozzi, 1670, are named as later owners of the codex.

Ethics[27]—owned a parchment codex with Bruni's translations of the *Economics* (212) and *Politics*. An exquisite early copy (198) of Bruni's entire version of the *Economics*, penned in 1425, belonged to the scholarly Sicilian humanist Nicolaus Scyllacius, who bought it from the copyist.[28] The Pisan notary and classical scholar ser Piero Roncione had in his collection one copy of Bruni's translation with the Preface and another copy which contained the commentary only (97, 121).[29]

The social classes that we have discovered so far to be Bruni's public audience are what we would expect. But the broad and fairly rapid diffusion of the first humanistic version of the *Economics* is also greatly attributable to the clergy. Regular and lay clerics of all ranks, mostly those in Italy, Spain, and later in German-speaking countries, were intent on studying this pseudo-Aristotelian work in its humanistic garb. In the fifteenth century the *Economics* was an integral part of Aristotelian moral philosophy and it held, after the *Ethics* and *Politics*, a third place in this segment of the curriculum in secular and clerical institutions of higher learning. Furthermore, it must be kept in mind that the higher ranking members of the clergy were scholars and very erudite members of the upper classes. They patronized the humanists and they shared their literary tastes and preferences with their families and friends. What appears, at first glance, to be somewhat surprising is the fact that clerics showed no hesitation in preferring Bruni's humanistic Latin version to the later medieval Latin translation authored by a cleric. In recent years experts on scholasticism have made much of the controversy between Leonardo Bruni and Alphonsus [Alonso] of Cartagena, bishop of Burgos,

---

27. Manetti, dissatisfied with Bruni's translation of the *Nicomachean Ethics*, prepared a new Latin version of it and also translated the *Magna Moralia* and the *Eudemian Ethics* which he dedicated, as mentioned earlier (p. 72), to King Alfonso of Aragon. Cf., Garin, *op. cit.*, pp. 17–19.

28. For a description of this manuscript and its significance for the transmission of Bruni's work see above p. 60.

29. The copy of Bruni's version of the *Economics* is now Cod. 1436 [L.148, rubro 139], fols. 101–106, of the Biblioteca Governativa at Lucca; I received a detailed description of it from Dott. ssa Marta Figgeri, director of the library. The copy of the commentary is now Cod. 690 [Roncioni 11], fols. 233–247v, of the Biblioteca Universitaria at Pisa. C. Vitelli, who described the codex in *Studi Italiani di Filologia Classica*, X (1902), 29–39, did not recognize the Bruni commentary. Kristeller corrected Vitelli in his *Iter Italicum*, II (1967), 74. According to A. Mancini, ser Piero Roncione purchased the first codex, now in Lucca, on April 26, 1466; but we do not know when he acquired the second one, now in Pisa, which was written in 1442, according to J. A. Fabricius, *Bibliotheca Latina Mediae et Infimae Aetatis*, I (Florence, 1858), 397. In the early eighteenth century both volumes were in the possession of Martius Michelli, canon of Lucca Cathedral.

concerning the merits of the medieval Latin version of the *Ethics* by Robert Grosseteste. This feud, on the part of the defenders of Grosseteste, was carried on until the late fifteenth century.[30] It is easy to show that the liberties Bruni took in his translation of the *Ethics* met with equal resistance from the humanists and their opponents. I have mentioned already Manetti, who sought to avoid the pitfalls of Bruni's translation in a new version which, however, remained unprinted and therefore could not rival as successfully the work of Bruni as did the translation by Argyropulos, done at the request of Cosimo de' Medici in response to criticism by various scholars.[31] Yet Bruni's version was widely read as the impressive number of manuscripts and printed editions indicates. Only as time went on, the public preferred the Argyropulos translation to Bruni's. Between 1495 and 1535 the Argyropulos version was printed twice as often as that by Bruni, and after 1535 the Bruni translation practically disappeared from the market while the Argyropulos translation was reissued, without interruption, until 1592.[32] As far as the clerics in the fifteenth century are concerned—if one may generalize—it seems that they, quite as much as the secular scholars dedicated to the *studia humanitatis*, regarded the celebrated "controversia Alphonsina" as a singular instance which did not prejudice their evaluation of other works by Bruni.

30. On Bruni's controversy with Alonso Garcia of Cartagena (1384–1435), see Angelo Paredi, *La Biblioteca del Pizolpasso* (Milan, 1961), p. 48 and n. 76 and Riccardo Fubini, "Tra umanesimo e concili. Note e giunte a una pubblicazione recente su Francesco Pizolpasso *(1370 c–1443)*." *Studi Medievali*. 3d. series. VII, 1 (1966), 323–353, esp. 337–343; also, E. Franceschini, "Leonardo Bruni e il 'vetus interpres' dell' Etica a Nicomaco," *Medioevo e Rinascimento*, I (Florence, 1955), 299–319.

31. Garin, *op. cit.*, p. 10, cites Pizolpasso, Poggio, Filelfo, Decembrio, Bessarion, Argyropulos, and Acciaiuoli as humanists who participated in this controversy concerning the merits of Bruni's version as compared with that by Grosseteste. The dissatisfaction of Gianozzo Manetti with Bruni's translation and his own version have been mentioned before (p. 78, n. 27).

32. Bertalot suggested that the translation of the *Ethics* by Argyropulos was printed twice as often as Bruni's ("Zur Bibliographie der Uebersetzungen des Leonardus Brunus Aretinus," p. 189). My own observations in studying the editions of the collected works of Aristotle in Latin translations which were printed in the cited forty-year period support Bertalot's suggestion. My further investigations of Latin translations of Aristotle's writings on moral philosophy published in the sixteenth century yielded the results submitted in the text. The translation of the *Ethics* by Argyropulos, in turn, was replaced by that of Denis Lambin (Dionysius Lambinus), which was first published in 1558 and which, from 1593 on, became the standard Latin version of the *Ethics* in the Latin and Graeco-Latin editions of the collected works of Aristotle. Immanuel Bekker adopted it in his collection of Latin translations of the works of Aristotle (vol. III of the Royal Prussian Academy edition). *Aristotelis Opera*, ed. Academia Regia Borussica. 5 vols. (Berlin, 1831–1870). III (1831), 537–589.

Among the members of the higher and even highest Catholic hierarchy we find two popes who had in their libraries copies of Bruni's
version of the *Economics*. The one was Nicholas V (reigned 1447–1451),
himself a humanist scholar with a passionate concern for the moral
philosophy of Aristotle and for still better Latin versions of the works by
the Greek philosopher than existed in his time. It was on his behalf that
Gregorio Tifernate rendered a new translation of the *Eudemian Ethics*
which had been translated earlier by Giannozzo Manetti. Nicholas' intimate acquaintance with Bruni's translations of Aristotle dated back to the
years when he drew up a program for a library for Cosimo de' Medici.[33]
Nicholas' copy of Bruni's version of the *Economics* with the Preface but
without the commentary (192) is part of a miscellaneous manuscript, containing the translations of the *Ethics* and *Politics* by Bruni, the translation
of the *Rhetorics* by Georgius Trapezuntius and the versions by Gregorio
Tifernate of the *Magna Moralia* and of the *Eudemian Ethics*; this collection
of Aristotelian writings on moral philosophy is headed by Bruni's sketch
of the life of Aristotle (*Vita Aristotelis*). On the first leaf of this parchment
codex is the papal coat of arms of Nicholas V.[34] A richly illuminated
parchment copy of the entire work by Bruni on the *Economics* (70), bound
together with a theological treatise, was owned by Pope Clement VII
(reigned 1523–1534), the former Cardinal Giulio de' Medici. His papal
coat of arms ornaments the first page of the codex, now in the Biblioteca
Laurenziana.[35]

Between 1451 and 1453, while he was residing at Bressanone (Brixen),
Cardinal Nicolaus Cusanus acquainted himself with Bruni's translations of
Aristotle. There he acquired copies of Bruni's versions of the *Politics* and
Economics, the latter complete with Preface and commentary and in an
arrangement that a few years earlier had become the standard form (48).
He had his secretary copy the *Ethics*. In the margins Cusanus added his
own glosses on Bruni's translation of the *Politics*. The three manuscripts

33. On the interest of Nicholas V in Aristotelian studies and translations, cf. Garin,
op. cit., pp. 18–19, and Kristeller, *Studies*, p. 341 n. 12; on his plan for a library composed
for Cosimo de' Medici, see Kristeller, *ibid.*, p. 573 n. 58.

34. The content of Cod. Vat. lat. 2096 is described in Kristeller, *Iter Italicum*, II, 311;
the ownership of the codex and the text of Bruni's version of the *Economics* were verified by
Monsignor José Ruysschaert.

35. Bandini Catalogue, III, 180; Dott. ssa Irma Merolle Tondi, director of the
Laurenziana, kindly supplied me with the corrected folio numbers of the *Economics* text
which are different from those given by Bandini. She also verified the composition of the
text.

were later bound together with some humanistic treatises, three of them by Bruni, and the codex, with the coat of arms of Cusanus, became part of his book collection at Kues.[36] The humanist scholar and collector of hand-written books at a time when the printed book was the order of the day, Cardinal Domenico Grimani (d. 1523) had in his library a manuscript containing the commentary by Bruni on his *Economics* translation (40), now in the Bibliothèque Nationale at Paris, which bears the marks of a faithful copy of the text as penned by Antonio di Mario. Among the manu-scripts of the Bruni version from the libraries of archbishops and bishops the one in the Biblioteca Ambrosiana (102) should be noted first on account of its owner. It belonged to Francesco Pizolpasso, who became archbishop of Milan in 1435. Pizolpasso, himself a scholar and theologian, was a lifelong friend of Bruni; the latter dedicated to him one of his earlier translations from the Greek (1407), the Latin version of the Demosthenes oration *Pro Ctesiphonte*. Both men were, as the Bruni *Epistolarium* testifies, in frequent correspondence with each other and Bruni sent Pizolpasso an extensive letter about the "controversia Alphonsiana" via their mutual friend Decembrio. The annotated *Economics* version by Bruni in the codex Ambrosianus is not complete and also not properly bound. In the first eight leaves of the volume there is the commentary on Book I only, and it is separated from the translation of both books with the Preface of a copy of the *Ethics* commentary (*conclusiones*) by Walter Burley. The manu-script of the prefaced commentary on the *Economics*, with the coat of arms of Pizolpasso on the bottom of its first leaf (fol. 25*v*), is in turn followed by a copy of Bruni's translation of the *Ethics* with marginal notes from the hand of Pizolpasso which indicate that he compared the Greek text with the controversial Bruni version.[37] A copy of the Preface and Book I of the translation of the *Economics* by Bruni (140) in a codex containing a variety

36. J. Marx, *Verzeichnis der Handschriften-Sammlung des Hospitals zu Cues bei Bernkastel a. Mosel* (Trier, 1905), pp. 167–169, No. 179.

37. Codex J 115 sup. and its texts are well described by Ezio Franceschini, "L'‘Aris-totele Latino' nei codici dell' Ambrosiana," *Miscellanea Galbiati*, III [=*Fontes Ambrosiani*, XXVII (1951)], 241–242, and 241 n. 6, and by Paredi, *op. cit.*, pp. 125–126. Dott. Paredi verified for me some minute points in the texts of Bruni's version and of the commentary. On Francesco Pizolpasso, who was born into the noble Bolognese family Lambertini and who died in 1443, his humanistic interests and friends, and his notable collection of hand-written books, see Paredi, *op. cit.*, pp. 3–65, and R. Fubini, *op. cit.* pp. 323–353, both mentioned above in n. 30. The letter from Bruni to Decembrio requesting him to transmit to Pizolpasso his long epistle concerning his controversy with Alonso of Cartagena (X, 24, in Mehus' edition) is described by Baron, *Leonardo Bruni Aretino*, p. 227, and the dedication of the Demosthenes oration to Pizolpasso is cited *ibid.*, p. 162.

of humanistic writings was in the Palace Library of the bishops of Trent.[38] Johannes Roth, bishop of Wrocław at the turn of the sixteenth century, possessed a codex with the translation of the *Ethics* by Argyropulos and Bruni's version of the *Economics* (222), both penned in Italy in the fifteenth century. He donated the volume to a monastery in his diocese "pro remedio anime sue et suorum" and from the convent it took its way into the free market of collectors.[39] We also know of a copy of the entire work by Bruni (49), most likely written in Germany before 1477, which belonged to a Canon Paul Megk, who gave it to the Dominican monastery at Regensburg.[40]

Cathedral libraries were favored repositories for codices containing among other humanistic treatises and Latin translations, Bruni's version of the *Economics*. The library of Florence cathedral had one such codex with the Aristotle translations by Bruni, among them the *Economics* (78), and also some of his versions of works of Plato; the texts in this parchment volume were exquisitely written, and the initials of each book of the translated works were illuminated. Francesco Pizolpasso left his collection of handwritten books, including the codex just discussed containing Bruni's version of the *Economics*, to the Biblioteca Capitolare del Capitolo Metropolitano at Milan, where it was deposited in the second half of the fifteenth century and where it remained until 1607 when Cardinal Federico Borromeo purchased it for the Biblioteca Ambrosiana. The copy done for the library of the cathedral of Constance (51) has been mentioned

38. The codex was removed in the second half of the eighteenth century from Trent to Austria, and early in the nineteenth century became part of the Imperial Court Library at Vienna. It was returned to Italy after World War I and is now on fiduciary deposit in the Biblioteca Comunale at Trent. It was described first in the catalogue of the Viennese collection (*Tabulae*, II (1868), 225, No. 3191 [Salisb. 8.g.]) and most recently by A. Cetto, "I codici viennesi della Biblioteca Vescovile di Trento," *Studi Trentini di Scienze Storiche*, XXXVII (1958), 494–495, No. 22. Professor Cetto furnished me with some details on this codex and its adventurous history, in addition to what he has written in the cited study.

39. In 1926 the codex was offered for sale by the Munich booksellers Weiss & Co. [see their catalogue, I (June, 1926), 9–10, item 5, with a detailed description]. Thus far I have not come across it in any public library. The donor's hope of a spiritual reward for his gift represents another instance of such motivation for giving handwritten books to convents, and it should be added to the other three examples cited on pp. 76–77.

40. C. Halm and others, *Catalogus codicum latinorum Bibliotheca Regiae Monacensis*, II, 2 (1876), 113, No. 985; Dr. W. Hoerman, director of the Manuscript Division of the Bayerische Staatsbibliothek, described for me the composition of the text in the copy and supplied me with information about the previous owners of the codex.

earlier. We find copies in the collections of several Spanish cathedrals but we have no information as to when they were deposited there.

The part the regular clergy played in disseminating Bruni's version of the *Economics* can hardly be overrated. We do have a few data on copies that were in convent libraries in the fifteenth century, but we cannot say how many manuscripts circulating outside monasteries were penned in their scriptoria. Many copies are written in a script pointing toward this origin and the explicits or brief notes at the end of the text are formulated in a manner characteristic of clerical scribes. Relatively, the largest numbers of manuscripts of the Bruni version were in the collections of Benedictine and Dominican convents. Among the six pieces traceable to Benedictine monasteries, two were in the library of the Florence abbey: the one (86), which probably originated there, is contained in a codex of the Aristotle translations by Bruni arranged according to the dates of their compositions, now in the Florence Biblioteca Nazionale Centrale; the other (80), combined with the translation of the *Ethics* by Bruni, belonged at a later time to the Strozzi collection and is now deposited in the Laurenziana. A copy in a codex at Holkham Hall (15) which, in addition to the *Economics*, has the translation of the *Ethics* by Argyropulos and Bruni's version of the *Politics*, originally came from the Benedictine monastery at Piacenza in Italy. The Benedictine Stift Melk possesses a copy (1) in a voluminous manuscript of miscellaneous writings which belonged to its library in 1491. A copy penned in the late fifteenth century by a Northern hand (50) forms part of a miscellaneous manuscript in the Archives of the Benedictine abbey at Ottobeuren in Bavaria. The now dissolved Benedictine monastery at Wiblingen in southern Germany is reported to have owned the earlier mentioned copy (219) which, according to a note at the end of it, was written at Basel. Since it is listed in a catalogue of the library from 1432, it must have been completed before that year. Next to the six copies from or in Benedictine collections there have turned up thus far five from Dominican monasteries. One copy (59), now in the University Library of Bologna, in a codex containing Bruni's three translations of Aristotle, comes from the Dominican convent in that city, and another (161), now in the Biblioteca Nacional in Madrid, comes from the Dominican convent in Piasencia (Spain). The University Library of Barcelona received as a gift from the Dominicans in that city an illuminated parchment codex with copies of Bruni's versions of the *Politics* and *Economics* (152), penned by a humanistic hand. The Bayerische Staatsbibliothek took over from the Dominican monastery of St. Blasius at

Regensburg a paper codex which contains, besides the already mentioned copy of Bruni's version of the *Economics* (49), Bruni's treatise *De studiis*, and some of his translations of Plato's works. The Dominican monastery at Vienna possessed before 1513 a codex of Aristotelian writings in medieval and renaissance Latin translations, among them Bruni's version of the *Economics* (219). The monastery still exists, but the codex cannot be located. Copies of Bruni's translation of the *Economics* were also in the libraries of older orders such as the Augustinians, Carthusians, Cistercians, Premonstratensians, and Carmelite friars. The two copies (182, 186) in the Swiss Carthusian and Carmelite convents and the one (162) in the famous Cistercian Abbey at Poblet were discussed in earlier contexts. To them should be added a copy (6) in Gothic script in a codex from the Premonstratensian Abbey de Parc in Louvain, now in the Bibliothèque Royale at Brussels. The Laurenziana received from the Franciscan convent S. Croce at Florence a richly illuminated and exquisitely written copy of Bruni's Aristotle translations, the last one being the *Economics* (76). The Biblioteca Ambrosiana, at the time of its founding (1606), was given in trust a parchment codex containing Bruni's translations of the *Ethics* and *Economics* (101); the codex belonged originally to the library of the Augustinian convent of S. Maria Incoronata at Milan. The library of the Augustinian convent of Santo Spirito at Florence possessed, according to an inventory of 1451, a miscellaneous manuscript of Bruni writings with Bruni's Preface to his version of the *Economics* at the beginning (218). The library was dispersed in the seventeenth century and the codex with whatever parts it contained of the annotated *Economics* version by Bruni presumably got lost.[41]

High-ranking members of the Augustinian and Franciscan orders were also among the earliest commentators of the *Economics* in the translation by Bruni. The first commentary in the traditional scholastic style

41. Professor Antonia Mazza of the Catholic University at Milan drew my attention to this copy. A. Goldmann, "Drei italienische Handschriftenkataloge s. XIII-XV," *Centralblatt fuer Bibliothekswesen*, IV (1887), 137–155, edited the 1451 inventory and sketched the fate of the convent library. He maintained (pp. 138–155) that the library perished in a fire in the night of March 22–23, 1471. Professor Mazza informed me that this belief, also shared by other scholars, is incorrect. The truth is that only the church burned while the library remained untouched. It is known that books in that library were consulted by scholars after 1471. The whole "parva libraria" of Santo Spirito was dispersed (in part sold or perhaps stolen) in the seventeenth century; only a few codices found their way into public collections and they are now deposited in Florence (Biblioteca Laurenziana, Biblioteca Riccardiana) and in Milan (Biblioteca Ambrosiana). Mazza is preparing a new edition of the inventory which will appear in a forthcoming issue of *Italia medievale e umanistica*.

was authored by the Augustinian General Guglielmo Bechi (Guilelmus Becchius), at one time bishop of Fiesole, who completed his work, dedicated to King Ferrante of Aragon, in 1467, after he had written a commentary on the *Ethics* (1465) and before he prepared a commentary on the *Politics* (1476), both also based on the translations by Bruni. The commentaries by Bechi remained unprinted.[42] The second commentary on the *Economics* with Bruni's translation as text was authored by Pedro de Castrovol (Fr. Petrus de Castrovole), who was Provincial of the Franciscan convents of Aragon in 1489–1491. Like Bechi, Pedro composed commentaries on the three central Aristotelian works on moral philosophy in the translations by Bruni. The commentary on the *Economics* was completed as early as 1481, but it was printed, together with his commentary on the *Politics*, only in 1496 at Pamplona (Hain-Copinger 4654).[43] Finally, one of the two printed commentaries from the beginning of the sixteenth century on Bruni's version of the *Economics* was the work of the Scottish scholar Gilbert Crab, a Carmelite friar who was active in Paris and Bordeaux.

IV. Among University Teachers; Scholastic Commentaries versus Humanistic Anthologies

One group of potential readers of Bruni's version of the *Economics* is practically missing in the list of the fifteenth-century owners of its handwritten copies—scholars and teachers connected with universities where Aristotelian moral philosophy was part of the curriculum. University courses exclusively devoted to the study of the *Economics* were rare, while in courses dealing with moral philosophy in general the *Economics* had its

42. A copy of the commentary on the *Economics* by Bechi is Cod. Ed. [Flor. Eccl.] 152 of the Laurenziana. It is a well-written and profusely illuminated parchment manuscript of forty-two leaves and belonged to Bechi himself (Bandini Catalogue, Supplement, I, 453–456). Another copy, although fragmentary, is Cod. Magl. VIII, 1404, fols. 145–154*v* of the Biblioteca Centrale at Florence (Kristeller, *Iter Italicum*, I, 133). Bechi's commentaries on the *Ethics* and *Politics* are in the codices Ed. [Flor. Eccl.] 153 and 154 of the Laurenziana (Bandini, *op. cit.*, cols. 455 and 455–456). On the commentaries, see Garin, *op. cit.*, p. 17 n. 1. Bechi received his academic training at the universities of Padua, Bologna, and Florence and, in addition to being a highly esteemed and fully occupied administrator, was a proficient teacher, preacher, and author. On his life and writings, see D. A. Perini, *Bibliographia Augustiniana. Scriptores Itali*, I (Florence, 1929), 103–105.

43. His commentary on the *Ethics* was printed by Henry Botel at Lerida on April 12, 1489 (Copinger 1481). On Pedro de Castrovol see *Dictionaire de Théologie Catholique*, X (Paris, 1910), col. 1837.

place. The various abbreviations, surveys (*tabulae*), compendia, and particularly the so-called *auctoritates* with summaries of chapters and paraphrases of salient passages from the works by Aristotle, composed for the benefit of students preparing for examinations, invariably contained a page or more of quotations from Books I and III (the *liber secundus* in the Durand and Bruni version) of the *Economics*.[1] The quotations indicate that in such cases the *Economics* was read in the later medieval Latin version. For more intensive studies scholars and university teachers resorted to the older medieval Latin translation of all three books.

With occasional exceptions the late scholastics of the fifteenth century ignored Bruni's translation and annotations. One such exception may be the anonymous scribe who copied both books with the annotations in the margins (211), but omitted the preface and superscribed the first book with the words "*Differentie Economice et Politice*," the traditional title of the scholastic commentaries on the first book.[2] It is symptomatic that few copies of Bruni's version are known to have been in the libraries of universities leading in Aristotelian studies in the fifteenth century. The University of Paris may serve as an example. At the end of that century its library possessed one copy (39) as compared with six copies of the two medieval Latin translations. University study of the Aristotelian works on moral philosophy dates back, of course, to the thirteenth century, and study of the *Economics*, in particular, to the last two decades of that century. Thus we should not be surprised to find five copies of Durand's version of the *Economics* dating from the late thirteenth and the fourteenth centuries. The single manuscript of the older anonymous medieval translation is of the latest vintage. It was penned in 1455 for Guillaume Fichet when this humanist, who was to become rector of the university in 1467, was still at the beginning of his splendid career.[3]

1. A survey of this literature may be found in Martin Grabmann, *Methoden und Hilfsmittel des Aristotelesstudiums im Mittelalter*. Sitzungsberichte (1939) der Bayerischen Akademie, Phil. Hist. Klasse. No. 5 (Munich, 1939).

2. This copy is part of Cod. Pal.lat. 1010 of the Vatican Library which is described in Kristeller's *Iter Italicum* II, 392. I received detailed information about the copy of the *Economics* from Monsignor José Ruysschaert.

3. Four of the five copies of Durand d'Auvergne's translation of the *Economics* which belonged to the library of the Sorbonne at the end of the fifteenth century are now in the Bibliothèque Nationale. They are contained in its codices lat. 16089, 16133, 16147, and 16490 (*Aristoteles Latinus*, I [1939], pp. 557–558, No. 664; pp. 563–565, No. 672; p. 567, No. 678, and pp. 573–574, No. 690). The fifth copy is in Cod. Bibliothèque de l'Université 1032 (*ibid.*, p. 592, No. 732). The copy of the anonymous medieval translation of the three books of the *Economics* is part of Cod. Bibliothèque Nationale, Lat. 16107 which includes, besides this text (*ibid.*, p. 561, No. 669) and other works, copies of the fragmentary com-

Resistance to the humanistic Latin translations of Aristotelian works began to weaken in the late 1480s. We can observe this change first in the teaching practices of the colleges, then in the printed editions of the collected works of Aristotle in Latin translations, and finally in the commentaries on works belonging to the Aristotelian *corpus morale*.

One center of this movement favoring humanistic translations of Aristotle was at the colleges in Paris. In 1486 a professor at the Collège de Laon, Odon Charlier, copied or had a scribe copy for him Bruni's version of the *Economics* (42) as well as Bruni's *Ethics* translation and *Isagogicon*. More famous for its humanistic tendencies was the Collège de Cardinal Lemoine where in the late 1480s and early 1490s Jacques Lefèvre d'Étaples taught Aristotelian moral philosophy from the translations by Bruni and other humanists. A few years later he edited them and accompanied them with his own commentaries reflecting humanistic critical scholarship at its best.[4]

---

mentary on the *Politics* by St. Thomas and a compendium of the *Ethics* with the commentary by St. Thomas. On the study of the *Economics* at the University of Paris in the late thirteenth century, see R.-A. Gauthier, O.P., "Deux témoignages sur la date de la première traduction latine des Économiques," *Revue Philosophique de Louvain*, L (1952), 273–283. I followed the author of this notable essay in assuming that the *translatio vetus* should be dated "about 1280" (see above, p. 63). On Guillaume Fichet and his interests in Aristotelian philosophy, ancient classical, patristic, and humanistic literature, see Kristeller, "An Unknown Humanist Sermon on St. Stephen by Guillaume Fichet," *Mélanges Eugène Tisserant*, IV [*Studi e Testi*, CCXXXVI, Vatican City, 1964], 459–497. On the manuscript of the *Economics* transcribed for Fichet, see p. 471 and n. 44. In 1455 Fichet was listed among the *licenciandi* and the *incipientes in artibus* at the Sorbonne (p. 462). Fichet's desire to read the *Economics* in the only complete Latin translation then available illustrates what I have said about the study of this spurious Aristotelian work by fifteenth-century university teachers.

4. On humanistic tendencies in Aristotelian studies in the Paris colleges during the last quarter of the fifteenth century, see A. Renaudet, *op. cit.*, pp. 126–133. The copy of Bruni's *Economics* version penned by or for Odon Charlier was mentioned above pp. 70–71 and p. 71 n. 10. Lefèvre began his prolific and eminently successful work of editing and commenting on humanistic translations of Aristotelian writings on moral philosophy shortly after 1490 with an introduction to the *Politics* which, however, was printed only eighteen years later as edited by one of his disciples, Wolfgang Pratensis. The first of his works in this field to be published immediately after its completion was an introduction to the *Ethics*, issued for the first time by Caillaut in 1494 (GW 9640) and reprinted nineteen times within the ensuing twenty-three years. It was followed by a copious commentary on the translation of the *Ethics* by Argyropulos, first printed by Higman and Hopyl in 1497 (GW 2359) together with his editions of the *Ethics* versions by Grosseteste and Bruni. Finally, in 1506, Lefèvre edited Bruni's translations of the *Politics* and *Economics* and provided them with annotations and commentaries. To these he added a compilation of excerpts from Plato's *Republic* and *Laws* and a humanistic Latin version of the genuine

While the Sorbonne remained adamant in its opposition to humanistic versions and methods of interpretation, faculty members of and scholars trained at universities less outstanding in the cultivation of Aristotelian moral philosophy than the University of Paris began to take interest in humanistic Latin translations of Aristotle. The commentary based on Bruni's version of the *Ethics* written by the professor at the University of Salamanca, Pedro de Osma, indicates such leanings at a leading Spanish university.[5] In Germany we can observe this tendency at the University of Freiburg im Breisgau. Its library owns a copy of the first printed edition of Bruni's translations of Aristotle published early in 1469 by Johann Mentelin at Strasbourg (GW 2367). In the margins of the *Ethics* a magister Friburgensis wrote a commentary which he completed on July 3, 1469.[6] This early use of Bruni's text in a commentary by a master from that university may not be accidental; already in the last quarter of the fifteenth century poetry and eloquence were taught by humanists at Freiburg.[7] The library also has a manuscript of Bruni's version (45) penned in 1507 by a certain Conrad Schraude from Allenspach who may have copied it from a printed edition.[8]

Book II of the *Economics*. At the end of this collection he presented Bruni's annotations of the *Economics*, which he titled "*explanatio*," as Bruni himself had done in his preface; he thereby indicated that Bruni's annotations are not a commentary in the traditional meaning of this term. This last work by Lefèvre on Aristotle's moral philosophy was first printed and published by Henry Estienne August 5, 1506. For a bibliography of Lefèvre's editions, first prints and reissues until 1517, see Renaudet, *op. cit.*, pp. lii–liii; in some instances I have corrected and augmented Renaudet's listings.

5. *Petri osmensis . . . in ethicorum Aristotelis commentarii*, ed. Ferdinandus de Roa. Salamanca, 1496 (Hain-Reichling 12122).

6. The exact date when the printing of this celebrated edition was completed is unknown. Incunabula experts presume from circumstantial evidence that it was completed or published before April 10, 1469. Included in this evidence is the marginal commentary on the *Nicomachean Ethics* by the magister Friburgensis, who completed writing it on July 3; see *Gesamtkatalog der Wiegendrucke* (referred to as GW with serial number of the cited item). 8 vols. (Leipzig, 1925–1940), II (1926), 596–597.

7. Friedrich Paulsen, *Geschichte des Gelehrten Unterrichts auf den deutschen Schulen und Universitäten*, 3rd ed., rev. R. Lehmann; I (Leipzig, 1919), 140–141.

8. The copy by Conrad Schraude of Bruni's version with the Preface, followed by a copy of Ovid letters from the same hand, is bound together with printed Latin texts from the years 1505 to 1512. Dr. Hennig, director of the Manuscript Division of the Freiburg University Library, described the entire volume and the copy for me. As to the version by Bruni in the libraries of Italian universities, renowned for their Aristotelian studies during the fifteenth century, the situation is not clear enough to warrant discussion in the text above. I submit here some facts which have come to my attention. Toward the end of the fifteenth century the library of the University of Bologna seems to have owned

In the last decade of the fifteenth century the increasing popularity of humanistic Latin translations of Aristotelian works had a marked effect on editions of the collected works of Aristotle in Latin translations (*Opera Omnia*), a novel form of publication which soon assumed an important role for the study of Aristotelian philosophy in general. In 1483 the Paduan professor Nicoletto Vernia prepared the first edition of Latin versions of the Aristotelian *corpus*, which at that time were used at the University of Padua. It was, in fact, a collection of Averroës' commentaries on Aristotle's writings, so far as then available. The Aristotelian texts were given in the medieval translations. As for the *Economics*, Vernia selected the older medieval version of the three books.[9] Vernia's compilation was printed at Venice in three folio volumes by the printer-publishers Andreas Torresanus and Bartholomaeus de Blavis and issued in two different typographical arrangements (GW 2337 and 2338). This luxurious parchment edition was not reissued. When Vernia's disciple Agostino Nifo prepared a new edition of Averroës' commentaries with the texts of the Aristotelian writings in 1495, these texts were humanistic Latin translations. In the second part of the second volume, printed on April 26, 1496, by the brothers de Gregoriis for the publisher Octavianus

three copies of Bruni's version (in addition to a copy of Durand's translation, written in the fourteenth century, in Cod. Biblioteca Universitaria, Lat. 1119; *Aristoteles Latinus*, II [1955], p. 888, No. 1283). Of the three copies of the Bruni version, two (60, 61) may have belonged to its collection in the fifteenth century. No copy of Bruni's version traceable to the library of the University of Padua has come to my attention. Two circumstances suggest that at Padua in the 1470s and 1480s, the *Economics* was read in medieval versions. One is the fact that as prominent a teacher at that university as Nicoletto Vernia adopted for his edition of the collected works of Aristotle in Latin translations (printed in 1483) the anonymous medieval translation of the three books of the *Economics*, albeit conflated with the later version of Durand. Secondly, in 1476, Ermolao Barbaro possessed a collection of medieval translations of the *Ethics*, *Politics*, and *Economics*, penned at the end of the fourteenth century—now Cod. Columbia University, Plimpton 17—and he wrote glosses in the margins of the translation of the *Ethics* by Grosseteste in which he compared this version with the Greek original. On the codex see S. De Ricci and W. J. Wilson, *Census of Medieval and Renaissance Manuscripts in the United States and Canada*, II (1937), 1756–1757; *Aristoteles Latinus*, I, 244, No. 17, item 5: *Economica, recensio Durandi*, fols. 181–185; on the Barbaro glosses, see Kristeller, *Studies*, pp. 384–352.

9. Vernia adopted his text from a manuscript which contained not a pure copy of the anonymous medieval Latin version of the three books (*translatio vetus*), but one in which the older translation of Books I and III is conflated with the version of Durand. A manuscript of this kind is the copy of the *translatio vetus* in Cod. Conv. Soppr. 95, fols. 199–201 of the Biblioteca Laurenziana (*Aristoteles Latinus*, II, 921, No. 1334) which in the fifteenth century belonged to the Florence Badia. On Vernia's edition, see F. Susemihl, *Aristotelis quae feruntur Oeconomica* (Leipzig, 1878), p. xviii.

Scotus (GW 2340), the *Economics* appeared in Bruni's version and—since there is no commentary by Averroës on the *Economics*—with Bruni's commentary. What may have induced the editor and publisher to make this change was that six years before the Venetian printer-publisher Bernardinus Stagninus had, with obvious success, put on the market a collection of Aristotelian works in humanistic translations (GW 2339). In the same year in which the de Gregoriis brothers finished their part of Nifo's edition they began to print for the publisher Benedictus Fontana another collection of Aristotelian texts in humanistic versions (GW 2341), among which the *Economics* again appeared in the translation by Bruni, but without the commentary. The tide had turned.

From 1495 on, scholastic commentaries by contemporary authors on Aristotelian works on moral philosophy were based on humanistic Latin translations, and commentaries by early scholastics were often combined with the modern Latin versions. At the beginning of the last decade of the fifteenth century, about 1491, the Cologne printer-publisher Heinrich Quentell brought out the *Economics* in the translation by Durand (GW 2431) with the commentary by Johannes Versor, a master of the Sorbonne and a scholar of Thomistic orientation.[10] It was the first late-scholastic commentary on the *Economics* to appear in print and the only one printed together with a medieval Latin translation. The next scholastic commentary, printed and published about 1495 by Henry Mayer at Toulouse (GW 2436), was already combined with the Bruni version. The commentary ascribed to the famous Augustinian Dionigi dei Roberti da Borgo San Sepolcro (Dionysius Burgensis, *ca.* 1280–1342), the correspondent of Petrarch and later bishop of Monopoli, is actually, as I detected, a kind of paraphrase and augmentation of the commentary on the *Economics* by Albert of Saxony (*ca.* 1316–1390). The genuine commentary by Albert of Saxony was frequently copied in the fourteenth and fifteenth centuries, and in several instances it was erroneously thought to be the work of St. Albert the Great or of other equally famous scholastics.[11] One year

10. On Versor and his method of commenting, see M. Grabmann, *Die mittelalterlichen Kommentare zur Politik des Aristoteles*. Sitzungsberichte (1941) der Bayerischen Akademie, Phil. Hist. Klasse. Vol. II, No. 10 (Munich, 1941), 65–75. Versor also wrote commentaries on the *Ethics* and *Politics* which, too, were printed and published by Heinrich Quentell. His commentary on the *Ethics* appeared first in 1491 (Hain 16053) and again in 1494 (Hain 16054); his commentary on the *Politics* appeared first in 1492 (GW 2444) and again in 1497 (GW 2445).

11. The only known copy of the Toulouse print is in the University Library at Grenoble. I compared a microfilm copy of it with microfilm of two manuscripts of the commentary by Albert of Saxony. One manuscript is Cod. C.14.b [Weingarten K.55],

after the publication of this edition the publisher Guillen at Pamplona put on the market a print of the Bruni version with the commentary by the Franciscan Pedro de Castrovol which was really based on it (Hain-Copinger 4654).[12]

---

fols. 237–268, of the Hessische Landesbibliothek at Fulda (*Aristoteles Latinus*, I, 678, No. 926), written in the late fifteenth century. The scribe noted at the end that it was the commentary by Albert of Saxony, and he copied it together with the version by Durand on which the commentary is based. The other manuscript is Cod. 7804, fols. 119–135*v*, of the Biblioteca Nacional at Madrid, presumably penned in France in the late fifteenth century. The scribe copied the commentary without the Aristotelian text—there are merely brief references to it at the beginning of each section of the commentary—and he ascribed the work he had copied to St. Albert the Great. The manuscript of the supposed St. Albert commentary is preceded by a copy of Bruni's annotated version of the *Economics* (161). Since the commentaries in both manuscripts are identical not only with each other but with descriptions of several copies of the commentary by Albert of Saxony, I presume that the ascription of the commentary in the Madrid manuscript is erroneous. The commentary in the Toulouse print, ascribed to Dionigi dei Roberti, is identical in content with the commentary in the two manuscripts, but is only similar to it in wording. The unknown editor of the Toulouse print took so much liberty in expanding and para-phrasing the terse comments and notations by Albert of Saxony that it is often difficult to recognize the original. Furthermore, he added short expositions to each portion of the commentary, probably written by himself, which merely rehash Albert's observations. But the contours of the commentary are preserved and, as in the Fulda manuscript, each portion of the commentary is accompanied by the corresponding portion of the Aristot-elian text for which the editor chose Bruni's version. What caused him to ascribe the com-mentary to Dionigi dei Roberti is difficult to say; there is no documentary evidence that Dionigi authored a commentary on the *Economics*. A critical edition of the commentary by Albert of Saxony (although presumed by its editor to be the commentary by St. Albert the Great) was prepared by Father Vicente Beltrán de Heredia in his study "Comentarios de San Alberto Magno a los Económicos de Aristóteles," *La Ciencia Tomista*, XLVI (Salamanca, 1932), 299–329. Ascription of this commentary to St. Albert the Great was questioned by Martin Grabmann in 1928 and later refuted by A. De Poorter, *Catalogue Général des Manuscrits des Bibliothèques de Belgique*, Vol. II: *Catalogue des Manuscrits de la Bibliothèque de la Ville de Bruges* (1934), 577. On Dionigi dei Roberti as commentator, see Rudolph Arbesmann, O.S.A., "Der Augustinereeremitenorden und der Beginn der humanistischen Bewegung," *Augustiniana*, XIV (Louvain, 1964), fasc. 1–2, p. 264 [re-printed in *Cassiciacum*, XIX (Würzburg, 1965), 23]. According to contemporary reports accepted by Arbesmann in agreement with earlier scholars (Fabricius, Goetz, Berlin-court), Dionigi composed commentaries on the *Politics* and *Poetics* but not on the *Eco-nomics*. Perini, *op. cit.*, II (Florence, 1931), 26–28, included among the writings of Dionigi the commentary on the *Economics* on the strength of the Toulouse print. The microfilm of the Toulouse print was kindly supplied me by the University Library at Grenoble; the microfilms of the manuscripts in the Hessische Landesbibliothek at Fulda and in the Biblioteca Nacional at Madrid were furnished by the respective libraries.

12. See above p. 85 and p. 85 n. 43.

In the early years of the sixteenth century three more commentaries on the pseudo-Aristotelian *Economics* were published; in two of them the commentators used the Bruni version as their textual basis. In the third the Bruni version was printed after the commentary, but in the commentary no direct reference is made to the text. The oldest of these three commentaries is from the pen of the Scottish scholar and Carmelite friar Gilbert Crab (1482–1522) who was at one time regent at the Collège de Bourgogne in Paris. His commentary, published by Jean Petit at Paris at an unknown date (*ca.* 1503?), consists of two parts; the first is an annotation of Bruni's version and the second contains questions in the nominalist tradition. To this commentary on the two books of the *Economics*, Crab added a humanistic Latin version or a humanistic adaptation of the older anonymous medieval Latin translation of the genuine Book II, which he named *economiarum publicarum liber unus*.[13] The second of our commentaries, by Jacques Lefèvre d'Étaples (also using Bruni's version) is part of a collection of texts related to Aristotle's *Politics* and *Economics*; the work was

---

13. The title of the commentary is *Aristoteles de convenientia politice et economice.* J. F. Kellas Johnstone and A. W. Robertson, the editors of the *Bibliographia Aberdonensis*, 2 vols. (Aberdeen, 1929–1930), I, 5–6, date the first edition *ca.* 1502 on the strength of the early printer's device used on the title page by Jean Petit. I think the date ought to be set at a time after 1503 because Crab refers to himself as master of arts. The records on his career indicate that he acquired this degree in 1503. The commentary was reissued in expanded form in 1510 by the Lyons publisher Simon Vincent, and was reprinted *ca.* 1515. Whether the copy listed by Copinger (No. 1834) corresponds to the *editio princeps* or represents another edition, as Johnstone and Robertson are inclined to presume, cannot yet be established. The humanistic version or humanistic adaptation of the medieval Latin translation of the genuine Book II of the *Economics*, which he titled *Economiarum publicarum Aristotelis liber unus*, and which he added to the two books translated by Bruni, was later adopted by Lefèvre in his 1506 edition of the *Politics* and *Economics* (see above p. 87 n. 4). For several years Crab was a regent at the Collège de Bourgogne and later he became a professor of philosophy at the University of Bordeaux where he died in 1522. While still in Paris, he collaborated with his colleague at the Burgundian College, Nicholas Dupuy (Nicolaus Bonaspes), in editing the *questiones* on the *Ethics* by John Buridan and Martin Lemaistre which, together with the medieval version of the *Ethics*, were published by Denis Roce at Paris in 1509. Crab later wrote his own commentary on the *Ethics* based on the Argyropulos translation; it was published in Paris by Henri Estienne on February 5, 1514, and then reissued by Simon Vincent in Lyons in 1517. On the life of Crab, who descended from an old Flemish family long settled at Aberdeen, and his academic career see *Scottish Notes and Queries*, X (Edinburgh, 1896), fasc. 3, pp. 33–34, and the *Bibliographia Aberdonensis*, I, 5–6. I am indebted to Professor F. Edward Cranz for first drawing my attention to the work of Crab, and to Dr. W. Douglas Simpson, librarian of the University Library, King's College, Aberdeen, for informing me of the literature on Crab and providing me with a microfilm copy of the *editio princeps* of the commentary on the *Economics* preserved in that library.

first published by Henry Estienne at Paris in 1506 and was reprinted several times until 1543. Lefèvre accompanied each chapter of the two books of Bruni's version with annotations in the humanistic manner and a commentary in the scholastic fashion. In another part of his collection Lefèvre presented the Latin version of the genuine Book II which he adopted from the Crab edition and, finally, Bruni's own annotations to his translation. The third *Economics* commentary was the work of Virgilius Wellendoerffer, a bachelor of theology and master of philosophy of the University of Leipzig and a professor of both subjects at his alma mater. His commentary, published by Wolfgang Stoeckel at Leipzig in 1511, is patterned after the commentaries on Aristotle by Walter Burley; it consists of "Conclusions" reached in the treatment of each passage of the Aristotelian text. The method of commenting chosen by Wellendoerffer was in tune with the Thomistic orientation of the arts faculty at the Leipzig University which prevailed until the humanistic reform of 1519.[14]

The rivalry of humanistic and scholastic tendencies in the study of Aristotelian moral philosophy has to be kept in mind if we want to understand the significance of five late copies of Bruni's version. One copy (149), penned in 1518 by Christopher Koszucki, a nobleman from Poznań, consists of Bruni's version of the *Economics*; on the pages containing the text of Book I we find glosses between the lines and an unidentified commentary in the margins.[15] Another manuscript (150) which originated probably in the late fifteenth century is a copy of Bruni's *liber secundus*

14. The title of the *Economics* commentary by Wellendoerffer is *Oecologium ex duobus Aristotelis Oeconomicorum libellis accumulatum. Conclusiones centum et quattuor : ac nove traductionis textum duplici cum regesto complectens* . . . (Georg Panzer, *Annales typographici ab anno MDI ad annum MDXXXVI*. 6 vols. [Nuremberg, 1798–1803]. II, 171, No. 338). Wellendoerffer also composed a commentary on the *Ethics* published in 1509, and a commentary on the *Politics*, first published in 1513 and reissued in 1516, all at Leipzig by Wolfgang Stoeckel. We know next to nothing about the life of the author; Zedler's *Universal Lexicon*, LII (Leipzig-Halle, 1747), col. 1637, contains only a list of his printed works (there are some more in manuscripts), and Chr. J. Joecher, *Allgemeines Gelehrten-Lexicon*, IV (Leipzig, 1751), col. 1879, adds no further information. Dr. Johannes Müller, director of the library of the Leipzig Karl-Marx-Universität, kindly supplied me with the following data from the university registers: Wellendoerffer (whose name is spelled in seven different ways in the documents), a native of Salzburg in Bavaria, was first matriculated in the summer semester of 1481 and received his baccalaureate in theology in 1483 and his master of arts degree in 1487. Only in 1500 is he mentioned as holding official positions in the faculties of the arts and theology, and in the summer semester of 1502 he served as rector of the university.

15. Rev. Dr. Joseph Nowacki, director of the Archives of the Poznań archdiocese, furnished me with a description of the codex and with microfilm of the copy of the *Economics*. Kristeller had brought the manuscript to my attention.

alone, accompanied by an unidentified commentary in the margins.[16] Also from the late fifteenth century is a manuscript in a hand, probably German (50), written and still preserved in the Benedictine Abbey of Ottobeuren. The text of the two books is separated into passages and each passage is followed by the corresponding portion of an unidentified commentary.[17] The Bruni version in a manuscript (46) penned by a northern hand, possibly in 1515, is also partitioned into passages which serve as textual basis for a very elaborate late-scholastic commentary.[18] A somewhat puzzling piece is a manuscript (148) which the Polish humanist Bernard of Lublin wrote in 1505. It contains excerpts from Bruni's version.[19] Bernard did not indicate the purpose of his excerpts. I would venture to guess that he may have intended them for that kind of textbook which in Aristotelian studies was known as "*auctoritates.*" As observed previously, quotations from the *Economics* in the "*auctoritates*" were taken from the Durand version. Perhaps Bernard planned to substitute for them quotations from the Bruni version, which became popular in Poland about that time. What makes me believe that this may have been his aim is that, contrary to the custom of teachers of eloquence, he deleted all sentences of purely literary character and concentrated on matters of Aristotelian doctrine to which alone the scholastics paid attention. The manuscript from the hand of Bernard of Lublin as well as the four others are therefore not the sort of faithful copies of Bruni's work or of parts of it made in the fifteenth century; they are editions of Bruni's text designed to be used in scholastic studies of the ancient work.

16. See above, p. 64 n. 5; a microfilm copy was made available to me by the director of the University Library at Wrocław.

17. Kristeller described for me the codex and the copy of Bruni's version, and Father Aegidius Kolb, O.S.B., the archivist of the abbey, took considerable pains in providing me with a microfilm copy of the *Economics* text.

18. The codex is at present on deposit in the Deutsche Staatsbibliothek at Berlin; while visiting there Professor Kristeller gathered for me the data on the codex, and Dr. Hans Luelfing, director of the Manuscript Division of that library, supplied me with a microfilm copy of the *Economics* text. My assumption that the commentary probably was penned in 1515 is based on the fact that the copy of Horace letters preceding it was made by a Philip Gruenfeld and was completed on March 10, 1515. The *Economics* text seems to be written by the same hand.

19. The manuscript of Bernardus Lublinius is not mentioned in the description of the Krakow codex by Jan Czubek in his *Katalog Rękopisów Akademii Umiejętności w Krakowie*, Supplement I (1912), 28. Professor Kristeller found it when he inspected the codex in that collection. I received a microfilm copy of it through the good offices of Dr. Marian Pelczar, director of the Biblioteka Gdańska Polskiej Akademii Nauk.

The inclination of late scholastics to combine their own commentaries with Bruni's version is understandable. In the preface and in the annotations to his translation of the *Economics* Bruni had failed to come to grips with some of the basic issues that the authors of these pseudo-Aristotelian treatises [20] posed to their interpreters. He informed his readers in the subtitle and in the Preface of his version that the *Economics*—he was referring to Book I only—deals with that part of Aristotle's practical philosophy which has come to be known by its Latin name as the area of the *res familiaris*. Exactly what the subject matter of this science is—in addition to precepts on how to increase the wealth of the "family"—he did not further explain. Nor did he go deeper into the difference between this discipline and the related science dealing with the *res publica*. Topics of this sort were important issues for schoolmen passionately concerned with the classification of the sciences and with the assignment of the variegated problems arising in human experience to their proper disciplines in a well-organized system of learning.

Moral philosophy in general, Bruni himself had maintained, "revolves . . . around action." [21] As to its three branches, he had adopted the traditional triad of *Ethics*, *Economics*, and *Politics*. He had assigned to the science of *Politics* the formulation of precepts concerning the better conduct of government, and to the science of *Economics* the deliberation of precepts on how to acquire in honest ways the wealth which "is useful indeed as it provides those who possess it with distinction as well as the ability to practice virtue." [22] Bruni's simplification of Aristotelian practical philosophy and of its three branches seems to have been widely accepted by

20. The authors of Books I and III of the pseudo-Aristotelian *Economics* are unknown. The Greek philosopher Philodemus (fl. *ca.* 60 B.C.), an Epicurean and contemporary of Cicero, ascribed the authorship of Book I to Theophrastus. His ascription has been accepted by most, if not all, modern Graecists. See O. Regenbogen, art. "Theophrastus," *Pauly-Wissowa Real-Enzyclopaedie der Classischen Altertumswissenschaft*, Supplementband VII (1950), col. 1521. V. Rose believed that Book III is identical with a treatise on marriage ascribed by Suidas to Aristotle. The text as we know it from the Latin version is obviously not the original but, as suggested by literary references, a revision by an editor of the first or second century A.D. See V. Rose, *Aristoteles pseudepigraphus* (Leipzig, 1883), pp. 644–665; on the revision, R. Bloch, "Liber secundus yconomicorum Aristotelis," *Archiv für Geschichte der Philosophie*, XXI (1908), 335–351; 441–468; esp. 465–466.

21. ". . . . duas philosophiae esse partes, quarum altera in cognitione rerum, altera in agendo versatur . . . ." Preface; H. Baron (ed.), *Leonardo Bruni Aretino*, p. 121, ll. 11–12.

22. "Sunt vero utiles divitiae, cum et ornamento sint possidentibus et ad virtutem exercendam suppeditent facultatem . . . ." *Ibid.*, p. 120, ll. 26–28.

later humanistic scholars,[23] but appeared to professional philosophers and university teachers too vague and general to be acceptable as sufficient characterizations of these disciplines. Bruni's eloquence and proficiency in the art of translation, although increasingly acknowledged as a valuable help in studies of the Aristotelian text, were not of prime importance to them; his annotations were not considered to be a satisfactory substitute for genuine commentaries.[24] Educated laymen and students of ancient literature, on the other hand, exclusively interested in the precepts for proper action, believed that the guidance available in the supposed Aristotelian treatise should be linked to the other ancient and modern humanistic authors read on matters of moral philosophy. In a letter dated December 5, 1443, Enea Silvio Piccolomini gave this advice to Duke Sigismund of Austria:

> If you want to know how one ought to govern a state then you have to read the books on *Politics* which Aristotle composed and Leonardo Bruni Aretino translated into Latin. But do not acquire the older [medieval] translation because it corrupts the eloquence and strains the mind too much. [For a knowledge] as to how to govern your family and yourself, the *Economics* and *Ethics* by Aristotle will be useful, also Cicero's *De Officiis* and the letters of Seneca and all books by this author. On how to guide one's wife, Francesco Barbaro of Venice has written a treatise [*De Re Uxoria*] and how to educate one's children, Plutarch [*De Liberis Educandis*, translated by Guarino].... If one educated outside Italy were to read what I am writing he would scold me vehemently because among the authors you would have to read I

23. See Bartolommeo della Fontes' (professor of poetry and oratory at the University of Florence) *Oratio in bonas artes* (1484) which explained the essence of moral philosophy: "Moral philosophy consists entirely in action and is in its turn divided into three parts. 'Personal' ('propria') philosophy instructs man himself and teaches the morals of man in the best manner. Domestic philosophy disposes of the home and family. Civil philosophy moderates and rules the city." See Charles Trinkaus, "A Humanist's Image of Humanism: The Inaugural Orations of Bartolommeo della Fonte," *Studies in the Renaissance*, VIII (1961), 115.

24. In the dedication to King Alfonso of his commentary on the *Economics* Bechi said that thus far (1467) no one had written a commentary on Bruni's version (". . . comentari institui . . . in Oeconomicorum libros . . . qui, quum latini a Leonardo Arretino viro eloquentissimo facti sint, neminem usque huc, qui eos commentaretur, habuerunt. Ego autem hanc curam lubens suscepi et commentum istud . . . tuo nomini dedicavi . . . ." Quoted from Bandini, *Bibliotheca Leopoldina Laurentiana*, I [1791], col. 454). Georg Voigt, *Die Wiederbelebung des classischen Alterthums*, 3rd. ed., prepared by Max Lehnerdt (Berlin, 1893), p. 392 n. 3, inferred from this remark by Bechi: "Mithin ist es ein Irrthum, wenn mitunter Bruni selbst ein solcher zugeschrieben worden."

did not enumerate Thomas Aquinas, Alexander of Hales, Albert the Great, Peter de Blois, Nicolaus de Lira and Alanus [Alanus ab Insulis or Alain de Lille] and the crowd of newer ones [i.e., scholastics]. But beware of listening to them![25]

The advice given by Piccolomini was apparently heeded by some partisans of his cause. They had Bruni's version of the *Economics* either written or bound together with texts related to the subject matter of the Aristotelian work. Or perhaps Piccolomini was merely describing a practice current in certain circles at his time. In a good number of codices from the fifteenth century, we find, indeed, besides Bruni's version of the *Economics*, writings by Cicero and Seneca on similar topics.[26] In some others, the *Economics* is followed by Plutarch's treatise on education, *De liberis educandis* (in the Latin translation by Guarino of Verona), as well as modern humanistic writings on education. Four examples of these volumes are: Cod. Ottob. lat. 1353 of the Vatican Library, Cod. Nouv. acq. lat. 650 of the Bibliothèque Nationale, Cod. 17403 [D'Orville 525] of the Bodleian Library, and Cod. O 71 sup. of the Biblioteca Ambrosiana.

The most significant of the four is the miscellaneous manuscript in the Bodleian Library. It comprises copies of Vergerio's *De ingenuis moribus*, Bruni's version of the *Economics*, and Guarino's translation of Plutarch's *De liberis educandis*, in that order. Some humanists, as Piccolomini indicated, apparently considered these three works as complementary writings. In two others of our four miscellanies—Cod. Ottob. lat. 1353 of the Vatican Library and Cod. Nouv. acq. lat. 650 of the Bibliothèque Nationale—Guarino's version of *De liberis educandis* is assigned to Bruni. In the Vatican codex, penned by a disciple of Ciriaco of Ancona, the scribe committed the further mistake of regarding the version of the *Economics* by Bruni as the treatise *De ingenuis moribus* by Pier Paolo Vergerio. The three texts in the Cod. 17403 [D'Orville 525] were written by the

25. Translated from the Latin text in *Enea Silvio Piccolomini, Papst Pius II. Ausgewaehlte Texte aus seinen Schriften*, ed. Berthe Widmer (Basel, 1960), pp. 284–287. G. Toffanin in his review of her edition in *Renaissance News*, XV (1962), 152, refers to this letter as a testimony of Piccolomini's dislike of medieval scholastic commentaries.

26. In Cod. lat. 6616 of the Bibliothèque Nationale, Bruni's version (35) is combined with Cicero's *De amicitia* and *Cato maior de senectute*; in Cod. 379 of Holkham Hall, the *Economics* (14) follows Cicero's correspondence with Quintus; in Cod. 1639 [lat. 856] of the Biblioteca Universitaria of Bologna, the *Economics* (59) is followed by Seneca's *De beneficiis*, while in Cod. 29438 [MS. Add. C.264] of the Bodleian Library the same work by Seneca precedes the *Economics* (26); in Cod. 114 of the Biblioteca de la Universidad at Madrid, we find between Bruni's translations of the *Politics* and *Economics* (165), Seneca's *De remediis fortuitorum*, and the spurious correspondence of Seneca with St. Paul.

same hand at Rome in 1454 and 1456–1457 respectively. In the Cod. O 71 sup. of the Biblioteca Ambrosiana, Bruni's version is followed by Guarino's translation of Plutarch's treatise.[27]

While the treatises by Plutarch and Vergerio deal with subjects only slightly touched upon in the *Economics*, the *De re uxoria* by Francesco Barbaro, also mentioned by Piccolomini, enlarges on a topic treated extensively in Book III (the *liber secundus* in the Bruni version) and discussed at some length in Book I. Barbaro devoted an entire chapter of his study of all aspects of marriage (II, 8), to the duties of a married woman in the house. This chapter is based largely on Xenophon's *Oeconomicus*, on the pseudo-Aristotelian *Economics*, and on the *De liberis educandis* by Plutarch.[28] It is therefore logical that in some codices a copy of the Barbaro treatise should be found next to Bruni's version of the *Economics*. Thus, for example, the texts in Cod. lat. 11 138 of the Bibliothèque Nationale—a paper codex—penned in 1471 by a Bartholomaeus Cersolus who noted at the end of the *De re uxoria* (fol. 47) that he completed his copy on May 31, 1471. The leaves following Barbaro's work contain Bruni's version of the *Economics* (38). Another such manuscript is a volume consisting of various texts written on parchment and paper leaves, now Cod. XIV E 26 of the Biblioteca Nazionale at Naples. The translation of the *Economics* by Bruni without the Preface (115) is here preceded by Barbaro's treatise, entitled *Precepta yconomica ex libro suo* [i.e., Barbaro's] *de re uxoria breviter tracta*.[29]

Such combinations—a sort of anthology—of writings concerning the

27. On the ascription to Bruni of the Guarino version and the confusion of Bruni's version of the *Economics* with the treatise by Vergerio in the Vatican codices, see Baron, *Leonardo Bruni Aretino*, p. 185. The Paris codex with the Guarino version (fols. 20–41*v*), erroneously ascribed to Bruni, is briefly described, without correction of this mistake, by H. Omont, "Nouvelles acquisitions du département des manuscrits de la Bibliothèque Nationale pendant les années 1896–1897," *Bibliothèque de l'École des Chartes*, LIX (1898), 93–94. For a detailed description of the codex of the Bodleian Library see F. Madan, *A Summary Catalogue*, IV (1897), p. 134. On the codex of the Biblioteca Ambrosiana, cf., Franceschini, *op. cit.*, p. 243 and note 2.

28. Francesco Barbaro probably wrote his treatise early in 1416 as a wedding gift for Lorenzo de' Medici, the brother of Cosimo, whom Barbaro had met half a year before on a visit to Florence. In Chapter 8 of Book II Barbaro refers to Xenophon's *Oeconomicus* eight times, to the *Economics* three times, and to *De liberis educandis* once. Francesco Barbaro, *De re uxoria*, ed. A. Gnesotto in *Atti e Memorie della R. Accademia di Scienze ed Arti in Padova*, N.S., XXX (1916), 7–100. On Francesco Barbaro's treatise, see Percy Gothein, *Francesco Barbaro: Früh-Humanismus und Staatskunst in Venedig* (Berlin, 1932), pp. 61–99.

29. For the Paris codex see above, p. 56 n. 8; the Naples codex was described for me by Dott.ssa G. Guerrieri.

res familiaris were not without parallels in the scholastic tradition. The Durand version of the *Economics* was occasionally accompanied by a short medieval tract, the *Epistola de cura rei familiaris ad Raymundum militem*, composed by an anonymous author but most frequently ascribed to St. Bernard of Clairvaux. This *Epistola* is a "treatise on domestic economy; it contains advice of how to manage servants, wives, and children, as well as directions on when to spend, and when to spare."[30] It appears, together with the Durand version, for example, in two Vatican codices. One is Cod. Ross. 569, a fourteenth-century manuscript penned by a French scribe. The other is Cod. Urb. lat. 1392, whose texts were written in the middle of the fifteenth century.[31] The *Epistola* also accompanied the Bruni version. Among the various codices which contain both works, one originated in Germany in the late fifteenth century and belonged at one time to the Dominican convent at Regensburg; the copy of Bruni's version (49) at the beginning of the volume is separated from the medieval tract by several texts. In another codex, which was in the library of the bishops of Trent, the pseudo-St. Bernard epistle immediately follows the copy of Bruni's version (140). There is, however, an essential difference between the combination of a Latin translation of the *Economics* with a medieval treatise and the combination of Bruni's version with ancient and renaissance treatises related to the management of family affairs. While the spurious Aristotelian work and the medieval tract cover identical ground, the writings by Plutarch, Vergerio, and Barbaro complement and augment the topics discussed in the *Economics*.

30. From the preface by J. R. Lumby to his edition of the Scottish translation of the *Epistola*. This tract circulated very widely in the fourteenth and fifteenth centuries to judge by the enormous number of copies. Hauréau counted sixteen copies alone in the Bibliothèque Nationale and there is hardly a major collection of medieval manuscripts without at least three copies. Ordinarily it was ascribed to St. Bernard of Clairvaux, occasionally to Bernardus Silvestris or to an otherwise unknown Bertrandus. It certainly was not the work of St. Bernard or of Bernardus Silvestris. For the Latin text, see Migne, *Patrologia Latina*, CLXXXII cols. 647a–651a; on the author, see B. Hauréau, *Notices et extraits de quelques manuscrits latins de la Bibliothèque Nationale*, I (Paris, 1890), 334–337, and M. Manitius, *Geschichte der Lateinischen Literatur des Mittelalters*, III (Munich, 1931), 209; on the Scottish translation, see J. Rawson Lumby (ed.), "Bernardus de cura rei familiaris with some Early Scottish Prophecies, etc.," *Early English Text Society*, No. 42 (London, 1870).

31. In Cod. Ross. 569 (*Aristoteles Latinus*, II, 1202–1203, No. 1806), the pseudo-St. Bernard epistle (fols. 90v–91) precedes Durand's version (fols. 189v–191). In Cod. Urb. lat. 1392 (*Aristoteles Latinus*, II, 1210, No. 1821), penned in 1441 and 1446, the Durand version is followed by a spurious commentary by Averroës on the *Economics* and a fragmentary copy of the pseudo-St. Bernard epistle.

CONCLUSION

Bruni made a significant contribution to the study of Aristotelian moral philosophy with his translation from the Greek of the *liber primus* and his humanistic adaptation of the medieval Latin text of the *liber secundus* of the pseudo-Aristotelian *Economics*, and with the Preface and annotations to his version. He did not influence the teaching of the *Economics* at such centers of Aristotelian studies as the universities of Paris, Padua, or Bologna so long as studies were conducted by conservative scholars who relied on traditional commentaries based on the medieval Latin translations. But by the end of the fifteenth century and in the early sixteenth century his work affected instruction in both secular and clerical schools of higher learning that prepared students for the university, and in some faculties of arts at universities in Italy, Spain, France, and Germany. For scholars dedicated to the *studia humanitatis* his version provided an example of elegance in the Latin translation of an ancient Greek philosophical text, and his annotations provided a novel way of elucidating Aristotle. To laymen and clerics sympathetic to humanistic learning he presented a long cherished treatise on the *res familiaris* in a new and attractive garb. It was in this form that members of the nobility, wealthy businessmen, professionals, and educated men from all walks of life became acquainted with the spurious Aristotelian work.

Bruni thus stimulated the nonacademic and to a lesser degree academic study of this branch of Aristotelian moral philosophy during the century after the publication of his annotated version of the *Economics*. But he did not open a path to the science which was to bear the name of *Political Economy* and developed in Italy and France about the mid-sixteenth century. Many fundamental socio-economic changes in the sixteenth century necessitated a different approach to economic problems. New intellectual currents modified the viewpoints of those pensive practitioners who were to lay the foundation of an autonomous science concerning the wealth of governments and nations. Yet there is in the philosophical foundation of this science a recognizable strain derived from the pseudo-Aristotelian *Economics*. Most probably it would not be there had the fathers of the new science not become familiar with this work, known so widely and exclusively until 1540 in the version prepared by Bruni.

APPENDIX I

INCIPITS AND EXPLICITS OF BRUNI'S WORK AND OF ITS PARTS*

Aristotelis Oeconomicorum Libri Duo.
Leonardo Aretino Interprete.

1. praefatio: Preciosa sunt interdum parvi corporis . . . Nunc ad textum Aristotelis veniamus.

2. liber primus: Res familiaris et res publica inter se differunt . . . sic enim parata non requirentur.

3. liber secundus: Probam mulierem omnibus quae sunt intus . . . multum etiam ad uxorem et filios et parentes.

4. commentarium super primum librum: Res familiaris et res publica inter se differunt. Diximus supra in prooemio . . . huiusmodi dictum valet.

5. commentarium super secundum librum: Probam mulierem omnibus. In rei familiaris disciplina consideratio habetur . . . quod antecessit in littera.

---

* The title of each part varies in the manucripts. The *praefatio*, e.g., is also called *prologus* or *prooemium*, the *commentarium super primum librum* sometimes *commentarius* [*in*] *super librum primum*, etc. The main title, if at all extant, is ordinarily found in the Explicit; sometimes it is entered by a later hand in the form of a superscription. Equally varying is the spelling. No standardization of titles or wording is herewith intended; this task remains to be done by the prospective editor of a critical edition.

101

APPENDIX II
SURVEY OF THE EXTANT MANUSCRIPTS

No bibliographer can claim that his compilation is complete, but I do hope that this survey of extant manuscripts comprises the bulk of the handwritten copies of Bruni's annotated Latin version of the pseudo-Aristotelian *Economics* preserved in known collections. Listed are also a few copies which are thought to be lost or reported to have circulated in the recent past but could not be located. My main source of primary information about the extant copies were the printed catalogues of manuscript collections.

Had I relied exclusively on this source, I would have found no more than half the number of items listed here. It was my good fortune that Professor Kristeller made available to me in 1957 the typescript of the major part of his *Iter Italicum: A Finding List of Uncatalogued or Incompletely Catalogued Humanistic Manuscripts of the Renaissance in Italian or other Libraries*, Vol. I: (London-Leiden, 1963); Vol. II: (*Ibid.*, 1967). Copies listed in the two volumes are marked by reference to the page in the *Iter*, I and II. Copies which will be included in future volumes are identified as being derived from this source by unspecified reference to the *Iter*. From 1957 to 1966 Professor Kristeller furnished me with additions to the material which I had seen in the above-mentioned typescript. These were copies which he located in Spain and in countries in Central and Eastern Europe; they are deposited in collections for which no printed inventories exist. Although only 35 per cent of the items in the survey bear reference to the *Iter*, an additional 15 per cent would not be there had they not been spotted by Professor Kristeller in inventories which failed to identify the copies as Bruni's work or in rare catalogues to which I had no access. For his help and his continuous and most patiently tendered advice at every stage of my labors I owe Professor Kristeller more than can be expressed in strongest words of grateful acknowledgment.

The description in the survey of each copy of Bruni's annotated Latin version of the *Economics* is confined to an indication of the leaves in which it is contained and whether the entire work or merely part of it was penned. The copied parts are enumerated in the order in which they appear in the manuscript. If the copy is bound separately, the notation "cod." precedes the signature of the codex. Not included in the survey are data on the codices containing a copy; they are submitted in the preceding study whenever the analysis of the transmission of Bruni's work or of its proliferation calls for it.

In ascertaining the components of the copied texts and the qualities, contents, and provenance of the codices containing them I received generous help from many sides. The *American Council of Learned Societies* gave me financial support for procuring microfilms of copies that required closer study. Extensive descriptions of copies of Bruni's work and of the codices in which they are contained as well as microfilms of copies were supplied by librarians and scholars in an admirable spirit of helpfulness. My special thanks are due to Dr. Max Burckhardt (Basel), Dr. W. O. Hassal (Holkham Hall and Bodleian Library), Dr. R. W. Hunt (Bodleian Library), and Rev. Dr. José López de Toro (Biblioteca Nacional, Madrid) for providing me with detailed descriptions of items in their collections; to Dr. Marian Pelczar (Gdańsk) for establishing for me contacts outside his library; to Monsignor José Ruysschaert (Vice-prefetto, Vatican Library) whose magnanimous help exceeded by far what I was entitled to expect; to Dott. Irma Merolle Tondi (Biblioteca Medicea Laurenziana) who assisted me in many ways in order to assure correctness of my descriptions; and to Mlle Jeanne Vielliard (Institut de Recherche et d'Histoire des Textes, Paris) who aided my work with her personal initiative and the assistance of her resourceful staff.

I also feel indebted to the following librarians and scholars not named in the footnotes of the study who answered my inquiries to an extent beyond the call of duty: Prof. M. Bersano Begey (Torino), Prof. Alberto Broglio (Rovigo), Dr. Butzmann (Wolfenbüttel), Dott. Attilio Carosi (Biblioteca Provinciale, Viterbo), Sig. Valentino Chiocchetti (Rovereto), Dott. Lucia Tammaro Conti (Orvieto), Dott. Domenico Corsi (Archivio di Stato, Lucca), Dott. Giuseppe Cortesi (Ravenna), Prof. Don Ireneo Daniele (Biblioteca del Seminario Vescovile, Padova), Dr. Charles J. Ermatinger (Vatican Microfilm Library, Saint Louis), Mrs. Irena Fabiana-Madeyska (Gdańsk), Dott. Pierrina Fontana (Biblioteca Casanatense), Dott. Gino Carosi (Siena), the late Dott. Alberto Giraldi (Biblioteca Nazionale Centrale, Florence), Dr. Hermann M. Goldbrunner (Deutsches Historisches Institut, Rome), Dr. J. Hornung (Universitätsbibliothek, Tübingen), Dr. Wolfgang Irtenkauf (Württembergische Landesbibliothek), Dr. Kern (Badische Landesbibliothek), Sr. Felipe C. R. Maldonado (Fundación Lázaro Galdiano, Madrid), Dott. Berta Maracchi (Biblioteca Riccardiana), Rev. Prof. Florencio Marcos (Salamanca), Dott. Lucilla Mariani (Biblioteca Angelica), Dott. Olga

Marinelli (Perugia), Dr. François Masai (Bibliothèque Royale de Belgique), Dott. Biaga Mosulli (Biblioteca Angelica), Mr. Wallace Nethery (University of Southern California, Los Angeles), Mr. H. V. Pink (University Library, Cambridge, England), Dott. Pietro Puliatti (Modena), Dr. Reginald (Stiftsbibliothek Melk), Dott. Giovanni Simonato (Palermo), Signorina Bianca Toschi (Arezzo), Dr. C. E. Wright (Deputy Keeper, British Museum), and the librarians of the Biblioteca Palatina, Parma, and of the Biblioteka Uniwersytecka, Wrocław. Mr. Kenneth Freyer of the Paul Klapper Library of Queens College deserves my warmest thanks for his help so freely given.

AUSTRIA

MELK, Stiftsbibliothek

1　　1064 (708), fols. 406v–418v: Preface, Books I and II
　　　　Kristeller, *Iter Italicum.*

SCHLAEGL, Stiftsbibliothek

2　　Clp. [454.b] 59, fols. 62–63v: Preface, Book I
　　　　G. Vielhaber and G. Indra, *Catalogus codicum Plagensium manuscriptorum.* (Linz, 1918), 249, No. 143.

VIENNA, Oesterreichische Nationalbibliothek

3　　960 [Philol. 106], fols. 82–86: Preface, Book I
　　　　Tabulae codicum manuscriptorum praeter graecos et orientales in Bibliotheca Palatina Vindobonensi asservatorum. I (1864), 164–165.

4　　3240 [Philol. 325], fols. 1–10v: Preface, Books I and II
　　　　Tabulae II (1868), 240.

5　　3420 [Philos. 240], fols. 124–125v: Preface, Book I
　　　　Tabulae II, 286.

BELGIUM

BRUSSELS, Bibliothèque Royale de Belgique

6　　11 466–478, fols. 63–66: Preface, Books I and II
　　　　J. Van den Gheyn and others, *Catalogue des manuscrits de la Bibliothèque Royale de Belgique,* III (1903), 82–83, No. 1690; corrected by Dr. F. Masai.

7   14 602–606, fols. 1–34: Preface, Books I and II, Commentaries
on both Books
J. Van den Gheyn, *Catalogue*, IV (1904), 340–341, No.
2914; corrected by Dr. F. Masai.

CZECHOSLOVAKIA

OLOMOUC, Statni Archiv, Capitolní Knihova
8   344, fols. 2–23*v*: Preface, Books I and II, Commentaries on
both Books
Průvodce po státnich archivech XIV; svazek 3: J. Bistřický,
M. Boháček, F. Čáda, "Seznam rukopisů Metropolitní
Kapituly v Oloumouci." (Prague, 1961), p. 133.

PRAGUE, Strahovska Knihovna (Památník Národního Písemnictví)
9   DB V 6, fols. 13–36: Preface, Book I, Commentary on Book I
L. Bertalot, "Uno zibaldone poetico umanistico del
Quattrocento a Praga," *La Bibliofilia*, XXVI (Florence,
1925), 65–66.

ENGLAND AND SCOTLAND

CAMBRIDGE, Collection of Mr. A. N. L. Munby
10   s.n., fols. 16–26*v*: Preface, Books I and II
Kristeller, *Iter Italicum*.

Sidney Sussex College
11   [C.M.A. 730], fols. 58*v*–62: Preface, Books I and II
M. R. James, *A Descriptive Catalogue of the Manuscripts in the
Library of Sidney Sussex College, Cambridge*. (Cambridge,
1895), pp. 48–49, No. 67.

University Library
12   Add. 6 180, fols. 29–54: Preface, Books I and II, Commentaries
on both Books
Kristeller, *Iter Italicum*.

EDINBURGH, University Library
13   D.b.V.16, fols. 48–56*v*: Preface, Books I and II
C. R. Borland, *A Descriptive Catalogue of the Western Medieval
Manuscripts in Edinburgh University Library*. (Edinburgh,
1916), p. 190, No. 119.

HOLKHAM HALL, Library of the Earl of Leicester

14   379, (fols. 1–7): Preface, Books I and II

S. De Ricci, "A Handlist of Manuscripts in the Library of the Earl of Leicester at Holkham Hall," *Supplement to the Bibliographical Society's Transactions.* No. 7 (Oxford, 1932), p. 32.

15   444, fols. 231–237v: Preface, Books I and II
Ibid., p. 39.

LONDON, British Museum

15a   cod. Harley 3 399: Preface, Books I and II, Commentaries on both books

A Catalogue of the Harleian Manuscripts in the British Museum. III (London, 1808), 23.

15b   Harley 3 651, fols. 34–41: Preface, Books I and II
Ibid., p. 49.

15c   Harley 4 883, fols. 123v–130v: Preface, Books I and II
Ibid., p. 214.

16   Arundel 373, fols. 40–52: Preface, Books I and II
Catalogue of Manuscripts in the British Museum. N. S. Vol. I, Part I (London, 1834), 109.

17   cod. Add. MS. 6 885: Preface, Books I and II, Commentaries on both books

Index to the Additional Manuscripts . . . acquired in the years 1783–1835. (London, 1849), pp. 14, 67.

18   Add. MS. 26 784, fols. 48–59v: Preface, Book I, Commentary on Book I

Catalogue of Additions to the Manuscripts in the British Museum, 1854–75. Vol. 2 (1877), 284–286.

19   Add. MS. 39 654 [Parham MS. 72], fols. 32v–50: Preface, Books I and II

Catalogue of Additions . . . 1916–1920. (London, 1933), p. 133.

(MALVERN, Collection of C. W. Dyson Perrins)

20   64, fols. 199–205: Preface, Book I

G. Warner, *Descriptive Catalogue of Illuminated Manuscripts in the Library of C. W. Dyson Perrins.* I (Oxford, 1920), 164–165; auctioned by Sotheby & Co., December 9, 1958, acquired by an unknown private collector.

OXFORD, Bodleian Library

21 1 731 [MS. Digby 130], fols. 34–51: Preface, Books I and II, Commentary on Book I
Catalogi codicum manuscriptorum Bibliotheca Bodleianae. Pars Nona comp. G. D. Macray (1883), p. 137.

22 17 403 [MS. D'Orville 525], fols 27–51: Preface, Books I and II, Commentaries on both books
F. Madan, H. H. E. Craster and N. Denholm-Young, *A Summary Catalogue of Western Manuscripts in the Bodleian Library at Oxford.* IV (1879), 134.

23 18 870 [MS. Canon. Class. Lat. 289], fols. 199–215v: Preface, Books I and II, Commentaries on both books (fragmentary at the end of Book I and at the beginning of Book II)
Catalogi codicum manuscriptorum . . . Pars Tertia, comp. H. O. Coxe (Oxford, 1854), col. 235, with old pagination.

24 19 701 [MS. Canon. Lat. Misc. 225], fols. 69v–71: Preface, Book I
Ibid., col. 604.

25 19 828 [MS. Canon. Lat. Misc. 352], fols. 103–116: Commentaries on both books
Ibid., col. 700.

26 29 438 [MS. Add.C.264], fols. 107–119: Preface, Book I, Commentary on Book I, Book II, Commentary on Book II (Commentaries in margins)
F. Madan and others, *A Summary Catalogue.* V (1905), 623.

27 40 037 [MS. Bywater 5], fols. 32–44v: Preface, Books I and II, Commentaries on both books
Kristeller, *Iter Italicum.*

FRANCE

PARIS, Bibliothèque de l'Arsénal

28 1131 [1 B L], fols. 21–65v: Preface, Books I and II, Commentaries on both books
Catalogue des Manuscrits de la Bibliothèque de l'Arsénal, comp. H. Martin, II (1886), 297.

Bibliothèque Nationale

29   lat. 6 310, fols. 111–117: Preface, Books I and II
Catalogus codicum manuscriptorum Bibliothecae Regiae. IV
(1744), 227; G. Mazzatinti, *La Biblioteca dei Re d'Aragona
in Napoli.* (Rocca S. Casciano, 1897), pp. 36–37.

30   lat. 6 312, fols. 105–123: Preface, Books I and II, Commentaries on both books
Catalogus, IV, 228; pagination of this and of the following
six manuscripts supplied by Mlle J. Vielliard.

31   lat. 6 313, fols. 76v–91v: Commentaries on both books; Preface,
Books I and II
Ibid.

32   lat. 6 315, fols. 1–25v: Preface, Books I and II, Commentaries
on both books
Ibid.

33   lat. 6 581, fols. 145–156: Preface, Books I and II, Commentaries
on both books
Ibid., 258.

34   lat. 6 582, fols. 4–37: Preface, Books I and II, Commentaries
on both books
Ibid., 259.

35   lat. 6 616, fols. 56–80v: Preface, Book I, Commentary on Book
I, Book II, Commentary on Book II
Ibid., 262.

36   lat. 7 662, fols. 166–168v: Preface, Book I, résumé of Book II
Ibid., 382.

37   lat. 10 193, fols. 87–92v: Preface, Books I and II
L. Delisle, "Inventaire des manuscrits conservés à la
Bibliothèque Impériale, sous les Nos. 8823–11503 du
fonds latin," *Bibliothèque de l'École des Chartes.* XXIII
(1862), 501; detailed description from the Institut de
Recherche et d'Histoire des Textes.

38   lat. 11 138, fols. 49–65v: Preface, Book I, Commentary on Book I
Delisle, *op. cit.,* XXIV (1863), 221; description from the
before mentioned Institut.

39   lat. 16 087, fols. 48*v*–51*v*: Preface, Books I and II
      Delisle, "Inventaire des manuscrits latins de la Sorbonne,
      conservés à la Bibliothèque Impériale sous les nos.
      15176–16718 du fonds latin," *op. cit.*, XXXI (1870), 37.

40   nouv.acq.lat. 566, fols. 59–72: Commentaries on both books
      H. Omont, "Nouvelles acquisitions du département des
      manuscrits de la Bibliothèque Nationale pendant les
      années 1894–1895," *op. cit.*, LVII (1896), 167.

41   nouv.acq.lat. 650, fols. 2–10: Preface, Books I and II
      Omont, "Nouvelles acquisitions . . . pendant les années
      1896–97," *op. cit.*, LIX (1898), 93–94.

      Université de Paris
42   570, fols. 4*va*–6*vb*: Preface, Books I and II
      *Catalogue général des Manuscrits des Bibliothèques Publiques de
      France. Université de Paris et Universités des Départements.*
      (Paris, 1918), pp. 139–140.

GERMANY

BERLIN, Deutsche Staatsbibliothek
43   Diez B (Santen) 73, fols. 131–137: Books I and II
      Kristeller, *Iter Italicum.*

      (Depot: Tübingen)
44   lat. fol. 582, fols. 21*ra*–29*va*: Preface, Books I and II, Com-
      mentaries on both books
      H. Baron (ed.), *Leonardo Bruni Aretino. Humanistisch-Philoso-
      phische Schriften.* (Leipzig, 1928), pp. 120, 237.

FREIBURG i.Br., Universitätsbibliothek
45   450, fols. (mss.) 2*v*–9: Preface, Books I and II
      Kristeller, *Iter Italicum.*

HAMBURG, Staats- und Universitätsbibliothek
46   Philol.quarto 128, pp. 161–226: Books I and II interspersed
      with unidentified commentary
      Kristeller, *Iter Italicum.*

KARLSRUHE, Badische Landesbibliothek

47   Reichenau 22, fols. 183–187v: Preface, Books I and II
       A. Holder, "Die Reichenauer Handschriften; Die
       Papierhandschriften," *Die Handschriften der Grossherzogl.*
       Badischen Hof- und Landesbibliothek in Karlsruhe. VI (1914),
       36–37.

KUES, Bibliothek des St. Nikolaus-Hospitals

48   179, fols. 157–174v: Preface, Books I and II, Commentaries on
       both books
       J. Marx, *Verzeichnis der Handschriften-Sammlung des Hospitals*
       zu Cues bei Bernkastel a. Mosel. (Trier, 1905), pp. 167–169.

MUNICH, Bayerische Staatsbibliothek

49   Clm 13 572 [Rat.Dom.172], fols. 1v–31v: Preface, Books I and
       II, Commentaries on both books
       Catalogus codicum latinorum Bibliothecae Regiae Monacensis,
       comp. C. Halm, G. Laubmann and others. II, 2 (1876),
       113, No. 985.

OTTOBEUREN, Archiv der Benediktinerabtei

50   II 389 b, f.(1–23v:) Books I and II, interspersed with un-
       identified commentary
       Kristeller, *Iter Italicum.*

STUTTGART, Württembergische Landesbibliothek

51   HB X 12, fols. 70v–74v: Preface, Books I and II
       K. Loeffler, "Die Handschriften des Klosters Wein-
       garten," *Beihefte zum Zentralblatt für Bibliothekswesen,* XLI
       (1912), 127.

WOLFENBÜTTEL, Herzog August Bibliothek

52   Extravagantes 299, fols. 59–76v: Preface, Books I and II
       Kristeller, *Iter Italicum.*

HOLLAND

LEIDEN, Bibliotheek der Rijksuniversiteit

53   cod. Perizonianus Q 18: Preface, Book I, Commentary on Book I
       Bibliotheca Universitatis Leidensis. Codices manuscripti. Vol. IV:
       Codices Perizoniani (comp. T. P. Sevensma, 1946), 71–72.

HUNGARY

BUDAPEST, Országos Széchényi Könyvtár
54   Clmae 292, fols. 69v–78: Preface, Books I and II
      E. Bartoniek, *Codices latini medii aevi.* Catalogi Bibliothecae
      Musaei Nationalis Hungarici, XII. (Budapest, 1940),
      269–271.

55   Clmae 515, fols. 60–73: Preface, Books I and II, Commentaries
      on both books
      Kristeller, *Iter Italicum.*

ITALY

AREZZO, Biblioteca della Fraternità dei Laici
56   cod. 118: Preface, Books I and II, Commentaries on both books
      G. Mazzatinti and A. Sorbelli, *Inventari dei Manoscritti
      delle Biblioteche d'Italia.* VI (1896), 193; corrected by
      Kristeller, *Iter Italicum,* I, 2.

57   154, pp. 89–174: Commentaries on both books; Preface,
      Books I and II
      Mazzatinti and Sorbelli, *op. cit.,* 197; corrected by Kristel-
      ler, *Iter Italicum,* I, 2.

58   459, fols. 50–60: Preface, Books I and II
      Kristeller, *Iter Italicum,* I, 4.

BOLOGNA, Biblioteca Universitaria
59   1 639 [lat. 856], fols. 214–219v: Preface, Books I and II
      L. Frati, "Indice dei codici latini conservati nella R.
      Biblioteca Universitaria di Bologna," *Studi Italiani di
      Filologia Classica.* XVI (1908), 371.

60   1 733 [lat. 889], fols. 141–168v: Preface, Books I and II,
      Commentaries on both books
      L. Frati, *op. cit.,* 382–383.

61   2 828 [lat. 1512], fols. 147v–158v: Preface, Book I
      L. Frati, "Indice . . .," *Studi Italiani.* XVII (1909), 114.

BRESCIA, Biblioteca Civica Queriniana
62   A.VII.1, fols. 96–117: Preface, Book I, Commentary on Book I
        A. Beltrami, "Index codicum classicorum latinorum qui
        in Bibliotheca Quiriniana Brixiensi adservantur," *Studi
        Italiani di Filologia Classica.* XIV (1906), 50.

FLORENCE, Biblioteca Medicea Laurenziana
63   Plut. 54. 10, fols. 22–23: Preface
        A. M. Bandinius, *Catalogus codicum latinorum Bibliothecae
        Mediceae Laurentianae.* 5 ₊vols. (Florence, 1774–1778). II
        (1775), 645.

64 cod. Plut. 77. 12: Commentaries on both books; Preface, Books I
        and II
        Bandini, III (1776), 136.

65   Plut. 78. 12, fols. 21–36*v*: Preface, Book I, Commentary on
        Book I, Book II, Commentary on Book II (fragmentary)
        Bandini, III, 163–164.

66   Plut. 79. 1, fols. 121*v*–127: Preface, Books I and II
        Bandini, III, 170–171.

67   Plut. 79. 17, fols. 1–6*: Preface, Books I and II
        Bandini, III, 177.

68   Plut. 79. 18, fols. 2–13*v**: Preface, Book I, Book II, Commen-
        tary on Book II
        Bandini, III, 178–179.

69 cod. Plut. 79. 19: Preface, Book I, Commentary on Book I, Book II,
        Commentary on Book II
        Bandini, III, 179.

70   Plut. 79. 20, fols. 1–25*v**: Preface, Books I and II, Commen-
        taries on both books
        Bandini, III, 180.

71 cod. Plut. 79. 21: Preface, Books I and II, Commentaries on both
        books
        Bandini, III, 180–181.

72   Plut. 79. 23, fols. 120–126: Preface, Books I and II
        Bandini, III, 181.

73   Plut. 89. sup. 52, fols. 85*v*–88*v**: Preface, Books I and II
        Bandini, III, 316.

    * Present pagination and different from Bandini.

| 74 | Plut. 89. sup. 53, fols. 155–187*v**: Preface, Books I and II, Commentaries on both books |
| | Bandini, III, 317. |

75   Plut. 90. sup. 54, fols. 61–71: Preface, Books I and II
      Bandini, III, 633–635.

76   Plut. 12. sin. 8, fols. 189–194*: Preface, Books I and II
      Bandini, IV (1777), 99.

77   Plut. 42. 15, fols. 164*v*–166*v**: Preface, Books I and II
      Bandini, V (1778), 182–183.

78   Edil. [Flor.Eccles.] 140, fols. 177–180*v*: Preface, Books I and II
      A. M. Bandinius, *Bibliotheca Leopoldina Laurentiana*. 3
      vols. (Florence, 1791–1793); cited hereafter as Supple-
      ment; I (1791), 461–464.

79   Strozzi 54, fols. 71–76*v*: Preface, Books I and II
      Bandini, Supplement II (1792), 392–393.

80   Strozzi 56, fols. 100–106*: Preface, Books I and II
      Bandini, Supplement II, 394.

81   Conv.Soppr. 605 (Castellina 55.92), fol. 1–40: Preface, Book I,
      Commentary on Book I, Book II, Commentary on Book II
      Kristeller, *Iter Italicum*, I, 73.

82 cod. Ashb. 1405 (1329): Preface, Books I and II, Commentary on
      Book II (fragmentary toward the end)
      Ibid., 86.

      Biblioteca Moreniana (Annexed to the Biblioteca Riccardiana)
83   Frullani 23, fols. 71–91: Preface, Books I and II, Commentaries
      on both books
      Ibid., 110.

      Biblioteca Nazionale Centrale
84   II, IX, 15, fols. 315–321: Preface, Books I and II
      Mazzatinti and Sorbelli, XI (1901), 259–260.

85   Magliabechi XXI 7, fols. 119–126*v*: Preface, Books I and II
      Kristeller, *Iter Italicum*, I, 120.

86   Conv.Soppr. C.7.2677, fols. 66*v*–70*v*: Preface, Books I and II;
      fols. 147–156*v*: Commentaries on both books
      Baron, *Leonardo Bruni Aretino*, pp. 120, 236.

87   Tordi 343, fol. 125v: Preface (fragmentary)
        Kristeller, *Iter Italicum*, I, 169.

88   Nuovi Acquisti 354, fols. 9–18: Preface, Books I and II
        Kristeller, *Iter Italicum*, I, 173–174.

        Biblioteca Riccardiana
89   112 [L I 26], fols. 1–8: Preface, Books I and II
        J. Lamius [Lami], *Catalogus codicum manuscriptorum qui in Bibliotheca Riccardiana Florentina adservantur.* (Livorno, 1756), p. 42; corrected by Kristeller, *Iter Italicum*, I, 185.

90   135, fols. 156–161: Books I and II
        Kristeller, *Iter Italicum*, I, 186.

91   159 [N II 18], fols. 1–32v: Commentaries on both books; Preface, Books I and II
        Lami, *op. cit.*, p. 42; Kristeller, *Iter Italicum*, I, 189.

92   166 [L I 32], fols. 240–246v: Preface, Books I and II
        Ibid.

93   523, fols. 90–94v: Preface, Books I and II
        Kristeller, *Iter Italicum*, I, 193.

94   710 [N II 8], fols. 82–91v: Preface, Books I and II
        Lami, *op. cit.*, p. 42; Kristeller, *Iter Italicum*, I, 198–199.

95   899, fols. 2–9: Preface, Books I and II
        Baron, *Leonardo Bruni Aretino*, p. 236.

        LUCCA, Biblioteca Capitolare
96   534, fols. 1–13v: Preface, Book I, Commentary on Book I
        Kristeller, *Iter Italicum*, I, 254.

        Biblioteca Governativa
97   1436, fols. 101–106: Preface, Books I and II
        A. Mancini, "Index codicum latinorum publicae bybliothecae Lucensis," *Studi Italiani di Filologia Classica.* VIII (1900), 213–214.

        MACERATA, Biblioteca Comunale
98   5, 3 D 8, fols. 142–146v*: Preface, Book I, Book II (fragmentary)
        G. Mazzatinti, *Inventari dei Manoscritti delle Biblioteche d'Italia.* Vol. I, fasc. 1 (Turin, 1887), 143–144.

* New pagination.

MANTOVA, Biblioteca Comunale
99   A IV 16, fols. 65–87: Preface, Book I, Commentary on Book I
        Giornale delle Biblioteche, III (1869), 31, No. 110.

MILAN, Biblioteca Ambrosiana
100   J 11 sup., fols. 1–13*v*: Preface, Books I and II
        Kristeller, *Iter Italicum*, I, 332.

101   J 98 sup., fols. 99–105: Preface, Books I and II
        E. Franceschini, "L' 'Aristotele Latino' nei codici dell'
        Ambrosiana," *Miscellanea Galbiati*, Vol. 3 [=*Fontes
        Ambrosiani*, XXVII] (1951), 242 and n. 5.

102   J 115 sup., fols. 1*v*–8*v*: Commentary on Book I; fols. 25*v*–32:
        Preface, Books I and II
        Ibid., 241–242 and 241 n. 6.

103   cod. L 59 sup.: Preface, Books I and II, Commentaries on both
        books (slightly fragmentary at the end)
        Ibid., 243 and n. 1.

104   O 71 sup., fols. 6–14*v*: Preface, Books I and II
        Ibid., 243 and n. 2.

105   H 184 inf., fols. 106*v*–113: Preface, Books I and II
        Ibid., 242 and n. 4.

106   J 33 inf., fols. 70–82*v*: Preface, Books I and II, Commentaries
        on both books
        Ibid., 243 and n. 3.

107   Sussidio B 166 [G S VI 1], fols. 269–277*v*: Preface, Books I
        and II
        Ibid., 242 and n. 6.

MODENA, Biblioteca Estense
108   Est.lat. 2 [Alpha Q 9, 16], fols. 1–10: Preface, Books I and II;
        fols. 25–37: Commentaries on both books
        Kristeller, *Iter Italicum*, I, 377.

109   Est.lat. 113 [Alpha Q 9, 13], fols. 1–22: Preface, Books I and
        II, Commentaries (in the margins) on both books
        Ibid., 369.

110   Campori 18 [Gamma E 6, 3], fols. 1–30: Preface, Books I and
        II, Commentaries on both books
        L. Lodi, *Catalogo dei codici e degli autografi posseduti dal
        Marchese Giuseppe Campori*. 2d. ed. (Modena, 1895), pp.
        19–20.

111   Campori 74 [Gamma W, 2, 29], fols. 1–55*v*: Preface, Books I
           and II, Commentaries on both books
               R. Vandini, *Appendice prima (seconda) al catalogo dei codici e
               manoscritti posseduti dal Marchese Giuseppe Campori.* (Modena,
               1886–1894), p. 38.

           NAPLES, Biblioteca Nazionale
112   VIII G 12, fols. 87*v*–93: Preface, Books I and II
               Kristeller, *Iter Italicum*, I, 404.

113   VIII G 30, fols. 116–120: Books I and II
               Ibid., 428.

114   VIII G 45, fols. 1–31: Preface, Book I, Commentary on Book I
               L. Bertalot, "Forschungen über Leonardo Bruni Aretino,"
               Archivum Romanicum. XV (1931), 302; Kristeller, *Iter
               Italicum*, I, 428.

115   XIV E 26, fols. 43–46*v*: Books I and II
               Kristeller, *Iter Italicum*, I, 433.

           ORVIETO, Biblioteca Comunale "Luigi Fumi"
115a   Fumi IX E 39 (2712), fols. 94–95*v*: Preface, Books I and II
               Kristeller, *Iter Italicum*.

           PADOVA, Biblioteca del Seminario
116   43, fols. 80–85: Preface, Books I and II
               Kristeller, *Iter Italicum*, II, 7.

           PALERMO, Biblioteca Nazionale
117   I C 9, fols. 117–137: Preface, Books I and II
               Ibid., 29.

           PARMA, Biblioteca Palatina
118   cod. Pal. 239: Commentaries on both Books; Preface, Books I and II
               Ibid., 33.

119   Parm. 170, fols. 91*v*–97*v*: Preface, Books I and II
               Ibid., 44

           PERUGIA, Biblioteca Comunale (Augusta)
120   169 [C.52], fols. 117–123*: Preface, Books I and II
               Mazzatinti and Sorbelli, V (1895), 94.

       * New pagination, different from Mazzatinti.

PISA, Biblioteca Universitaria

121   690 [Roncioni 11], fols. 233–247*v*: Commentaries on both books (three words missing at the end)

C. Vitelli, "De Codice Roncioniano scholiorum in Iuvenalem," *Studi Italiani di Filologia Classica.* X (1902), 31–32; Mazzatinti and Sorbelli, XXIV (1916), 58, referring to the codex as no. 680 as Vitelli did.

Seminario Arcivescovile, Biblioteca Cateriniana

122   136, fols. 65–67*v*: Preface, Books I and II

C. Vitelli, "Index codicum latinorum qui Pisis in Bybliothecis Conventus S. Catherinae et Universitatis adservantur," *Studi Italiani*, VIII (1900), 381–391, esp. 387–388; Mazzatinti and Sorbelli, XXIV (1916), 83–84, No. 114.

RAVENNA, Biblioteca Classense

123   343, fols. 90–109*v*: Preface, Books I and II, Commentaries on both books

Mazzatinti and Sorbelli, IV (1894), 219.

ROME, Biblioteca Angelica

124   141 [B.5.10], fols. 11–34*v*: Preface, Books I and II, Commentaries on both books

E. Narducci, *Catalogus codicum manuscriptorum praeter Graecos et Orientales in Bibliotheca Angelica olim coenobii S. Augustini de Urbe.* (Rome, 1893), p. 73.

125   234 [C.3.15], no. 3, fols. 28–37: Preface, Books I and II

126   no. 6, fols. 44*v*–61*v*; 63*v*–65: Preface, Book I, Commentary on Book I; Commentary on Book II

Ibid., pp. 134–135.

127   1023 [R.7.4], fols. 2–17: Preface, Books I and II, Commentaries on both books

Ibid., p. 424.

128   1373 [T.5.11], fols. 82–86: Preface, Books I and II

Ibid., p. 579.

Biblioteca Casanatense

129   294 [D V 13], fols. 90–96*v*: Preface, Books I and II

Kristeller, *Iter Italicum*, II, 97.

130   656, fols. 109*v*–126*v*: Preface, Books I and II, Commentaries on both books
           Ibid., 94.

131   1549, fols. 111–119: Preface, Books I and II
           Ibid., 102.

132   4265, fols. 2–11*v*: Preface, Books I and II
           Ibid., 96.

      Biblioteca Nazionale Centrale Vittorio Emanuele II
133   Vittorio Emanuele 238, fols. 116–127*v*: Preface, Books I and II, Commentaries on both books
           Baron, *Leonardo Bruni Aretino*, p. 232.

      ROVERETO, Biblioteca Civica
134   12, fols. 1–22*v*: Preface, Book I, Commentary on Book I, Book II, Commentary on Book II (fragmentary; breaks in the middle)
           E. Benvenuti, *I manoscritti della Biblioteca Civica di Rovereto descritti.* Part I (1908), pp. 22–24.

      ROVIGO, Biblioteca Comunale (Biblioteca dell' Accademia dei Concordi)
135   Silvestriano 126, fols. 112*v*-117*v*: Preface, Books I and II (one leaf missing)
           Mazzatinti and Sorbelli, III (1893), 6, No. 20, and different pagination.

      SAVIGNANO, Biblioteca dell' Accademia dei Filopatridi (Rubiconia)
136   75, fols. 12–13: Preface
           Mazzatinti and Sorbelli, I (1890), 105.

      SIENA, Biblioteca Comunale degli Intronati
137   C VIII 3, fols. 192–202*v*: Preface, Books I and II; fols. 203–216*v*: Commentaries on both books (fragmentary at the beginning); fols. 227–238*v*: Beginning of Commentaries, missing before folio 203
           L. Ilardi, *La Biblioteca Pubblica di Siena disposta secondo le materie.* 7 vols. (Siena, 1844–1848), IV, Part II, 87; VI, 125.

138   L VI 56, fols. 1–15: Preface, Books I and II
           Kristeller, *Iter Italicum*, II, 158.

TORINO, Biblioteca del Re

139   Varia 7, fols. 50–72: Preface, Books I and II, Commentaries on both books
        Ibid., 185.

TRENTO, Biblioteca Comunale

140   Vindob.lat. 3191, fols. 144–150: Preface, Book I
        Tabulae II (1868), 225; A. Cetto, "I codici viennesi della Biblioteca Vescovile di Trento," *Studi Trentini di science storiche.* XXXVII (1958), 494–495.

TREVISO, Biblioteca Comunale

141   630, fols. 29–38*v*: Preface, Book I
        Kristeller, *Iter Italicum*, II, 198.

VENICE, Biblioteca Nazionale Marciana

142   Z.1. 491 [1857], fols. 5–20: Preface, Books I and II
        J. Valentinelli, *Bibliotheca Manuscripta ad S. Marci Venetiarum.* IV (1871), 11.

143   Z.1. 501 [1712], fols. 126–131: Preface, Books I and II
        Ibid., 198.

144   Marc.lat. VI 251 [3469], fols. 134*v*–140*v*: Preface, Books I and II
        Ibid., 69.

145   Marc.lat. XIV 214 [4674], fols. (MSS) 50–76: Preface, Books I and II, Commentaries on both books
        Kristeller, *Iter Italicum*, II, 284.

VITERBO, Biblioteca Capitolare

146   37, fols. 1–15*: Book I (fragmentary at the beginning), Book II, Commentaries on both books
        L. Dorez, "Inventaire Sommaire des Manuscrits de la Bibliothèque Capitulaire de Viterbe," *Revue des Bibliothèques.* V (1895), 243, No. 17.

POLAND

GDAŃSK, Biblioteka Gdańska Polskiej Akademii Nauk

147   2369, fols. 1–24: Preface, Books I and II
        Katalog der Danziger Stadtbibliothek. Vol. III (1909): *Katalog der Handschriften. Teil 3*, comp. O. Günther, 274.

---

* Newest pagination; one leaf in the beginning of the codex is missing; presumably it contained the Preface and the beginning of Book 1.

KRAKÓW, Biblioteka Polskiej Akademii Nauk

148   1717, fols. 199*v*–202*v*: Excerpts from Books I and II
       Kristeller, *Iter Italicum*.

POZNAŃ, Archiwum Archidiecezjalne

149   196, fols. 40–54: Books I and II (marginal and interlinear
       notes in fols. 40–45)
       Ibid.

WROCŁAW, Biblioteka Uniwersytecka

150   IV F 67, fols. 52–55*v*: Book II (with unidentified commentary)
       G. Lacombe (ed.), *Aristoteles Latinus*, I (1939), 761, No.
       1117; without identification of the Bruni text.

PORTUGAL

LISBON, Biblioteca Nacional

151   Alcobacense 284, fols. 130–138*v*: Preface, Books I and II
       *Biblioteca Nacional de Lisboa. Inventário dos codices alco-
       bacenses.* Part IV (1932), 254–255.

SPAIN

BARCELONA, Biblioteca Universitaria

152   752, fols. 122–129: Preface, Books I and II
       F. Miquel Rosell, *Inventario General de Manuscritos de la
       Biblioteca Universitaria de Barcelona.* II (1958), 280–281.

CORDOBA, Archivo Catedralicio (Biblioteca del Cabildo)

153   132, fols. [?]: Preface, Books I and II
       Kristeller, *Iter Italicum*.

EL ESCORIAL, Real Biblioteca

154   f. II. 2., fols. 107–114: Preface, Books I and II
       G. Antolin, *Catálogo de los códices latinos de la Real Biblioteca
       del Escorial.* II (1911), 149–150.

155   f. III. 7., fols. 143–147: Preface, Books I and II
       Ibid., 179–180.

156   f. III. 25., fols. 100–107: Preface, Books I and II
       Ibid., 197–198

MADRID, Biblioteca de la Fundación Lázaro Galdiano
156a   216 (15029), fols. 129–137*v*: Preface, Books I and II
       Kristeller, *Iter Italicum*.

       Biblioteca Nacional
157   6 565, fols. 165–176: Preface, Books I and II
       Ibid.

158   6 927 [T 129], fols. 185–189*v*: Preface, Books I and II
       Ibid.

159   7 321, fols. 168–173*v*: Preface, Books I and II
       Ibid.

160   7 687, fols. 139–143*v*: Preface, Book I, Book II (fragmentary;
       breaks in the middle)
       L. Bertalot, "Zur Bibliographie der Uebersetzungen des
       Leonardus Brunus Aretinus," *Quellen und Forschungen
       aus italienischen Archiven und Bibliotheken.* XXVII (1937),
       186.

161   7 804, fols. 100–118*v*: Preface, Book I, Commentary on Book I,
       Book II, Commentary on Book II
       Kristeller, *Iter Italicum*.

162   12 692, fols. 100–119*v*: Preface, Books I and II, Commentaries
       on both books
       Bertalot, "Zur Bibliographie," 186.

163   13 521, fols. 122–129*v*: Preface, Books I and II
       Ibid., 186 n. 2.

       Biblioteca de la Universidad
164   109, fols. 112ra–120ra: Preface, Books I and II
       J. Villa-Amil y Casto, *Catálogo de los manuscritos existentes
       en la Biblioteca del Noviciado de la Universidad Central.* Part I:
       Codices. (Madrid, 1878), 39–40.

165   114, fols. 164–171*v*: Preface, Books I and II, Commentaries on
       both books
       Ibid., 41–42.

       SALAMANCA, Biblioteca Universitaria
166   2 265 [Palacio 2007; 2 N 3; VII J 2], fols. 158–162: Books I
       and II, Commentary on Book I (fragmentary; last third of the
       text is missing)
       Kristeller, *Iter Italicum*.

167   2 603 [Palacio 380; 2 E 2; VII E 2], fols. [?]: Preface,
         Books I and II
         Bertalot, "Zur Bibliographie," 186.

SEGOVIA, Biblioteca de la Catedral
168   Vitrina 33 [old nos. 86, 295], fols. 89–94v: Preface, Books
         I and II
         Kristeller, *Iter Italicum*.
169   Vitrina 29 [old nos. 129, 134], pp. 372–389: Commentaries
         on both books
         Ibid.

SEO DE URGEL, Archivo de la Catedral
169a   51 P [Costa No. 145], fols. 107–114: Preface, Books I and II
         Ibid.

SEVILLA, Biblioteca Colombina
170   5-3-13 [BB 145-4], fascicle 2: Preface, Books I and II, Com-
         mentaries on both books.
         Ibid.
171   7-4-16, fols. 145–156: Preface, Books I and II, Commentaries
         on both books.
         Ibid.

TARAZONA (Province Zaragoza), Biblioteca de la Catedral
172   111, fols. 114–121: Preface, Books I and II
         Ibid.

TOLEDO, Biblioteca del Cabildo
173   13-7 [Octavio No. CX], fols. 172v–185v: Books I and II
         J. M. Octavio de Toledo, *Catálogo de la Libreria del Cabildo
         Toledano*. Vol. I: *Manuscritos* (1903), 60.
174   94–15 [Octavio No. XXXIX], fols. 131–136v: Preface, Books
         I and II
         Ibid., 28–29.
175   95–18 [Octavio No. III], fols. 75–90: Preface, Books I and II
         Ibid., 9–10.

VALENCIA, Biblioteca Universitaria
176   389 [Gutiérrez No. 359; De Marinis II, 27], fols. 145–153:
         Preface, Books I and II
         M. Gutiérrez del Caño, *Catálogo de los manuscritos existentes
         en la Biblioteca Universitaria de Valencia*. I (1914), 140.

177   cod. 721 [Gutiérrez Nos. 130, 131; De Marinis II, 17]: Preface,
        Books I and II, Commentaries on both books
        Ibid., 46.

178   828 [Gutiérrez No. 129; De Marinis II, 14], fols. 202–222:
        Books I and II, Commentaries on both books
        Ibid., 45–46.

        ZARAGOZA, Biblioteca Capitular (de la Seo)
179   16–54, fols. [?]: Preface, Books I and II (fragmentary at the
        end)
        Kristeller, *Iter Italicum.*

SWITZERLAND

        BASEL, Oeffentliche Bibliothek der Universität
180   F. I. 2., fols. 84–94*v*: Preface, Books I and II, Commentaries
        on both books
        G. Haenel, *Catalogi librorum manuscriptorum qui in biblio-
        thecis Galliae, Helvetiae, Belgii, Britanniae M., Hispaniae,
        Lusitaniae asservantur.* (Leipzig, 1830), col. 525.

181   F. II.10., fols. 325–336: Preface, Books I and II, Commentaries
        on both books
        Ibid.

182   AN. IV.14 [F.IV.1], fols. 81–91: Preface, Books I and II,
        Commentaries on both books
        Ibid.

183   F. VI. 1., fols., 144–150: Preface, Books I and II
        Ibid.

184   O. II.32., fols. 21–41*v*: Preface, Books I and II, Commentaries
        on both books
        Ibid., col. 657 bis.

185   O. III.23., fol. 142 *r,v*: Preface
        Ibid., col. 658 bis.

        ZÜRICH, Zentralbibliothek
186   267 [Car. C 101], fols. 87–100*v*: Preface, Books I and II,
        Commentaries on both books
        Katalog der Handschriften der Zentralbibliothek Zürich. I:
        Mittelalterliche Handschriften, comp. C. Mohlberg. Fasc. 1–2
        (1932), 112–113.

U.S.A.

chicago, The Newberry Library
187   MS. 78.1, fols. 72*v*–79: Preface, Book I
         Communication from H. Baron.

los angeles, The Library of the University of Southern California
188   RL 091–A 717 e, fols. 1–14: Preface, Books I and II, Com-
         mentaries on both books
         W. H. Bond and C. U. Faye, *Supplement to the Census of
         Medieval and Renaissance Manuscripts in the United States and
         Canada.* (New York, 1962), 16.

189   RL 093–C 586 do, fols. 123–134: Preface, Books I and II
         S. De Rici and W. J. Wilson, *Census of Medieval and
         Renaissance Manuscripts in the United States and Canada.*
         Vol. I: (New York, 1935), 18.

U.S.S.R.

leningrad, Publichnaja Biblioteka
190 cod. Cl.lat.O.v.1: Preface, Books I and II, Commentaries on both
     books
     Kristeller, *Iter Italicum.*

Vatican City

vatican city, Biblioteca Apostolica Vaticana
191   Vat.lat. 1 494, fols. 65ra–68rb: Books I and II, Preface
         Codices Vaticani Latini, III, comp. B. Nogara (1912),
         24–25.

192   Vat.lat. 2 096, fols. 126*v*–134: Preface, Books I and II
         Kristeller, *Iter Italicum*, II, 311.

193   Vat.lat. 2 099, fols. 87–92*v*: Preface, Books I and II
         Ibid., 311.

194   Vat.lat. 2 100, fols. 193–198*v*: Preface, Books I and II
         Ibid.

195   Vat.lat. 2 101, fols. 166*v*–174: Preface, Books I and II, Commentaries (in the margins) on both books
        Ibid.

196   Vat.lat. 2 103, fols. 90–95*v*: Books I and II
        Ibid.

197   Vat.lat. 2 108, fols. 216*v*–223: Preface, Books I and II
        Bertalot, "Forschungen über Leonardo Bruni Aretino," 291.

198   Vat.lat. 3 347, fols. 38*v*-56*v*: Preface, Book I, Commentary on Book I, Book II, Commenatry on Book II
        Baron, *Leonardo Bruni Aretino*, pp. 120, 228–229.

199   Vat.lat. 4 506, fols. 1–44: Preface, Books I and II, Commentaries on both books
        Kristeller, *Iter Italicum*, II, 328.

200   Vat.lat. 4 510, fols. 114–126*v*: Preface, Books I and II
        Ibid.

201   Vat.lat. 5 109, fols. 99–106*v*: Preface, Books I and II
        Ibid., 331.

202   Vat.lat. 5 144, fol. 118: Preface (fragmentary)
        Ibid., 370.

203   Vat.lat. 5 336, fols. 1–23*v*: Preface, Books I and II, Commentary on Book I
        Ibid., 374.

204   Vat.lat. 8 750, fols. 272–283: Preface, Book I, Commentary on Book I (fragmentary; last fourth of the text is missing)
        Ibid., 385.

205   Vat.lat. 11 453, fols. 33–43: Books I and II
        Codices Vaticani Latini, 11414–11709, comp. J. Ruysschaert (Vatican City, 1959), 80–82.

206   Chig. J IV 118, fols. 72*v*–83: Preface, Books I and II, Commentaries on both books
        Kristeller, *Iter Italicum*, II, 482.

207   Ottob.lat. 1 348, fols. 38*v*–74*v*: Preface, Books I and II
        Ibid., 429.

208   Ottob.lat. 1 353, fols. 272*v*–285*v*: Preface, Books I and II
        Baron, *Leonardo Bruni Aretino*, p. 185.

209   Ottob.lat. 1 398, fols. 1–16v: Preface, Books I and II, Commentaries on both books
        Ibid., p. 187.

210   Ottob.lat. 1 705, fols. 147–165v: Preface, Books I and II, Commentaries on both books
        Kristeller, *Iter Italicum*, II, 419.

211   Pal.lat. 1 010, fols. 156–163v: Book I, Commentary on Book I, Book II, Commentary on Book II (Commentaries in the margins)
        Ibid., 392.

212   Pal.lat. 1 029, fols. 1–9: Preface, Books I and II
        Baron, *Leonardo Bruni Aretino*, pp. 120, 231.

213   Reg.lat. 1 189, fols. 1–38v: Preface, Books I and II, Commentaries on both books
        Kristeller, *Iter Italicum*, II, 401.

214   Ross. 784 [X 164], fols. 62–75: Preface, Books I and II, Commentaries on both books
        Ibid., 467.

215   Urb.lat. 1 326, fols. 150v–160: Preface, Books I and II
        C. Stornaiolo, *Codices Urbinates Latini*. Vol. III (Rome, 1921), 267.

216   Urb.lat. 1 339, fols. 136–161: Preface, Books I and II, Commentaries on both books
        Ibid., 273–274.

217   cod. Urb.lat. 1 342: Preface, Books I and II, Commentaries on both books
        Ibid., 1342.

SUPPLEMENT

A. LOST (or probably lost)

    FLORENCE, Biblioteca di Santo Spirito (dispersed in the seventeenth century)

218   Banco III, No. 4 a miscellaneous MS containing writings by Bruni listed in an inventory of 1451 (now FLORENCE, Biblioteca Laurenziana, Ashburnham 1897, fols. 37v–41); on fol. 38v it is described as follows:

> Plura opuscula Leo⸰ ardi Aretini ligatus et semicoper-
> tus corio viridi ⸰ ⸰ius principium est *Pretiosa sunt
> interdum* [= Bruni' . Preface] . . .

A. Goldmann, "Drei italienische Handschriftenkataloge
s. XIII–XV," *Centralblatt für Bibliothekwesen*, IV (1887),
147.

VIENNA, Dominikanerkloster

219 R 7 a miscellaneous MS listed in an inventory of 1513;
Bruni's annotated *Economics* version is described as follows:

> Econonomicorum Aristotelis textus, incipit: Res
> familiaris . . . Leonhardi Aretini commentum super
> eo, incipit: Sicut liber in se.

*Mittelalterliche Bibliothekskataloge Oesterreichs. I: Niedero-
esterreich*, ed. Th. Gottlieb. (Wien, 1915), 392–393.

WIBLINGEN, Benedictinerkloster (dissolved 1806)

220 s.n. listed in an inventory of 1432 thus:

> Explicit commentarium Leonardi Aretini in libros
> oeconomicorum Aristotelis . . . finitus Basileae in die
> sancti Benedicti . . . .

*Mittelalterliche Bibliothekskataloge Deutschlands und der Schweiz.
I: Die Bistümer Konstanz und Chur*, ed. P. Lehmann. (Munich,
1918), 435.

WROCŁAW, Biblioteka Uniwersytecka

221 IV F 29, fols. [?]: Preface, Books I and II
Probably lost in World War II.
Kristeller, *Iter Italicum*.

B. NOT LOCATED (listed in catalogues of dissolved collections,
booksellers, or auctioneers, but not found in extant public
collections)

MUNICH, (Booksellers) Weiss & Co.

222 I, 5, fols. 117–123: Preface, Books I and II
Codices, Manuscripti, Incunabula, Typographica. Katalog I
(1926), 9–10.

ROME, Collection of D. B. Boncompagni (dissolved 1911)

223 133 (149), fols. 95v–103: Preface, Book I
E. Narducci, *Catalogo di manoscritti da D. B. Boncompagni*. 2d ed. (Rome, 1892), 84.

THE LISTED MANUSCRIPTS ACCORDING TO COMPLETENESS AND CONTENTS*

A. Preface
    63, 87 (frag.), 136, 185, 202 (frag.)

B. Preface, Book I
    2, 3, 5, 20, 24, 61, 140, 141, 187, (223)

C. Preface, Book I, Résumé of Book II
    36

D. Preface, Books I and II
    (1) In the above order
        1, 4, 6, 10, 11, 13, 14, 15, 15b, 15c, 16, 19, 29, 37, 39, 41, 42, 45,
        47, 51, 52, 54, 58, 59, 66, 67, 72, 73, 75, 76, 77, 78, 79, 80, 84, 85,
        88, 89, 92, 93, 94, 95, 98 (frag.), 100, 101, 104, 105, 107, 112, 115a,
        116, 117, 119, 120, 122, 125, 128, 129, 131, 132, 135 (frag.),
        138, 142, 143, 144, 147, 151, 152, 153, 154, 155, 156, 156a, 157,
        158, 159, 160 (frag.), 163, 164, 167, 168, 169a, 172, 174, 175, 176,
        179 (frag.), 183, 189, 192, 193, 194, 197, 200, 201, 207, 208, 212,
        215, (221), (222)
    (2) Books I and II, Preface
        191

E. Books I and II
    (1) Without Bruni's commentary
        43, 90, 113, 115, 173, 196, 205
    (2) With unidentified commentary
        149
    (3) Interspersed with unidentified commentary
        46, 50

F. Book II
    150 (with unidentified commentary)

G. Books I and II, Commentary on Book I
    166 (fragmentary at the end of commentary; followed by vacant
    leaves which were prepared for continuation of commentary)

H. Books I and II, Commentaries on both books
    146 (frag.; Preface probably missing), [166], 178, 211 (Commentaries
    in the margins)—see also below O. (1)

* Parentheses ( ) indicate a manuscript lost or not located; brackets [ ] indicate
that the manuscript, if completed, would belong to the group in which it is inserted; the
manuscript is listed elsewhere in its present form.

I. Preface, Book I, Commentary on Book I
    9, 18, 38, 53, 62, 96, 99, 114, 204 (frag.)

K. Preface, Books I and II, Commentary on Book I
    (1) In the above order; title of Commentary: *Commentariolus*
        21, 203
    (2) Commentary on Book I; Preface, Books I and II
        102 (twenty-four leaves between Commentary and prefaced version)

L. Preface, Book I, Book II, Commentary on Book II
    68 (vacant page after Book I)—see also below N. (1)

M. Preface, Book I, Commentary on Book I, Commentary on Book II
    126 (leaves with unrelated text between the commentaries)—see also below N. (1)

N. Preface, Book I, Commentary on Book I, Book II, Commentary on Book II
    (1) Commentary following the respective book
        35, 65 (frag.), [68], 69, 81, [126], 134 (frag.), 161, 198
    (2) Commentaries in the margins
        26, 109, 195

O. Preface, Books I and II, Commentaries on both books
    (1) In the above order
        7, 8, 12, 15a, 17, 22, 23 (frag.), 27, 28, 30, 32, 33, 34, 44, 48, 49, 55, 56, 60, 70, 71, 74, 82 (frag.), 83, 86, 103, 106, 108, 110, 111, 123, 124, 127, 130, 133, 137, 139, 145, [146], 160, 162, 165, 170, 171, 177, 180, 181, 182, 184, 186, 188, 190, 199, 206, 209, 210, 213, 214, 216, 217, (219?)
    (2) Commentaries on both books; Preface, Books I and II
        31, 57, 64, 91, 118

P. Commentaries on both books
    25, 40, 121 (frag.), 169

Q. Excerpts from Books I and II
    148

R. Unknown arrangement of the parts
    (218), (220)

APPENDIX III
MANUSCRIPTS AND EARLY PRINTED BOOKS
DISCUSSED IN THE TEXT AND FOOTNOTES*

MANUSCRIPTS

Copies of Bruni's Annotated Version of the Economics

BARCELONA, Biblioteca Universitaria
752:83

BASEL, Oeffentliche Bibliothek der Universitaet
AN. IV. 14 [F.IV.1]:76–77; III, 23; 84

BOLOGNA, Biblioteca Universitaria
1 639 [lat. 856]:83; IV,26
1 733 [lat. 889]:IV,8
2 828 [lat. 1512]:58; I,16; IV,8

BRESCIA, Biblioteca Queriniana
A.VII.1:56; I,6; 69

BRUSSELS, Bibliothèque Royale de Belgique
11 466–78:84

CHICAGO, The Newberry Library
MS. 78.1:58; I,15

CORDOBA, Archivo Catedralicio
132:69

EL ESCORIAL, Real Biblioteca
f. III. 7:73; III,18

---

* Arabic numerals after the shelf-number of the codex denote pages of the text; Roman numerals followed by Arabic numerals denote part and footnote in the respective part.

FLORENCE, Biblioteca Medicea Laurenziana
Plut. 54. c.10:74–75; III,21
Plut. 79. c. 1:75; III,22
Plut. 79. c.19:55; 59; 74
Plut. 79. c.20:80; III,35
Plut. 79. c.21:74
Plut. 79. c.23:74
Plut. 12. sin.8:84
Edil. [Flor.Eccles.] 140:82
Strozzi 54:77; III,26
Strozzi 56:83

Biblioteca Nazionale Centrale
II. IX. 15:75
Conv. Soppr. C.7.2677:55; 61; 83

Biblioteca Riccardiana
135:69; 77

Biblioteca di Santo Spirito (dispersed)
Banco III, no. 4 (listed in 1451):84; III,41

FREIBURG i.Br., Universitätsbibliothek
450:88; IV,8

HAMBURG, Staats- und Universitätsbibliothek
Philol. quarto 128:94; IV,18

HOLKHAM HALL, Library of the Earl of Leicester
379:IV,26
444:83

KRAKÓW, Biblioteka Polskiej Akademii Nauk
1717:27; 71; 94; IV,19

KUES, Bibliothek des St. Nikolaus-Hospitals
179:80–81; III,36

LEIDEN, Bibliotheek der Rijksuniversiteit
Perizonianus Q 18:56; I,9

LONDON, British Museum
Harley 3 651:77; III,24

LUCCA, Biblioteca Governativa
1436:78; III,29

VATICAN CITY, Biblioteca Apostolica Vaticana
Vat.lat. 2 096:80; III,34
Vat.lat. 3 347:60; I,18; 69; 78
Vat.lat. 5 144:76
Ottob.lat. 1 353:61; I,22; 97
Pal.lat. 1 010:86; IV,2
Pal.lat. 1 029:77–78
Urb.lat. 1 326:73
Urb.lat. 1 339:73
Urb.lat. 1 342:73–74; III,19

VENICE, Biblioteca Nazionale Marciana
Marc.lat. VI 251 [3469]:69; 75

VIENNA, Dominikanerkloster
R 7 (lost):84
Oesterreichische Nationalbibliothek
Vindob. 3 420 [Philos. 240]:58; I,14

WIBLINGEN, Benedictinerkloster (dissolved)
s.n. (listed in 1432):70; 83

WROCŁAW, Biblioteka Uniwersytecka
IV F 67:II,5; 93–94

ZÜRICH, Zentralbibliothek
267 [Car. C 101]:70; 76; III,23; 84

Handwritten Commentaries on Bruni's Version

FLORENCE, Biblioteca Medicea Laurenziana
Ed. [Flor.Eccl.] 152—Bechi commentary:84–85; III,42; IV,24
Biblioteca Nazionale Centrale
Magl. VIII, 1404—Bechi commentary (frag.):III,42

Handwritten Copies of Medieval Economics Versions

1. Older Anonymous Translation

FLORENCE, Biblioteca Medicea Laurenziana
Conv. Soppr. 95:IV,9
MACERATA, Biblioteca Comunale
5,3 D 30:II,5
PARIS, Bibliothèque Nationale
lat. 16 107:86; IV,3

2. *Translation by Durand d'Auvergne*

BOLOGNA, Biblioteca Universitaria
  lat. 1 119:IV,8

NEW YORK, Columbia University Library
  Plimpton 17:IV,8

PARIS, Bibliothèque Nationale
  lat. 16 089:IV,3
  lat. 16 133:IV,3
  lat. 16 147:IV,3
  lat. 16 490:IV,3

  Université de Paris
  1 032:IV,3

VATICAN CITY, Biblioteca Apostolica Vaticana
  Ross. 569:99; IV,31
  Urb.lat. 1 392:99; IV,31

3. *French Version by Oresme based on the Durand Translation*

BRUSSELS, Bibliothèque Royale de Belgique
  2 904:71–72; III,11

EARLY PRINTED BOOKS

Bruni's Version with or without Annotations

1. *In Separate Editions or Combined with Other Aristotle Translations*

Aristoteles: Ethica Nicomachea. Politica. Oeconomica. Translated by Bruni. Strasbourg: Johann Mentelin, before April 10, 1469. (GW 2367):26; I,20; 70; 88; IV,6

[*Aristoteles: Oeconomica.* Annotated Bruni Version.] Venice: Christophorus Valdarfer [*ca.* 1470]. (GW 2435):I,20.

Aristoteles: Ethica ad Nicomachum. Politica. Oeconomica. [Valencia: Lambert Palmart, *ca.* 1475–77]. (GW 2370):70.

Aristoteles: Politica. Oeconomica. Translated by Bruni. Paris: George Wolff for Durand Gerlier, January 19, 1489/90. (GW 2447):71.

Oeconomicorum Aristotelis libelli cum commentariis Leonardi Aretini. Edited by Bartholomaeus de Lombardia. Siena: Simon Nardi, February 1, 1508. (DK 6.6882):60; I,20

Aristoteles: Sophistici Elenchi. Oeconomica (translated by Bruni). Cracow: Floryan Ungler, 1512. (Estreicher XII, 214):71.

2. In Latin Editions of the Collected Works of Aristotle

[Aristotelis Opera Omnia]. Venice: Bernardus Stagninus (de Tridino), June 23, 1489. T.5:... Economica (Annotated Bruni version) ... (GW 2339):90.

... Omnia Aristotelis Opera ... Ed. Agostino Nifo. Venice: (Johannes & Gregorius de Gregoriis) for Octavianus Scotus, 1495–1496. T.II,2:... Economica (Annotated Bruni version) ... April 26, 1496. (GW 2340; BMC V,384):89–90.

[Aristotelis Opera Omnia]. Venice: Johannes & Gregorius de Gregoriis for Benedictus Fontana, July 13, 1496. Contains the Bruni version without annotations. (GW 2341):90.

Commentaries on Bruni's Version of the Economics

[Aristoteles: Oeconomica]. Bruni version with the commentary by Dionigi dei Roberti da Burgo S.Sepolcro. [Toulouse: Heinrich Mayer, ca. 1495]. (GW 2436):90; IV,11

Fr. Petrus de Castrovole. Commentum ... super libros Yconomice; Commentum ... super libros Politicorum ...; Pamplona: Guillen, 1496. (Hain-Copinger 4654):85; 90–91

Gilbert Crab, Aristoteles de convenientia politice et economice. First edition. Paris: Jean Petit, ca. 1502 (Bibl. Aberdonensis, I, 5–6):92; IV,13

Jacques Lefèvre d'Etaples (ed.). Politicorum libri 8. Economicorum libri 2 (Bruni's version with the commentary by Lefèvre) ... Explanationis Leonardi in oeconomica duo. First edition. Paris: H. Stephanus [H. Estienne], August 5, 1506 (DK 6.7126):87; IV,4; 92–93

Virgilius Wellendoerffer, Oecologium ex duobus Aristotelis Oeconomicorum libellis accumulatum. Conclusiones centum et quattuor.... Leipzig: Wolfgang Stoeckel, 1512. (Panzer VII, p. 171, No. 338):93; IV,14

Medieval Latin Translations of the Economics

[Aristotelis Opera Omnia]. Edited by Nicoletto Vernia. Venice: Andreas Torresanus & Bartholomaeus de Blavis, 1483. T. III,2:... Economica (Conflated translatio vetus). February 3, 1483. (GW 2337):89; IV,9

Liber yconomicorum Aristotelis ... cum commento Johannis versoris.... [Cologne: Heinrich Quentell, ca. 1491]. (GW 2431):90; IV,10

STATE AND CHURCH IN BRANDENBURG-ANSBACH-KULMBACH 1524–1526

Gottfried G. Krodel

Valparaiso University

ABBREVIATIONS

Ansbach I	See p. 172 n. 10
Ansbach II	See p. 171 n. 5
APB	*Ansbachisches Pfarrerbuch*, ed. M. Simon (*EAKGB*, XXVIII, 1957)
ARC	*Acta Reformationis Catholicae* (Regensburg, 1959 ff.)
BBayKG	*Beiträge zur Bayrischen Kirchengeschichte*
BPB	*Bayreuthisches Pfarrerbuch*, ed. M. Simon (*EAKGB*, XII, 1930)
CIC	*Codex Iuris Canonici*
DRTA. JR	*Deutsche Reichstagsakten unter Kaiser Karl V.* (Reprint: Göttingen, 1962 ff.)
DuCange	*Glossarium mediae et infimae latinitatis*, 6 vols. (Paris, 1840 ff.)
EAKGB	*Einzelarbeiten aus der Kirchengeschichte Bayerns*
FB	*Die Fränkischen Bekenntnisse*, ed. W. F. Schmidt, K. Schornbaum (Munich, 1930)
FKO	*Fränkische Kirchenordnungen. Die evangelischen Kirchenordnungen des XVI. Jahrhunderts, XI: Bayern*, section I: *Franken*, ed. M. Simon (Tübingen, 1961)
Flugschrift	See p. 180 n. 61
LW	*Luther's Works.* American Edition (Philadelphia–St. Louis, 1955 ff.)
Rurer I	See p. 181 n. 68
Rurer II	See p. 184 n. 78
WA	*Luthers Werke.* Kritische Gesamtausgabe (Weimar, 1883 ff.)
WA, Br	*Luthers Werke.* Kritische Gesamtausgabe, section Briefwechsel (Weimar, 1930 ff.)
WKO	*Wendelsteiner Kirchenordnung;* see p. 151
ZBayKG	*Zeitschrift für Bayrische Kirchengeschichte*
ZevKR	*Zeitschrift für evangelisches Kirchenrecht*
ZKG	*Zeitschrift für Kirchengeschichte*
ZRG	*Zeitschrift der Savigny-Stiftung für Rechtsgeschichte*

STATE AND CHURCH IN BRANDENBURG-ANSBACH-KULMBACH
1524–1526*

I. INTRODUCTION

Ever since Rudolph Sohm's contributions to ecclesiastical law[1] and the resulting controversy with Adolf Harnack,[2] historians have sought to discover the essence of ecclesiastical law and the structure of the territorial church of the Reformation.[3] As might be expected, the work has centered

* The following pages are dedicated to Professor Wilhelm Maurer, Erlangen, in appreciation of his friendship. The research for this article could not have been undertaken and completed without the generous help of the Bayrische Staatsbibliothek in Munich, of the Newberry Library in Chicago, of the libraries of the University of Erlangen, of Concordia Theological Seminary in St. Louis, of Union Theological Seminary in New York, and of the Committee on Creative Work and Research, Valparaiso University, Valparaiso, Indiana. To all, my gratitude.

1. This term has been adopted for the German *Kirchenrecht*, which is the general term for all law used in the church. *Kirchenrecht* is divided into two parts, the Canon Law of the Roman church, based on the *Corpus* and *Codex Iuris Canonici*, and the *Kirchenrecht* as it is used in the Protestant churches. In the following work "Canon Law" designates the law which was and is used in the Roman church, while "ecclesiastical law" designates *Kirchenrecht* in general, and the law which is used in the Protestant churches in particular.

2. For Sohm's contribution to ecclesiastical law, see e.g., Excursus IV; W. Maurer, "Von Ursprung und Wesen kirchlichen Rechtes," *ZevKR*, V (1956), 1 ff., his *Pfarrerrecht und Bekenntnis* (Berlin, 1957), pp. 27 ff., and his "R. Sohms Ringen um den Zusammenhang zwischen Geist und Recht in der Geschichte des kirchlichen Rechtes," *ZevKR*, VIII (1961), 26 ff.; D. Stoodt, *Wort und Recht. Rudolf Sohm und das theologische Problem des Kirchenrechts* (Munich, 1962); rev.: *Theol. Lit. zeitung*, LXXXVIII (1963), 939 ff. On the controversy between Sohm and Harnack, see W. Maurer, "Die Auseinandersetzung zwischen Harnack und Sohm um die Begründung eines evangelischen Kirchenrechtes," *Kerygma und Dogma*, VI (1960), 194 ff.

3. See e.g., G. Schwanhäusser, *Das Gesetzgebungsrecht der evangelischen Kirche unter dem Einfluss des landesherrlichen Kirchenregiments im 16. Jahrhundert* (Erlangen: Jur. Diss., 1957); H. Liermann, *Deutsches Evangelisches Kirchenrecht* (Stuttgart, 1933), pp. 3 ff., 42 ff., 47 ff., 60 ff.; H. E. Feine, *Kirchliche Rechsgeschichte: Die katholische Kirche*; 4th ed. (Cologne-Graz, 1964), pp. 465 ff., 489 ff., 502 ff.; K. Holl, *Gesammelte Aufsätze zur Kirchengeschichte* I: *Luther*; 4th ed. (Tübingen, 1932), pp. 326 ff.; E. Wolf, "Kirchenbegriff und Kirchenrechtslehre," *Theol. Lit. zeitung*, LXXXV (1960), 641 ff.; W. A. Mueller, *Church and State in Luther and Calvin* (Nashville, 1954), pp. 5 ff.; L. W. Spitz, Jr., "Impact of the Reformation on Church-State Issues," *Church and State under God*, ed. A. G. Huegli (St. Louis,

on Luther, Melanchthon, and the situation in electoral Saxony.[4] More recently, historical research has branched out from electoral Saxony and has begun to focus upon other territories of the Empire.[5] The following work is the first contribution to the state-church question in the margraviate Brandenburg-Ansbach-Kulmbach. This small territory, spread out through the Franconian Circuit of the Empire,[6] was, together with the imperial city of Nuremberg, the center of the Reformation in south-

---

1964), pp. 59 ff.; E. Berggrav, "State and Church—The Lutheran View," *The Lutheran Quarterly*, IV (1952), 363 ff.; H. H. Schrey, "Church, State, and Society—A Protestant View," *Lutheran World*, V (1958), 2 ff.; G. W. Forell, H. A. Preus, J. J. Pelikan, "Toward a Lutheran View of Church and State," *The Lutheran Quarterly*, V (1953), 280 ff.

4. For the older literature, see Holl, *op. cit.*, pp. 288 ff. For the more recent literature, see J. Heckel, *Lex charitatis. Eine juristische Untersuchung über das Recht in der Theologie Martin Luthers* (Munich, 1953), pp. 11 ff., 19 ff., 136 ff., 194 ff.; hereinafter cited as Heckel I. On Heckel I, see E. Wolf, "Der christliche Glaube und das Recht," *ZevKR*, IV (1955), 225 ff., and F. Lau, "Leges charitatis. Drei Fragen an J. Heckel," *Kerygma und Dogma*, II (1956), 76 ff. See further W. Maurer, "Die Enstehung des Landeskirchentums in der Reformation," *Staat und Kirche im Wandel der Jahrhunderte*, ed. W. P. Fuchs (Stuttgart, 1966), pp. 69 ff.; N. Stein, *Luthers Gutachten und Weisung an die weltlichen Obrigkeiten zum Aufbau eines evangelischen Kirchenwesens* (Freiburg: Phil. Diss., 1961); F. K. Wentz, "The Development of Luther's View on Church-Organization," *The Lutheran Quarterly*, VII (1955), 217 ff. For Melanchthon, see F. Lau, "Melanchthon und die Ordnung der Kirche," *Philipp Melanchthon. Forschungsbeiträge zur vierhundertsten Wiederkehr seines Todestages, dargeboten in Wittenberg 1960*, ed. W. Elliger (Göttingen, 1961), pp. 98 ff.; J. Heckel, "Cura religionis, ius in sacra, ius circa sacra," *Festschr. f. Ulrich Stutz. Kirchenrechtliche Abhandlungen*, CXVII–CXVIII (1938; reprint Darmstadt, 1962), pp. 6 ff., 24 ff.; cited as Heckel II; see also M. Heckel, "Zur Entwicklung des deutschen Staatskirchenrechtes von der Reformation bis zur Schwelle der Weimarer Verfassung," *ZevKR*, XII (1966), 1 ff.

5. See e.g., H. Reller, *Vorreformatorische und reformatorische Kirchenverfassung im Fürstentum Braunschweig-Wolfenbüttel* (Göttingen, 1959); W. Maurer, "Franz Lambert von Avignon und das Verfassungsideal der *Reformatio ecclesiarum Hassiae* von 1526," *ZKG*, XLVIII (1929), 118 ff.; A. Hancock, "Philipp of Hesse's View of the Relationship of Prince and Church," *Church History*, XXXV (1966), 157 ff.; H. Bornkamm, "Kurfürst Moritz von Sachsen zwischen Reformation und Staatsräson," *Zeitschr. f. deutsche Geisteswiss.*, I (1938), 398 ff. With the continuation of the publication of *Die Evangelischen Kirchenordnungen des XVI. Jahrhunderts* one may expect that the territorially oriented research will increasingly concentrate on the *beginnings of the Landeskirchen*.

6. Emperor Maximilian (on July 2, 1500) and Emperor Charles V (on May 26, 1521) organized the German territories into ten *Reichskreise*. The Franconian Circuit was made up of the territories of the bishops of Würzburg, Bamberg, and Eichstätt, the imperial city of Nuremberg and some smaller imperial cities at the Franconian-Swabian border, several smaller Estates, and the margraviate. See *The New Cambridge Modern History*, I: *The Renaissance*, ed. G. R. Potter (Cambridge, 1964), 199 ff., 208 ff., 211 f.; *Ibid.*, II: *The Reformation*, ed. G. R. Elton (Cambridge, 1962), 477 f.; K. Zeumer, *Quellensammlung zur Geschichte der deutschen Reichsverfassung in Mittelalter und Neuzeit* (Tübingen, 1907), pp. 241

central Germany. In the third decade of the sixteenth century it was ruled by Margrave Casimir, a member of the Hohenzollern family.

The root of the Hohenzollern dynasty and its many branches was the small county of Zollern in Swabia, with Hechingen as its center. In spite of territorial acquisitions—Sigmaringen being the most important one—the Swabian Hohenzollerns have remained geographically unimportant and politically powerless throughout German history. In 1191/92 one of the Hohenzollern counts married the heiress of the *Burggrafschaft* Nuremberg, and the Franconian and Swabian territories were divided among their children.

Nuremberg was a *Königshof*, that is, a property of the German king entrusted to a governor, or *Burggraf*. In the king's behalf, the Burggraf administered the military and judicial affairs of a small territory surrounding the castle. As soon as the Hohenzollerns had established themselves in Nuremberg, they tried to expand the Burggrafschaft. Since the situation was already stabilized at the northern, southern, eastern, and western borders of the Burggrafschaft, the Hohenzollern drive for expansion was aimed in a northeastern and southwestern direction. In the thirteenth century the *Burggrafen* acquired the Rangau (southwest of Nuremberg) from the heritage of the counts of Abenberg, and in 1331 they bought Ansbach. As early as 1248 the Burggrafen had expanded into the northeast when they had acquired the territory surrounding Bayreuth from the Andechs-Meran heritage. In 1340 the *Burggrafen* also acquired the territory of Kulmbach (with the famous Plassenburg) from the Orlamünde heritage. By the beginning of the fifteenth century the territories of the Burggrafen stretched, with some interruptions, in a northeasterly-southwesterly direction from Hof almost to the Danube. It had two centers, the *Oberland* with Kulmbach in the north, the *Unterland* with Cadol· burg and Ansbach in the south.

The growth of the political prestige of the Burggrafen paralleled the growth of their territory: in 1363 they became imperial sovereigns (*Reichsfürsten*). One big thorn in the flesh of the Burggrafen was Nuremberg, which had become an imperial city at the beginning of the thirteenth century. As such, Nuremberg jealously guarded its privileges, tried successfully to increase them, and blocked the plan of the Burggrafen to

ff., 263; *DRTA.* JR, II, No. 21, (p. 228); F. Hartung, *Geschichte des Fränkischen Kreises, Darstellungen und Akten: 1521–1529* (Leipzig, 1910), and his *Deutsche Verfassungsgeschichte vom 15. Jahrhundert bis zur Gegenwart*; 8th ed. (Stuttgart, 1950), pp. 7, 14, 25 f., 42; H. Rössler, *Fränkischer Geist, Deutsches Schicksal* (Kulmbach, 1953), pp. 13 ff., 36 ff.; H. H. Hofmann, "Ständische Vertretung in Franken. Versuch eines Überblicks," *Jahrb. f. Fränkische Landesforschung*, XXIV (1964), 111 ff.

unite the Oberland and Unterland through the accession of Nuremberg, which would have formed a land bridge between the two centers of Hohenzollern territories.[7] The Burggrafen then cast about for other means of expansion. A prime opportunity arose during the Council of Constance, when, in appreciation of faithful service, Emperor Sigismund entrusted Burggraf Frederick VI with the Mark Brandenburg, and shortly thereafter invested him as Frederick I, elector and margrave of Brandenburg-Ansbach-Kulmbach. Thus the Burggrafen became margraves and increasingly divorced themselves from the city of Nuremberg. In 1422 the city acquired the famous castle, and in 1427 Frederick VI (I as margrave) sold the judicial rights of the Burggraf to the city, retaining only the title and the privilege of the imperial *Landgericht*.

Frederick divided the Hohenzollern territories into three major parts, designating one to each of his three sons: to Frederick went the Mark and the electorate, to Albrecht Achilles went Ansbach, and to John went Kulmbach. After the death of his brothers, Albrecht Achilles was again able to unite the whole Hohenzollern territories in Franconia and Brandenburg. In his famous *Dispositio Achillea* of 1473, Achilles established the north-German branch of the Hohenzollern dynasty. His son John Cicero inherited the Mark and the electorate. In John Cicero, Brandenburg had its first elector who was no longer tied to Franconia and who considered the Mark as the center of his activity. Cicero's sons were Joachim I, elector of Brandenburg, and Albrecht, archbishop of Mainz, the two great antagonists of Luther. Frederick and Sigismund, the two younger sons of Albrecht Achilles, followed in the Franconian territories; after Sigismund's death in 1495, Frederick combined the Unterland and the Oberland. Frederick had been blessed with many sons. By dynastic law, established by one of the Burggrafen in 1372 and 1385, the Franconian territories could be divided only into two parts, the Oberland and the Unterland. Thus only the two oldest sons could expect any inheritance; the others had to look for a livelihood elsewhere. Casimir, the oldest son, stayed at home,[8] while George, the second-born, went into the service of the king of Bohemia-Hungary,[9] and acquired the right to inherit some territories in Silesia. Two of Frederick's younger sons, William and

7. On the rise of Nuremberg, see G. Pfeiffer, "Der Aufstieg der Reichsstadt Nürnberg im 13. Jahrhundert," *Mit. d. Ver. f. Gesch. d. Stadt Nürnberg*, XLIV (1953), 14 ff.

8. On Casimir, see K. Schottenloher, *Bibliographie zur deutschen Geschichte im Zeitalter der Glaubensspaltung* (Leipzig, 1933 ff.; reprint: Stuttgart, 1956 ff.) III, Nos. 29147c–29156.

9. On George, see Schottenloher, *op. cit.*, III, Nos. 29097a–29128; G. Pfeiffer, in *Neue Deutsche Biographie* (Berlin, 1953, ff.), VI, 204; K. Müller, "Markgraf Georg von Brandenburg-Jägerndorf," *Jahrb. f. d. schlesische Kirche und Kirchengeschichte*, XXXIV (1955), 7 ff.

John Albrecht, became bishops, Albrecht became grand master of the Teutonic Order, Frederick became dean of the collegiate cathedral chapter in Würzburg, and Gumprecht became a member of the Würzburg cathedral chapter.

In 1515, Casimir deposed his father Frederick, charging him with senility and insanity, and placed him in protective custody. In 1516, Casimir took over the government of the Oberland, George of the Unterland. Since the territories could not bear the burden of the budget for two princely households and since George was more interested in his Silesian territories, Casimir was in full charge of the Franconian affairs.

During the reign of Margrave Casimir, the Reformation movement began to penetrate the margraviate.[10] How did Casimir react to the Reformation? How did the relationship of the state to the church develop between 1524 and 1526?

II. Legal Problems Created by the Beginnings of the Reformation in the Margraviate and Their Possible Solution

The people of the Franconian territories enthusiastically supported Luther as soon as he appeared on the stage of German history.[1] Already in

10. For bibliographical information on the Reformation in Hohenzollern Franconia, see *FKO*, p. 1 ff., 61 f. For details on events, see M. Simon, *Evangelische Kirchengeschichte Bayerns* (Munich, 1942), I, 161 ff., 215 ff.; hereinafter cited as Simon, *EKGB*; only the first edition of Simon, *EKGB*, can be used for our work, since the second edition (Nuremberg, 1952) has no documentary apparatus.—The ecclesiastical jurisdiction in the Franconian Hohenzollern territories was divided between the dioceses of Würzburg (see e.g., W. Engel, "Zur Geschichte des spätmittelalterlichen Sends in Bistum Würzburg," *Würzburger Diözesan Geschichtsblätter*, XIV–XV [1953], 357 ff.; see also F. Merzbacher, "Verfassung und Gerichtsbarkeit der Würzburger Archidiakone in der ersten Hälfte des 16. Jahrhunderts," *Archiv. f. Kath. Kirchenrecht*, CXXV [1951], 326 ff.), Bamberg (see E. von Guttenberg, *Germania Sacra: Das Bistum Bamberg, Kirchenprovinz Mainz*, I [Berlin, 1937]; J. Kist, *Fürst-und Erzbistum Bamberg*; 3d ed. [Bamberg, 1962]), Eichstätt, and Augsburg. The archbishop of Mainz was the metropolitan bishop for the whole territory; from 1515/16 it was Albrecht of Brandenburg (a cousin to Casimir and George) who is best known for his involvement in the indulgence controversy.

1. According to Simon, *EKGB*, I, 166 ff.; for a Roman Catholic view see J. B. Götz, *Die Glaubenspaltung im Gebiete der Markgrafschaft Ansbach-Kulmbach, 1520–1535* (*Erläuterungen und Ergänzungen zu Jansens "Geschichte des deutschen Volkes,"* ed. L. Pastor; V, Part IV (Freiburg, 1907), 14 ff.; A. Amrhein, *Reformationsgeschichtliche Mitteilungen aus dem Bistum Würzburg, 1517–1573* (Münster, 1923). Still highly informative is E. Engelhardt, *Ehrengedächtnisz der Reformation* (Nuremberg, 1861); although this booklet is now over one hundred years old, it is still reliable and heavily used in more recent works.

June, 1520, Sylvester von Schaumberg, one of the Franconian nobles, offered asylum to Luther and promised, if necessary, to protect the Reformer with one hundred horsemen.[2] While attending the Diet of Worms in 1521, George Vogler,[3] the chancellor of the government of Brandenburg-Ansbach-Kulmbach, and Lazarus Spengler,[4] the chancellor of the Nuremberg city council, were deeply impressed by Luther's ideas and steadfastness; both men returned from Worms convinced followers of the Reformer, and they became the most influential representatives of the Reformation in Franconian territories. Town and country seem to have been equally moved by Luther's teachings; some of the towns, especially some of the imperial cities, were the centers from which the Reformation penetrated the countryside.[5]

The Diet of Worms, the first official gathering of the German Estates over which Charles V presided, reconstituted the Council of Regency.[6] The council was to serve as a caretaker government in the absence of Charles, who immediately after the Worms diet was caught in a web of political and military action all over Europe; consequently he had neither the energy nor the interest to dedicate himself to the affairs of the German portions of his vast empire. The council took up residency in the imperial

2. *WA*, Br, II, No. 298; *LW* XLVIII, 169, 223 n. 3.

3. On Vogler, see Schottenloher, *op. cit.*, III, Nos. 21936–21939; K. Schornbaum, *Die Stellung des Markgrafen Kasimir zur reformatorischen Bewegung in den Jahren 1524–1527* (Nuremberg, 1900), pp. 21, 152 n. 55; hereinafter cited as Schornbaum I. E. Grünewaldt, "Das Porträt des Kanzlers Georg Vogler," *Mainfränkisches Jahrbuch f. Geschichte und Kunst*, II (1950), 130 ff. To the best of my knowledge there is still no comprehensive biography of Vogler, who played such an important role in Franconian Reformation history.

4. On Spengler, see G. Wolf, *Quellenkunde der deutschen Reformationsgeschichte* (Gotha, 1915 ff.) II, Part I, 203; Schottenloher, *op. cit.*, II, Nos. 20354–20372; VII, Nos. 58286, 58287; U. Ohlau, "Neue Quellen zur Familiengeschichte der Spengler," *Mit. d. Ver. f. Gesch. d. Stadt Nürnberg*, LII (1963), 232 ff.; H. von Schubert, *Lazarus Spengler und die Reformation in Nürnberg*, ed. and intr. H. Holborn (Leipzig, 1934); H. J. Grimm, "The Relations of Luther and Melanchthon with the Townsmen," *Luther and Melanchthon in the History and Theology of the Reformation*, ed. V. Vajta (Philadelphia, 1961), pp. 32 ff. On Vogler's and Spengler's visit to Worms, see Simon, *EKGB*, I, 166 f. Vogler's title was *Sekretär*, and Spengler's title was *Schreiber*. At first glance it seems as if both men held minor positions of clerks. In reality, however, both men stood at the center of the "executive branch" of the government; hence "chancellor" seems an appropriate translation of their titles.

5. Schornbaum I, pp. 18 ff.; *FKO*, pp. 4 f.; Simon, *EKGB*, I, 161 ff.

6. *DRTA*. JR, II, No. 21 (pp. 222 ff.); L. von Ranke, *Deutsche Geschichte im Zeitalter der Reformation*, krit. ed. P. Joachimsen; 6 vols. in 3 (Meersburg-Leipzig, 1933) I, Part I, 262 ff. (pp. 223 ff.); hereinafter cited as Ranke; the references to the English translation by Sarah Austin (London, 1905) are given in parenthesis or brackets. Elton, *op. cit.*, pp. 81 ff., 338 ff., 477 ff.

city of Nuremberg. Among other topics, it had to deal with the enforcement of the Edict of Worms.[7] While the Council of Regency and the Diets of Nuremberg discussed the touchy problem of what to do with Luther and the swiftly spreading Reformation movement,[8] the margraviate Brandenburg-Ansbach-Kulmbach flung open its doors to the new teachings. Peasants, townspeople, craftsmen, administrative officials of all levels,[9] and some preachers[10] constituted the moving powers. In the general excitement there was little initial opposition to the spread of the Reformation. Margrave Casimir[11] did little or nothing to stop the Reformation; he did not even try to enforce the Edict of Worms. His chancellor Vogler[12] apparently convinced

7. See *DRTA.* JR, II, Nos. 92, 93.

8. *DRTA.* JR, III, Nos. 74, 78–82; IV, No. 149 (pp. 603 ff.); Simon, *EKGB*, I, 213 ff.; Ranke I, Part II, 23 ff. (pp. 263 ff.); E. Franz, *Nürnberg, Kaiser und Reich. Studien zur reichsstädtischen Auszenpolitik* (Munich, 1930), pp. 81 ff.

9. E.g., Hans Herbst, the judge of Schwabach (see pp. 148 n. 18, 150 n. 24, 154 n. 35); Wolf Christoph von Wiesenthau, the *Amtmann* (district magistrate, bailiff) in Schwabach (Schornbaum I, p. 19).

10. E.g., John Rurer, called sometimes the German Chrysostom, who was a canon and city pastor in Ansbach and chaplain to the Margrave; *APB*, No. 2501; Schottenloher, *op. cit.*, II, Nos. 18400–18404; Wolf, *Quellenkunde*, II, Part II, 164 f. Lic. Adam Weisz, pastor in Crailsheim; *APB*, No. 3237; Wolf, *Quellenkunde*, II, Part II, 204 f.; Schottenloher, *op. cit.*, II, Nos. 22245–22251a. Kaspar Löner, pastor in Hof; *BPB*, No. 1472; Schottenloher, *op. cit.*, I, Nos. 10731–10735; A. Behr, "Loener, Kaspar," *Die Religion in Geschichte und Gegenwart*, 3rd ed. (Tübingen, 1957–1965), IV, col. 428. According to Simon (*FKO*, pp. 4, 63; *EKGB*, I, 166 ff.), the Reformation was a *Volksbewegung*; for more details, see Schornbaum I, pp. 18 ff.; *FKO*, pp. 63 ff. For a Roman Catholic view of the events, see Götz, *op. cit., passim*; Amrhein *op. cit., passim*.

11. On Casimir's relationship to the Reformation, see Schornbaum I; *FKO*, pp. 65 ff.; *FB*, p. 6. It is the great merit of Schornbaum (I) to have clarified (on the basis of a thorough analysis of all available source material) the position taken by Casimir in relation to the Reformation, a matter which has been highly controversial since the days of the Reformation. In contrast to Schornbaum I, the work by Götz is of little value.

12. On Vogler, see p. 146 n. 3. Since April, 1524, Vogler had been actively supported by Hans von Schwarzenberg, who at that time, having left the service of the bishop of Bamberg, came as *Landhofmeister* (minister in charge of the court) to Ansbach. On Schwarzenberg, the author of the *Bamberg Criminal Code* of 1507, see W. Scheel, *Johann Freiherr von Schwarzenberg* (Berlin, 1905); Schottenloher, *op. cit.*, II, Nos. 19531–19546a; V, Nos. 49221–49223; VII, Nos. 58071–58075; Rössler, *op. cit.*, pp. 156 ff. In issues pertaining to the Reformation, Vogler's political opponent was Hans von Seckendorf-Aberdaar, for whom the whole Reformation was nothing more than a political issue; see Schornbaum I, pp. 21, 153 n. 56; K. Schornbaum, *Zur Politik des Markgrafen Georg von Brandenburg vom Beginne seiner selbständigen Regierung bis zum Nürnberger Anstand, 1528–1532* (Munich, 1906), p. 249 n. 47; hereinafter cited as Schornbaum II.

him that such an attempt would only stir up restlessness among the people,[13] and the people themselves were eager to listen to the new kind of preaching. In many places a deep-seated animosity, even hostility, against the papal clergy became evident. In some cases the people boycotted those papal clergymen who stubbornly refused to preach the Gospel and administer the sacraments in the manner of the reformers in Wittenberg.[14] If the local priest refused to preach the gospel, or to abandon his benefice, the people often voluntarily supported an evangelical preacher,[15] who sometimes, unfortunately, was of dubious character or of little learning.

There was great readiness among the people to listen to the preaching of the unadulterated Word of God; there was also great confusion among them concerning theological and legal questions. As a first step toward documenting their desire for the gospel and the new teachings, the people demanded that the Sunday sermon be preached in the vernacular and strictly adhere to a text from Scripture, and that baptism be administered in the vernacular.[16] Next, following the example set by Leisnig and Nuremberg,[17] the people pulled all ecclesiastical financial resources in a Common Chest.[18] And finally, after 1523/24, the people seriously

13. The traditionalists in the territory (guided from the outside by Casimir's brother Frederick, the dean of the collegiate cathedral chapter in Würzburg, and actively represented in Ansbach by the margrave's wife Suzanna, a former Bavarian princess, and by the dean of the St. Gumbertus chapter in Ansbach, a certain Dr. Weinhardt; see Schornbaum I, pp. 21, 190 n. 191, 275 ff.; Schornbaum II, p. 248 n. 46) therefore saw in Vogler their archenemy and did all they could to discredit him and have him removed from office. When in 1526 they finally accomplished this (see p. 170), it was too late to do any good, since in the meantime the Reformation had put down such deep roots in the territory that it could no longer be uprooted.

14. E.g., Hans Link, the city pastor at Schwabach; Schornbaum I, p. 19; *FKO*, p. 65; H. Clauss, *Die Einführung der Reformation in Schwabach* (Leipzig, 1917), pp. 42 ff. For the organization of the church in Schwabach, see G. Heckel, "*Die Schwabacher Pfarrer bis zur Reformationszeit,*" *ZBayKG*, XXI (1952), 1 ff., 143 ff.

15. See e.g., the situation in Wendelstein, pp. 151 ff.

16. See pp. 152.

17. For the financial system of the medieval church and its reorganization through Luther, see Excursus I.

18. E.g., in Kitzingen, where the citizens were highly dissatisfied with the services rendered to them by their pastor, who had a benefice as a canon in Eichstätt and who spent all his time there. Consequently the citizens changed a mass benefice into a position for a preacher and called a certain Christoph Hofmann (see *APB*, No. 1242), who had studied with Luther. In agreement with Casimir they then, in August, 1523, created the Common Chest, for which they wrote an ordinance which was based on that of Nuremberg; Schornbaum I, p. 20; *FKO*, p. 64; text of the Kitzingen Ordinance: *FKO*, pp. 72 ff. For similar events in Ansbach, see Schornbaum I, p. 21, and his "Wann wurde in Ansbach

demanded that the mass, the center of the worship in the papal church, be replaced with an evangelical communion-liturgy.[19]

All these steps raised serious questions. Who was to examine and watch over the teachings and the morals of the clergy? How could the position of the pastor within the parish and the functioning of the pastoral office be protected from any arbitrary actions on the part of the people?[20] How could the faith and morals of the parishioners be examined and supervised in an orderly fashion? The church, moreover, was responsible for many functions which today are handled by the state. To name only the most important: the church supervised matrimony through a carefully developed and highly complicated legal machinery. How should canonical obstructions to marriage and divorce be dealt with?[21]

These problems had to be solved with greatest speed, since the people were rejecting the traditional religious-legal authority, the Canon Law, by which all such and similar matters had been decided. The situation was complicated by two facts. On the one hand, the bishops of Würzburg, Bamberg and Eichstätt were unwilling to remain idle while one parish after another was taken over by the Reformation.[22] On the other hand, Margrave Casimir was decidedly willing to step into the existing confusion

---

der erste evangelische Gottesdienst gehalten?" *BBayKG*, IX (1903), 26 ff. In Ansbach the contributions to the mass benefice of the main city pastor declined so rapidly that the pastor resigned; *FKO*, p. 64. In Schwabach, the Reformation had its roots in the congregation which assembled regularly in the house of Hans Herbst (see p. 147 n. 9), boycotting Hans Link, the city pastor (see p. 150 n. 24). In the spring of 1524 in Schwabach, too, a Common Chest was organized.

19. E.g., February, 1524, Wolfgang Gallus, the pastor at Oberampfrach, ceased celebrating mass; *FKO*, p. 65; *APB*, No. 860. For further material, see Simon, *EKGB*, I, 183 f. In view of the material presented, Zeeden's statement that *Lutheranism was introduced* in the margraviate by the territorial sovereigns as *Landeskonfession* (i.e., the "official faith" of the people living within the boundaries of the territory) can not be maintained; see E. W. Zeeden, *Die Entstehung der Konfessionen* (Munich-Vienna, 1965), p. 16. The material presented on the following pages will further substantiate this argument.

20. It seems that in Ansbach, e.g., the decline of the pastor's income, which caused him to resign (see p. 148 n. 18), was not the result of a leaning toward the Reformation on the part of the people, but rather of confusion in the legal framework and procedures among the various ecclesiastical institutions in that city; see Schornbaum I, pp. 250 f.; G. Kuhr, "Der katholische Pfarrer Johannes Mendel und die Anfänge der Reformation in Ansbach," *ZBayKG*, XXXII (1963), 74 ff.

21. For a glimpse into the complicated situation, see P. Rassow, "Der Kampf um das Eherecht im 12. Jahrhundert," *Die geschichtliche Einheit des Abendlandes* (Cologne-Graz, 1960), pp. 263 ff. This is a collection of essays, all by Rassow himself. Feine, *op. cit.*, pp. 543 ff.

22. See e.g., Amrhein, *op. cit.*, *passim*.

in order to deprive the bishops of as many rights and privileges as possible; he wanted to stabilize his position as territorial lord by increasingly expanding his authority over the church in his territory.[23] When Casimir was *patronus parochiae* he made as many concessions to the people who were demanding reforms as were convenient to him. When the nobles of the territory, or the bishops, complained about the ever-increasing Reformation movement in the country, or when harassed priests appealed to Casimir for help against unruly parishioners, he procrastinated in making a decision; and when he finally decided any particular issue, he did it in such a way that he only added to the general confusion. Casimir's whole attitude clearly reveals that he had not the least understanding of the religious situation in his country.[24]

23. The oath of loyalty which the margraves had demanded from their clergy for some time makes quite clear the ambition of the sovereigns to subordinate the clergy to the state. In the later middle ages it was customary in some areas for patrons to bind a pastor to themselves by demanding an oath of loyalty; e.g., see F. X. Buchner, "Zur Geschichte der Pfarrei Rehlingen am Ausgang des Mittelalters," *ZBayKG*, XXI (1952), 140 ff.; M. Simon, "Movendelpfründe und landesherrliches Kirchenregiment," *ZBayKG*, XXVI (1957), 1 ff.; Feine, *op. cit.*, pp. 391 f., 402 ff., 433. The margraves, however, interfered with the Canon Law directly. They obligated the clergy for whom they held the patronage to refer all matters controversial between laity and clergy, and all controversial faith-and-marriage-issues, to the margraves' court, and to refer nothing to the ecclesiastical courts without "approval" of the government. Text of the oath: M. Simon, "Vom Priestereid zum Ordinationsgelübde in Brandenburg-Ansbach-Bayreuth und in Bayern," *Das Wort in Geschichte und Gegenwart* (Munich, 1957), pp. 172 ff., *Beilage* I (pp. 191 ff.). This interference with the ecclesiastical jurisdiction cannot be explained, however, exclusively on the basis of absolutistic tendencies on the part of a sovereign. Other factors (such as a feeling of responsibility for the subjects, or the decay in the ecclesiastical judicial system) are of equal importance. See Excursus IV; J. Hashagen, "Zur Charakteristik der geistlichen Gerichtsbarkeit vornehmlich im späteren Mittelalter," *ZRG* Kan. Abt., VI (1916), 274 ff., 281 ff.; Feine, *op. cit.*, pp. 489 ff.; K. Frölich, "Die Rechtsformen der mittelalterlichen Altarpfründen," *ZRG* Kan. Abt., XX (1931), 457 ff. The oath of loyalty has to be viewed against the background of what Ulrich Stutz has called the *Eigenkirche* principle which had developed in Western Christendom during the early middle ages and which was at least partially responsible for the controversy between pope and emperor during the high middle ages. For details, see Feine, *op. cit.*, pp. 160 ff., 205 ff., 255 ff.

24. When Hans Link, the city pastor of Schwabach, e.g., complained to Casimir about the Lutheran movement in his town (see p. 148 n. 18), Casimir ordered everyone in the town to maintain law and peace. The people of the town then called a layman to be their preacher. Casimir removed him when Link again complained. Next, the people called three "Lutheran" preachers, and they were promptly expelled by the bishop of Eichstätt, without Casimir doing anything about it. The margrave even tolerated the incarceration of his judge in Schwabach, Hans Herbst (who may be considered the leader of the Reformation movement in that city), by the ecclesiastical officials for breaking

In the fall of 1524, in the village of Wendelstein, near Nuremberg, a highly promising possibility developed for ending the confusion in ecclesiastical affairs.[25] The peasants and small craftsmen of this community had boycotted their pastor for some time and had instead, at their own expense, maintained an evangelical preacher.[26] Tired of this obstinacy on the part of his parishioners, the pastor resigned from his office; whereupon the margrave as *patronus parochiae* appointed a new pastor.[27] When the new pastor took up residency, the people greeted him through a representative (who is unknown to us) with a speech which was contrary to all the legal principles of that day:[28]

> Honorable, dear brother!... According to the testimony of Holy Scripture, it is the duty of a Christian congregation to ask God, the Lord, to send workers into his harvest; [*a Christian congregation*] *also has the power unanimously to seek an honorable man with good reputation from within* [*the congregation*] *who would* [*preach*] *the Word of God* according to the true understanding.... A Christian congregation also has the

fast-regulations. When the people of Schwabach *asked* the margrave for an evangelical preacher, however, he went out of his way to find one for them. See Simon, *EKGB*, I, 179. The custodian of the church at Hornhaid argued that he was not responsible to the pastor but to the parishioners. When the pastor and his colleagues complained about this to the bishop in Würzburg, who in turn asked Casimir for intervention, the margrave made some statements to the effect that he would not tolerate anyone being robbed of his rights; he did nothing, however, to improve the situation. Schornbaum I, pp. 25, 160 n. 81. When during the first *Ansbacher Landtag* in September, 1524, the bishop of Würzburg requested Casimir to stop all discussion of the Reformation issue and wanted to proclaim a mandate in Ansbach by which all clergy would have been prohibited from participating in any such discussions under threat of severest punishment (see Götz, *op. cit.*, p. 34), Casimir simply prohibited the publication of the mandate. See Schornbaum I, p. 177 n. 151. For a general evaluation of Casimir's position on the Reformation, see Schornbaum I, pp. 17 f., 26. It would be a challenging task to investigate Casimir's religiosity and character. How deep were the margrave's religious convictions? What kind of a person was this—even more, what kind of a sovereign—who was unable to take any firm stand in the face of the religious turmoil around him?

25. For the events in Wendelstein, see Schornbaum I, pp. 25 f.; Wiedemann, "Die Frühmesse zu Wendelstein," *BBayKG*, XXVI (1920), 69 ff.; *Flugschrift*, pp. 190 f.; *FKO*, p. 65; see also E. Wiedemann, "Zur Geschichte Wendelsteins bei Nürnberg," *Mit. d. Ver. f. Gesch. d. Stadt Nürnberg*, XXIV (1922), 261 ff.

26. *Flugschrift*, p. 191; *FKO*, p. 65.

27. *Flugschrift*, p. 190 f.

28. See Simon, *FKO*, p. 65. See, however, also K. S. Bader, "Universitas subditorum —des pfarrers untertanen. Zur Auffassung und Bezeichnung der spätmittelalterlichen Pfarrgemeinde," *Festschr. f. Hans Liermann*, ed. K. Obermayer *et al.* (Erlangen, 1964), pp. 11 ff.; and D. Kurze, *Pfarrerwahlen im Mittelalter* (Cologne-Graz, 1965).

authority to dismiss [this man] again and to appoint someone else in his stead. . . . Now, in these final days, this aforementioned custom has been taken from the Christian congregation through the Anti-Christ. . . .

Now, dear brother and good friend, *since you came here of your own accord to be our servant* on orders of our Gracious Lord . . . [Casimir] (although we did not call you), *you should become acquainted with our wishes and ideas.* . . .

First, we shall acknowledge you not as a lord over, but only as a servant . . . of the congregation; you are not to give us orders, but we will give you orders. And so we command you to present the gospel to us faithfully . . . in its purity . . . according to the truth, [and] free and uncontaminated [by human doctrine].

Second, [we command you] to live in the community and congregation as a faithful servant of Jesus Christ [in word and] deed according to the gospel. You should distribute the sacrament of the Testament of Jesus Christ, and you should deal with it no differently than the Lord has taught and ordered us [to do].

In the same way you should publicly deal with the sacrament of baptism in such a way that many people can understand it. . . . In no way should you be influenced or terrified by the teachings or commandments of men [to abandon God's Word] . . . . *If you will do this* (as it is stated) *then we shall acknowledge you as a true shepherd and faithful servant of Jesus Christ.*

Should you, however, pursue the contrary . . . then you should know that *we shall not only brand you as an unfaithful servant but also shall drive you as a ravenous wolf into the net, and shall under no circumstances tolerate you in our midst.* . . .

Further, should the occasion arise that you think there is a just cause or complaint against one or more parishioners, then you should not accuse him in Eichstätt, or anywhere else, but only before his duly appointed judge and lord. In the same way [we shall deal with you]: no one shall accuse you anywhere else than at the court of the local judge, or of our gracious lords, the margraves. . . .[29]

Anyone familiar with Reformation history will see that this document reflects Luther's writing of 1523[30] concerning the authority of a Christian congregation and its right to judge all doctrine and to call and

29. *FKO*, pp. 77 ff., italicized by this writer. This speech is known as the *Wendelsteiner Kirchenordnung (WKO)*.

30. Simon has already pointed this out; *FKO*, p. 77 n. 1. So far as I have been able to determine, an exact comparison of Luther's writing with *WKO* is unfortunately not yet available.

dismiss pastors and teachers.[31] On the basis of I Cor. 2:15, Luther had maintained that the congregation of believers, of those who were redeemed and reborn through the power of the Holy Spirit, has the right and privilege to put in order its own affairs, to judge all doctrines taught in the church, to scrutinize all laws by which the church operates, and if necessary to create new laws.[32] The people of Wendelstein justified their refusal to bow to the Canon Law and their rejection of the competence of the bishop's court in Eichestätt on the basis of the fundamental rights of all true Christians.[33] The people replaced the law of the bishop, the

31. *WA*, XI, 401 ff.; *Works of Martin Luther*; Holman ed. (Philadelphia, 1931), IV, 75 ff. On Luther's thoughts in this booklet, see K. D. Schmidt, "Luthers Ansatz zur Neuordnung der Gemeinden im Jahre 1523," *Luther* (Berlin, 1958), I, 14 ff.; W. Brunotte, *Das geistliche Amt bei Luther* (Berlin, 1959), pp. 60 ff. (rev.: *ZRG. Kan. Abt.*, XLIX [1963], 520 ff.); Holl, *op. cit.*, pp. 351 ff.

32. For Luther's views on these issues, see Heckel I, pp. 136 ff.; J. Heckel, *Das blinde, undeutliche Wort 'Kirche.' Gesammelte Aufsätze*, ed. S. Grundmann (Cologne-Graz, 1964), pp. 132 ff.; hereinafter cited as Heckel III. Also H. Liermann, "Luther ordnet seine Kirche," *Lutherjahrbuch*, XXXI (1964), 29 ff.; E. Schott, "Kirchliche Gesetzgebungsgewalt im Urteil Luthers," *Wissenschaft. Zeitschr. d. Universität Halle.*, Gesellschafts-und-Sprachwissenschaftliche Reihe, IV (1954/55), 141 ff.; H. Hermelink, "Zu Luthers Gedanken über Idealgemeinde und *Von weltlicher Obrigkeit*," *ZKG*, XXIX (1908), 479 ff.; H. Dörries, "Geschichte der vocatio zum kirchlichen Amt," *Stat crux dum volvitur orbis. Festschr. f. Hans Lilje*, ed. G. Hoffmann, *et al.* (Berlin, 1959), pp. 108 ff.; F. Refoulé, "L'Eglise et le Saint-Esprit chez Luther et dans la théologie catholique," *Rev. d. Scien. phil. et théol.*, XLVIII (1964), 428 ff.; R. Prenter, *Spiritus Sanctus* (Philadelphia, 1953), pp. 3 ff., 101 ff., 184 ff.

33. Without actually saying so, the author of *WKO* here deals with the fundamental rights of the Christian, a notion which is taken over from Luther, without, however, quoting the Reformer. According to Luther, the three fundamental rights of all Christians are: equality of all Christians in the eyes of God, spiritual freedom, and the right to love the brother as well as the claim on a brother's love. For Luther, the consequences of these fundamental rights for the structure of ecclesiastical law (see also Excursus I) are, among others, the nullification of the special religiously qualified status of the clergy as opposed to the laity, and the concept of the priesthood of all believers; this is based on the equality of all Christians as truly spiritual people. To this comes the right of the congregation to appoint pastors and to judge all laws used within the church, and if necessary to create new laws; this congregational form of church-polity is based on the equality and freedom of all Christians. And finally, the right to love and the claim to be loved forms one of the principles by which, according to Luther, all ecclesiastical law is to be structured (the other being the constitutionality of ecclesiastical law; see p. 174). For Luther, see especially his *Address to the Christian Nobility of Germany* and his *On the Freedom of a Christian*; see further Heckel I, pp. 40 ff., 140 ff.; Holl, *op. cit.*, pp. 317 ff., 326 ff.; R. Prenter, "Die göttliche Einsetzung des Predigtamtes und das allgemeine Priestertum bei Luther," *Theol. Lit. zeitung*, LXXXVI (1961), 322 ff.; H. Brunotte, "Sacerdotium und Ministerium als

representative of false doctrine, with the law of the congregation of true believers,[34] of those who are truly filled with the Holy Spirit.

So far as we know, this speech was drawn up for the people of Wendelstein by a certain Hans Herbst, who was city judge in Schwabach.[35] He pointed out the direction in which a possible solution could be sought for the problems created by the Reformation in the field of ecclesiastical law and in the state-church relationship.[36] Obviously he left many questions unanswered. What good could the *Wendelsteiner Kirchenordnung* do, if the *patronus*, that is, the margrave, would not allow his right to appoint the pastor to be jeopardized, no less nullified? What would happen if the margrave refused to respect the fundamental rights of the Christian congregation—rights that were the presuppositions of Herbst's argu-

---

Grundbegriffe im lutherischen Kirchenrecht," *Staatsverfassung und Kirchenordnung. Festg. f. Rudolf Smend*, ed. K. Hesse, *et al.* (Tübingen, 1962), pp. 263 ff.; Kl. Tuchel, "Luthers Auffassung vom geistlichen Amt," *Lutherjahrbuch*, XXV (1958), 61 ff.; H. Brunotte, *Das Amt der Verkündigung und das allgemeine Priestertum aller Gläubigen, Luthertum*, XXVI (Berlin, 1962), 7 ff.; W. Grundmann, "Sacerdotium und ministerium," *ZRG*. Kan. Abt., XLIX (1963), 236 ff.; S. Grundmann, "Kirche, allgemeines Priestertum und Kirchliches Amt," *ZevKR*, IX (1962), 1 ff.; E. Sommerlath, "Amt und Allgemeines Priestertum," *Schrift. d. Theologischen Konvents Augsburgischen Bekenntnisses*, V (1953), 40 ff.; W. Brunotte, *Das Geistliche Amt bei Luther* (Berlin, 1959), *passim*; H. Lieberg, *Amt und Ordination bei Luther und Melanchthon* (Göttingen, 1962), *passim*; B. A. Gerrish, "Priesthood and Ministry in the Theology of Luther," *Church History*, XXXIV (1965), 404 ff.; G. Hök, "Luther's Doctrine of the Ministry," *Scottish Journal of Theology*, VII (1954), 16 ff.; W. Maurer, *Von der Freiheit eines Christenmenschen* (Göttingen, 1949), p. 29. On the fundamental rights of the Christian in *WKO*, see for equality above, the italicized lines in the introduction, and in paragraphs one, two, and five; for freedom, above, the italicized lines in the introduction and in paragraph four.

34. This becomes especially clear in the introduction and in the first paragraph of *WKO*; see above.

35. See pp. 147 n. 9, 148 n. 18, 150 n. 24. Pertinent information on Herbst has been collected by J. B. Riederer, *Nachrichten zur Kirchen-, Gelehrten-und Büchergeschichte*; 4 vols. (Altdorf, 1764–1768); III (1766), 317 ff.; Schornbaum I, p. 19 n. 29; Clauss, *op. cit.*, *passim*; *Flugschrift*, pp. 189 ff.

36. Herbst apparently had thought that *WKO* should be used not only for Wendelstein, but as a model for other congregations. This conclusion is almost inescapable since *WKO* was printed as a pamphlet; Simon, *EKGB*, I, 179; *Flugschrift*, pp. 190 f.; bibliographical information: *FKO*, p. 77; G. W. Panzer, *Annalen der älteren deutschen Literatur* (Nuremberg 1788–1805; reprint: Hildesheim, 1961), II, Nos. 2502, 2503. Although it is not known who gave the manuscript to a press, it can be assumed that it was Herbst, since it is highly dubious that the people of Wendelstein had any connection with printing houses.

ments?[37] Who or what should guarantee that the pastor would preach the unadulterated Word of God and administer the sacraments "correctly"? Who or what, in turn, should protect the pastor from the vacillation of the people? How could the claims of the congregation be defended against the claims of the bishop?

Despite these unanswered questions, Herbst clearly defined the competence of the congregation in all matters pertaining to the regulation of its affairs. The Canon Law was replaced by the legal statements prepared by the congregation. In addition to emphasizing the congregational form of church-polity, Herbst underscored the competence of the secular court for the legalities between the congregation and its pastor. Should pastor or parishioners have complaints against one another, then the margrave's court was to decide the case. But what if the secular power would not accept this responsibility? This question was beyond the interest of Herbst and the people of Wendelstein. They exhorted their territorial sovereign to step into the existing legal chaos in ecclesiastical affairs and confirm their rights; they expected the margrave to function as arbiter between the congregation and the pastor, and thus establish legal norms.[38]

37. This raises the problem of the essence of the Christian's resistance to the government, which Herbst did not see. It is interesting to note that in the same way in which for Luther the Christian's resistance to the government was closely connected with the roots of ecclesiastical law (see Heckel I, p. 140; Heckel III, pp. 111 ff., 132 ff., 288 ff.), so in *WKO* the question of the Christian's resistance to the government was implicitly present.

38. The appointed pastor, a certain Kaspar Krantz, accepted the conditions, certainly not being aware of all that was involved (see *Flugschrift*, p. 191). The pastor did not, however, care for his parish as the people had demanded. Consequently, in January, 1525, the people complained to the *Amtmann* of the margrave in Schwabach, Wolf Christoph von Wiesenthau, asking that the evangelical preacher whom they had maintained since Pentecost, 1524, and with whom they were satisfied, be officially appointed as their pastor; nothing is known of this preacher. The *Amtmann* approved this petition and referred it to the government in Ansbach. Unfortunately what further happened is not known; thus Simon in *Flugschrift*, p. 191. In August, 1527, however, a certain George Reischenbeck was appointed to the Wendelstein parish; see *APB*, No. 2356. During the Brandenburg-Nuremberg Church Visitation of 1528/29, the visitation commission rated Reischenbeck as doing his job quite well. The representatives of the parish made no complaints against him; to the contrary they voiced their complete approval of his teaching, preaching, and general conduct. See M. Simon, "Zur Visitation der Nürnberger Landpfarreien im Jahre 1528," *ZBayKG*, XXXV (1966), 16, 27, 39. The opinion of the people should perhaps be taken cautiously; nevertheless, if it is combined with the evaluation of the visitation commission, we may be justified in assuming the following course of events: The government in Ansbach dismissed Krantz at a date and for reasons unknown. Even

Margrave Casimir does not seem to have understood this appeal from his people. In the summer and fall of 1524 he did, however, abandon his spectator's position in relation to the Reformation. He yielded to the pressure for decisive action which came from three different directions. There was pressure from the top: in April, 1524, the Diet of Nuremberg passed a resolution that the problem of Luther be solved by the imperial Estates, and ordered the Estates to take the necessary preliminary steps. There was pressure from below: appeals such as the one by the people of Wendelstein for decisive action became more urgent, and could no longer be by-passed—especially in view of the appearance of the enthusiasts, and the growing unrest among the peasants. And there was pressure from outside of the territory: the bishops loudly protested the growing Reformation movement and threatened to undertake sharp legal, and perhaps even military, countermeasures. Casimir was ready to act. He was convinced that the settlement of the problems created by Luther would coincide with his own political plans.[39] It was Casimir's tragedy that he was ready to act decisively regarding the legal and religious situation in his country, but that he was not ready, or able, to affirm clear religious convictions. Consequently he subordinated the religious problem of his territory to his

---

though it is highly dubious that the government intended to appoint an evangelical preacher and thus comply with the people's wishes—Reischenbeck was appointed at a time when the papal party dominated the Ansbach government (see pp. 169 f.)—nevertheless Reischenbeck, Krantz's successor, turned out to be a good evangelical preacher, and thus the people's demand was finally met.

39. Casimir was dreaming of a united and powerful Empire, based on strong territorial states and a smoothly functioning imperial administration under the Council of Regency. He saw enemies of these hopes in the imperial cities (see pp. 143 f.) with their political independence and their economic "egocentricity," in the bishops with their ties to Rome, and in the Swabian League with its transterritorial power. Casimir therefore did everything to nullify these three factors. He first tried to eliminate the power of the bishops. After lengthy discussions and quarrels he finally succeeded somewhat by replacing with his own candidate the bishops' candidate for the Franconian Circuit's seat in the Council of Regency and the Imperial Supreme Court. See Schornbaum II, p. 258 n. 83. He failed totally, however, in his ambitious plan to secularize the diocese of Würzburg and to entrust it as the Duchy of Franconia to his brother Frederick, then dean of the collegiate cathedral chapter in Würzburg. For further details, see Schornbaum I, pp. 16 f., 27 ff., 37 ff., 45 f., 51, 57, 64, 170 n. 113; see also K. S. Bader, "Kaiserliche und ständische Reformgedanken in der Reichsreform des endenden 15. Jahrhunderts," *Historisches Jahrbuch*, LXXIII (1954) 74 ff.; E. Wolf, "Die deutsche Reichstheorie in der Reformationszeit," *Zeitschr. f. deutsche Kulturphilosophie*, X (1944), 115 ff.; P. Rassow, "Forschungen zur Reichs-Idee im 16. und 17. Jahrhundert," *Die geschichtliche Einheit des Abendlandes*, pp. 294 ff.; K. Brandi, "Der Reichsgedanke Karls V.," *Europ. Revue*, XVI (1940), 271 ff.

own political ambitions and failed to do anything to resolve the religious chaos in his land. On the other hand, Casimir's imperial policies did not succeed. Only ruthlessly determined, courageous political action could have overcome the opposition which the margrave encountered on all sides, opposition in which religious and political elements were combined. Casimir was not the person to act clearly in matters of religion, or courageously in matters of politics.

III. MARGRAVE CASIMIR'S ECCLESIASTICAL POLICY, 1524–1526

The resolution passed by the Diet of Nuremberg in April, 1524, charged the imperial Estates with the task of finding a solution for the problems created by the Reformation. According to this resolution,[1] the Edict of Worms was to be enforced by the Estates as strictly as possible; the diet was to convene again in November, 1524, in order to settle the ecclesiastical affairs, and this settlement was to be in effect until a general council of the church would decide the issues raised by Luther. In order to prepare for the diet and the council, the Estates were ordered to have abstracts drawn up containing the controversial points in the reformers' recently published books. Together with the Gravamina,[2] these controversial points were to be discussed during the diet. In the meantime the gospel was to be preached in accordance with the mandate issued by the Council of Regency in March, 1523,[3] and no further innovations were to be enacted or tolerated. Margrave Casimir used this resolution as legal basis and moral justification[4] for interfering both with the disorder in the parishes of his territory, and with the situation of the church in the whole Franconian Circuit.[5] In the late summer and early fall of 1524, he

1. *DRTA.* JR, IV, No. 149 (pp. 603, 10 ff.); Ranke I, Part II, 78 ff. (pp. 310 ff.).

2. I.e., the complaints of the German secular Estates—and ecclesiastical Estates (see Hashagen, *op. cit.*, pp. 283 ff.)—against the church, especially the papacy in Rome; on the Gravamina, see B. Gebhardt, *Die Gravamina der Deutschen Nation gegen den römischen Hof. Ein Beitrag zur Vorgeschichte der Reformation*; 2d ed. (Breslau, 1895); G. M. Weber, *Die hundert Beschwerden der gesammten deutschen Nation dem römischen Stuhle übergeben im Jahre 1523* (Erlangen, 1829); A. Störmann, *Die städtischen Gravamina gegen den Klerus am Ausgang des Mittelalters und in der Reformationszeit* (Münster, 1916); *ARC* I, 419 ff.

3. *DRTA.* JR, III, No. 84 (p. 450, ll. 1 ff.).

4. When the bishop of Würzburg protested the discussions of the Reformation issue held by the *Ansbacher Landtag* in September, 1524 (see p. 150 n. 24), Casimir rejected this protest, pointing out that the discussions were not directed against the church, but were only the faithful execution of the resolution of the diet; Schornbaum I, pp. 38, 177 n. 115.

5. On the Franconian Circuit, see p. 142 n. 6.

feverishly sought support among the secular Estates of the Franconian Circuit for his campaign against the power and privileges of the bishops. Circuit representation at the Imperial Supreme Court and the Council of Regency (an issue on which the margrave and the bishops did not agree),[6] the Gravamina,[7] the abstracting of the points which were controversial between religious traditionalists and followers of Luther—all these points coincided for Casimir and were labeled by him as the Reformation issues. His efforts resulted in the well-known meeting of the secular Estates of the Franconian Circuit held in August, 1524, in Windsheim,[8] in the first *Ansbacher Landtag*[9] (September, 1524), and in a series of *Ratschläge*[10] which were drawn up by the theologians of the Franconian Circuit, both the traditionalists and the reformers.[11]

The XXIII Articles,[12] which to the best of our knowledge were drawn up by John Rurer, Casimir's court chaplain,[13] and George Vogler, Casimir's chancellor,[14] were the basis for all discussions among the secular Estates of the Franconian Circuit.[15] In these articles all points of

6. See p. 156 n. 39.

7. See p. 157 n. 2.

8. On this meeting, see Schornbaum I, pp. 33 ff.; *FB*, pp. 9 f.; *FKO*, pp. 65 f.; Simon, *EKGB*, I, 213 ff.; Götz, *op. cit.*, pp. 29 ff.

9. I.e., the assembly of the secular and ecclesiastical Estates of the territory. On this *Landtag*, see Schornbaum I, pp. 37 ff.; Simon, *EKGB*, I, 214 f.; *FKO*, p. 66; K. Schornbaum, "Das Protokoll des Ansbacher Landtages 1524," *57. Jahresb. d. Hist. Ver. f. Mittelfranken* (1910), 98 ff. The designations first, second, third for the Ansbacher Landtage are added here for clarification only and do not coincide with the actual number of times the Landtag assembled in Ansbach during Casimir's reign.

10. I.e., a brief on a particular issue. The *Ratschläge* prepared by the theologians of the Franconian Circuit are catalogued in *FB*, p. ix, and analyzed in *FB*, pp. 13 ff., 54 ff. For our work the most important one is *Ansbach I* (*FB*, pp. 183 ff.), the *Ratschlag* of some evangelical pastors of the margraviate, handed over to Casimir on September 30, 1524.

11. The pro-Reformation documents began that period in the policies of the margraviate which ended in June, 1530, when Casimir's brother, Margrave George, together with other Lutheran imperial Estates, signed the *Augsburg Confession*. For details on this development, see H. von Schubert, "Beiträge zur Geschichte der evangelischen Bekenntnis-und Bündnisbildung, 1529/30," *ZKG*, XXX (1909), 28 ff., and his *Die Anfänge der evangelischen Bekenntnisbildung bis 1529/30* (*Schrif. d. Ver. f. Reformationsgeschichte*, No. 143 [Leipzig, 1928]); E. Fabian, *Die Entstehung des Schmalkaldischen Bundes und seiner Verfassung*; 2d ed. (Tübingen, 1962), pp. 18 ff.

12. Text: *FB*, pp. 180 ff.

13. On Rurer, see p. 147 n. 10.

14. On Vogler, see p. 146 n. 3; see also *FB*, p. 9; *FKO*, p. 5.

15. See Schornbaum I, pp. 35 ff.; *FB*, pp. 9 f.

controversy between Rome and the Reformation were compiled, and views and counterviews contrasted. Casimir called his territorial Estates to meet at Ansbach on September 25, 1524, to work out a joint resolution on these articles. This resolution was to be further discussed at the meeting of the Franconian Circuit, already called to meet in Rothenburg on October 11. The circuit was then to act by presenting a joint resolution to the upcoming diet at Speyer.[16] In spite of the serious opposition voiced by many of the territory's clergy, the Reformation issue was fully discussed during the first Ansbacher Landtag.[17] Nothing could stop Casimir from dealing with this problem, not even an imperial mandate issued on July 15 canceling the diet which had been scheduled for Speyer and forbidding any further discussion of the Reformation issue.[18] Having already exposed his plans, Casimir needed a unanimous decision on his XXIII Articles. If his Estates could not work out such a decision, then he would have to expose himself even further by publicly siding with one or the other of the positions presented in the articles; he was neither ready to do this, nor would he have considered it expedient to do so. As may be expected, the differences of opinion could not be compromised. On October 1, in a politically ingenious resolution, the whole matter was tabled, pending further discussion.[19] As a result the legal problems of the Reformation

16. See p. 157.

17. See pp. 150 n. 24, 157 n. 4, and Schornbaum I, pp. 45 ff.

18. Schornbaum I, pp. 46 f.; Götz, *op. cit.*, p. 45. The mandate reached Ansbach on September 27. In order not to handicap the negotiations at the Landtag, the margrave laid the mandate aside and said nothing of it until the Landtag was over. Casimir was convinced that the emperor was ill-advised in cancelling the diet and that the Empire and the general council were served best if the discussions and preparations for the diet were continued.

19. Text: *FKO*, pp. 80 f.: "[Resolved] . . . that throughout His Grace's domain and territories the holy gospel and divine Word be preached clearly and purely . . . according to the right and true understanding, and that nothing [be preached] that is contrary [to the divine Word], so that the common Christian people are not scandalized and misled [.Resolved] that all pastors and preachers of the divine Word should in their sermons restrain themselves from speaking evil of anyone in particular, [or from preaching in such a way as] to cause quarrels, scandals or uproar; as it is stated above, they should preach only God's Word unadulteratedly and purely, so that only God's praise and honor, and the salvation of the common Christian people are . . . promoted." *FKO*, p. 80; this resolution followed a draft prepared by Hans von Seckendorf (see p. 147 n. 12). This resolution of the Landtag (proclaimed as law by the margrave) could of course be understood as not only permitting, but even ordering the preaching of the gospel as the reformers understood it. Since in this resolution, however, the phrase "preaching of the gospel" was not defined, and since the Margrave was effectively preventing any positive

were left in abeyance. Casimir, and thus the state, supported neither the traditionalists nor the reformers; he hoped to escape difficulty by dealing only in generalities, and consequently, in view of the tense situation, satisfied no one. In order not to jeopardize his political ambitions, Casimir postponed any decision on the religious and legal issues which somehow had to be settled. It is a sign of the spiritual dynamics of the Reformation as a people's movement that the Reformation continued to spread across the Franconian countryside although the sovereign had not thrown his support behind it.

Totally ignoring the fact that the religious problems and the legal questions arising from the Reformation had in no way been put in order, Casimir for the next two years pursued a course which was determined by three goals: (a) he wanted to maintain peace in his country; (b) he intended to use the religious and social tensions to buttress his rule over the church in the territory; (c) he planned to use the reform mood of his people to initiate and foster good foreign relations in his drive toward fulfillment of his political plans. In seeking to carry out this program, Casimir interfered not only with the external but also with the internal, spiritual matters of the church. Although he was an expert in playing one party against another and skillfully combined one aim with the other, he was only partially successful—and anything he did achieve he was unable to secure and protect.

The margrave took sharp measures against the enthusiasts who were disturbing the peace of the land.[20] However, he adopted a wait-and-see

---

results from such gospel-preaching (see p. 164), it is quite clear that this resolution was not a green light for the Reformation in the margraviate. See Excursus II. It would seem, therefore, that H. Westermayer (*Die brandenburgisch-nürnbergische Kirchenvisitation und Kirchenordnung 1528/33* [Erlangen, 1894], p. 1) saw in this resolution somewhat more than actually was there when he called it a public affirmation of the Reformation. Schornbaum's opinion (Schornbaum I, pp. 56 f.) that in this resolution Casimir took no position at all on the Reformation likewise does not do justice to this resolution. See further, pp. 163 ff.

20. See Simon, *EKGB*, I, 182 f., 195 ff.; G. Krodel, "Nürnberger Humanisten am Anfang des Abendmahlsstreites," *ZBayKG*, XXV (1956), 40 ff. The documents dealing with the enthusiast: *Quellen und Forschungen zur Geschichte der Wiedertäufer*, II, *Bayern*, I: *Markgrafentum Brandenburg*, ed. K. Schornbaum (Leipzig, 1934). In December, 1524, Casimir prohibited the sale of Münzer's writings in his territories; Schornbaum I, p. 195 n. 18. In February, 1525, he refused to grant a residency-permit to Andrew Carlstadt; Schornbaum I, pp. 165 n. 97, 163 n. 96. For further material, see P. Schattenmann, *Die Einführung der Reformation in der ehemaligen Reichsstadt Rothenburg ob der Tauber, 1520–1580* (*EAKGB*, VII [1928]), pp. 50 ff.

policy[21] toward the rebellious peasants. He was forced to do this because he lacked financial resources for a concerted military drive against the peasants, and because his plan to unite the whole Franconian Circuit for military action failed due to the resistance of the Franconian bishops.[22] Taking a middle course, Casimir mobilized his military strength as much as he could; at the same time he made concessions to the religious-social movement,[23] without, however, openly siding with it.[24] Then in June, 1525, when the peasants' luck had run out and the sovereigns began to be victorious,[25] Casimir entered the war and took brutal revenge on the defeated peasants.[26]

Casimir used the Peasants' War to promote his second aim: the consolidation of the authority of the secular government over the clergy and the parishes in the territory.[27] His over-all aim[28] was to eliminate the authority of the bishops in all ecclesiastical affairs, with the possible exception of ordination, and to replace it with his own authority.

For quite some time the margraves had exercised a certain control over those priests for whom they had the patronage. The margraves demanded that, prior to his installation in one of their parishes, a priest

21. According to G. Franz, *Der Deutsche Bauernkrieg*, 4th ed. (Darmstadt, 1965), p. 203. For Casimir's ambiguous position in the Peasants' War, see C. Jäger, "Markgraf Casimir und der Bauernkrieg in den südlichen Grenzämtern des Fürstentums unterhalb des Gebirgs," *Mit. d. Ver. f. Gesch. d. Stadt Nürnberg*, IX (1892), 17 ff.; M. Thomas, *Markgraf Casimir von Brandenburg im Bauernkrieg* (Gotha, 1897); see also W. Sellmann, *Die Marktbibarter Bauernverschwörung, 1525, und ihre Auswirkung auf das Haus des Ritters von Seckendorff in Sugenheim* (Erlangen: Phil. Diss., 1952). For general information, see Ranke, I, Part II, 106 ff. (pp. 334 ff.); Elton, *op. cit.*, 86 ff.; for Luther and the Peasants' War, see R. N. Crossley, "Luther and the Peasants' War. A Brief Summary," *The Dawn of Modern Civilization. Studies in Renaissance, Reformation and Other Topics Presented to Honor Albert Hyma*, ed. K. A. Strand (Ann Arbor, 1962), pp. 129 ff.

22. Schornbaum I, p. 66.

23. *Ibid.*, pp. 67 f.; *FKO*, p. 67.

24. Casimir refused, e.g., to attend the meeting which the peasants had called for June 1, 1525, in Schweinfurt, and to which he had been invited. This meeting was designed to prepare peace negotiations with the sovereigns. See Franz, *Der Deutsche Bauernkrieg*, pp. 204 f., and his *Quellen zur Geschichte des Bauernkrieges* (Darmstadt, 1963), No. 125.

25. June 2, 1525: Battle at Königshofen; June 4: Battle at Ingolstadt; June 8: Conquest of Würzburg; and June 17: Conquest of Bamberg by the troops of the Swabian League. See Franz, *Der Deutsche Bauernkrieg*, pp. 176 ff., and his *Quellen*, Nos. 126–128.

26. June 5 to July 2: 80 persons decapitated, 69 crippled; Franz, *Quellen*, No. 130.

27. Schornbaum I, pp. 68 f.

28. Documented by the various instructions for his ambassadors to the spring and summer 1525 meetings of the Estates of the Franconian Circuit; see e.g., Schornbaum I, pp. 69 f.

sign an oath of loyalty and obedience.[29] This oath was an act of private law, which bound two parties, the margrave as *patronus* and his priest as *parochus loci*. In 1525/26 Casimir tightened his grip on the clergy—and now not only on those for whom he was *patronus* but on all the clergy of the territory—by acts of public law. As territorial sovereign he made certain pronouncements, either independently or with the consent of his Estates. First, he suspended the clergy's tax privileges,[30] and thus took an important step toward establishing equality between clergy and laity.[31] Then he ordered all property of the monasteries to be catalogued, and he confiscated part of it.[32] Next he ordered the monks and nuns to wear secular clothing in order, so he argued, to avoid provoking the smoldering hatred of the common people toward monks and nuns.[33] In March, 1526, he demanded one-tenth of the income of each clergyman in the land.[34] And finally, he established the competence of the secular courts for the clergy.[35]

29. See p. 150 n. 23.

30. Resolution of the second Ansbacher Landtag, April, 1525; *FKO*, pp. 82 f.; Schornbaum I, pp. 67 f.

31. The church's tax privileges were at all times one of the sore points in the relationship of the state to the church, and even in our country some serious rethinking of this issue is now going on. Already Constantine the Great had granted the church exemption from real estate taxes; later the church and the clergy were exempted from sales and professional taxes, as well as from the tax levied on the individual. Then came exemption from all *munera civila* (e.g., guard and fire duty, public construction duty). During the reigns of Pope Alexander III (1159–1181) and of Pope Innocent III (1198–1216) the theory was promoted that ecclesiastical persons and properties were to be exempted from all taxes and duties to be paid to the secular community and that voluntary contributions by the clergy to the secular community were subject to special papal dispensation. The third (1179) and the fourth (1215) Lateran Council incorporated this theory in the Canon Law. Although in 1220 Emperor Frederick II acknowledged this principle by imperial law, the German territorial sovereigns of the later middle ages tried more or less successfully to circumvent it. See DuCange, *s. v. Immunitas; Corpus Iuris Canonici*, 4, 7, X, *de imm.* III, 49 (ed. Ae. Friedberg [Graz, 1959] II, cols. 654 ff.); Feine, *op. cit.*, pp. 71 f., 393 f., 453 ff., 493 ff.

32. Schornbaum I, pp. 66, 68, 200 n. 207, 211 n. 237; Götz, *op. cit.*, p. 62; *FKO*, p. 67; K. Schornbaum, "Zur Klostersaekularisation des Markgrafen Kasimir. 1525," *BBayKG*, X (1904), 129 ff.; Schottenloher, *op. cit.*, III, No. 29168.

33. Schornbaum I, pp. 67 f.; *FKO*, p. 67. Perhaps this can be called a step on the way to the Reformation (see Schornbaum I, pp. 68, 90 f.; Simon in *FKO*, p. 67); this action was not based on religious considerations, however, but on considerations of state; see p. 164.

34. Schornbaum I, p. 92.

35. Mandate of August 30, 1525; *FKO*, pp. 68, 85. Casimir justified his break with the traditional legal structure of the state-church relationship with a mixture of reasons taken

While Casimir was pursuing these measures so detrimental to the papal church, he was also attempting to gain the support of the pro-Reformation party, without, however, publicly endorsing the Reformation. In the resolution of the second Ansbacher Landtag (April, 1525), the margrave ordered, for instance, that the holy gospel be preached in its purity[36]—but he did not qualify this statement. In the same year he published two mandates which served only to muddy further his position on the Reformation. In these mandates Casimir did not publicly endorse the Reformation; he did not even silently tolerate the reform of religious life throughout the territory.[37] To understand these mandates as a positive statement on the Reformation[38] is to misunderstand them completely. Both mandates were exclusively designed to maintain the peace of the land. In them, on the one hand, the duty of the subjects to obey secular authority was given a religious basis, and a "correct" understanding of the freedom of a Christian was developed; and this was directed toward the country's social-revolutionary movement. On the other hand, by ordering the preaching of the unadulterated Word of God, the margrave wanted to present himself in these mandates as friend and promoter of the Reformation; and this was directed toward the reformers. Whatever concessions the margrave made to the Reformation in 1525 were

---

from *raison d'état* and natural law: The common man complained about the privileges of the clergy, and these complaints had to be properly handled to avoid unrest among the people (*FKO*, p. 82). The state needed money for the war against the peasants, by which war the people were protected, which of course included the clergy; the clergy should therefore share in the expenses of the war. Had the clergy not led such a godless life, but lived as men of God, fulfilled their duty, and fed their flocks with the true gospel, the peasants would not have rebelled. (See Schornbaum I, pp. 92 f., 108, 238 n. 306.) Thus it is clear that Casimir's actions against the papal church have nothing to do with an affirmation of the Reformation. In defending himself, Casimir did not cite one of the fundamental laws of all Christians, equality, as Luther would have done (see p. 153 n. 33). It appears that between April, 1525, and October, 1526, a change took place in Casimir's argumentation. For in the resolution of the third Ansbacher Landtag (October, 1526), Casimir justified the elimination of the clergy's tax exemption by pointing out that "peace and Christian equality have to be maintained" (*FKO*, p. 96). But even here the idea of *Christian* equality did not become basic to Casimir's thoughts; he still emphasized that the *peace* in the territory would be jeopardized if the clergy would not share in the common tax burden.

36. For a detailed analysis of this phrase, see Excursus II.

37. Mandate of April 7, 1525 (Schornbaum I, p. 67, 198 n. 203), with which Rurer I (see p. 181 n. 68) was mailed to the clergy of the territory; mandate of August 30, 1525 (*FKO*, pp. 84 ff.; Schornbaum I, p. 90).

38. See Simon, *FKO*, pp. 67 f.; see Excursus II.

local only;[39] this may clearly be seen from the fact that Casimir rejected the various petitions of the cities to introduce the Reformation officially throughout the territory.[40]

Casimir used the social disturbances in the territory to interfere not only with the external and financial sides of church life, but also with the spiritual side. In the resolutions of the first and second Ansbacher Landtage (October, 1524; April, 1525), and in the mandates of 1525, may be found, if not always with identical words, the formula which had been used in the resolution of the Nuremberg diet of April, 1524: "clear preaching of the pure gospel and of the Word of God."[41] Casimir adopted this ambiguous[42] formula and clarified it, not in a religious-confessional sense, but in a state-church sense. In the resolution of the first Ansbacher Landtag, the formula was simply taken over from the resolution of the Nuremberg diet.[43] The clergy was to preach the Holy Gospel and the divine Word clearly and purely. Only those statements which might create offense or error among the people, could seduce the people to quarreling, and would not contribute to the salvation of souls and the honor of God, were to be excluded from the sermons. In their preaching the clergy was to focus on the corporeal[44] and spiritual well-being of the people; consequently all sermons were to be scrutinized carefully by state officials. Pastors not complying with this order were to be held responsible—by whom, it is not said. So long as the peace of the land was not disturbed, and so long as the people did not get any "wrong" ideas, Casimir did not care *what* was preached.

This situation changed in 1525. Together with the mandate of April, 1525, the margrave sent out a sermon (Rurer I) which was to be preached

39. Casimir, e.g., apparently did not intervene when in the spring of 1525 all papal ceremonies were abolished in Feuchtwangen, or when Rurer (see p. 147 n. 10) celebrated the first evangelical Lord's Supper in Ansbach on April 9, 1525. The margrave even gave permission to some congregations in the Oberland to give the cup to the laity during communion, as long as it was done secretly. For further material, see *FKO*, p. 67 f.; Schornbaum I, pp. 90 f., 220 n. 254; Schornbaum, "Wann wurde in Ansbach."

40. See p. 172 n. 6.

41. See p. 157; *DRTA*. JR, IV, No. 149 (p. 605); *FKO*, pp. 80, 82, 84, 85; see also Excursus II.

42. That this resolution was intended to be ambiguous becomes clear beyond doubt if one examines the discussions (see *DRTA*. JR, IV) that preceded this resolution and observes the tug-of-war between the propapal and pro-Reformation parties of the diet. See *FKO*, p. 80.

43. See *FKO*, p. 80.

44. I.e., the clergy ought to avoid making any statements which would shock or scandalize the people, cause unrest among them, or in any way stir up trouble, so that the people's "corporeal" well-being is not disturbed; see *FKO*, p. 80, where this thought is expressed in the term "*ergernus*," which in turn is placed *before* "*irrung*."

from all the pulpits in the territory on a specifically designated Sunday.[45] That is, the margrave told the clergy of the territory *what* to preach, at least on that one Sunday. This sermon, which to the best of our knowledge Casimir had ordered Rurer to draft, contained some of Luther's thought. It is impossible to say whether Casimir was aware of this, and whether he knew that in ordering the proclamation of this sermon he was in reality promoting the Reformation. The sermon was important to him, not for its religious thoughts, but for its political aspects. Casimir had become well aware that the preaching concerning the freedom of a Christian could be misunderstood and was, at least in part, responsible for the social unrest in the territory. Therefore the margrave felt that a clarification of the term "freedom," which would put the duty to obey the appointed authorities on a religious foundation, would be the best weapon against the restlessness that disturbed the country. And Rurer I was to do precisely this.

This interpretation of Rurer I is confirmed by a close examination of the mandate of August 30, 1525.[46] In the covering letter with which this mandate was sent to the local officials, the margrave emphasized that the Peasants' War was caused by the godless preaching and conduct of the clergy,[47] and that similar events could be avoided only through the faithful preaching of the Word of God in its purity and through conduct on the part of the clergy which would be in keeping with their high office. The mandate was therefore designed to regulate the preaching of the gospel. The local officials had to supervise the execution of the mandate, and all offenses against it were to be punished in property and body by the secular courts.[48]

The margrave here assumed the role of a bishop. He ordered the clergy to preach and told them exactly *what* to preach; he supervised the clergy so that they would comply with his regulation, and he claimed jurisdiction over them, at least insofar as this particular mandate was concerned. This was the first and at the same time the decisive step toward the assumption of full ecclesiastical jurisdiction.[49] The margrave interfered with the external affairs of the church,[50] as well as with the spiritual affairs, by ordering and controlling the preaching of the clergy in his country.[51] From this first step it was only a matter of time until the church in its totality would be controlled by the territorial sovereign. It

45. See pp. 163 n. 37, 181 f.; Excursus II.
46. *FKO*, pp. 84 ff.
47. See also the margrave's argumentation on p. 162 n. 35.
48. *FKO*, pp. 84 f.; see also Schornbaum I, pp. 95 f.
49. Götz, *op. cit.*, p. 76; for the ecclesiastical jurisdiction, see Excursus IV.
50. E.g., vestments and finances; see p. 162.
51. And both actions were a gross breach of law.

must be pointed out that *a religious break with Rome on the part of Casimir was not at all necessary for arriving at this idea of a state-controlled church.* Principles of natural law and *raison d'état* were used by Casimir to defend this break into the legal sphere of the papal church.[52] And so the development which had begun with the priests' oath of loyalty was now concluded. Because of the oath, the clergy over which the margraves held patronage could not *freely* transmit controversial matters of faith or life to the bishop's court.[53] Without reading anything into the document, it can be said that in the legal arrangement envisioned by the margraves in demanding the oath, the secular authorities functioned, however, *only as a checkpoint* to prevent abuses on the part of the clergy, or to remedy grievances on the part of the laity.[54] Now, in 1525/26, the bishop's court was completely eliminated and its functions absorbed by the secular court, and *this applied to the clergy of the entire territory.*[55]

The mandate of August, 1525, therefore, had nothing to do with the Reformation, but was designed exclusively to establish the authority of the territorial sovereign in the church, beginning with legal and financial questions, and then pursuing into questions of faith and life. This becomes especially clear if one focuses on the formula "clear preaching of the pure gospel and of the Word of God."[56] How did Casimir clarify this formula in August, 1525? In order to avoid rebellion among the people, Casimir stipulated that the clergy should preach the Word of God in its purity. Emphasis was to be given to the following: if a pastor preaches that faith alone is necessary for salvation then he also has to preach that this faith must bear the fruit which God expects of it; if a pastor deals with Christian freedom in his sermon, then he also has to emphasize that this Christian freedom is the spiritual liberation from sin, death, and the devil; and a pastor has to point out the biblical foundation of the citizens' obedience toward the government; furthermore, he has to make it clear to his congregation that Christian freedom includes this obedience.[57]

The difference between that understanding of the formula which we find in the resolution of the first Ansbacher Landtag (October, 1524), and that which we find in this mandate of August, 1525, is quite obvious. In

52. *FKO*, pp. 84 f.

53. See p. 150 n. 23.

54. See Hashagen, *op. cit.*, pp. 281 ff.

55. And this not only for the clergy for whom the margrave was *patronus*. It is one of the ironies of history that the bishops themselves were, at least in part, responsible for this development, since, according to Simon (see p. 150 n. 23), they were silent at the very beginning when the margraves initiated the oath of loyalty.

56. See p. 164.

57. *FKO*, pp. 85 ff.

1524, Casimir had no interest in *what* the clergy preached, as long as this preaching did not cause unrest among the people.[58] In August of 1525 Casimir gave, however, exact orders concerning the content of the sermon. The August mandate used thoughts which were at the center of Luther's theology.[59] It is not amazing, therefore, that the representatives of the Reformation in the margraviate understood this pronouncement of the government as an order to go ahead with the reformation of religious life, and as a promise of the good will of the sovereign for those who would comply with this order. To understand the mandate in such a framework was natural,[60] and no alterations of the text were necessary, though Casimir later charged Vogler with having made some alterations.[61] If one considers the whole conduct of Casimir,[62] however, one has to ask seriously whether this mandate was an affirmation of the Reformation or whether it

58. See p. 164.

59. The hopeful evangelicals in the territory understood this mandate as an endorsement of Luther's Reformation (see below n. 60). Indeed, strong traces of Luther's understanding of faith and its relationship to works, of the Christian's freedom, of his obligation to the secular government, and of the nature of secular government can be found in this mandate (see *FKO*, pp. 85 ff.), although the Reformer is never directly quoted. How this mandate received its Lutheran character is unknown, and perhaps also unimportant. The important question, however, is whether Casimir here actually affirmed Lutheranism, or whether the Lutheran character of this mandate was not a clever bit of duplicity on the margrave's part. It seems to me that the latter was the case; see below n. 62, and Excursus II.

60. Adam Weisz (see p. 147 n. 10), e.g., understood this mandate in such a way; see *FKO*, p. 68; Schornbaum I, pp. 91 f., 220 n. 256. It must be asked whether in view of its contents *Flugschrift* (see pp. 179 f.) would not have had to be dated after this mandate, i.e., after August, 1525, and not, as Simon has suggested (*Flugschrift*, pp. 186 ff.), prior to the April mandate. In Simon's argumentation one question remains open. In the title of *Flugschrift* the punishment of those who preach the gospel and draw the necessary conclusions from such preaching is mentioned; see *Flugschrift*, p. 183. Simon provides no material by which it could be documented that prior to April, 1525 (i.e., around the change of the years 1524/25, the time when, according to Simon, *Flugschrift* had been composed), Casimir took legal action against the evangelicals of his territory. Whether such proceedings can be established for the period after the August mandate must also remain a question. In any case, Simon's dating of *Flugschrift* is not as much beyond doubt as it appears to him.

61. Schornbaum I, pp. 90, 219 n. 251.

62. E.g., the margrave's order in 1526 to celebrate the Corpus Christi Festival. Casimir's order was directed only to the cities, either because the cities no longer observed the festival, or because the margrave considered himself *able to order* the citizens to celebrate the festival again. The order was not directed to the rural areas, either because the festival was still observed there, or because the margrave felt that such an order might antagonize the peasants and thus stir up new trouble. See Schornbaum I, p. 91. Another example of Casimir's position would be his refusal to take positive action on the petitions of the cities to introduce the Reformation (see pp. 163 n. 36, 172 n. 6).

was not rather an ingenious attempt to play the evangelical movement against the social unrest within the territory, while at the same time consolidating the sovereign's power over the church.

Casimir used the evangelical movement within the margraviate in order to construct alliances. He sought support from other imperial Estates for the reform of the imperial administration, and for that which he considered to be the reform of the church, that is, the elimination of the political power of the ecclesiastical hierarchy in Germany. In these efforts he even went so far as to seek contact with his natural enemy, the imperial city of Nuremberg.[63] When these plans failed, he concentrated on consolidating his relationship with electoral Saxony, with which he had cooperated since the days of the Peasants' War. After initial successes,[64]

63. The Franconian Circuit meeting at Windsheim (see p. 158) eased the tension between the margrave and the city, a tension which had existed at least since the early fifteenth century; see pp. 143 ff. Nuremberg too had worked out *Ratschläge* on Casimir's XXIII Articles and forwarded them to Ansbach; see *FB*, pp. 71 ff., 411 ff. Already at the Rothenburg meeting in October, 1524 (see pp. 158, 159), however, the tension between the two Estates reappeared. The Peasants' War, and the imperial policies of the margrave in the summer and autumn of 1526, made it obvious to the Nurembergers that they had little in common with Casimir. See Schornbaum I, pp. 35 ff., 62 f.

64. For the general historical setting, see Ranke I, Part II, 85 ff., 136 ff. (pp. 316 ff., 395 ff.). Elector John of Saxony was the only sovereign who helped Casimir against the peasants; Schornbaum I, pp. 73, 207 n. 218. At the beginning of August, 1525, both sovereigns met in Saalfeld (Schornbaum I, pp. 73 ff.; G. Buchwald, "Lutherana," *Archiv f. Reformationsgeschichte*, XXV [1928], 41) in order to discuss how any further unrest among the people could be prevented. During this meeting it was decided, regarding the Reformation issue, that the secular Estates of the Empire should jointly prepare themselves for the next diet, and then jointly act. (The first step planned was an exchange of documents concerning the controversial religious issues, in an attempt to find out who stood where on matters of faith. Casimir therefore forwarded *Ansbach I* to Electoral Saxony. On September 6, 1525, the Wittenberg Theological Faculty, led by Luther, approved of *Ansbach I*, pointing out some minor differences concerning the evaluation of religious pictures and statues; *WA*, Br III, No. 918; H. von Schubert, "Beiträge zur Geschichte der evangelischen Bekenntnis-und Bündnispolitik 1529/30," *ZKG*, XXIX [1908], 323 ff., esp. 342 ff.; XXX [1909], 28 ff.). Both sovereigns agreed that the Reformation issue would have to be settled by the diet and not by the pope or a general council, that those Estates who had a positive position on the Reformation would have to cooperate, and that the emperor would have to be enlisted to aid in this plan. These ideas were the reason for Casimir's refusal to join the papal efforts to bring about a political alliance among traditionalistic Estates; although strongly urged by a special envoy, Casimir did not attend the 1524 Regensburg meeting of the pro-Roman Estates; Schornbaum I, pp. 16 f.; Ranke I, Part II, 92 ff. (pp. 321 ff.); *ARC*, I, 294 ff. In order to assure the emperor's backing for his plan, Casimir boycotted an anti-Habsburg meeting of south-German Estates in Ingolstadt in the summer of 1525 (Schornbaum I, p. 208 n. 224), while at the same time attempting to organize a meeting of sovereigns in Esslingen; see Schornbaum I, pp. 77 ff., 80.

all of Casimir's efforts in this connection, however, were nullified by a politically brilliant move by Habsburgs. The emperor and his brother Ferdinand appointed Casimir to be an imperial commissioner for the Diet of Augsburg (November, 1525) and for the Diet of Speyer (June, 1526); they also appointed him to the position of supreme commander of the imperial army, charging him with directing the war against the Turks.[65] In so doing, they neatly separated Casimir from any anti-Habsburg coalition that might have developed within the Empire and blocked Casimir's flirtations with those sovereigns who openly supported the Reformation; at the same time they tied him more closely to Habsburg and papal interests. Since Casimir was convinced that his political salvation was based on the good will of the Habsburg family,[66] he let himself be drawn deeply into Habsburg politics; this, in turn, created the catastrophic situation within the margraviate which was brought about through the resolution adopted by the third Ansbacher Landtag in October, 1526.[67]

When Casimir left the margraviate shortly after this Landtag to go to Hungary and supervise the preparation of the war against the Turks, he left utter chaos behind. The treasury was bankrupt, or close to it.[68]

65. Ranke I, Part II, 136 ff., 208 ff. (pp. 359 ff., 417 ff.); Elton, *op. cit.*, pp. 346 ff.; Schornbaum I, pp. 80 ff., 95 ff.; *FKO*, p. 68.

66. The bishops of the Franconian Circuit took the necessary legal and political measures against Casimir's secularization of church properties and the taxation of the clergy. It was due only to the intervention of Ferdinand (the emperor's brother) that court procedures were abandoned; Schornbaum I, pp. 88 f. In May, 1526, at the court of the Swabian League, Weigand von Redwitz, bishop of Bamberg (see O. Erhard, *Die Reformation der Kirche in Bamberg unter Bischof Weigand*, 1522–1556 [Erlangen, 1898]; R. Schmitt, *Die Reformation im Bistum Bamberg* [Erlangen: Phil. Diss. 1954]), accused the margrave of being at fault insofar as the demand for the one-tenth of the clergy's income was concerned (see p. 162). And in June of the same year the bishops decided to act jointly, and initiated legal action against Casimir; Schornbaum I, pp. 93 ff., 98 f. Had the margrave been found guilty (and this no doubt would have been the case), then his country would have been subject to the execution of the judgment by the league, and this would have been precisely at the moment when Casimir was preparing for the action in Hungary.

67. On this *Landtag*, see Schornbaum I, pp. 98 ff.; for an analysis of the resolution, see Excursus III.

68. On the financial situation of the margraviate, see Schornbaum II, pp. 12 f., 251 n. 59. According to Schornbaum, between 1515 and 1525 the deficit in the budget rose from 186, 314 fl. 3 ort 1 to 551, 414 fl. 2½ ort 5½. Whatever this sum may mean in present-day currency, it was sufficiently large for Margrave George seriously to consider resigning and letting one of his brothers take over the government of the territory. The exchequer was plunged into this dilemma not only through Casimir's mismanagement, but also—and this was the main reason—because the Habsburg family was unwilling, and most of the time unable, to fulfill its financial obligations to the Franconian Hohenzollern.

Urged by the papists, Casimir finally dismissed Vogler and had him imprisoned; thus the one politician who had a clear vision of the religious and secular needs and possibilities of the country was abruptly removed from the scene, and the Reformation was denied its strongest supporter.[69] The people were utterly confused as to the legal aspects of the ecclesiastical affairs.[70] The territory stood legally[71] and politically[72] wide open to the claims of the papal church. Casimir's time to straighten out the affairs of his territory had run out; he died on September 21, 1527.

IV. The Expectations of the Evangelicals Concerning the Relationship of the State to the Church

Casimir failed in his ecclesiastical policy as well as in his political plans.[1] He saw clearly what should be done in order to straighten out the religious chaos that existed in his country,[2] but he lacked determination to take the decisive step. Hans von Schwarzenberg[3] pointed out what had to be done when on October 1, 1524, he addressed the territorial Estates

69. See pp. 146 n. 3, 148 n. 13. Vogler courageously resisted the resolution of the Landtag and protested it publicly. He was therefore imprisoned in October, 1526, but was not brought to trial; Schornbaum I, pp. 231 n. 292, 232 n. 296; Schornbaum II, p. 270 n. 95. Thus political support for the Reformation was eliminated in the territory, since Hans von Schwarzenberg (see p. 147 n. 12) had been, since May, 1526, at the court of Margrave Albrecht, grand master of the Teutonic Order; Schornbaum I, p. 232 n. 293.

70. This becomes obvious from the unrest that developed when, in 1527, the government in Ansbach tried to enforce the resolution. For details, see Schornbaum I, pp. 108 f., 239 nn. 312–314, 241 n. 315, 242 n. 316, 245 n. 320.

71. See p. 169 n. 66. The Franconian bishops took steps against the margrave either at the court of the Swabian League, or at the Imperial Supreme Court, or at the Council of Regency. They did so either individually or jointly, but mostly individually, and this markedly weakened their cause. Here is not the place to trace these steps. The complaints of the bishops can be summarized in the following three points: (a) With the October, 1526, Landtag resolution, Casimir abolished the traditional legal structure of the state-church relationship and created a new order; (b) the margrave replaced ecclesiastical jurisdiction with his own jurisdiction; (c) taxation of clergy and confiscation of church-property is contrary to all law and custom. At the meeting of the Swabian League in in Donauwörth on April 4, 1527, Casimir was successful in placating the bishop of Bamberg, at least temporarily; DRTA.JR, VII, Part I, 101 ff. Tension with the bishop of Würzburg remained strong, however, right to the end of Casimir's life, and Margrave George inherited this problem. See Schornbaum II, p. 248 n. 46.

72. During Casimir's absence in Hungary, Hans von Seckendorf (see p. 147 n. 12) was entrusted with the governmental affairs of the territory; Casimir's brothers in Würzburg (see p. 145) were to assist him in a rather decisive way.

1. For Casimir's ambitions, see pp. 156 n. 39, 168 n. 64.

2. This becomes obvious from some of Casimir's letters to his brother, Margrave George; see e.g., Schornbaum I, pp. 62 f., 186 n. 186, 104 f.

3. See p. 147 n. 12.

assembled in Ansbach and urged them and the Margrave to take the
following steps:

1. To affirm [and maintain] the pure and clear Word of God, regardless of all papal or imperial orders, for God is mightier and more to be
feared than all people. The present issues concerning God's Word
should, however, not be forced. To the contrary, now is the time to
pass a . . . resolution to the following effect:
   a. The fact is that our Gracious Lord [Casimir] is aware that at
present there are two types of [Christian] messages being proclaimed [in the land]. Our Gracious Lord's order is [therefore] to
preach God's Word in its purity and in an unadulterated way, as
it can be found in the Old and New Testaments, and [to preach]
nothing that is contrary [to God's Word].
   b. Our Gracious Lord [has been informed that] there are some
people [in the country] who preach and talk in such a fashion that it
causes strife. This should be prohibited. Concerning this matter the
local officials should be ordered not to tolerate [such preaching and
talking]; should someone dare to do it anyway, then have him
arrested and brought [to the court of the margrave].
   c. Preachers should be forbidden to call one another [from the
pulpit] "Lutheran," "papist," or "heretic" in a derogatory way.
No one should call himself "Lutheran," or ridicule someone else
[with this name].
2. Regarding the other Articles, our Gracious Lord should not punish
anyone who conducts himself according to the gospel. [That is, our
Gracious Lord should not interfere] if a priest marries, or another
distributes the whole sacrament; [he] should neither punish nor
prohibit it, if people eat meat. . . .[4]

The progressives in the territory (Hans von Schwarzenberg spoke for
them) expected some decisive action from Casimir by which the representative of the state would sanction Reformation preaching and the reform
of the religious life, at least in part. These expectations are documented in
theological briefs, especially in *Ansbach I*,[5] in petitions turned over to

4. Schornbaum I, p. 52. On von Schwarzenberg as the author of this speech, see
Schornbaum I, p. 180 n. 161. The "Articles" mentioned in the second paragraph of this
speech are the XXIII Articles; see p. 158.
5. *FB*, pp. 183 ff.; see p. 172 n. 10. *Ansbach II* (*FB*, pp. 340 ff.) was the reply of some of
the evangelical preachers of the territory to the document drawn up by the papal preachers
on the XXIII Articles (see p. 158). A carefully worked-out evaluation of the religious and
legal situation within the territory, turned over to the margrave by Adam Weisz (see p.
147 n. 10; Schornbaum I, pp. 91, 220 n. 256; K. Schornbaum, "Zum Briefwechsel des
Adam Weisz," *BBayKG*, V [1899], 226 ff.), also belongs in this category of documents.

Casimir asking permission to conduct officially the reform of the whole church life in many cities of the territory,[6] and in a number of anonymously published pamphlets.[7] As time passed, the question of reforming the liturgy became dominant.[8] Since the papal church rejected the Reformation movement and attempted to suppress the new teachings by every possible means, the progressives expected, hoped, and even demanded from their sovereign a break with the papal church. Without actually saying so, they assigned to the sovereign the *ius reformandi*[9] and exhorted him to use it against the papal church. On what legal and religious principles did they base their thoughts?

Ansbach I[10] begins with a statement on the nature of the true church

6. Already during the first Ansbacher Landtag, September, 1524 (see pp. 158 f.), some of the territory's cities had turned over a petition to Casimir asking for permission to conduct a thorough reform of the church life within their walls. Schornbaum (I, pp. 46 f.) assumes on the one hand that this petition was given to the margrave at the *beginning* of the Landtag and that the sovereign did not act upon it in order to avoid hampering the business of the Landtag. On the other hand, however, Schornbaum suggests (I, p. 180 n. 161) that the cities turned their petition over to Casimir *on the last day* of the Landtag, after it had become quite clear that no joint action would come forth from the Landtag; he further suggests that this petition could have formed the basis for the speech of Hans von Schwarzenberg (see pp. 170 f.) to the final plenary meeting of the Landtag. Urged by Vogler (see p. 146 n. 3), some cities acted independently in early 1525, and again petitioned the margrave for permission to conduct a thorough reform of the church life; see Schornbaum I, p. 191 n. 193; *Flugschrift*, pp. 187 f. On February 4, 1525, Casimir rejected these petitions without exactly saying so; see Schornbaum I, pp. 65 f.; for Casimir's answer in excerpt, see *Flugschrift*, pp. 188 f. The petitions of various congregations for an evangelical preacher also belong in this category of documents; e.g., Wendelstein (see p. 155 n. 38), and Schwabach (see p. 150 n. 24).

7. E.g., *WKO*, *Flugschrift*, Rurer II; for other documents, see *Flugschrift*, p. 183; Simon, *EKGB*, I, 179. The prevailing mood within Germany at that time is reflected in a pamphlet entitled: *Ein Christlicher Rathschlag vnd Unterrichtung, welcher gestalt sich alle Christliche Personen . . . halten sollen dasz sie das in Vermög vnd nach Anzeigung eines sondern Artickels im Abschied desz jüngst gehaltenen Reichstages zu Speyer dieses* 1526 Jahrs . . . *mögen verantworten*. Text: Fr. Hortleder, *Ausschreiben . . . von den Ursachen des Deutschen Krieges*, I (Frankfurt, 1617), Buch I, Kap. 2, 27 ff. Ranke (I, Part II, 263 n. 1 [p. 464 n. 1]) refers to this *Ratschlag* in connection with the events in the margraviate, without specifically assigning the origin of this document to the territory; it is interesting to observe that many thoughts and arguments found in this *Ratschlag* can also be found in Rurer II.

8. This problem can of course also be found in the 1524/25 material; but in the document drawn up by Weisz (see p. 171 n. 5), e.g., it is more detailed than in the earlier documents.

9. See p. 193 n. 127.

10. *FB*, pp. 183 ff. In this document, in 169 paragraphs of widely varied length and value, the unknown authors—John Rurer certainly must have been one of them (see pp. 147 n. 10, 158)—dealt with the XXIII Articles (see p. 158). From note 11 through note 59 below, the unqualified page references are to be found in *FB*.

(Article I);[11] then follow the articles on the power of the keys [12] and on the interpretation of Scripture.[13] Based on this material, the authors of *Ansbach I* develop the main points of the Christian faith in constant dialogue with the views held by the papal church. In addition to the first three basic articles, the article[14] on the "*gaistlichen stand*"[15] is of special significance for the topic under discussion in this study.

The true church is an object of faith, the authors of *Ansbach I* affirm; consequently all statements that can be made about the church are statements of faith, and the article on the church deals with matters of faith and not with anything that can be seen or touched.[16] The church is the *corpus Christi*, the body of all God-elected believers,[17] who shall live forever in the unity-of the Holy Spirit, of faith, love, and hope. The church is the congregation of those sanctified people who have been reborn through God's living Word. Christ, the head of the church,[18] rules this congregation through his Holy Spirit, who is all-effective in his Word.[19] This government of the church through Christ guarantees, therefore, that the church cannot err and cannot be overcome, not even by the gates of hell.[20]

The church is not a *civitas platonica*[21] or an entity unto itself. The church has a mission which can only be discharged within the framework of this world. And this mission is a work of brotherly love through which

11. Pp. 44 ff., 187 ff.

12. Pp. 195 ff.

13. Pp. 217 ff.

14. Pp 290 ff.

15. I.e., the ecclesiastical Estate, especially the clergy who administer the "spiritual" gifts, but also the members of the orders.

16. Pp. 188 f. For Luther (with whom the authors of *Ansbach I* agree at this point, although they do not quote the Reformer), see *WA*, VII, 710, ll. 2 ff., 719 f. (*Against Ambrosius Catharinus*, 1521); see further E. Kinder, "Die Verborgenheit der Kirche nach Luther," *Reformation: Schicksal und Auftrag. Fest. f. Joseph Lortz*, ed. E. Iserloh, *et al.* (Baden-Baden, 1958) I, 173 ff., and his *Der evangelische Glaube und die Kirche* (Berlin, 1958), pp. 57 ff.; P. Althaus, *Communio Sanctorum* (Munich, 1929), pp. 23 ff., 85 ff.; G. Rupp, *The Righteousness of God. Luther Studies* (London, 1953), pp. 310 ff.; H. Preuss, *Communion of Saints* (Minneapolis, 1948), pp. 75 ff.; C. C. Eastword, "Luther's Conception of the Church," *Scottish Journal of Theology*, XI (1958), 22 ff.

17. P. 187. "Metaphysische Schlüsse und Folgerungen [concerning predestination] vermeiden aber unsere Bekenntnisse ganz grundsätzlich." See Schmidt, *FB*, p. 45.

18. Pp. 187, 188, 230.

19. Pp. 187 ff.

20. Pp. 188, 189; see also Schopper's *Ratschlag, FB*, p. 394.

21. P. 188. As far as I have been able to determine, *Ansbach I* does not discuss whether unbelievers, too, may belong to the church in the world, although they are not members of the *ecclesia vera*.

the grace of God is proclaimed to sinners.[22] Through this proclamation of the gospel, Christ's lordship is activated in the church, while at the same time Christ's claim for sovereignty over the world is established. The mission to proclaim the gospel is the point at which the church takes on a concrete shape within this world. No one can judge which person lets himself be truly grasped by this proclamation, comes to faith, and becomes thereby a member of the true church; consequently no one can determine the social limits of the true church;[23] nevertheless the true church exists and has its mission within the limitations of time and space.[24]

The church's center is the fact that God in Christ reconciled the world unto himself; it constitutes the church and gives the church its breath of life.[25] In the same way in which the members of this church cannot exist without external things, so the church, too, cannot exist in the world without external things.[26] The center of the church is unfolded in the proclamation of the Word of God and the administration of the sacraments, that is, in events which take place within time and space. The gospel concerning Christ's lordship and man's salvation is, then, the divine basic law, the constitution for the church in time and eternity.[27]

In order to fulfill its mission in agreement with its constitution, the church needs an ordinance, a law, by which it governs its functioning. This law is necessary for the earthly existence of the church, but neither the law in itself nor its fulfillment by the Christian is a prerequisite for

22. Pp. 188 f., 194 f.

23. Pp. 188 ff.

24. See *FB*, p. 46.

25. Pp. 188 (par. 5), 194 f., 196 f., 198 f. For Luther, see *WA*, VIII, 491 (*The Misuse of the Mass*, 1521; *LW*, XXXVI, 133 ff.); see further Heckel I, pp. 37 ff., 46 ff., 117 ff., 136 ff.

26. Pp. 188 f., 195.

27. For the titles which describe the constitution of the church, see below, p. 176 n. 43. On the nature of ecclesiastical law, which, in turn, unfolds the constitution into the day-by-day life of the church, see above, pp. 141 n. 2, 153 nn. 32, 33, below, p. 178 n. 52; see also Excursus IV; E. Kinder, "Das Wesen kirchlicher Ordnung nach den lutherischen Bekenntnisschriften," *Festschr. d. Augustana Hochschule u. d. Nürnberger Predigerseminars f. Hans Meiser*, ed. G. Merz (Munich, n.d.), pp. 10 ff.; M. Schmidt, "Kirchliches Recht und Rechtfertigung auf dem Boden der Reformation," *Materialdienst d. Konfessionskundlichen Institutes Bensheim*, XII (1961), 61 ff.; H. Liermann, *Grundlagen des kirchlichen Verfassungsrechtes nach lutherischer Auffassung. Luthertum*, XI (Berlin, 1954); G. Masur, "Naturrecht und Kirche. Studien zur Evangelischen Kirchenverfassung Deutschlands im 18. Jahrhundert," *Historische Zeitschrift*, CXLVIII (1933), 30 ff.; G. Forck, *Die Königsherrschaft Jesu Christi* (Berlin, 1960); rev.: *Theol. Lit. zeitung*, LXXXVII (1962), 53 ff.; E. Kohlmeyer, "Die Bedeutung der Kirche für Luther," *ZKG*, XLVII (1928), 474 ff.

salvation.[28] The church's basic law and the church's mission to preach the gospel are given to the church *iure divino*.[29] They are not rights which the church can claim, of course, but rather privileges with which the church has been endowed; and inherent in these privileges is the obligation of making full use of them, as is expressed by the various New Testament commands, "go and preach," and also by some of Christ's parables.[30] On the other hand, law and order in the church are *iure humano* and have the exclusive function of serving the divine basic law, the church's constitution, by securing it in the various fields of ecclesiastical activities. And so the church in the world needs, for instance, an ordinance for governing the pastoral office, and statements which are legally binding for the pastor; it needs an ordinance for the liturgy, the diaconate, and for the church's physical properties.[31] If the divine basic law is distorted by the man-made ecclesiastical law, as happens in the Canon Law (according to *Ansbach I*), then the ecclesiastical law has to be reformed; if this proves to be impossible for any reason, then this law of the church has to be rejected as unconstitutional.[32]

Who has the task of conducting this reformation or creation of ecclesiastical law?[33] Who has the right to shape the external make-up of the church and to supervise the functioning of it? According to the authors of *Ansbach I*, it is the duty and the privilege of all believers to create, in cooperation with their bishop, that is, their pastor, that law and order which is necessary for the existence of the church in this world.[34] The believers have this duty and privilege *iure divino*; it is derived from the church's divine basic law. The believers, reborn through the living Word,[35] are invested with the three fundamental Christian rights:

28. Pp. 188 f., 195, 196 ff., 200. The proclamation of the gospel alone is sufficient for salvation. See also G. Ritter, *Die Neugestaltung Europas im 16. Jahrhundert* (Berlin, 1950), pp. 86, 104 ff., 114 ff.

29. Pp. 188, 189 ff., 194 f., 197 ff.

30. Pp. 194 f., 196 f., 198 f.

31. Pp. 195, 234 f., 237, 287, 290 ff.; for the liturgy, see the material on the individual sacraments and on the forms of worship developed throughout *Ansbach I*.

32. Pp. 189 f., 191 ff., 194 f., 196 ff., 202 ff., 229 ff., 291 (par. 114, at the end).

33. In connection with the Ansbach material of the period 1524–1526, Schmidt promises to investigate this problem in a special chapter (*FB*, p. 102 n. 6). In *FB, Buch 3, Kap. 2, Abschnitt III*, he deals with the *Reformationsrecht der Obrigkeit*, but he does not work with the 1524–1526 material. He deals exclusively with the 1528–1530 material, and here he concentrates on the *Ratschläge* of 1530.

34. Pp. 195, 205 ff., 234.

35. Pp. 188, 221–229, 230 ff.

freedom,[36] equality,[37] and love.[38] As a negative consequence of this fact the authors of *Ansbach I* reject the differentiation between the ecclesiastical and the secular estate, between priest and layman, as it is maintained in the Canon Law,[39] and affirm the priesthood of all believers.[40] As a positive consequence, they posit the right of the believer to judge and evaluate all things.[41] The congregation of the *homines spirituales* (understood in the frame of the priesthood of all believers)[42] has the right, even the duty, to organize the life of the congregation by creating ecclesiastical law. The norms which have to be activated in this process of putting the church in order are furnished by the divine basic law which constitutes the church. This divine basic law, and consequently also the norms for the ecclesiastical law, are more closely described by the three Reformation principles—the *sola scriptura*, the *solus Christus*, and the *sola fide*.[43] Since the Canon Law of the papal church is not shaped by these three principles, it has to be rejected as a whole, although after careful examination[44] individual statements may retain validity.

The authors of *Ansbach I* strongly affirm the congregational form of church-polity. They develop those principles which have already appeared in the *Wendelsteiner Kirchenordnung*.[45] Agreeing with Luther (whom,

36. For the fundamental rights of the Christian, see above, p. 153 n. 33; for freedom in *Ansbach I*, see *FB*, pp. 229 (par. 37)–232 (par. 41).

37. Pp. 194 f., 294 ff.

38. Pp. 295, 291.

39. Pp. 209 ff., 234 ff., 237 f., 246 ff., 285–292. The authors of *Ansbach I* go even so far as to reject any kind of supervision by anyone; see below, p. 178.

40. Pp. 194 ff., 265 f.; see also Schopper's *Ratschlag*, *FB*, p. 383.

41. Pp. 22 ff., 223 ff., 230 ff.; see also *Ansbach II*, *FB*, pp. 344 ff.

42. See above, pp. 153 n. 33, 176 nn. 39, 40.

43. Pp. 198 f., 217 ff., 221, 230, 292 ff.

44. Pp. 195 ff., 199, 226, 228 f., 230 f. On the problems connected with the adoption of certain material of the Canon Law by the reformers, see W. Maurer, "Reste des Kanonischen Rechtes im Frühprotestantismus," *ZRG* Kan. Abt., LI (1965), 190 ff.

45. For our discussion the question of priority is unimportant. Since the speech on which *WKO* was based (see above, p. 151) was delivered on October 19, 1524 (see *Flugschrift*, p. 190; *FKO*, p. 65), the author of *WKO* could have made use of *Ansbach I*, had he been acquainted with it; were he not acquainted with it, then his arguments are even more remarkable. The main difference between *Ansbach I* and *WKO* lies in the fact that *WKO* only points out the right of the parish to examine the pastor, and if necessary to discharge him; it deals only with the legalities concerning the pastor (*Pfarrerrecht*). In *Ansbach I*, on the other hand, basic statements on the nature of ecclesiastical law are developed, and from them some—unfortunately not many—details are derived.

incidentally, they never cite),[46] the authors emphasize the autonomy of the local congregation in questions pertaining to the spiritual and to the legal life of the church—an autonomy derived from and limited by the divine basic law.[47] Arguing from this presupposition, the authors of *Ansbach I* reject the Canon Law and justify this break with traditional legal norms by emphasizing the biblical basis of the three Reformation principles. They proceed only sporadically in detailing the ecclesiastical law. Concerning the formation of doctrinal statements, they do not go beyond a biblicistic, fundamentalistic framework.[48] Concerning the organization of the external life of the congregation, its finances for example, they offer only general ideas.[49] The area on which the authors of *Ansbach I* concentrate is the reform of the liturgy and of religious life; and here they stress the *dogmatic presuppositions* almost exclusively, while *liturgical details* are neglected.[50] *Ansbach I* sees the freedom of the Christian and his privilege of shaping the life of his congregation (of making, for instance, necessary reforms in the liturgy) as being constantly limited by his obligation to consider those in other congregations. Such freedom leaves no room for any arbitrary or capricious decisions by any one congregation insofar as the liturgy is concerned.[51] In conducting reforms, Christians are to be considerate of their brethren. If uniformity in the liturgy cannot be accomplished, then at least any particular congregation has to avoid offending any other congregation. Unfortunately the authors

46. This of course does not mean that the authors of *Ansbach I* were not familiar with many of Luther's writings. Despite the fact that they apparently never quoted Luther, they leaned heavily on many of the Reformer's writings; see *FB*, pp. 54 ff. It would be a highly challenging task to analyze Luther's position on *Ansbach I* (see p. 168 n. 64) and compare it with his position on the work done by the Homberg Synod in 1526.

47. See above, p. 174.

48. See Schmidt, *FB*, p. 13 ff., 62 ff. This is correct, although the *sola scriptura* is christologically qualified (see the references above, p. 176 n. 43), a fact which Schmidt has not sufficiently emphasized.

49. Pp. 290 ff.; on the endowments for the parish, see pp. 261 ff. Regarding details in the *Pfarrerrecht*, the authors of *Ansbach I* point out that the local congregation has the right to elect the pastor, or at least to confirm his appointment after examining him; see pp. 234, 287. *Ansbach I* is more concerned with the development of critical principles than with detailed constructive statements.

50. Consequently one cannot agree with Schmidt's argument that in Ansbach the principles for organizing the worship service had not been developed prior to 1526; *FB*, p. 102.

51. Pp. 292, 295. This notion is especially emphasized in an undated brief drafted by Adam Weisz (see above, p. 147 n. 10) to which Schmidt referred (*FB*, p. 103), and an anonymous, also undated brief which Schornbaum edited in *FB*, pp. 400 ff.

of *Ansbach I* do not elaborate on any way of achieving a common liturgy. The church at large, be it all the congregations of the margraviate, or of the Empire, or even of the world, is de-emphasized in favor of the local congregation. Consequently all legal problems concerning the coexistence of one congregation with other congregations are not even glimpsed.

The autonomy of the congregations within the framework of the divine basic law is absolute, and any other supervision of either spiritual or external affairs is strictly rejected. The authors of *Ansbach I* refute the papal understanding of the pastoral office; they consider this office exclusively in the framework of the proclamation of God's Word. They therefore cannot understand or coordinate the two functions of the pastoral office, that of proclaiming the Word (of shepherding the sheep) and that of governing not only the sheep but also the shepherds. In their theology of the pastoral office, the authors of *Ansbach I* do not allow for a responsible supervision of the congregations.[52] They thus allow a vacuum to develop, into which elements alien to the nature of the church can move. And such elements had to penetrate the church at that moment when law and order within the congregations of the territory had to be supervised but no office was available to discharge this responsibility, since the congregations had never provided for such an office. Five years later the margrave, no longer Casimir but his brother and successor George, enters this vacuum as "supreme pastor of souls" and takes over full responsibility for the congregations of his country.[53]

The relationship between state and church is not considered at all in *Ansbach I*. In the preface the authors refer briefly to the circumstances under which the document originated;[54] occasionally they mention that secular authorities have the duty to judge external matters.[55] But they

52. *Ansbach I* (*FB*, pp. 194 f., 209 ff., 234) and *Ansbach II* (*FB*, pp. 342 ff.) have no room for the *potestas iurisdictionis* (see Excursus IV) of the pastoral office. In an apparent attempt to eliminate even the slightest possibility of pastoral, episcopal "tyranny," or of explaining ecclesiastical law iure divino, the authors of these documents focus exclusively on the *potestas clavium* of the church. The *Ratschlag* on the XXIII Articles (see above, p. 158) issued by the city of Rothenburg speaks of the pastor as "*Wächter*" and "*Aufseher*"; see Schattenmann, *op. cit.*, p. 174. But here, too, there is no development of the two functions of the pastoral office. For the Ansbacher theologians *Kirchenregiment* meant exclusively the spiritual shepherding of the sheep; see *FB*, p. 196.

53. Margrave George to his vice-regents and councillors: Schleiz, June 29, 1529; K. Schornbaum, "Zur Reformationsgeschichte im Bayreuther Oberland," *ZBayKG*, VI (1931), 203 ff., esp. 205.

54. Pp. 183 f.; see also above, p. 158.

55. P. 212.

develop no theory as to the nature of secular authority, nor do they elaborate on the rights of the sovereign, especially on his ius reformandi.[56] As far as I can determine, this problem is touched only once. In the discussion on the privilege of a congregation to create the laws necessary for its existence, the following statement appears:

> How should one deal with the present large crowd [of preachers] who altogether, as is obvious, do not serve the congregation[s], either through preaching or through other services? Answer: We shall turn this problem over to the secular government for a solution. [After all,] how are other bad situations corrected? In this case, however, one has to proceed in an especially Christian way, because love teaches [us] that one should spare and be especially kind to those who have lived in error and now wish to be corrected. Therefore one must live in peace with them.[57]

Without further elaboration, the authors of *Ansbach I* here assign to the government the privilege of doing away with certain evil conditions in the organizational[58] life as well as in the spiritual life[59] of the church; they claim the assistance of the state for the re-establishment of the church's divine basic law in the day-by-day life of the church, which law has been destroyed through practices tolerated in the papal church. The legal or religious basis, however, for this interference of the state in the affairs of the church is not developed.

It should not amaze us that we find in *Ansbach I*[60] no details on the relationship of the state to the church. Within the boundaries of the territory, this relationship was by no means controversial at the time *Ansbach I* was written. The authors of this document could hope that Casimir would openly support the Reformation. But the margrave's indecision nullified this hope. Consequently the material presented in *Ansbach I* was further developed in *Flugschrift*, in Rurer I and II, and in the requests of the cities of the margraviate to Casimir to introduce the Reformation officially.

56. See below, p. 193 n. 127.

57. P. 292.

58. P. 291; at issue are abuses in the diaconate, the office of the church sexton, and the office of the grave digger.

59. Pp. 291 f.; at issue is the organization of the preaching office.

60. *Ansbach II* does not go beyond the material offered in *Ansbach I*, as far as I have been able to determine.

According to the title, it is the purpose of *Flugschrift*[61] faithfully to admonish secular authorities who do not take a clear and positive position on the proclamation of God's Word.[62] The little book is designed to drive into the minds of the rulers that they are guilty in God's eyes if they do not permit the Reformation in their territories. Whosoever prohibits the preaching of God's Word could not even pretend to be a Christian. Consequently, the author of *Flugschrift* argues, certain sovereigns tolerate or even command the preaching of the pure and unadulterated gospel. When, however, any reforms are conducted which directly result from this new way of preaching, then these sovereigns prohibit them, and threaten with severe punishments those who initiate such a reform program. The sovereigns, in turn, justify their position by pointing out three facts: (*a*) The understanding and meaning of the divine Word is not at all clear, but to the contrary is ambiguous, even controversial. (*b*) Consequently all reforms within the religious life have to be postponed until the church has decided, in a general council, how God's Word is to be understood. (*c*) Only by affirming this position can peace be maintained in the land. In the detailed counterargument to the sovereigns' position, the author emphasizes that this vacillation on the issues raised by the Reformation makes the sovereigns just as guilty as were Herod, Pilate, and the Jews through their dealings with Jesus; he makes clear that it is the duty of a sovereign to make up his mind on any religious issues without delay. The author of *Flugschrift* presupposes, of course, that such a decision can only be in favor of the Reformation.[63]

The author of *Flugschrift* allotted to secular authority the *duty to arrive at a clear position on religious questions, and to tolerate the Reformation* in the territory. The author wanted tolerance, and no interference in the religious affairs of the territory, be that interference negative or positive insofar as the Reformation was concerned. It has been assumed that Hans Herbst authored *Flugschrift*, and that this booklet was aimed at Margrave Casimir.[64] If this is correct—and there seems no reason to doubt it—

61. *Getrewe, Christenliche vnd nützliche warnung etlicher obrigkait, die das Euangelion zu predigenn zulassen vnd befehlen, Vnd straffen doch desselben volziehung. 1525.* See Panzer, *op. cit.*, II, Nos. 2907, 2908; copy in the Archiv of the Evangelical Lutheran Church of Bavaria in Nuremberg. The following presentation is based on M. Simon, "Eine unbeachtete Flugschrift zur Reformationsgeschichte der Markgrafschaft Brandenburg-Ansbach," *ZBayKG*, XXII (1953), 183 ff.

62. *Flugschrift*, pp. 183 f.

63. *Ibid.*, pp. 184 f.

64. According to Simon (*Flugschrift*, pp. 189 ff.), on the basis of a most detailed argumentation; for other works by Herbst, see Simon, *EKGB*, I, 179.

then Herbst developed in *Flugschrift* the same ideas as in the *Wendelsteiner Kirchenordnung*,[65] only from a different point of view. In the *Wendelsteiner Kirchenordnung*, he focused on the relationship of the state to the church from the viewpoint of the church: the Christians of Wendelstein wanted the margrave to respect their God-given privilege of deciding all legal and spiritual questions of church life. In *Flugschrift*, Herbst elaborated on the relationship of the state to the church from the viewpoint of the state: it is the sovereign's duty to respect the privileges of the congregation and to tolerate the Reformation; should he not fulfill this duty, then he is guilty in God's eyes.

Thoughts similar to those expressed in the *Wendelsteiner Kirchenordnung* and *Flugschrift* were set forth in the petitions which the cities turned over to Casimir in September, 1524, and January/February, 1525.[66] In these petitions, the city delegates asked the sovereign to sanction, on behalf of the state (that is, through the law of the land), the preaching of the gospel as the reformers understood it; to tolerate the reforms which had to be enacted as a direct result of this preaching; and legally to protect the citizens of the territory who openly affirmed the Reformation.

But what would happen if the sovereign would not fulfill these hopes of his people? This question had been latent since the material presented in the *Wendelsteiner Kirchenordnung*.[67] The question was never posed from 1524 to 1526, so far as I have been able to determine. John Rurer was nevertheless apparently aware of this problem, because in one of his first major extant writings (Rurer I) [68] he did touch upon it—though only indirectly.

Rurer I develops an evangelical understanding of Christian freedom which may be summarized in three statements: (*a*) The believer has the spirit of freedom since he is liberated—through Christ—from the bondage of the law, of sin, and the power of death. (*b*) The believer has the spirit of love through Christ living in him, so that he voluntarily, and out of

---

65. See pp. 151 f., and *Flugschrift*, pp. 190 f.

66. See p. 172 n. 6; text in excerpt in *Flugschrift*, pp. 186 ff.

67. See p. 155 n. 37.

68. *Ein Christlich Predig wider die vnchristlichen Empörung vnnd vngehorsam etlicher vnterthanen, So sie itzt vnter dem scheyn des Euangelions vnd Christenlicher Freyheyt, on grund wider Gott, sein heyligs wort, Vnd jr selbs Eere, Glübd vnd Ayde fürnemen.* E. Weller, *Repertorium typographicum* (Nördlingen, 1864–1874; reprint: Hildesheim, 1961), No. 3615; copy in Bavarian Staatsbibliothek in Munich. On Rurer as author, see Schornbaum, "Zum Briefwechsel des Adam Weisz," 229 ff.; Schornbaum I, p. 198 n. 203; *FB*, p. 101. The text, without the title page, consists of fifteen pages which are numbered with arabic numerals in order to facilitate the citing. From note 69 through note 75 below, the unqualified page references refer to the Munich copy of Rurer I.

love for Christ and the brethren, strives to fulfill the ten commandments; thus the believer is liberated to true ethics, exclusively centered on Christ and the brethren, and free from any expectations of reward. (c) The Christian freedom is a freedom in things spiritual, and not in things external.[69] These ideas develop in two directions: the freedom of the Christian is activated in the fulfilling of the ethics of the Sermon on the Mount;[70] and it is activated in the obedience to and respect for the state.[71] Christ, his conduct and his teachings are the best example for the practice of the Christian freedom.

Rurer then analyzes the nature of the state. On the basis of Rom. 13, he emphasizes the duty of the Christian to obey the state in all external, temporarily restricted matters.[72] This duty of obedience is not based on the religiously understood nature of the state, as might be expected, but on the Christian's love for his brother: as a Christian I am deeply aware of the fact that the state, through the sword, checks the evil, demonic, sinful powers in this world, which may harm my fellow man; therefore, out of love and care for my neighbor, I do respect and honor the state, and obey its orders and laws.[73] The Christian is also subject to the "unchristian" state, in which, contrary to God's law, the citizens are tyrannized and oppressed.[74] The Christian owes obedience not only to the good and pious sovereign, but also to the evil and tyrannical one. Rurer bases this thought on five arguments: (a) The state is and remains God's institution, notwithstanding the fact that a tyrant may abuse or distort the nature of this institution. (b) One wrong does not set right another one; that is, disobedience to the sovereign cannot be justified on the basis of that sovereign's arbitrary abuse of a divine institution. (c) The life of the Christian is marked by the Cross; consequently to disobey the tyrannical sovereign and rebel against this cross of tyranny would be a rejection of Christian life under the Cross. (d) God alone is the judge, and in his own time he will take revenge on the tyrant; it is, therefore, not the Christian's task to interfere with God's plan. (e) Disobedience to the government is the root of revolution, and in the course of a revolution both guilty and innocent people are harmed—but mostly the innocent ones.[75]

69. Pp. 2 f.
70. Pp. 3 ff.
71. Pp. 6 ff.
72. P. 11.
73. Pp. 6 ff., 8 f.
74. Pp. 10 f.
75. Pp. 1 f., 11 ff. Rurer I here follows Luther completely. The Reformer had argued that the Christian has no right to rebel against the government on the basis of the gospel

Rurer I has to be viewed against the background of the Peasants' War,[76] and if so viewed, its purpose is clear: the pacification of the citizens, and an attempt to put the citizens' obedience to the state on a religious foundation. Although the framework of Rurer I is determined by the circumstances of the time, this booklet presents some concepts of the relationship of the Christian to the state, and of the state to the church, concepts which are basic to the Lutheran Reformation in Germany.[77] Three ideas are developed concerning the sovereign's duty to sanction the congregational form of church-polity: (*a*) The government as secular authority is and remains an institution ordained by God, notwithstanding the fact that a sovereign may act in an unchristian manner. (In connection with the topic under discussion, "unchristian" means that the sovereign does not respect the privilege of the congregation to manage its own affairs, or does not tolerate the reforms enacted by the congregation, or protect the reformers against the persecutions by the papal church.) (*b*) The Christian's duty to obey, however, is restricted to externals. In view of the Peasants' War, we cannot be amazed that Rurer does not elaborate on the essence of the resistance against the government if it interferes with things spiritual. (*c*) If the government hinders, restricts, or opposes the freedom of the Christian congregation to manage its affairs, then the individual Christian has to bear this cross.

By the spring of 1525, the representatives of the Reformation in the margraviate had developed the following principles concerning the relationship of the state to the church, or more precisely, concerning ecclesiastical law and the right of the sovereign to interfere with the spiritual or the external affairs of the church: (*a*) On the basis of the divine basic law of the Christian congregation, believers have the privilege of managing the legal affairs of the congregation. (*b*) This privilege supersedes any privileges or laws claimed or practiced by the papal church.

---

and of faith, or for the sake of the establishment of the kingdom of God. Here the Christian can only passively resist, i.e., he can document his resistance by suffering for the sake of God's Word and by living under the Cross. Quite different circumstances arise, however, when the Christian feels compelled to resist the government, e.g., for constitutional reasons. Luther's main thrust was directed toward the elimination of any justification for a "Christian" revolution. For details, see Heckel I, pp. 157, 186, 189, 151 ff., 180 ff.; Heckel III, pp. 243 ff., 288 ff.; W. A. Johnson, "Luther's Doctrine of the Two Kingdoms," *The Lutheran Quarterly*, XV (1963), 239 ff.; L. C. Green, "Resistance to Authority and Luther," *The Lutheran Quarterly*, VI (1954), 338 ff.; G. W. Forell, "Luther and Politics" *Luther and Culture. Martin Luther Lectures*, IV (Decorah, Iowa, 1960), 3 ff.

76. See pp. 160 f., 164 f.

77. For the relationship between church and state according to the Lutheran Reformation, see pp. 141 nn. 2, 3, 182 n. 75; Heckel III, pp. 307 ff.

(c) To the sovereign is attributed the *right to tolerate* reforms in the religious life, thus jeopardizing the jurisdiction of the papal church. (d) If such reforms originate in the true, that is, Reformation, understanding of the Word of God, then the sovereign has the religious *duty to tolerate* these reforms and to protect those who enact them, notwithstanding the existing law of the papal church. (e) Should the sovereign refuse to do this, then he is guilty in God's eyes. (f) This guilt does not, however, justify disobedience to the sovereign in external matters.

The emphasis in all these thoughts was placed on the sovereign's duty to arrive at a clear position concerning religious issues, and to sanction the Reformation movement within his territory. In addition to this, it was emphasized that the sovereign had the right, even the duty, to break with the law of the papal church. At the center of these considerations were tolerance and protection. How did the evangelicals of the margraviate develop these ideas in the period from the spring of 1525 to the third Ansbacher Landtag in October, 1526? The most important source for dealing with this question is Rurer II.[78]

Rurer II is divided into two parts of almost equal length. In the first major part,[79] the author offers a "*Summa*"[80] of the evangelical faith in forty articles. These articles are short theses, well supported with biblical passages, rather than long elaborations. In the second major part,[81] Rurer uses all his eloquence to convince his reader that the Lutheran doctrine is completely based on the Bible and is therefore correct.[82]

In the first major part, Rurer places his thoughts on Christian freedom,[83] as developed in Rurer I, into the totality of the Christian faith.

---

78. *Christliche vnterrichtung eins pfarhern an seinen herrn, ein fursten des heyligen Reychs, auff viertzig Artickel vnd puncten gestelt, was eins rechten, waren, Euangelischen Pfarhern oder Predigers Predigen vnd lere sein soll . . . Das des Pfarhern namen ytz nit lauter angezeygt oder gesetzt, ist ausz guten Christenlichen vraschen vnterlassen, aber seinem herren vnd vilen deszselben Rethen wol bekant. 1526.* Panzer, *op. cit.*, II, Nos. 3125, 3126; copy available in the library of the University of Erlangen. On Rurer as the author of this booklet, see K. Schornbaum, "Zur religiösen Haltung der Stadt Ansbach in den ersten Jahren der Reformation," *BBayKG*, VII (1901), esp. 150 f.; Schornbaum I, pp. 109, 238 n. 11. The text, without the title page, consists of forty-one pages which are numbered with arabic numerals in order to facilitate the citing. From note 79 through note 117 below, "Articles" refers to the articles in the first major part of Rurer II, and the unqualified page references refer to the pages of the Erlangen copy of Rurer II.

79. Pp. 3–21.

80. P. 21.

81. Pp. 21–41.

82. See Schmidt, *FB*, p. 102.

83. Articles XVIII–XX.

He begins with the doctrine of man (Art. I–IV), which he develops in the framework of the dialectic of law and gospel (Art. V–X). When setting forth his thoughts on Christ, on the act of redemption, and on the nature of man's salvation, Rurer rather one-sidedly emphasizes the *work* of Jesus, neglecting the *person* of Jesus, and puts his thoughts under the *solus Christus* (Art. XI–XV). Then, following Article XV, Rurer adds twenty articles in which he analyzes the nature of faith (Art. XVI). He begins with a discussion of the roots of faith, which he sees in the work of the Holy Spirit (Art. XVII–XX); then he discusses the topics "Faith and Works" (Art. XXI–XXVI), "Spirit and the Word of God" (Art. XXVII–XXX), and "Word and the Office of Preaching" (Art. XXXI–XXXV). In conclusion Rurer analyzes the nature of the church (Art. XXXVI–XXXIX) and the nature of the state (Art. XL).

In connection with the elaboration or *Christian freedom* (Art. XVIII–XX), Rurer repeats thoughts which he had already presented in Rurer I and which can also be found in *Ansbach I*. The Holy Spirit, who is active in the believers, frees them from the power of sin and the devil.[84] Christian freedom is therefore a spiritual freedom; it is freedom within man's spirit and conscience, and not a freedom of, or in, external matters.[85] Christian freedom is the freedom of that new life which is given to all who die and are raised again with Christ through faith.[86] Faith, in turn, is God's gift; he creates this faith through the preaching of his Word.[87] Rurer discusses the preaching of the Word in connection with the power of the keys which are entrusted to the pastoral office.[88] And this office, which is to function according to the *sola scriptura* principle, is the only institution which the church needs.[89]

The preaching of God's Word "gives birth to, sanctifies, and governs the *church*."[90] Although the church exists in the world, it has no secular nature; therefore the church needs no laws for ruling souls. Only God's

84. Articles XVI, XVII, XVIII.
85. Article XIX.
86. Article XX.
87. Articles XXVI, XXVII.
88. Article XXVIII.
89. Articles XXXII, XXX, XXXIV. In Article XXXII, Rurer states that only he who is called by God and sent (Rurer does not say by whom) should preach. Unfortunately Rurer does not say how this calling and sending takes place. Through the congregation? Through a spiritual experience? Or the calling through an experience, and the sending through the congregation? And how should a congregation know that a call was "legitimate"?
90. Article XXXVI.

Word rules in the church.[91] In external matters, however, such as the singing of hymns, the reading of Scripture, and the administration of the sacraments, good order has to exist among the Christians; this order, in turn, contributes to the spiritual edification of the Christians and helps to maintain peace and unanimity within the church.[92]

In discussing the nature of the *state*,[93] Rurer points out first that secular authority is from God, to be used for the good of the citizens. Then he states that a Christian sovereign has to be concerned with God's honor, with the salvation of the subjects, and the common good. The subjects, on the other hand, are obligated to be obedient to the sovereign with both body and goods, regardless of his moral, spiritual, or religious qualifications. If the government commands something which is contrary to God's Word, however, this duty to obey is nullified.

In the first subdivision[94] of the second major part, Rurer demonstrates that the preaching of the Lutheran preachers is filled with "God's spirit and doctrine;"[95] contrary to this, the preaching of the papal priests "does not originate in God's spirit but in that of the Anti-Christ."[96] This argumentation concluded

> that now the people everywhere desire that God's Word be preached to them; they are so eager to hear it, and work so hard for it, that frequently they walk . . . many miles to [listen to an evangelical sermon], regardless of the fact that . . . they are often severely punished for this. What else does [this situation] document than that there has been a big famine of God's Word on earth . . . and that until now the people lacked the proper food . . . ?[97]

In the second subdivision,[98] the following three arguments of the papists against the thesis developed in the first subdivision are discussed: (*a*) The Lutheran preachers spread among the people an "incorrect" understanding of Christian freedom; consequently they are responsible for the social unrest in the country.[99] (*b*) The message of the Lutheran

91. Articles XXX, XXXII, XXXIV–XXXVIII.
92. Article XXXIX.
93. Article XL.
94. Pp. 21–27.
95. P. 22.
96. P. 23.
97. P. 26.
98. Pp. 27–31.
99. P. 28: ". . . ausz was vrsach aber solch vngeschickt prediger erweckt vnd aufgestanden sind, ist leichtlich zugedencken, wann wir vnser sünd, hinlesigkeit vnd vndanckbarkeit in allen wolthaten gottes wöllen bedencken vnd zu hertzen nemen, davon hierin

preachers does not contribute to the moral improvement of the people. (*c*) It is impossible that all this time there has been error in questions of faith.

The third subdivision[100] is introduced with a question:

Gracious Sovereign and Lord, since the aforementioned articles [those of the first major part], together with all which is taught . . . by the . . . evangelical preachers, are nothing but God's Word . . . Your Sovereign Grace [should] consider first of all whether one should not mourn and weep tears of blood over the fact that many sovereigns . . . who otherwise want to be good Christians and want to be called [good Christian sovereigns] still do have doubts whether this sacred evangelical and Christian teaching is God's Word. Is this not remarkably great blindness and harm?[101]

In answering this question, the author emphasizes that it is both stupid and blasphemous to reject the message of the evangelical preachers in order to remain true to the "faith of the fathers."

In his fourth subdivision[102] the author argues more strongly:

[a.] Therefore, Gracious Sovereign and Lord, be it far from Your Sovereign Grace . . . even to think such a . . . horrible thought, or to harbor a similar opinion, that the presently proclaimed teaching of the evangelical preachers is new, wrong, Lutheran, heretical, or devilish. . . .

Your Sovereign Grace be on guard, if you are interested in . . . God's blessing [upon you] and, for the sake of God, let no one convince you to . . . hinder and persecute such evangelical or divine teaching, or to plan and undertake anything against it. For should Your Sovereign Grace dare to do such a thing (may God guard against this and protect Your Sovereign Grace from so doing), I want to have Your Sovereign Grace warned . . . and told that Your Sovereign Grace will not succeed in so doing. All who despised God's Word, or who dared to oppose it, always had misfortune and could not execute what they had

---

nit stat ist weitter zu melden." It is by no means stretching too far to assume that this passage was directed against Casimir personally. This passage would then have to be understood as needling Casimir and would have to be paraphrased as follows: If you, Casimir, would not have been so stubbornly ungrateful for God's present blessings (i.e., for the preaching of God's Word as the reformers understood it), then the unrest in the country (Peasants' War) could have been avoided. Although Rurer does have a point here, he nevertheless oversimplifies the issue.

100. Pp. 31–35.
101. P. 31.
102. Pp. 35–40.

planned; they received, however, their just punishment, went down and perished . . . .

In view of this, Your Sovereign Grace should not hinder the spreading of the gospel which is now breaking to the fore around us. Do consider that it is not [the plan and work] of a man but the plan and work of God that now in so many territories . . . the gospel and God's Word is preached again . . . .

[b.] Therefore Your Sovereign Grace should not touch fiery coals, as the saying goes, and dare to hinder or persecute the gospel out of fear of your own misfortune and catastrophe. To the contrary, let [the gospel] be promoted and handled in peace, and protect and shield it, together with its preachers. Your Sovereign Grace also should refrain from punishing those who, according to content and authority of the divine Word and Christian freedom, act without wrongdoing, according to their needs . . . [follows Rom. 13:3].

[c.] If Your Sovereign Grace desires to rule well the territory and the people, to possess and retain them in peace and unanimity, then Your Sovereign Grace should keep the divine Word and its preachers before your eyes, and love and respect them. Your Sovereign Grace should also take care whenever you can and have the urge to listen to Holy Scriptures or the Word of God, to read it and meditate upon it in preference to all other business, so that Your Sovereign Grace may learn from it God's counsel, will, and work. For if one rules without God's counsel, neither land nor people prosper . . . .

[d.] Your Sovereign Grace should take special care that all things which are contrary and offensive to God's honor, to his Word, to faith and brotherly love are abolished, especially the great horror of the daily celebration of masses . . . .

[e.] Your Sovereign Grace should also command and become involved in the task of having God's Word preached with one accord in your territories, cities and villages, and of having a uniform evangelical and not popish [church] ordinance and [liturgy] maintained as much as possible, according to the opportunities and desires of the local congregations.[103]

In these sentences the sovereign is charged with the *cura religionis*.[104] He *has to tolerate the preaching of the gospel* as well as the *liturgical reforms* which are the necessary outgrowth of this preaching. Even more, the sovereign *must be involved* in the *creation of an evangelical church-ordinance* in

103. Pp. 35–38.

104. On this term and the way it was understood in the middle ages, and in the Reformation, see p. 193 n. 127; Heckel II, pp. 2 ff.; Heckel I, pp. 192 ff.; Heckel III, pp. 296, 325, 337, 395.

accordance with the wishes of the congregations.[105] The idea of early 1525 that it is the sovereign's *duty to tolerate* the preaching of the gospel as the reformers understood it[106] has now been developed to the point that the sovereign has the *duty to interfere* in the religious and ecclesiastical chaos, to conduct a reform of the whole church life, and to participate in the creation of new ecclesiastical law. The sovereign has the duty to break with the law of the papal church, and nothing should hinder him from fulfilling this duty. Neither protests of the bishops, nor any threats of the emperor to maintain the legal claims of the papal church, even with arms if necessary, should influence the sovereign. Rurer uses Rom. 8:31 in order to counsel the sovereign, and makes the seriousness of the situation quite clear.[107]

Rurer points out that it is the duty of the sovereign not only to tolerate the Reformation and protect those who break with the law of the papal church, but also to create new ecclesiastical law,[108] always, however, in cooperation with the church, or more specifically, with the congregations of the territory.[109] Unfortunately, Rurer does not detail how this should be done. Theoretically he does not exclude the possibility that the sovereign will *rule* the church of his territory by decree. Rurer makes it quite clear, however, that the new ecclesiastical law is not to stand above the congregations as a means by which the sovereign could exercise control over the church. On the contrary, the new ecclesiastical law should stand within the congregations as an element for securing the divine basic law of the church. The new law of the church cannot, therefore, be shaped according to the necessities of the state, but only according to those of the church. Based on the ideas presented in Article XXXIX of the first major part, Rurer here maintains the congregational form of church-polity while at the same time emphasizing unity and order for all the congregations in the territory. The principles which govern the creation of the new ecclesiastical law are the divine basic law of the church on the one side, and love for the brethren on the other side.[110] The

---

105. Pp. 37 f.; see above, p. 188, position(*e*), and Excursus V.

106. See above, p. 180.

107. Pp. 38 ff.

108. According to Rurer, the *cura religionis* always functions both negatively (by breaking with the unconstitutional Canon Law) and positively (by creating a new ecclesiastical law); see also Heckel I, p. 192 n. 1501.

109. Here are the roots of the synodical form of church-polity which W. Guszmann (*Quellen und Forschungen zur Geschichte des Augsburger Glaubensbekenntnisses* [Leipzig, 1911] I, Part II, 65) found in the Ansbacher *Ratschläge* of 1530.

110. See Articles XXXVIII, XXXIX.

ecclesiastical law should secure the divine basic law, negatively, by breaking with the law of the papal church, and positively, by organizing the church as a legal entity on Reformation principles.

If we now seek the basis of this program, we must first ask whether Rurer even considers this problem. Rurer does not argue or attempt to prove his point in this fourth subdivision, but rather calls on his reader to act. As a result, it is not surprising that the author does not deal at any great length with the important question of the basis of the sovereign's cura religionis. We will find a different picture, however, if we look more closely at this fourth subdivision, keeping in mind that Rurer wishes to accomplish five different things with his reader, the margrave:[111] (a) that the sovereign abandon his resistance to the preaching of the gospel and no longer hinder the reformation of the liturgy and of religious life; (b) that he protect the evangelical preachers against connivance or open persecution on the part of the papal church; (c) that the sovereign himself come to the "true" faith;[112] (d) that he abolish the distortions of the gospel as practiced by the papal church; (e) that he "command" and supervise the creation of an evangelical ecclesiastical law, respecting the congregational form of church polity.[113] A glance at this list shows immediately that point (c) is the center of Rurer's thoughts. Filled with the zeal of a true court-preacher who is concerned for the soul entrusted to his pastoral care, Rurer wants the margrave to come to the "true" faith, that is, to learn God's will, counsel, and work. But he is also fully aware that the margrave might not do this. How could he not be aware of this, in view of Casimir's ambiguous position in the period from 1524 to 1526?[114] Watching Casimir daily and seeing that he is not yet a true believer, Rurer begins with points (a) and (b), emphasizing the sovereign's *duty to tolerance* of and *protection* for the Reformation, and only then injects point (c), the invitation and exhortation to come to faith. If the sovereign is caught up in the gospel, if he is a Christian sovereign, then, so Rurer continues in (d) and (e), the margrave "should take special care" to abolish the papal distortions, especially the daily celebration of masses, and introduce an evangelical church-ordinance and liturgy. This new ecclesiastical law has to be built on the divine basic law of the church, and has to respect the spiritual privilege of the Christian to exercise his fundamental right of freedom, by which the congregation of the believers creates its own laws.

111. Pp. 35–38; see above, pp. 187 f.
112. P. 37.
113. P. 37 f.
114. See above, pp. 160 ff.

When Rurer speaks of the sovereign's *cura religionis*, he is referring to the sovereign's duty to abolish—or to help in abolishing, by toleration and protection—the unconstitutional situation that exists in the church, and to restore the constitutionality of ecclesiastical law. The divine basic law, the constitution of the church, has to be restored and secured within the church itself. This is done by the believers themselves; the sovereign only acts as an overseer[115] so that chaos does not develop within the parishes of his territory. The divine basic law of the church has to be secured also outside the church, that is, in the relationship of the church to society at large, as symbolized by the state; this securing is done by the sovereign, who through the law of the land sanctions the privileges of the congregations, acknowledges the ecclesiastical law, and protects the evangelical preachers against the claims of the papal church. And this *cura religionis* is both the duty of the sovereign and the basis for his action in ecclesiastical affairs. Why? Because he is a Christian sovereign. According to Article XL of the first major part, it is the task of a Christian sovereign to be concerned with God's honor, the salvation of his subjects, and the common good.[116] Any individual who does not let himself be grasped by God's act of reconciliation through faith in Christ will be shattered by God's wrath. Likewise, a country whose sovereign and inhabitants do not accept Christ's redemptive lordship drifts into chaos, which is a sign of God's wrath and judgment over land and people. If a land falls under God's wrath and judgment, then this is primarily the fault of the ruler, because neither country nor people can prosper when the ruler reigns without counsel from God's Word.[117]

According to Rurer, the two titles "sovereign" and "Christian" coexist in the person of the *Christian sovereign*, and this coexistence furnishes the basis for the sovereign's duty and privilege of exercising the *cura religionis*. Through the divine basic law of the church, the *believing* sovereign is given the privilege to use the fundamental rights of the

115. See Excursus V. On the constitutionality of the ecclesiastical law, see above, pp. 174 f.

116. P. 20. It did not take long until Melanchthon argued that the sovereign is *custos utriusque tabulae*; see Heckel II, pp. 6 ff.; Heckel III, pp. 316 ff., 322 ff., 610 ff.

117. P. 37; see above, p. 188, position (*c*). Rurer applies this statement to the *believing sovereign*, i.e., to the sovereign who complies with the exhortation to study God's Word, meditate on it, and believe it. Consequently it is not a religiously understood raison d'état which justifies the sovereign's action in ecclesiastical affairs, but only his faith. (See Heckel I, p. 197, for Luther's opinion on this point, and for a critical evaluation of Holl's interpretation of Luther.) Raison d'état justifies only the *cura religionis* of the unbelieving sovereign (see above, pp. 187 f., position [*a/b*] and the beginning of [*c*]); then, however, the *cura religionis* has a different makeup; see below, p. 193.

Christian;[118] like any other Christian, a believing sovereign has the spiritual power to create law and order for the life and teachings within the congregation. This principle authorizes the sovereign to break with the papal church, to reject the Canon Law, and to cooperate in creating new ecclesiastical law, *but only as equal among equals*. Without being specifically mentioned, the priesthood of all believers is made the basis for the sovereign's participation in church government, a notion which is in direct agreement with Luther's position on this issue.[119] In Rurer's ideas there is no word of any legal claim, privilege, or power to command, which the sovereign holds in ecclesiastical affairs by virtue of his office.[120] The only claim or privilege held by the believing sovereign in regard to legal questions of the church is the right to serve the external make-up of the church, and this right he shares with all believers. But the *believing* sovereign is also a *sovereign*;[121] that is, he is a person who, before God, is *responsible* for the *spiritual and physical well-being* of those entrusted to him. And on this basis the sovereign is charged with the right and duty to see that the divine basic law is legally secured, both within the church and outside the church; that is, in the life of the church proper, and in the relationship of the church to the state. The two titles "sovereign" and "Christian" do not give the territorial sovereign authority to command and demand obedience from the congregations of his domain; they do not give him any power of control over the affairs of the church. But they do *authorize* the sovereign, even more, they *obligate* him, to a responsible cooperation with the church of his territory in setting up and administering constitutional church government.[122]

In developing a basis for the sovereign's cura religionis, Rurer like Luther emphasizes the two titles "sovereign" and "Christian"; he ignores, however, Luther's third principle, the "emergency situation." Luther argues that the church is exposed to an emergency situation, since the church itself, through its officials, refuses to undertake the necessary actions to correct the unconstitutionality within the church. Henceforth the sovereign, whom God has charged with the responsibilities of secular

118. See p. 153 n. 33.
119. For Luther, see Holl, pp. 329 ff.; Heckel I, pp. 136 ff.
120. For Luther, see Heckel I, p. 139 n. 1139: "Eine Obrigkeit mit einer Befehlsgewalt wie im weltlichen Recht gibt es im Kirchenwesen nicht."
121. About a decade after Rurer II, Melanchthon expressed this thought in the term *praecipuum membrum ecclesiae*, which he adopted from the imperial law; see Heckel II, pp. 24 ff.; for the roots in Luther, see *WA* VI, 413, ll. 27 ff.; Holl, *op. cit.*, pp. 333 ff., 349 ff.
122. For further details, see Excursus V.

government, has to step in as *Notbischof*.[123] Rurer does not say that it is actually the task of the church (that is, of the bishops) to create new ecclesiastical law, or that, since the church refuses to fulfill this obligation, the Christian sovereign can and must step into this situation. But all of Rurer's statements must be seen against the background of the situation in which the church found itself.[124] Rurer tries to impress his reader with the fact that the papal church is failing to fulfill its obligation, both in the area of theology and of ecclesiastical law; even more, that the officials of this church stubbornly refuse to improve the situation although admonished to do so. Consequently the officials of the church are guilty before God, and this guilt will extend over land and people.[125] The congregation of true believers is at hand, however, and seeks the sovereign's legal protection.

Rurer is not an idealist; he clearly envisions the possibility that the sovereign would not come to the "true" faith. Even then the sovereign is obligated to exercise the cura religionis; its nature, however, is basically different. The *unbelieving sovereign is obligated to tolerate* the evangelical preaching and *to protect* the evangelical preachers; he is obligated to secure the divine basic law of the church *outside* the church, that is, in the relationship of the church to the state. The reason for this sounds quite modern. It is a religiously interpreted essence of the state; should the sovereign refuse to fulfill his obligation, then the territory will be exposed to divine judgment; that is, without religion on the part of the people, a state cannot exist in peace and good order, and chaos replaces them.[126] The sovereign who does not believe is, however, not endowed with the privilege of exercising the three fundamental rights of the Christian. Therefore, he is not authorized to participate in the creation of new ecclesiastical law and in the administration of the affairs of the church.[127] Since Rurer wants to

123. For Luther, see Heckel I, p. 196; L. W. Spitz, "Luther's Ecclesiology and his Concept of the Prince as *Notbischof*," *Church History*, XXII (1953), 113 ff.; for Melanchthon, see Heckel II, 6 ff., 24 ff.

124. E.g., Rurer II, pp. 26 ff., 31.

125. Rurer II, pp. 23, 26 f., 35, 37.

126. Rurer II, pp. 21, 35 f.; then, on p. 37 (see p. 188, position [c]), appears the admonition of the sovereign to study God's Word and come to faith. Rurer here anticipated the religiously colored secularism of our age, in which a touch of religion is added to many secular events.

127. For Rurer, just as for Luther, secular governments do not have religious functions; consequently the cura religionis and the ius reformandi of the imperial Estates cannot be coordinated without qualifications. For Rurer it is *politically wise* that the sovereign exercise the cura religionis (Melanchthon's *conservatio religionis*; see Heckel III, p. 323). This cura is not combined with the ius reformandi, the privilege of the sovereign to enact ecclesiastical reforms (a privilege which has been constitutionally guaranteed by

gain the sovereign for the "true" faith, he does not make this last statement, but it is the necessary outgrowth of his whole argument.

V. Conclusion

Rurer II, with *Wendelsteiner Kirchenordnung* and *Ansbach I*, are the main documents dealing with the relationship of the state to the church as it was envisioned by the evangelicals[1] of the margraviate in the period from 1524 to 1526. These documents also set forth the plans of the Ansbach reformers for an evangelical ecclesiastical law and for the organization of the church on Reformation principles. The historian and theologian would like to have more material available, especially concerning the details of ecclesiastical organization. Nevertheless the material that is available gives a clear though sometimes quite sketchy picture of the aims of the evangelicals.

In the fall of 1524 (*Wendelsteiner Kirchenordnung, Ansbach I*) the evangelicals of the margraviate had high expectations regarding the religious position of their sovereign, Margrave Casimir, and the help he could and actually would give to the cause of the gospel. They also sought a congregational form of church-polity, according to which the organizational structure of the congregation would be determined by the believers themselves. But as early as the first *Ansbacher Landtag* (September, 1524) the evangelicals must have recognized that these plans would not materialize swiftly. Nevertheless they continued to hope for the support of the margrave (*Flugschrift*); and Rurer even worked out a basis for the cura religionis and the ius reformandi of the territorial sovereign, while strictly maintaining the legal autonomy of the church in the frame of the divine basic law (Rurer II).

The basic difference between Rurer's position and Margrave Casimir's plans is clear if one recalls the latter's maneuvers. The margrave's

---

the Diet of Augsburg in 1555). For Rurer the cura religionis is combined with the ius reformandi *only* if the sovereign is a truly believing Christian; and even then it is not an ius that can be enforced; see Excursus V. On the ius reformandi, see M. Heckel, "Staat und Kirche nach den Lehren der evangelischen Juristen Deutschlands in der ersten Hälfte des 17. Jahrhunderts," *ZRG*. Kan. Abt., LXXIII (1956), 117 ff.; LXXIV (1957), 202 ff.; see also U. Stutz, "Höchstes Regal," *ZRG*. Kan. Abt., XII (1922), 416 ff.; Heckel III, pp. 321, 393 ff.; DuCange, *s.v.*, Reformator.

1. The details of the relationship of Luther to the Ansbach reformers has to be investigated still further than Schmidt (*FB*) and Guszmann (*op. cit.*) have done.

ambition had been to replace the authority of the Franconian bishops with that of the territorial sovereign. He wanted to conclude the development which had begun in the latter middle ages (oath of loyalty to be signed by the priest) and organize the *landesherrliche Kirchenregiment,* thus closing his territory to any outside legal interference in ecclesiastical affairs. The substance of the church of his territory was unimportant to Casimir. On the basis of the resolution of the third *Ansbacher Landtag* (October, 1526) it is obvious, however, that this territorial church was papal in character, if we bypass some minor concessions to the evangelicals. To fulfill his ambitions, Casimir sometimes ruthlessly used the cura religionis which the representatives of the Reformation had attributed to him; he could not have cared less, however, for the responsibilities which were combined with this cura religionis. For the Ansbach reformers the cura religionis had a religious nature: toleration and protection of the Reformation, as in 1524–25; toleration, protection, and responsible cooperation on the basis of a personal religious decision (1526). Casimir, as a typical renaissance sovereign, saw in the cura religionis the possibility to subordinate the church to his government. The margrave aimed for a state church, and thus he anticipated the church-form which developed in England under Henry VIII, a few years after Casimir's death.[2] The representatives of the Reformation aimed for a new ecclesiastical organization, protected by the state, but free from any state control;[3] on the basis of available evidence it seems that such a solution could have settled the religious and legal chaos that had developed in the margraviate. The imbalance of these two principles overshadowed the last years of Casimir's life and condemned his religious policies to failure. The situation did not change until the end of 1527, when Casimir's brother, Margrave George, whom history has called the Pious, took over the government of Brandenburg-Ansbach-Kulmbach.[4]

2. It would be interesting to compare the legal and theological settlement of the Reformation created by the third Ansbacher Landtag, October, 1526, with the situation created by Henry VIII in England.

3. See Excursus V.

4. I am presently investigating the relationship of the state to the church in 1528, the first year of the rule of the Margrave George.

EXCURSUS I

LUTHER ON THE FINANCES OF A PARISH

In the middle ages the income of the individual parish came predominantly from three sources.[1] The first was a special tax levied upon all members of the parish, and the fees charged for ministerial acts. The second was the income derived from basic endowment, such as real estate, or the right to collect highway or bridge tolls, water rights, mining rights, etc. Individual contributions, either as cash gifts or as endowments (altar foundations), formed the third source of income; such contributions were designated as stipends for priests hired exclusively to celebrate mass. The entire income was administered solely by the clergy, and not always in the most correct ways. On the other hand, secular authorities (city councils, knights, barons, dukes, and kings) sometimes partially controlled the church finances if they were patrons, that is, if they had endowed a parish and yet had retained some control over it, or had hired the priests for their private service, or were responsible for their livelihood in one way or the other.[2] One of the points of irritation among the clergy themselves, and between clergy and laity, was a just distribution of the money among the clergy.[3] The more important problem, however, was the care of the sick and underprivileged in the parish—a problem not always successfully handled by the local clergy. Toward the end of the middle ages, therefore, religiously minded individuals, or independent religious brotherhoods, or even secular authorities, gradually stepped into the field of charities.[4]

The Reformation had to face the necessity of organizing a proper administration of the finances of the parish and of setting up a proper

1. On the financial structure of the church in the middle ages see, e.g., W. E. Lunt, *Papal Revenues in the Middle Ages*; 2 vols. (New York, 1934); J. Lederer, "Finanzwesen, kirchliches," *Lexikon für Theologie und Kirche*; 2d ed. (Freiburg, 1957 ff.), IV, cols. 133 ff.

2. The oath of loyalty demanded by the margraves of Brandenburg-Ansbach of their clergy originated in this situation; see p. 150 n. 23.

3. See e.g., the *Epistola de misera curatorum seu plebanorum*, published in 1489; see Hashagen, *op. cit.*, pp. 283 f.; A. Werminghoff, "Die Epistola de misera curatorum seu plebanorum," *Archiv f. Reformationsgeschichte*, XIII (1916), 200 ff.

4. Only studies oriented toward local history can document this. See, e.g., O. Winkelmann, *Das Fürsorgewesen der Stadt Strassburg vor und nach der Reformation bis zum Ausgang des sechzehnten Jahrhunderts* (Leipzig, 1922); Th. Stark, *Die christliche Wohltätigkeit im Mittelalter und in der Reformationszeit in den ostschwäbischen Reichsstädten*, EAKGB, IV (1926).

system for the care of the local poor and sick. Luther's radical criticism of the mass and of the understanding of charities and begging as means of "obtaining" salvation [5] raised the question of the proper use of available funds. The situation was more complicated than it might seem at first glance. In addition to Luther's criticism, which undermined the traditional structure of ecclesiastical finances, there was the eagerness of some secular Estates to confiscate as much of the church's wealth as possible.[6] And finally, many laymen, "freed from the yoke of the papal church" and abusing this freedom, refused to pay tithes and rents.[7]

Luther was convinced that it was the right and duty of the local parish, the congregation of the believers, to set up a system of handling the finances of the parish. According to Luther, the administration of the finances of the parish has to serve the spiritual center of the parish (that is, the preaching of the Word and the administration of the sacraments), has to guarantee the fundamental rights of a Christian (equality, freedom, and brotherly love),[8] and has to be conducted in an orderly fashion. This right of the parish superseded all other previous legal arrangements concerning finances in particular, and concerning the structure of parish life in general.[9]

The *Ordnung der Stat Wittenberg* (*Wittenberg City Ordinance*) of January, 1522[10]—which was drawn up by Andrew Carlstadt[11] but was based on some of Luther's suggestions—pulled all ecclesiastical finances of Wittenberg into a Common Chest, which was to be placed under the control of both laymen and clergy; its revenues were to be used exclusively for paying salaries of the clergy, maintaining buildings, and administering charities. According to this ordinance, the church finances in Wittenberg were to

5. See e.g., *WA*, VIII, 411 ff.; *LW*, XXXVI, 133 ff.; *WA*, VI, 512 ff.; *LW*, XXXVI, 35 ff.; *WA*, VI, 450 f.; *Works of Martin Luther*; Holman Ed. (Philadelphia, 1915), II, 134 ff.; *WA*, II, 742 ff.; *LW*, XXXV, 49 ff. For Luther's opposition to begging, see especially his *Long Sermon on Usury* (1520), *LW*, XLV, 281 ff., 286 ff.

6. A good example would be the situation in Leisnig (see below p. 199 n. 13), where the city council refused to release certain funds to the Common Chest.

7. In 1523 Luther, e.g., complained about the unwillingness of certain people to pay their ground-rents to the Wittenberg Augustinian monastery, and about the hardship which resulted from this; see *WA*, Br, III, Nos. 681, 687. The visitation in electoral Saxony uncovered many cases of delinquencies in the payment of rents and tithes; see, e.g., *WA*, Br, III, No. 950.

8. See p. 153 n. 33.

9. See especially Luther's *Address to the Christian Nobility of Germany* (1520).

10. *Die evangelischen Kirchenordnungen des sechzehnten Jahrhunderts*, ed. Ae. Richter (Weimar, 1846), II, 484 f.

11. On Carlstadt, see *LW*, XLVIII, 79 n. 12.

be handled by parties who were responsible to secular authorities (to the city council and to the department of revenue of the electoral government). It is interesting to observe that the cities, both the free imperial cities and those which were under the authority of a territorial ruler, were most eager to follow this example set by Wittenberg. In the early years of the 1520s many cities,[12] therefore, adopted ordinances for a Common Chest; among them was Leisnig, a small town in Electoral Saxony. The Leisnig Ordinance of a Common Chest was drawn up in fall of 1522 by the people of that town upon Luther's recommendations; the Reformer wholeheartedly approved of the ordinance in January, 1523, and published it together with a preface in spring of that year.[13] The Leisnig Ordinance deals not only with matters of congregational finances but with the whole organization of congregational life; consequently it is "almost a rudimentary congregational constitution."[14] In addition to the importance this ordinance has for the structure of congregational life, it gives insight into the understanding and structure of the community's welfare program. Rejecting begging and charities as means of "obtaining" salvation, Luther and the people of Leisnig affirmed[15] the community's responsibility to care for the socially underprivileged; the community has, however, also the duty to see to it that no dependence of the poor on the community can develop. The poor person has to be decently sustained by the Common Chest, but only in order to get him back on his own feet, so that he is able to take again his place in the community and share in its burdens. It was strongly emphasized that charity is never to deteriorate to a "handout," but that it is to be considered a "free loan" granted to the brother in need; in accepting charity the individual affirms his responsibility to share in the community's burden by "repaying" the loan, if and when he is able.

12. E.g., Augsburg, Nuremberg, Altenburg, Kitzingen, Strassburg, Breslau, Regensburg. For details, see *WA*, XII, 2; O. Winkelmann, "Die Armenordnungen von Nürnberg (1522), Kitzingen (1523), Regensburg (1523) und Ypern (1525)," *Archiv f. Reformationsgeschichte*, X (1912/13), 242 ff.; XI (1914), 1 ff. See also Grimm, *op. cit.* (p. 146 n. 4), and B. Möller, *Reichsstadt und Reformation* (Gütersloh, 1962; rev.: *ZBayKG*, XXXI [1962]), 254 ff. To what degree do these ordinances hang together? How much were they influenced by the Leisnig Ordinance? How much did Luther directly influence these ordinances? As far as I am able to determine, these questions are not yet completely answered.

13. For a detailed report on the situation in Leisnig and Luther's relationship to the ordinance, see W. I. Brandt, in *LW*, XLV, 161 ff. For the text of the ordinance, see *LW*, XLV, 176; for Luther's preface, see *ibid.*, 169 ff.

14. Brandt, *LW*, XLV, 162.

15. *LW*, XLV, 171 f., 173 f., 185 f., 189 ff.

EXCURSUS II

OBSERVATIONS ON THE TEXT OF THE RESOLUTION OF
THE SECOND ANSBACHER LANDTAG, APRIL, 1525

In the resolution of the second Ansbacher Landtag (April, 1525), it is
stated that the subjects of the margrave do

> not have to rebel or gather [in protest] because [they want the
> preaching of the gospel in its purity]. For it is generally known, and
> it is also true, that our Gracious Lord, Margrave Casimir . . . not
> only tolerates the fact that throughout His Grace's . . . territories the
> Holy Gospel and Word of God is preached clearly and purely, *sonder
> auch* [continuation from "not only" in the preceding part of this
> sentence] *solchs allenthalben zu tan ernstlich bevolhen haben* [subject:
> Casimir].[1]

The phrase given in the original poses some problems since it is not clear
with which preceding word, or group of words, "*solchs*" is to be connected;
consequently the object of "*zu tan*" is also unclear. In addition there is a
switch in tense; the first part of the sentence would have to be paraphrased as follows: The margrave does not only tolerate the pure[2]
preaching of the gospel, but he even *has* commanded that the gospel be
preached in all purity. As a result this statement would have to be
understood as an endorsement of the Reformation on the basis of a command already issued. This interpretation is apparently assumed by
Simon, who sees in this resolution a "*Genehmigung*" for preaching the
gospel as the reformers understood it.[3] He is apparently unaware, however, that linguistically this is not the only possible interpretation of this
sentence; he further overlooks the change in the tenses of the two parts of
the sentence.

In analyzing this sentence Simon simply does not adhere to the text.
To begin with the most obvious, when did Casimir command that God's
Word be preached in its purity so that he can now refer back to such a

1. *FKO*, p. 82.
2. I.e., as the reformers understood it.
3. *FKO*, p. 67.

command? Does Simon think of the formula in the resolution of the first Ansbacher Landtag (October, 1524)?[4] Then he would not only completely misunderstand this formula,[5] but he would also be contradicting himself, for he had already stated[6] that this October, 1524, resolution is *only* an affirmation of the resolution of the Nuremberg diet and not an endorsement of the Reformation. Simon takes an easy way out by arguing that here, in the resolution of the second Ansbacher Landtag (April, 1525), the margrave *exaggerated concerning the past*; that Casimir never really did command the gospel to be preached in all its purity (an argument which needs to be qualified in view of the resolution of the first Ansbacher Landtag, otherwise it remains highly ambiguous); but rather that, concerning the future, the margrave would act permissively. Simon does not say *what* this permission was for, but his whole argument demands the assumption that Casimir gave permission for the future preaching of God's Word as the reformers understood it. But in *this part of the sentence there is not a word said about the future*! Therefore it seems to me dangerous to read into this resolution a permission to preach the gospel as the reformers understood it. In addition to the general linguistic ambiguity, the terms "gospel" and "pure preaching" are not qualified, a fact which Simon does point out; having made this observation, he does, however, draw no conclusions from it for the interpretation of the text. Further, the question must be asked why Casimir, on February 4, 1525, a short time prior to this resolution, rejected the petitions of the cities in his territory to introduce the Reformation officially through the abolishment of the celebration of the mass?[7] Would Casimir have changed his stand in such a short time? And if so, why? Simon apparently wants to use *Flugschrift*[8] to justify this change in Casimir's stand, since he dates this pamphlet prior to this Landtag resolution, but after the cities had petitioned Casimir.[9] Whether this date can be upheld is unimportant.[10] But Casimir was too firm and unbending to have reacted to a proclamation of the people, as we have it in *Flugschrift*, in such a radical fashion. It is closer to actuality to see in this resolution not an endorsement of, or a concession to, the Reformation, but rather a political move by which Casimir wanted to lure the progressives to his side and play them against the social unrest in the territory.

4. See p. 164.
5. See p. 159.
6. *FKO*, p. 66.
7. *FKO*, p. 67; Schornbaum I, pp. 64 f.
8. See p. 180 n. 61.
9. *FKO*, p. 67.
10. See p. 167 n. 60.

This interpretation can be supported with the text of the resolution. "*Solchs . . . allenthalben zu tan*" can be connected with "gospel and Word of God," and not with "preaching." Then it would have to be paraphrased: Casimir not only tolerates the preaching of the gospel and the Word of God in its purity—how far this is true, or whether Casimir exaggerates here would be a matter all by itself—but he *has also commanded* that the Word of God *be done* throughout his territories, that is, be put into practice. Casimir would repeat here a command to the subjects to live an evangelical life; and this would mean, in view of the historical background of the second Ansbacher Landtag—the Peasants' War—that the subjects should practice that obedience owed by the Christian to the secular government.[11] The order which is now repeated, and to which the past "*bevolhen haben*" refers, can be found in the resolution issued by the first Ansbacher Landtag. Here it is pointed out that the preachers should preach, and that all subjects should act, so that no unrest is caused.[12] And in the concluding paragraph of this resolution the obedience owed by the Christian to the governing authorities is emphasized as (both religious and secular) *duty* of the individual. This is the order to which the resolution of the second Ansbacher Landtag refers when it states that the margrave *has commanded* that the subjects "*do*" the Word of God.

11. Rurer I confirms this interpretation; see pp. 164 f.
12. See *FKO*, p. 80, col. 2, par. 3.

EXCURSUS III

THE RESOLUTION OF THE THIRD ANSBACHER LANDTAG, OCTOBER, 1526

The resolution of the third Ansbacher Landtag (October 10, 1526)[1] secured the papal church in its essential parts: Latin language for the mass, even for the *verba consecrationis*; the tabernacle; auricular confession; the countless holidays of the church; foundations and endowments for ecclesiastical purposes; votive masses; religious brotherhoods; and celibacy—all this was maintained. There were some few concessions to the evangelical progressives: German language for the Epistle and Gospel in the mass, loud and clear recitation of the *verba consecrationis* in Latin, permission to sing German hymns during the mass, abolishment of payments for pastoral services, freedom for sponsors to decide which language should be used for baptism—if the liturgy was in Latin, then a sermon in German should be added—and there was to be a pastoral admonition in German prior to confession. In addition to these stipulations, the resolution urged that both laity and clergy intensify their religious commitment.

There were two major concessions to the evangelicals:[2] permission to celebrate the Lord's Supper by giving both the bread and the wine to the laity, and a new evaluation of the fast-regulations. The permission to give the cup to the laity was based on the resolution of the Diet of Speyer.[3] Concerning the fast-regulations, it was pointed out that they were to be maintained, but their meaning was qualified: The essential purpose of fasting is not to expose anyone to dangers of body and soul, or to cause sin to be committed if the fast-regulations were not maintained, but rather to help the earnest Christian to chasten and subdue his body; consequently the pastors were to admonish their people to fast, but they were not to threaten the people with punishments, or with loss of salvation, if the regulations were not properly fulfilled.[4] The margrave here

1. *FKO*, pp. 88 ff.

2. These two concessions constitute the only substantiation for Ranke's argument (I, Part II, 270 [p. 470]) that this resolution has an evangelical bent, an argument which does not do justice to this resolution in its other points.

3. See Ranke I, Part II, 208 ff. (pp. 417 ff.).

4. See *FKO*, p. 93.

adopted the idea of the Christian's freedom [5] in order to break the grip of the papal church over the laity at a very important point. The fast-regulations kept the people under the spiritual (matter of sin) and legal (matter of punishment) domination of the papal church, and Casimir acted against this domination with the statements of the resolution.

The resolution stabilized the rule of the territorial sovereign over the church: The sovereign regulates faith and liturgy in his country. He commands the preachers "to preach the sacred gospel and Word of God . . . clearly and purely . . . and nothing else which is contrary [to the gospel]." [6] He prohibits heresy, pulpit quarrels, and all disputations concerned with religious issues. He supervises the finances of the church, he secularizes property of the church, yet he also promises to return property to the monasteries, should they be in need of it. He places laity and clergy on an equal level regarding the civil burdens, and taxes the clergy directly. He goes even further and has a German liturgy for baptism prepared, which could be used if the sponsors so desire. [7] He reserves for himself the right to approve all clergymen who are to function in the territory and subordinates them to the authority of his courts. [8]

With this resolution, which was the law of the land, Casimir intended to organize the church in his territory on the basis of the resolution of the 1526 Diet of Speyer. [9] The resolution of the Landtag was intended to keep the Franconian bishops out of the ecclesiastical affairs of the margraviate. The resolution was not to protect or help either the evangelicals or the traditionalists, but was rather to stabilize the *landesherrliche Kirchenregiment*. The clause that the resolution should be valid only until a general council of the church had spoken on all issues was, in view of the basic nature of the resolution and the past conduct of the margrave, of minor importance. The resolution was so utterly useless—it neither stabilized the ecclesiastical situation in the territory, nor did it satisfy the bishops— that Margrave George, Casimir's successor, felt compelled to clarify the resolution during his first Landtag in March, 1528. [10]

5. See p. 153 n. 33.

6. *FKO*, p. 89. Casimir's statements concerning the liturgy and religious life (see above, at the beginning of this excursus) make it clear beyond doubt, however, that he did not take this phrase to be an endorsement of the Reformation.

7. Text: *FKO*, pp. 98 ff.

8. *FKO*, pp. 89 f.

9. See *FKO*, p. 88, and Casimir's letter to his brother Margrave George of October 15, 1525; Schornbaum I, pp. 104 f.

10. See Schornbaum II, pp. 14 f.

EXCURSUS IV

POTESTAS ECCLESIASTICA AND *IURISDICTIA ECCLESIASTICA* ACCORDING TO ROMAN CATHOLIC AND TO LUTHERAN UNDERSTANDING

Ecclesiastical law ˙combines religious and legal elements in church government.

Through the Holy Spirit, Christ is present in his church as the power which creates the church and gives life to its members, and as the power which rules the church. Based on this assumption, pre-Reformation and post-Reformation Roman theology differentiates between the church's *potestas ordinis* and *potestas iurisdictionis*. The iure divino exercised potestas ordinis, through baptism endows the individual with the immutable right of membership in the church, and through ordination endows the clergy with the hierarchically structured immutable ability to give to, or withhold from, the church's member Christ's life-giving power (that is, to shepherd the sheep by preaching and administering the sacraments); hence the differentiation between clergy and laity. The potestas iurisdictionis, the right to govern the church (*regere ecclesiam*) and make the necessary legal and administrative arrangements (both within and outside of the church)[1] for implementing the potestas ordinis, is restricted to the clergy, or more precisely, to the pope and the bishops. For them this potestas is established iure divino, while the "lower" clergy is entrusted with this power iure humano; that is, the clergy's potestas iurisdictionis is derived from the power of the bishops and of the pope. According to the curialistic theory as it was finally expressed by Vatican I, the potestas iurisdictionis is given iure divino alone to the pope as the vicar of Christ; according to the conciliar theory of the fifteenth century, this potestas is given iure divino to the pope *and* to the bishops. The power with which Christ has entrusted the church is the foundation of the *regimen ecclesiae*, which has two functions: the spiritual *and* the legal shepherding of the members of the church. These functions are exercised in the church iure divino, whereby the governing function is placed, however, in the

1. *CIC*, c. 196.

hierarchic structure which begins with the pope and ends with the lowest clergyman.[2]

The potestas iurisdictionis of the church forms the basis of the ecclesiastical jurisdiction. This jurisdiction is exercised iure divino by pope and bishops and is divided into administrative and disciplinary jurisdiction. According to *Codex Iuris Canonici*, cc. 1552, 1553, the ecclesiastical jurisdiction covers all cases for which ecclesiastical courts are competent. This competence is established iure divino and excludes any jurisdiction of state unless the church yields its jurisdiction to the state. The church has always claimed the right to punish any violation of its ordinances by either the clergy or the laity. As long as the church employed purely ecclesiastical or spiritual punishments, as in the early church, there was no conflict between state and church. Tensions had to develop, however, as soon as the church used worldly punishments and increasingly extended the competence of the ecclesiastical courts into the secular realm while at the same time demanding immunity from secular courts for clergy and church properties. Although points of friction can still arise today, the *Codex Iuris Canonici* and the concordats between the papal see and the secular governments have clearly established the competence of the ecclesiastical courts for *delicta mere ecclesiastica* and *causae spirituales* (sacraments, liturgy, doctrine). In order to avoid friction with the secular courts regarding issues dealing with ecclesiastical persons and properties, the *Codex Iuris Canonici* differentiates between the pure jurisdiction of the church and a jurisdiction *mixti fori*. Thus the point of great tension in the middle ages is somewhat clarified. In the early and high middle ages the church extended its jurisdiction increasingly into the secular, and this cannot be explained exclusively in terms of hunger for power, but must be seen against the background of the inefficient secular judicial system. In the high and later middle ages, the reverse occurred. The state extended its legal authority and increasingly jeopardized the ecclesiastical courts; this too cannot be explained exclusively as power hunger, but must be viewed

2. See DuCange, *s.v. Potestas, Rector* (1); Thomas Aquinas, *Sum. theol.*, Part II: 2, qu. 39, art. 3; Part III, qu. 63; *Catechismus Romanus*, Part II, cap. VII, qu. VI, VII; *Confutatio (Resp.* II, art. VII) of the *Confessio Augustana*: "Episcopos non solum habere potestatem ministerii verbi Dei, sed etiam potestatem regiminis et coercitativae correctionis ad dirigendum subditos in finem beautudinis aeternae. At potestatum autem regiminis requiritur potestas judicandi, definiendi, discernendi, et statuendi ea, quae ad praefatum finem expediunt et conducunt." See further H. Denzinger, K. Rahner, *Enchiridion symbolorum definitionum et declarationum de rebus fidei et morum*; 31st ed. (Freiburg, 1957), Nos. 570 ff., 717, 956 ff., 961 ff., 1821 ff., 1841; *CIC*, cc. 118–123, 196, 197, 199, 335, 948; Feine, *op. cit.*, pp. 42, 213 f., 546 ff.; M. Spinka, *Advocates of Reform from Wyclif to Erasmus*, The Library of Christian Classics, XIV (Philadelphia, 1953), 91 ff.; F. Vigener, *Bischofsamt und Papstgewalt*; 2d ed. (Göttingen, 1964).

against the background of the increasing complications in the ecclesiastical court procedures.[3]

The Lutheran Reformation sees the church iure divino endowed with one postestas, the *potestas clavium*, which is exercised in the *ministerium verbi*. This potestas constitutes the spiritual shepherding of the sheep (the preaching of the gospel, the administering of the sacraments, the forgiving and retaining of sins, the judging of doctrine, and the rejecting of that doctrine which is contrary to the gospel).[4] On the basis of the priesthood of all believers, this power is held by all believers and can be exercised by all faithful.[5] In order to avoid chaos, however, the believers call one out of their midst,[6] and charge him with exercising this potestas, without themselves relinquishing it. This charge, enacted iure humano,[7] endows the pastor with the power (granted to the church iure divino) to administer publicly the potestas clavium in his congregation, and makes him the spiritual shepherd. It also charges him with the responsibility of preparing and if necessary enforcing (in cooperation with the congregation)[8] good order by which the potestas clavium can be properly and best implemented; that is, this charge endows the pastor with the potestas iurisdictionis (which is strictly of iure humano origin) with governing the sheep, if necessary by force (excommunication).[9]

Consequently Sohm's argument (that the gospel suffices to govern the church and that *Kirchenregiment* for the Lutheran Reformation is only the spiritual shepherding of the sheep) cannot be maintained, as has been

3. See DuCange, *s.v. Iudicare, Poenitentia, Judicium* (3), *Ius ecclesiasticum*; *CIC*, cc. 100 (par. 1), 119–123, 1933, 2198, 2214, 2223, 2341; Hashagen, *op. cit.*, pp. 205 ff.; Feine, *op. cit.*, pp. 120 ff., 182 ff., 213 ff., 294 ff., 433 ff., 699 ff.; Heckel III, pp. 454 ff.; W. Bertrams, *Der neuzeitliche Staatsgedanke und die Konkordate des ausgehenden Mittelalters*; 2d ed. (Rome, 1950); J. J. Baierl, *The Catholic Church and the Modern State* (Rochester, 1956); C. Zollmann, *American Civil Church Law* (New York, 1917).

4. *Confessio Augustana*, Arts. VII, XIV, XXVIII, paragraphs 5, 21.

5. See Melanchthon's *De potestate et primatu papae tractatus*, paragraphs 22 ff.; *The Book of Concord*, ed. Th. Tappert (Philadelphia, 1959), pp. 323 ff.

6. See also p. 151.

7. *Confessio Augustana*, Art. XIV.

8. See p. 175.

9. *Confessio Augustana*, Arts. XV, XXVIII, paragraphs 53 ff.; E. Schlink, *Theology of the Lutheran Confessions* (Philadelphia, 1961), pp. 229 ff.; Kinder, *op. cit.* (p. 174 n. 27). On the New Testament and early church background, see H. von Campenhausen, *Die Begründung kirchlicher Entscheidungen beim Apostel Paulus*; 2d ed. (Heidelberg, 1965); E. Schweizer, *Church Order in the New Testament* (London, 1961); L. Goppelt, "Kirchenleitung in der palästinischen Urkirche und bei Paulus," *Reformatio und Confessio. Festschr. f. Wilhelm Maurer*, ed. F. W. Kantzenbach, *et al.* (Berlin, 1965), pp. 1 ff., and H. Dombois, "Altkirchliche und evangelische Kirchenverfassung," *ZevKR*, II (1952), 1 ff.; on Schweizer's work, see D. Stoodt, "Schrift und Kirchenrecht," *ZevKR*, VIII (1961), 340 ff.

pointed out repeatedly.[10] It was Sohm's great merit, however, to have demonstrated that the Lutheran Reformation had both a narrow and a broad understanding of *Kirchenregiment*, of governing the church.[11] According to the narrow understanding of the term, the church is "governed" by the Word of God alone, through the potestas clavium, and this has nothing to do with legalities or force, but is exclusively a work of grace. According to the broad understanding of this term, the church as a social entity is governed by the potestas iurisdictionis, by legalities and force. Luther made it quite clear that these powers have nothing to do with one another, and should not be mixed, or allowed to overlap, although they are necessary for the existence of the church in the world and coexist in one person (the pastor or the bishop). Due to the circumstances of the time (especially in view of the mounting resistance of the Roman church to the constitutional use of the potestas iurisdictionis within itself), the Lutheran Reformation was forced to entrust *Kirchenregiment* as a legal-administrative operation to the secular government. Luther was well aware, however, that this was only a temporary solution to the problems due to an emergency situation that existed in the church.[12] The Lutheran Reformation was further aware that the pastoral office has two functions: iure divino to shepherd the sheep spiritually, iure humano to shepherd the sheep legally in the framework of the parish. Thus the Lutheran pastor is both pastor and bishop.[13] He holds the potestas clavium and the potestas iurisdictionis (of the bishop in the Roman church, though this potestas is differently described) the former iure divino, sharing it with all Christians, the latter iure humano, so that the pastor is set aside from the rest of the congregation, not to dominate it but to serve it within the framework of the divine basic law of the church.

The potestas iurisdictionis is exercised in a unique way by the shepherd of both shepherds and sheep, the bishop. The Lutheran bishop shares, iure divino, with his fellow pastors and Christian laymen the potestas clavium. But iure humano, in order to establish good order in the church

10. See e.g., K. Rieker, *Die rechtliche Stellung der evangelischen Kirche Deutschlands* (Leipzig, 1893), pp. 100 ff.; see also W. D. Marsch, "Ist das Recht eine notwendige Funktion der Kirche?" *ZevKR*, V (1956), 117 ff.; Heckel I, pp. 13 ff., 196; see also p. 141 n. 2.

11. *Confessio Augustana*, Art, XIV, German Text: "*Das Kirchenregiment*." This phrase is translated in *Book of Concord* (*op. cit.*) if not incorrectly, then at least weakly as "Order in the Church."

12. See p. 192.

13. See p. 175.

at large and supervise its execution, the bishop is singled out to exercise the potestas iurisdictionis over pastors and parishioners, again not to dominate them, but rather to serve them within the framework of the divine basic law of the church, so that the potestas clavium is properly and best implemented.[14]

14. See W. Maurer, *Das synodale evangelische Bischofsamt seit 1918. Fuldaer Hefte: Schrif. d. Theologischen Konvents Augsburgischen Bekenntnisses*, X (1955); P. Brunner, "Vom Amt des Bischofs," *Schrif. d. Theologischen Konvents Augsburgischen Bekenntnisses*, IX (1955), 5 ff.

EXCURSUS V

THE EVANGELICALS AND THE BEGINNINGS OF THE *LANDESHERRLICHE KIRCHENREGIMENT* IN THE MARGRAVIATE

The decisive passage in Rurer II reads: "Befelhen und schaffen E.F.G. auch in jren Fürstenthumben . . . das das wort gotts eintrechtiglich geprediget, Vnd eynhellige Euangelische . . . ordnung nach gelenheyt . . . einer yeglichen . . . gemeyn souil müglich gehalten werde."[1] This could of course mean that in this phrase the roots of the future development were hidden, so that here some kind of commanding or supervisory privilege would be ascribed to the sovereign. Were this so, the church would thereby be robbed of its constitutional right to create its own law for its earthly existence; force, an element alien to the nature of the church, could thus penetrate the ecclesiastical law. Rurer would then here already be the caesaropapist he was called[2] on the basis of some of his later statements. Rurer II, however, does not support this interpretation.

To begin with, "befelhen" means to order or command, and this seems to make our argument impossible. However "befelhen" is coordinated with "schaffen," a word of two principle meanings. In the southwestern (Swabian) area of Germany "schaffen" meant then to work at a task, to create, to be actively involved in a task; in the southeastern (Bavarian-Austrian) area "schaffen" meant to order, to command, to organize.[3] Since Rurer II originated in Franconia, which was more closely aligned to the southwestern (Swabian) area of Germany, the first meaning of "schaffen" is the appropriate one.[4] Rurer apparently wanted to say that the sovereign should command, that is, promote, and be actively involved in the creation of new ecclesiastical law through co-operation rather than force; for the "befelhen" and "schaffen" are at

1. Rurer II, p. 38; see p. 188, position (*e*).
2. So by Schmidt (*FB*, p. 132), and by Guszmann (*op. cit.* I, Part I, 65 f., 67 f.).
3. Luther, e.g., used both these meanings; see *WA*, XII, 328, l. 16, and his translations of Gen. 1 : 1, Lev. 11 : 32, Num. 4 : 12. When Luther used *schaffen*, he usually used it in the sense of "working at."
4. See F. Kluge, *Etymologisches Wörterbuch der deutschen Sprache*; 11th ed. (Berlin, 1934), *s.v. schaffen*; A. Götze, *Frühneuhochdeutsches Glossar*; 5th ed. (Berlin, 1956), *s.v. schaffen*; *Trübners Deutsches Wörterbuch, s.v. schaffen.*

once qualified through the phrase "according to the opportunities and desires of the local congregations." Rurer did not envision force as the propelling power in the process of creating a new ecclesiastical law, but rather cooperation between congregation and sovereign: the sovereign does not *rule* the church by decree, but *serves* the church with his executive machinery. This fact has to be maintained, even though it must be granted that Rurer did not clearly state the limits of the sovereign's jurisdiction, nor did he give any details as to how this cooperation should be put into operation. Rurer did not elaborate on the differentiation between the sovereign's spiritual power (that is, the sovereign's right as a believing Christian to help in creating new ecclesiastical law), and the sovereign's secular, official power. Here, then, are indeed some of the roots of the further development of the state-church relationship which culminated in the *landesherrliche Kirchenregiment*. Nevertheless Heckel's statement that Luther did not belong to the forefathers of the landesherrliche Kirchenregiment[5] can also be applied to Rurer, although the statement has to be somewhat modified: Rurer was not striving for the landesherrliche Kirchenregiment because he was deeply convinced of the legal independence of the church. Rurer did not say anything about how the new ecclesiastical law was to be established (and this was not unique with him). For Rurer, the questions concerning the "how" belonged to the future; the present, however, demanded protection while the "corrupt" Canon Law was being abolished, and the sovereign was the only person who could grant this protection. Therefore Rurer sought refuge for the emerging church in the power of the sovereign, and he was willing to turn the existence of the church in the world over to the sovereign, *provided that the sovereign was a believing member of this church.* To which other secular power should Rurer have gone for protection? He was no optimist concerning the sovereign's position and plans; Rurer's thoughts were also not shaped by the pastor's desire to avoid legal and administrative tasks and to dedicate himself exclusively to the care of souls.[6] Rurer's arguments have to be seen against the background of the emergency situation which existed in the church due to the anticonstitutional—because it was contrary to the divine basic law of the church[7]—character of the Canon Law, the need for protection of the evangelical preachers and parishioners against harassment by the papal church, and a patriarchic understanding of the nature of the sovereign's office.

5. Heckel I, p. 194.
6. See Schmidt, *FB*, p. 134, on the basis of some of Rurer's later statements.
7. See p. 174.

How little some of the evangelical pastors of the territory, and some laymen, were thinking of the landesherrliche Kirchenregiment at that time may be seen from the detailed steps taken toward the development of a new ecclesiastical law and a new ecclesiastical organization. For the legalities concerning the pastor and his office, one must refer to the basic statements in the *Wendelsteiner Kirchenordnung* and *Ansbach I*. Beginnings of a reorganization of the chapter-meetings (the gathering of pastors in a certain area) may also be found. Bernhard Wurtzelmann, pastor in Dinkelsbühl,[8] gave considerable thought to the reorganization of the chapter-meetings, and asked Andreas Osiander in Nuremberg to draft a constitution for the chapters.[9] In connection with the first Brandenburg-Nuremberg Church Visitation in 1528/29, Adam Weisz[10] attempted to revive the brotherhoods of pastors, as well as the chapter-meetings. According to his plan, the pastors of a certain area would be organized into a pastors' conference which would elect the *superintendent* (dean or district president); he was to be entrusted, among other things, with the responsibility of the *censura fratrum*. The last article of the 1528 Church-Ordinance of Brandenburg-Ansbach-Kulmbach did envision the office of superintendent;[11] but unfortunately this concept was of little value, since the functions of this office were not clearly defined, and above all since no financial means were available to establish this office and make it work.[12]

How little on the other hand the politicians trusted the abilities of the clergy, and how strongly the government felt the need to step into the affairs of the church,[13] may be seen from a document drawn up by Hans von Schwarzenberg[14] during the Diet of Augsburg, 1525. According to

8. On Wurtzelmann, see *Pfarrerbuch der Reichsstädte Dinkelsbühl, Schweinfurt, Weiszenburg i.B. und Windsheim sowie der Reichsdörfer Gochsheim und Sennfeld*, ed. M. Simon, *EAKGB*, XXXIX (1962), 16, No. 76.

9. See Th. Kolde, "Andreas Osianders Entwurf eines für die Kapitelsversammlungen," *BBayKG*, IX (1903), 36 ff.

10. On Weisz, see p. 147 n. 10.

11. *FKO*, p. 139.

12. For details, see *FKO*, pp. 116, 294; G. Bossert, "Die ersten Schritte zur Neuordnung der Kapitel in der Markgrafschaft Brandenburg-Ansbach, 1528 ff.," *Blätter f. Bayrische Kirchengeschichte*, I (1887/88), 33 ff.; F. Vogtherr, "Die Verfassung der Evangelisch-Lutherischen Kirche in den ehemaligen Fürstentümern Ansbach und Bayreuth," *BBayKG*, II (1896), 211 ff.

13. As a first step, the clergy was to be allowed to marry; ecclesiastical finances were to be reorganized; the episcopal jurisdiction was to be checked by the state, and perhaps even eliminated completely.

14. On von Schwarzenberg, see p. 147 n. 12.

Schornbaum,[15] the final draft of this document is in the Nuremberg State Archive, *Ansbacher Religionsakten* 1, II, fols. 16–22; Schwarzenberg's autograph with corrections by Vogler is deposited in the *Ansbacher Religionsakten* 11, fols. 59–68. In this document Schwarzenberg presented a plan for creating a state-church with a Protestant orientation.

Between 1524 and 1526 we find, then, in the margraviate three interpretations of the relationship of the state to the church: (*a*) State-church and landesherrliches Kirchenregiment, without affirmation of Protestant theology, liturgy, and religious life (Casimir 1524–25), with affirmation of papal theology, liturgy, and religious life (Casimir in 1526). (*b*) State-church and landesherrliches Kirchenregiment with affirmation of Protestant theology, liturgy, and religious life (Schwarzenberg). (*c*) Legal independence of the Protestant church (*Ansbach I*, Rurer II), sanctioned by the state (*Wendelsteiner Kirchenordnung, Flugschrift*), and organized with the help of the state (Rurer II). The question would be, in view of the circumstances, which interpretation of the state-church relationship could finally dominate the situation?

15. See Schornbaum I, p. 210 n. 237.

POOR RELIEF, HUMANISM, AND HERESY: THE CASE OF LYON

Natalie Zemon Davis

University of Toronto

POOR RELIEF, HUMANISM, AND HERESY: THE CASE OF LYON*

"The vicar of the Bishop of Tournai is abusing my little book on the poor [*De subventione pauperum*]," the great Spanish humanist Juan Luis Vives wrote to a friend in 1527, "he rules that it is heretical and Lutheran."[1] A few years later the mendicant orders of Ypres were saying the same thing about the poor-relief system which the magistrates of that Flemish city had recently established: "Forbidding [anyone] to ask for alms . . . is evil, vicious, and in conformity with a principle of Luther which has been condemned." The eminent theologians at the Sorbonne thought the Ypres scheme was at least "salutary and pious," but they went on to warn in 1531 that the magistrates must not prohibit public begging and alms-giving in the streets; while any attempt to appropriate ecclesiastical revenues for poor relief "would be the part not of good Catholics, but of impious heretics, Waldensians, Wycliffites or Lutherans."[2] Not long after, the Dominican prior and Inquisitor of Lyon, one Nicolas Morin, raised the same issue there. In 1532 he wrote an attack on a passionate French sermon,[3] in which the cleric and humanist Jean de Vauzelles had urged the notables of Lyon to introduce sweeping new welfare measures. The book was filled with errors, Morin said, "and pernicious to Catholic piety." Lyon had much more to fear from a host of heretics and unfaithful than it did from an abundance of poor strangers.[4]

* This is a slightly modified and lengthened version of a paper presented to the Newberry Library Renaissance Conference in April, 1966, and to the Conférence de Recherches sur les Pauvres et la Pauvreté directed by Professor Michel Mollat at the University of Paris in May, 1967. I am grateful to the American Philosophical Society for a grant which aided this research.

1. Vives to Cranvelt, August 16, 1527, in Juan Luis Vives, *De l'assistance aux pauvres*, trans. R. A. Casanova and L. Caby (Brussells, 1943), p. 42.

2. J. Nolf, *La réforme de la bienfaisance publique à Ypres au XVIe siècle* (Ghent, 1915), pp. 51, 69; Charles du Plessis d'Argentré, *Collectio Judiciorum de novibus erroribus* (Paris, 1728), pp. 84–85.

3. *Police subsidaire a celle quasi infinie multitude des povres survenus a Lyon lan Mil cinq cens trente Ung/Avec les Graces que les povres en rendent tant a messieurs de leglise que aux notables de la ville. Le tout fort exemplaire pour toutes aultres citez* (Lyon: Claude Nourry, dit le Prince, n.d. [1531]).

4. *Tractatus Catholice eruditionis ad testimonium et legem recurrens, confutansque libellum perniciosum velamine elemosine pauperibus Lugduni impense propalatum* [sic], *Editione exaratus*

Blaming Protestantism for new poor-relief measures did not, of course, end with the sixteenth century. R. H. Tawney, while admitting that indiscriminate charity had had its critics before the Reformation, thought it had been undermined only by the Protestant attack on monasticism and hypocritical works. "The new medicine for poverty," to use his famous phrase—that is, harsh discipline or deprivation to uproot the poor from idleness—may have been prompted by political and economic changes, but it was prescribed by Puritan self-righteousness.[5] More recently Christopher Hill has argued in a study of the influential Puritan divine William Perkins that it was the Calvinist view of church polity that convinced the rich not to give alms indiscriminately and the poor not to expect them. The underserving poor were "outcasts, outside the law and outside the church," and thus, says Hill, fit only for being a large cheap labor supply for developing capitalism.[6]

In the sixteenth century the magistrates of Ypres said they were astonished to be called Lutherans when all they cared about was helping the poor.[7] And several modern scholars would agree with them that poor-relief reform was not necessarily connected with heresy. Brian Tierney, for instance, has proved that canon lawyers had always perceived the spiritual dangers of involuntary poverty and had also worked out some bases for discriminating among those asking alms.[8] Other historians have said that by the fourteenth and fifteenth centuries even voluntary poverty was losing its extraordinary allure for the morally sensitive: some Florentine humanists were preferring the civic uses of wealth to voluntary poverty, while northern thinkers like Jean Gerson were valuing inner detachment from material goods over literal abandonment of one's possessions.[9]

Fratris Nicolai Morini Blesensis Ordinis fratrum predicatorum doctoris theologi ac heretice pravitatis inquisitoris . . . (Lyon: Guillaume Boulle); Colophon: printed for Boulle by Jean Crespin, dit du Carré, September 4, 1532; 74^v, 66^v; hereinafter cited as Morin.

5. R. H. Tawney, Religion and the Rise of Capitalism (Holland Memorial Lectures, 1922; Harmondsworth, Middlesex: Penguin Books, 1964), pp. 262–264. W. Cunningham, in his Christianity and Economic Science of 1914, had already attributed the stern Scotch treatment of children and unemployed adults to Calvinism.

6. Christopher Hill, "Puritans and the Poor," Past and Present, 2 (Nov., 1952), 32–50. Hill has treated the subject at greater length in Chapter 7 of Society and Puritanism in Pre-Revolutionary England (London, 1964).

7. Nolf, op. cit., pp. 69, 51.

8. Medieval Poor Law. A Sketch of Canonical Theory and its Application in England (Berkeley and Los Angeles, 1959), chaps. 1 and 3.

9. Hans Baron, "Franciscan Poverty and Civic Wealth as Factors in the Rise of Humanistic Thought," Speculum, XIII (1938), 1–37. Charles Trinkaus has stressed in his "Humanist Treatises on the Status of the Religious: Petrarch, Salutati, Valla" (Studies in

If attitudes toward poverty were clearly changing before the sixteenth century, other scholars have shown that poor-relief measures of the seventeenth century were not always due to Protestantism either. The employment of children, says one economic historian, owed more to an "awareness, however crude, of basic demographic circumstances" than to Puritan doctrine.[10] And Emanuel Chill has demonstrated for seventeenth-century France that the movement to enclose the poor in disciplinarian "hospitals" was led not by Huguenots or even by government bureaucrats, but by the pious members of the Company of the Holy Sacrament.[11]

Finally, comparative studies of poor-relief institutions during the sixteenth century have uncovered striking similarities. Already in the 1880s, when German industrialization was prompting comparative economic history, Georg Ratzinger and Franz Ehrle pointed this out.[12] Building on their work, W. J. Ashley told English readers that reforms in poor relief had as intellectual sources both the continental reformers and the Catholic humanist Juan Luis Vives, while the magistrates of Ypres had cited in their support an argument from the late Conciliarist John Major. Sidney and Beatrice Webb followed Ashley's view in their well-known *English Poor Law*.[13]

the Renaissance, XI [1964], 23–27) how serious Salutati was in praising the vow of poverty to a friend who was a religious. But Salutati was able to resist the attractions of that status, and his justification for poverty, as Trinkaus points out, is very different from that of the twelfth century. Salutati talked of the socially useful actions of the moderately poor; the twelfth century of meeting Christ among the poor. See Michel Mollat, "Pauvres et pauvreté à la fin du XIIe siècle," *Revue d'ascétique et de mystique*, XLI (1965), 305–323. On northern thinkers, see F. Rapp, "L'église et la pauvreté en Alsace à la fin du moyen âge" in "Résumés des travaux présentés à la Conférenece de Recherches dirigés par M. Mollat" (mimeo, Faculté des Lettres et Sciences Humaines de l'Université de Paris, 1964–1965).

10. D. C. Coleman, "Labour in the English Economy of the Seventeenth Century," *Economic History Review*, V, 2nd ser., VIII (1956), 286.

11. Emanuel Chill, "Religion and Mendicity in Seventeenth-Century France," *International Review of Social History*, VII (1962), 400–425. Enclosing the poor was also supported by mercantilist thinkers irrespective of religion: J.-P. Gutton, "A l'aube du XVIIe siècle: Idées nouvelles sur les pauvres," *Cahiers d'Histoire*, X (1965), 87–97.

12. Georg Ratzinger, *Geschichte der Kirchlichen Armenpflege* (Freiburg im Breisgau, 1884); Franz Ehrle, *Beiträge zur Geschichte und Reform der Armenpflege* (Freiburg im Breisau, 1881).

13. W. J. Ashley, *An Introduction to English Economic History and Theory*; 4th ed. (London, 1906), II, 340–346. Sidney and Beatrice Webb, *English Local Government: English Poor Law History*; Part I: *The Old Poor Law* (London, 1927), pp. 1–60. Also see F. Salter, *Some Early Tracts on Poor Relief* (London, 1926), with an introduction by S. Webb.

Yet the ghosts of the mendicant orders of Ypres and the theologians of the Sorbonne, and now of the Inquisitor Nicolas Morin, live on to worry us with their accusations. They haunted the Belgian scholar Pierre Bonenfant when he described welfare reform in Catholic Mons and Ypres as "a curious and without doubt generally *unconscious* introduction of Lutheran principles."[14] They haunted G. R. Elton when he was trying to identify the anonymous author of an impressive draft proposal for poor-law reform in England in 1535. "Because of his opposition to indiscriminate alms," said Elton, he must be "a reformer in religion."[15]

Perhaps the trouble is that we have not sufficiently convinced ourselves of how and why European religious sensibility had changed in regard to begging and the charitable act even without the impact of reformed teachings on these subjects. Perhaps we have not been sufficiently aware of the extent to which Christian humanists other than Vives played a role in reforming poor relief on the Continent. Perhaps also we have not inquired closely enough whether certain assumptions underlying the new poor laws do not flow as naturally from Erasmian views of education, order, and charity as they do from Protestant ones about works and church polity. And finally perhaps we must ask once again whether business men and lawyers on European town councils did not, irrespective of their religious convictions, bring their vocational experiences to bear on the difficulties of urban life.

I want now to make such an inquiry about the institution of the Aumône-Générale of Lyon during the early 1530s. This organization, of which the Lyonnais were very proud, is typical of the urban welfare projects of northern Europe and even of a few municipal experiments in Spain.[16] The problems of urban disorder, misery, and illness which Lyon

14. Pierre Bonenfant, "Les origines et le caractère de la Réforme de la bienfaisance publique aux Pays-Bas sous le règne de Charles-Quint," *Revue belge de philologie et d'histoire*, VI (1927), 230. Italics mine. Jean Imbert seems to be following Bonenfant in talking of Vives' project as a "programme protestant" in *Les hôpitaux en France* (Paris, 1966), p. 24. In all other respects these works are immensely valuable.

15. G. R. Elton, "An Early Tudor Poor Law," *Economic History Review*, 2d ser., VI (1953), 65 and 65 n. 2, where he quotes the Sorbonne decision on Ypres. Whether or not the real author was a Protestant is not at issue here. The point is the assumption underlying Elton's inference.

16. Basic printed sources on the Aumône-Générale are: *Inventaire-sommaire des archives hospitalières antérieures à 1790*, ed. M. A. Steyert and F. Rolle, *Ville de Lyon. La Charité ou Aumône-Générale*; 4 vols. (Lyon, 1874); E. Richard, "Les origines de l'Aumône-Générale à Lyon," *Revue du lyonnais*, 5th ser., L (1886), 329–339; Henri de Boissieu, "L'aumône-générale de 1534 à 1562," *Revue d'histoire de Lyon*, VIII (1909), 43–57, 81–105, 205–223,

faced were more acute than in less rapidly expanding cities, but they were no different in kind. But what makes Lyon especially useful for analysis is that during the 1530s she was a Catholic city, whose clergy ran the spectrum from the Catholic reformer through the nonchalant canon; that she had important circles of humanist activity; and that she already had a small but fairly identifiable Protestant movement. Thus we can sort out what religious variables, if any, were involved in the creation and support of the Aumône-Générale.

Let us begin then with an examination of poverty in Lyon and its impact on city life and feeling. Later on we can take a look at the men who brought about welfare reform, and analyze the institutions which they created.

Lyon's population was already growing by 1490, and it had very likely doubled by the mid-sixteenth century. In the 1530s between 40,000 and 50,000 people were living within its expanded city walls. New subdivisions were laid out in neat rectangles, new houses went up, and the consulate began to talk of widening streets and squares.[17] Demographic recovery was of course general in Europe in the late fifteenth century as

255–276; *idem*, "L'Aumône-Générale sous la domination protestante," *Bulletin de la société littéraire historique et archéologique de Lyon*, III (1908–1909), 1–32; A Croze, "Statuts et règlements primitifs de l'Aumône-Générale de Lyon," *Revue d'histoire de Lyon*, XIII (1914), 363 ff. An interesting popular study of the Aumône-Générale through the eighteenth century is Gabriel Arminjon, *Banquier des pauvres* (n.p., 1957).

For Spain, Maria Jimenez Salas, *Historia de la Asistencia Social en España en la edad moderna* (Madrid, 1958); Antonio Rumeu de Armas, *Historia de la Prevision Social en España* (Madrid, 1944); Jean Sarrailh, "Note sur la réforme de la bienfaisance en Espagne à la fin du XVIIIe siècle," *Eventail de l'histoire vivante . . . Hommage à Lucien Febvre* (Paris, 1953), II, 371–380. The best data on sixteenth-century urban experiments in Spain comes from Juan de Medina, *De la orden que en algunos pueblos de Espanase ha puesto en la limosna* (Salamanca, 1545).

17. No definitive study has been made of the population of sixteenth-century Lyon. An unpublished thesis by Georges Breuillac computed the population for the first decade of the century as between 30,000 and 40,000. Roger Doucet calculated the high point of growth as 50,000–55,000, reached between 1535 and 1550 (*Histoire de Lyon*, ed. A. Kleinclausz [Lyon, 1939]), I, 487. Roger Mols gives a higher estimate for Lyon in *Introduction à la démographie historique des villes d'Europe du XIVe au XVIIIe siècle* (Louvain, 1955), II, 514–517. Professor Richard-Felix Gascon of the Université de Lyon, who is working on this problem, believes that the high point was reached about 1560, but that can at present specify the size only as lying between 60,000 and 100,000. I am assuming (on the basis also of my own research) that the high point was reached about 1560 and that the size was 65,000. On city growth, see A. Kleinclausz *et al.*, *Lyon des origines à nos jours* (Paris, 1925), pp. 22–30, 160, 166.

the death rate declined, but in Lyon, as in other cities, the population was swelled especially by immigration. Chances looked good in a city with four annual fairs, which the Italian banking houses had made a center for the European money market, where new shops were opening in printing, in the metal trades, and in finishing textiles. So they came—the sons and daughters of peasants from the Lyonnais and Burgundy and other provinces, young artisans from Flanders, Germany, and Italy, from Dijon and Troyes and Paris.

They came poor, and most of them stayed that way. But poverty was not a condition peculiar to newcomers; natives suffered it as well. What accounts for this? We expect it in the men who have no skills, the *gagnedeniers* who did odd jobs when they could find them for three *sous* a day.

TABLE 1

OCCUPATION OF THE MALE IN NINETY-ONE FAMILIES ADDED TO RELIEF ROLLS, MAY–DECEMBER, 1534 AND JANUARY–JULY, 1539*

OCCUPATION	FAMILIES WHERE HUSBAND ALIVE	FAMILIES WHERE HUSBAND RECENTLY DIED	TOTAL
Unskilled day laborers	23	0	23
Boatmen, wagoners	5	1	6
Urban winegrowers, gardeners	3	2	5
Soldiers	1	0	1
Butchers, pastry makers	3	0	3
Millers	0	2	2
Bakers	1	0	1
Candlemakers	0	1	1
Pouch makers	2	1	3
Shoemakers, cobblers	6	0	6
Combmakers	1	0	1
Cutlers, pinmakers	5	0	5
Glassmakers	1	0	1
Weavers, embroiderers	6	2	8
Dyers	5	1	6
Shearers	0	1	1
Tailors, dressmakers	4	0	4
Masons, carpenters, stonecutters	8	3	11
Printers, playing-card makers	2	0	2
Teachers	1	0	1
Total	77	14	91

* About 200 families are recorded in Arch. Char. E4 and E5 as being added to the rolls during this fifteen month period, but occupations are given for the males in only 91 instances. In the case of artisans, the records rarely state whether the man was a master or journeyman. In addition, the occupations of three women are given: a weaver, a wet nurse, and a glovemaker.

But poverty was also the plight of the skilled journeymen whose wages were two or three times that much, and poverty could sometimes grip their masters as well. For instance, seventy-seven families in which the husband was still alive were added to the relief rolls of the Aumône-Générale in a fifteen month period of the 1530s (see Table 1). Only 41 percent of these men were unskilled; the rest were artisans.[18] This was the case partly because the incomes of artisans had to stretch to feed so many mouths. "Poor householders and artisans heavily burdened with children," said the ordinances of the Aumône-Générale. The "heavy burden" was most likely to be three dependent children,[19] but some poor families had more (see Table 2). Is it surprising that the master weaver Pierre les Combes with his five children should need help even though he

TABLE 2

NUMBER OF DEPENDENT CHILDREN IN FORTY-ONE
FAMILIES AIDED BY THE AUMÔNE-GÉNÉRALE,
1534–1539*

NUMBER OF CHILDREN	NUMBER OF FAMILIES WHERE HUSBAND ALIVE	NUMBER OF WIDOWS	TOTAL FAMILIES
1	5	2	7
2	9	4	13
3	8	1	9
4	4	0	4
5	3†	0	3
6	1	1	2
7	3‡	0	3
Total	33	8	41
Median number of children	3	2	3
Average number of children	3	2.3	3

* Based on Archives de la Charité, E4, E5. Dependence is assumed because otherwise the records would not have mentioned the children.
 † Includes two women pregnant with sixth child.
 ‡ Includes one woman pregnant with eighth child.

18. The Norwich census of the poor in 1570 also shows a majority of the poor from skilled trades (J. F. Pound, "An Elizabethan Census of the Poor," *University of Birmingham Historical Journal*, VIII [1962], 139, 152–153).

19. J. F. Pound found in Norwich in 1570 that the average number of children in poor families where both parents were alive was 2.34 (*ibid.*, p. 142), whereas my figures from Lyon in the 1530s for such families give three children as both the median and the average. This could be due to a difference in sample, his being 351 families described in a census, mine being 33 families mentioned at random by the rectors among many more poor families. Yet there may be a real difference in standard of living between the two cities at the different periods: only 4 of his total 351 families have 7 children, while 3 of the 33 families found in Lyon have 7 children (see Table 2).

had two looms and a journeyman and one of his own sons to keep them busy? Or that the notary André Gouzebaud had sold most of his furniture to feed his seven children and pregnant wife?[20]

Even in families with one or two children, there were many emergencies in which savings were wiped out. Some trades, such as construction, just stopped during the damp, cold winters of Lyon; others were "reduced to nothing" by foreign competition. An expanding industry like printing had its troubles too, for demand was not always translated promptly into orders, and the presses of small shops were quieted from time to time.

One might be laid off, or one might get sick. By the early 1530s citizens were claiming that plague was "sprouting" in Lyon every year.[21] Visitors noticed that the Lyonnais always suffered with colds and pleurisy. Printers' journeymen complained that presswork gave them arthritis.[22] During one year in the 1530s, 544 poor people, most of them males still working at their trades in Lyon, entered the Hôtel-Dieu for ailments other than plague (see Table 3). About 30 per cent of them died there, while the families of the others suffered temporary loss of income. And these figures do not take into account the poor people who were sick at home. The period of lying-in for poor mothers was costly too,[23] since many of them worked or helped their husbands. Of course, the rich got sick and had babies as well, but on the poor the economic effects were devastating.

Finally, there was the other great scourge of preindustrial society— famine. In normal years an unskilled worker in Lyon paid more than half a day's wage for a weekly supply of low-quality bread for himself alone; but there were several years between 1500 and 1531 when grain and,

20. Archives de la Charité de Lyon [cited hereinafter as Arch. Char.], E4, 1^v, 172^r; E5, p. 296.

21. *Ibid.*, E4, 1^r. The epidemics of these years were mild, however. In the spring of 1531, there were only twelve victims at the plague hospital (E138, 90^v). The consuls began to become alarmed in March, 1532, when there were thirty-two victims, Archives communales de Lyon [cited hereinafter as Arch. com.], B51, 92^v. It was not until 1564 that there was a plague with a very high death toll and with large numbers of inhabitants fleeing the city. For an excellent discussion of disease in a sixteenth-century city, see Brian Pullan, "The Famine in Venice and the New Poor Law, 1527–1529," *Bollettino dell' Istituto di Storia della Società e dello Stato Veneziano*, V–VI (1963–1964), 159–168.

22. *Généralle description de l'antique et célèbre Cité de Lyon . . . par N. de Nicolay . . . cosmographe du Roy* (1573 MSS; Lyon, 1881), p. 17. *Remonstrances et Mémoires pour les Compagnons Imprimeurs de Paris et Lyon . . .* (n.p. [Lyon?], n.d. [1572], A i^r.

23. Numerous women asked the Aumône-Générale for special aid until they were up after childbirth (Arch. Char., Er, 61^r, 94^v, 172^r). In many cases in the Norwich census the wives of poor men worked (Pound, *op. cit.*, p. 137).

TABLE 3

ENTRIES AND DEATHS AT THE HÔTEL-DIEU
DURING SELECTED PERIODS OF THE 1530s*

Period of Time	Number of Entries	Number of Deaths	Ratio of Deaths to Entries
March, 1530	61	18	.30
Dec., 1530	51	17	.33
June, 1534	38	9	.24
Dec., 1534	26	8	.30
March, 1535	30	4	.13
March, 1537	38	7	.24
Oct., 1537	149	30	.20
March, 1539	34	11	.32
June, 1539	46	13	.28
Oct., 1539	50	11	.22
Dec., 1539	36	11	.31
March, 1539– April, 1540	544	162	.30

* Based on Archives de l'Hôtel-Dieu, F18, F19, F20.

accordingly, bread cost three to six times that price (see 271–272, Appendix I). This was largely the fault of a primitive agriculture and inadequate transportation, but (as food rioters believed and recent research has confirmed) hoarding by grain speculators made matters worse.[24]

Urban poverty had had all these components to some degree since the fourteenth century, but in the first decades of the sixteenth century they intersected with a period of population growth to increase greatly the dangers of city living. Poverty was not usually shamefaced, did not remain quietly sick behind closed shutters; instead it poured into the streets with begging, noise, crime, threat of disease, and rioting. Who were the beggars? A small minority were adult males, skilled and unskilled, who were temporarily out of work. Some were new to the town, others were regular inhabitants. But what the poor craftsman or day laborer was much more likely to do when times were hard was send his children out to beg. Even the consulate was turning out foundlings from the Hôtel-Dieu at the age of seven to ask alms in the street, with a sign explaining their plight.[25]

24. The placard of the 1529 grain riot in Lyon blamed the high price on "false usurers" hoarding grain until they got their price. The weather was good, said the placard, and there had been no military requisition of grain (Arch. com., BB46, 101^{r-v}). On the impact of speculation on grain prices, see C. Verlinden, J. Craeybeckx, E. Scholliers, "Mouvements des prix et des salaires en Belgique au XVIe siècle," *Annales: Économies. Sociétés. Civilisations*, X (1955), 179–189.

25. Archives de l'Hôtel-Dieu de Lyon [cited hereinafter as Arch. H.D.], E1, 3^{r}.

So townsmen complained of "the great number of little children crying and hooting with hunger and cold day and night through the town, making a marvellous racket in the churches, disturbing the devotion of the people . . . Oh, what confusion, heartbreak and scandal." The poor girls were getting pregnant and their futures were ruined. Seven out of thirteen cases of begging discussed by the rectors of the Aumône-Générale in its first months involved children.[26] The presence of many children among city beggars may well have been a new development, one associated with the population growth of the late fifteenth century. In any case, as we shall see, it was an important factor in welfare reform and in humanist interest in poor relief.[27]

Making noise and scandal in the streets along with the children were the professional beggars, men and women who rarely if ever worked for wages and who used all their skill to collect alms. Some were sick, old, or disabled, and made the most of their deficiencies. The rest were "*maraulx*," "*ribauds*," "*belitres*" and "*coquins*"—these terms from Jean de Vauzelles' sermon give a glimpse of the rich vocabulary of opprobrium which the higher orders throughout Europe had evolved to describe its vagrants and vagabonds, its bums, tramps, and loafers. Legislation against them began in Europe even before the Black Death,[28] but by the fifteenth century the magistrates of Basel could detail twenty-five distinct categories of phony beggars, and they missed a few that were current in France.[29] There were those who pretended to have epilepsy and those who

26. Arch. Char., E4, 1ʳ, 100ᵛ, 118ᵛ, 120ᵛ, 122ʳ, 150ʳ, 158ʳ.

27. The statute of the Ypres' poor-relief system also show special concern for child-beggars (Salter, *op. cit.* [above, n. 13], pp. 47, 53). During the later middle ages hospitals for foundlings were established, which kept the youngsters until they were seven or eight, and there were also a small number of hospitals for orphans (as one in Douai, F. Leclère, "Recherches sur la charité . . . au XIVe siècle à Douai," *Revue du Nord*, XLVIII [1966], 145). But the great period for the foundation of establishments for children *separate* from other hospitals is the late fifteenth and sixteenth centuries. See L. Lallemand, *Histoire de la Charité* (Paris, 1906), III, 139, 148; W. J. Marx, *The Development of Charity in Medieval Louvain* (Yonkers, N.Y., 1936), pp. 74–75; Jean Imbert, *Les hôpitaux en droit canonique* (Paris, 1947), p. 127; Jean Delumeau, *Vie economique et sociale de Rome dans la seconde moitié du XVIe siècle*, Bibliothèque des écoles françaises d'Athènes et de Rome, Fasc. 184 (Paris, 1957), p. 410.

28. C. Paultré, *De la repression de la mendicité et du vagabondage sous l'ancien régime* (Paris, 1906), pp. 17 ff. Lallemand, *op. cit.*, III, 346–347. Manuel Colmeira, *Historia de la economia politica en España* (Madrid, 1965), pp. 599–600.

29. Paultré, *op. cit.*, pp. 29, 34–35, 51–53. The *Liber vagatorum* of the late fifteenth century was based on the listing of the Senate of Basel made in the early fifteenth century. Also see Sebastian Brant's chapter on beggars in the *Narrenschiff* (1494) and Erasmus' colloquy "Beggar Talk" in *The Colloquies of Erasmus*, trans. Craig R. Thompson (Chicago, 1965), especially p. 251.

pretended to have been bitten by mad dogs; there were men who pretended to be hangmen on expiatory pilgrimages, and women who pretended
to be penitents, begging by day as Mary Magdalene and then "moon-
lighting" later at Mary Magdalene's former trade. The beggars' art had
its discomforts too: some asked alms almost naked even in winter; others
rubbed their skins with chemicals to give the impression of disease.

All of this behavior shaded off into confidence games, dishonest gambling, and other forms of petty crime—"the art of conny-catching" as it
was called in England.[30] (See Hieronymus Bosch's painting of the
conjurer playing the old shell game while his partner works the audience
lifting purses.)

To make matters worse, the numbers of beggars and vagabonds on the
streets of Lyon were constantly being swelled by strangers seeking alms—
vagrants passing through, beggars coming at fair time, and beggars
following the royal court, which stayed in Lyon, for instance, in 1524–
1525. Every June there occurred the big religious festival of the year, the
Pardon of Saint John the Baptist, and the cloister of the cathedral was
jammed with mendicants from nearby provinces, "running, jumping,
shouting and singing," to the annoyance of the canon-counts.[31] And
finally, when famine hit surrounding areas, the city not only had to worry
about provisioning its own inhabitants, but could always expect visitors
from the countryside. Sometimes they came in orderly processions, all bare-
foot and dressed in white as penitents calling "rain, rain" in the country
dialect of the Lyonnais. Sometimes, as in the terrible spring of 1531, they
came from as far away as Burgundy "in great troops and boatloads without any government among them."[32]

Under these circumstances it is hardly surprising that ecclesiastical and
lay sentiment had long since hardened against the professional beggar,
but the point is that it was now turning against *all* beggars in the city.
First of all, crowds of beggars deserving and undeserving were thought to
enhance the danger of plague. (In fact, rats and fleas do not need mendicants to thrive and migrate; but the spread of other diseases may well
have been facilitated by crowds of beggars, and these in turn may have
lowered the resistance of the population to plague). In Lyon and elsewhere

30. Thompson, *op. cit.*, p. 252; and Frank Aydelotte's delightful *Elizabethan Rogues
and Vagabonds* (Oxford, 1913).

31. A. Sachet, *Le pardon annuel de la Saint Jean et de la Saint Pierre à Saint Jean de Lyon*
(Lyon, 1918), I, 491–492.

32. Guillaume Paradin, *Memoires de l'histoire de Lyon* (Lyon: Antoine Gryphius,
1573), p. 281. *La Police de l'Aulmosne de Lyon* (Lyon: Sébastien Gryphius, 1539), p. 7.
The coming of country folk to the city in time of famine was an old and widespread
custom in Europe (Paultré, *op. cit.*, pp. 64–65; Pullan, *op. cit.* [above, n. 21]).

throughout Europe authorities had long made temporary prohibitions against begging whenever the Black Death struck.[33] Now that the consulate had gone to the trouble of building a special hospital on the outskirts of Lyon to isolate plague victims, it is not surprising that it would think of taking permanent measures against begging. Later on the Aumône-Générale was to be presented to archbishop and king as in part a way to keep down contagion. For the humanist Vives as well as for the Venetian Senate in its poor law of 1528, welfare reform was also a health measure.[34] Thus, a revulsion against mendicancy could grow independent of any religious critique of the merits of charitable acts.

At the same time, however, events in Lyon were leading not only Protestant sympathizers but many Catholics as well to ask whether an act of charity could best occur within the traditional pattern of giving. No one remembered experiencing anything so horrible as the spring famine of 1531. More than 1,500 country folk and at least 4,500 inhabitants of the city were in desperate need.[35] The mobs looked, said Jean de Vauzelles, like bodies dug up from the graves. Like corpses used for anatomical dissections, said a witness a few years later. "I am dying of hunger, I am dying of hunger," they cried; and they did die, right there in the streets. "My heart broke," wrote the Inquisitor Nicolas Morin, "I will never forget it." At first the inhabitants tried to feed people in the old way—individual handouts outside their houses. But all that happened, said Vauzelles, was that some of the starving gorged themselves so suddenly that they suffocated and died, while others threw themselves upon the donors so violently that the food was lost and they became afraid to give. And all the while "the poor were overwhelming us . . . with their clamor and laments . . . outside our doors."[36]

33. Charles Mullett, *The Bubonic Plague and England* (Lexington, Ky., 1956), pp. 22–23, 44–46. Sachet, *op. cit.*, I, 493: in 1468 beggars are chased from the cloister of Saint John because of danger of infection.

34. Arch. Char., E4, 6^v; A1, letter of Henri de Gabiano. Vives, *op. cit.* [above, n. 1], pp. 186–187. Pullan, *op. cit.*, 159, 167–168.

35. Morin, *op. cit.* [above, n. 4], 31^r, estimated a total of 8,000 poor fed by the temporary organization, while the *Police de l'Aulmosne* estimated 7,000–8,000 (pp. 11–12). My figures are based on the actual accounts for the distribution of 1531 (Arch. Char., E138, 89^r, 90^v).

36. Vauzelles, *Police subsidaire* [cited above, n. 3], A iii^r; *Police de l'Aulmosne*, p. 7. Rabelais had carried on public dissections in Lyon in 1537, and the author of the *Police de l'Aulmosne*, who may have been Vauzelles himself, had evidently been reminded of the 1531 famine while watching Rabelais' dissections. Morin, *op. cit.*, 24^v–25^r. The 1528 famine in Vicenza and Venice had a similar impact on witnesses (Pullan, *op. cit.*, 153, 157).

Under these circumstances, for Vauzelles, compassion was transformed into fear and horror, and the fruits of compassion were death, not life. Indeed, the city of which Vauzelles was so proud—"the refuge of the Gauls . . the emporium . . . of all the world"—had lost its identity, "so thickly sown with poverty that it resembled rather a hospital of the famished." It was only when the consulate and notables had set up an organization, a precursor of the Aumône-Générale, with all food distributed regularly in specified places, with everyone off the streets in temporary log cabins, only then could Vauzelles talk of charity in the city, of Jesus "by a new rebirth . . . enveloped in the misery of these poor and receiving a greater welcome than in his town of Bethlehem." It was only then that Vauzelles could think of Lyon as a city again, now "a holy city of Jerusalem." And since people do such execrable things when they are starving, Vauzelles concluded that it was better to prevent people from ever falling into such hunger than to lift them out of it.[37]

Poverty was threatening not only physical and spiritual health, but also property and power. Despite a hint of violence,[38] the mobs of 1531 were too far gone to organize an uprising; but in the spring of 1529 there had been a serious food riot, or *Rebeine* as the Lyonnais called it. Blaming the rather high price of grain on speculators and conniving magistrates, about two thousand inhabitants, most of them unskilled laborers, women and teen-agers, looted the municipal granary, the Franciscan monastery nearby, and the homes of several wealthy men, including that of Lyon's earliest humanist, the physician and former consul Symphorien Champier. The consulate promised concessions to restore order, but a few weeks later it was busier with whippings and hanging the rebel leaders than with reducing the price of bread.[39]

That the consulate at first put punishment above prevention is not surprising. For a day the rioters had been masters of the city. Meanwhile

37. Vauzelles, *Police subsidaire*, A ii[v]–A iii[v], B iiii[r–v], C ii[v].

38. Arch. com., BB48, 275[r], 276[v]; Vauzelles, *Police subsidaire*, B i[v].

39. The full archival sources for the Rebeine have been printed by M. G. and G. Guigue in *Bibliothèque historique du Lyonnais* (Lyon, 1886). Symphorien Champier's eyewitness account is also essential, but must be used with caution because of his false and unsubstantiated theory on the relation of heresy to the Rebeine: *Sensuyt ung petit traicte de la noblesse et anciennete de la ville de lyon. Ensemble de la rebeine ou rebellion du populaire de la dicte ville contre les conseillers de la cyte et notables marchans a cause des bledz . . .* (Paris: Jean Saint Denis, 1529); *Cy commence ung petit livre de lantiquite, origine et noblesse . . . de Lyon: Ensemble de la rebeine et coniuration ou rebellion du populaire . . .* (Lyon, January, 1529/30). P. Allut has reproduced the second edition in his *Étude biographique et bibliographique sur Symphorien Champier* (Lyon, 1859), pp. 333–382. Henri Hauser followed Champier's account in his "Étude critique sur la Rebeine de Lyon," *Revue historique*, LXI (1896), 265–307.

peasants in the Lyonnais were refusing to pay their tithes.[40] Nicolas Volcyr's hair-raising description of the Peasants' Revolt in Alsace was being read among the consular families, and Champier was imagining that the same thing could happen in Lyon.[41] In addition the people had become uppish and ungrateful. Champier was so insulted at the attack on his house that he wrote a book on the Rebeine, reminding the poor how he had persuaded the consulate, in speeches decked out with Hebrew, Greek, Egyptian, and Roman examples, to put a tariff on wine rather than on grain or flour.[42] If Champier stood alone among his contemporaries in believing that the rioters' disobedience was due to heresy (and my own research has shown that what Protestant sympathizers there were among the poor were *not* in the mob, but in the special troops set up to restore order and requisition grain by force from private granaries),[43] nevertheless the burghers and merchants were nervous about the danger of *sédition* for a long time. Three years later the consulate and royal officers were still tracking down and hanging the leaders of the Rebeine.

But punishment was no answer—"a hungry people cannot fear the gibbet," said Jean de Vauzelles—and the autumn of 1530 was to see well-armed and disciplined artisans, printers' and dyers' journeymen, marching through the streets and posting placards about the cost of living.[44] Champier told the consulate that these evildoers must be punished, but also that the bakers should be constrained to bake bread at a decent

40. "Vidimus des lettres patentes de François Ier, 1529," ed. N. Weiss, *Bulletin de la société de l'histoire du protestantisme français*, LIX (1910), 501–504.

41. Nicolas Volcyr, *L'histoire et Recueil de la triumphant et glorieuse victoire obtenue contre les seduyctz et abusez Lutheriens du pays Daulsays* . . . (Paris, 1526), in the library of lawyer Claude Bellièvre, who was a consul in 1523–1524 and also at the time of the Rebeine (Lucien Auvray, "La bibliothèque de Claude Bellièvre, 1530," *Mélanges offerts à M. Emile Picot* [Paris, 1913], II, 356). Volcyr and Champier had both been in the service of the Duke of Lorraine and Volcyr wrote a poem for one of Champier's works (Allut, *op. cit.*, p. 173). Volcyr's history stresses the connection of the Peasants' Revolt with Lutheran heresy.

42. Champier, *Rebeine*, in Allut, *op. cit.*, p. 356.

43. N. Z. Davis, "Strikes and Salvation at Lyons," *Archiv für Reformationsgeschichte*, LVI (1965), 56 n. 27; *idem*, "A Trade Union in Sixteenth-Century France," *Economic History Review*, 2nd ser., XIX (1966), 66. The *Mémoires* of the moderate Catholic Guillaume Paradin do not give heresy as the background to the Rebeine, though Paradin followed Champier's account in other ways. The arch-opponent of Protestants, Claude de Rubys, described the Rebeine as a simple grain revolt (*Histoire veritable de la ville de Lyon* . . . [Lyon, 1604]). In Paris, a citizen described it in his diary as a grain revolt: "y eust à Lyon grande mutinerie, à cause de la charté des bleds . . ." (*Journal d'un Bourgeois de Paris*, ed. V. Bourrilly, [Paris, 1910], p. 322).

44. Vauzelles, *Police subsidaire*, C ii[v]. Arch. com., BB49, 203[v]–204[v], 210[r]–211[r].

price "so there would be no cause for the people to get stirred up."[45] The next spring, of course, was the terrible famine, and not long after, the plague worsened. The temporary *aumône* of 1531 was repeated briefly in 1532. If the notables did not immediately make the aumône permanent, it was because they were considering at many a consulate meeting how they would finance such a novel and large-scale venture and whom among the "great multitude of poor" they could afford to support. But all the conditions which were making life intolerable for the inhabitants of this expanding and cosmopolitan city had come to a head in the 1530s and finally led in 1534 to the establishment of an organization "to nourish the poor forever."[46]

The new organization involved a dramatic shift of funds and power from ecclesiastical to lay hands, and a change in the act of charity. It was a *reformatio* of a kind, but one which was created not by a religious party, but by a coalition of notables: Catholics and Protestant sympathizers, and all of them goaded on by Christian humanists, who like Vives believed that cities had been founded "for the increase of charity and human fellowship."[47]

Let us see who some of the members of this coalition were. Only two of them were clerics, and those two were the only important literary figures in the Lyonnais clergy of their day. The priest and doctor of laws Jean de Vauzelles:[48] now in his thirties, descended from an old communal family of notaries, holder of a priory and of an important judicial post under the noble canon-counts of Saint John, one of the many protégés of Marguerite of Navarre. Though he liked to find antique precedents for everything—poor-relief included—and though the royal entry parade which he directed in 1533 was sprinkled with learned references,[49] it was the Italian language and letters rather than the classical ones that he knew well and adored. Almost all his published works, however, were in French, inexpensive, and intended to communicate to a wide public the simple essentials of the Gospel and to move them by stylistic and pictorial

45. *Ibid.*, 216[v].

46. *Ibid.*, 269[r]–273[v], 275[r]–276[r], BB51, 92[v], 100[v], BB52 6[r], 9[r], 56[r]–57[v], 77[v], 80[v], 133[v]; *Police de l'Aulmosne* [above, n. 32] p. 17; Paradin, *op. cit.* [above, n. 32], p. 290.

47. Vives, *op. cit.* [above, n. 1], p. 53.

48. On Vauzelles, see Ludovic de Vauzelles, "Notice sur Jean de Vauzelles," *Revue du Lyonnais*, 3rd ser., XIII (1872), 52–73; Emile Picot, *Les français italianisants au XVIe siècle* (Paris, 1906), I, 118 ff.; and N. Z. Davis, "Holbein's *Pictures of Death* and the Reformation at Lyons," *Studies in the Renaissance*, III (1956), 111–118.

49. Vauzelles, *Police subsidaire*, C ii[v]. *L'entree de la . . . Reyne Eleonor en la Cité de Lyon L'an mil cinq cens trente trois . . .*, in T. Godefroy, *Le Ceremonial François* (Paris, 1649), I, 804–816.

devices to live according to the teachings and example of Christ. Thus his French translation of a concordance of the Gospels; his translation of Aretino's Bible stories; his edition with commentaries of Holbein's *Pictures of Death*, from which the artist had banished the gruesome touches of the earlier *danse macabre* as Vauzelles wanted to banish disgusting sores and wounds from the streets of Lyon.[50] An opponent of persecution and a literary friend of Protestant sympathizers such as Etienne Dolet, he nevertheless held with Erasmus to a Catholic view of the merit of true charity. And as for the Lutherans, he was shocked by their impetuous iconoclasm and destructiveness, and thought Luther a scourge sent to rid the church of hypocrisy.[51]

In Santo Pagnini of Lucca,[52] Vauzelles' colleague in welfare reform, we see a rather different blend of humanist interests with Catholic orthodoxy: a Dominican of the convent at Fiesole, a doctor of theology, master of Greek and Hebrew at the encouragement of Savonarola, celebrated and eloquent orator in Florence, and finally protégé of the Medici. He taught Greek and Hebrew in Rome until Leo X's death; then he made his way to France, settling in 1526 in Lyon, where he was told by Italian residents that there were "many people infected with heresy" against whom he must raise his voice.[53] Though already in his

---

50. *Hystoire evangelique des quatre evangelistes en ung fidelement abregee* . . . (Lyon: Gilbert de Villiers, 1526), dedicated to Marguérite de France: Vauzelles wanted those who could not read Latin to be able to participate in the "riches" of the Gospel. *La Passion de Iesu Christ, vifvement descripte, par le Divin engin de Pierre Aretin* . . . (Lyon: Melchior and Gaspard Trechsel, March, 1539/40), dedication to the princess Jeanne de Navarre stressing the moral lessons to be learned from meditating on the Crucifixion. *La Genese de M. Pierre Aretin, Avec la vision de Noë* . . . (Lyon: Sébastien Gryphius, 1542), dedication to François I, "Monarque d'Eloquence," presenting to him the "divine eloquence" of Aretino. *Les Simulachres et Historiees Faces de la Mort* . . . (Lyon: Melchior and Gaspard Trechsel, 1538), dedication to the Abbess of Saint Peter's in Lyon. "The Pictures of Death . . . are the mirror by which one can correct the deformities of sin and embellish the soul."

Vauzelles was not a great stylist, but his writing in these works aimed at a wide audience is direct, colorful, and effective, in contrast to the many precious turns of phrases in his letters to Aretino and his poems for the Queen's Entry.

51. Vauzelles, *Police subsidaire*, C iv^v; *idem, Simulachres*, A iii^{r-v}. He said in the *Hystoire evangelique* in justifying his departure from the exact text of Scripture, that the words were not magical, but rather faith in the words was what counted. "Toutes choses ou la foy nest la principalle ouvriere sont supersticieuses et damnables" (fol. iii^v). This is an Erasmian view rather than the Lutheran "faith alone." He is also like Erasmus in criticizing ceremonialism but accepting the merit of true works.

52. T. M. Centi, "L'attività letteraria di Santi Pagnini (1470–1536)," *Archivum fratrum praedicatorum*, XV (1945), 5–51.

53. Pagnini to Clement VII in *In Utriusque Instrumenti nova translatio* (Lyon: Antoine du Ry, 1528); quoted Centi, *ibid.*, p. 20.

mid-fifties, Pagnini plunged actively into the life of his new city, preaching in Latin, French, and Italian; squeezing money for the plague hospital out of his rich Florentine relatives; making friends with French literary figures like Champier; and publishing: Hebrew grammars and dictionaries, a new translation of the Bible from Hebrew sources, and a defense of Catholic doctrine drawing heavily on the early Church Fathers.[54] Though he himself had made an unpublished translation of the *Odyssey* and part of the *Iliad*, he criticized people who were more ardent for the "fables of poets" than for the Scripture. Scholastic disputes about "instances, relations, quiddities and formalities" had nothing at all to do with salvation.[55]

What did Pagnini and Vauzelles do to help the Aumône-Générale get started? Vauzelles' sermon to the consuls and notables in late May, 1531[56] exhorted them by flattery, promises, and prophetic threats to continue the organized charity which they had just begun and to extend its scope (Don't stop now, don't look backward; remember what happened to

54. *Habes Hoc in libro candide Lector Hebraicas Institutiones* ... (Lyon: Antoine du Ry for François de Clermont, bishop of Avignon, 1526); dedication to Federico Fregoso, archbishop of Salerno, defending the usefulness of Hebrew letters in studying the Bible and the support of Saint Jerome for this view. *Hoc est, Thesaurus Linguae Sanctae. Sic enim inscribere placuit Lexicon hoc Hebraicum* (Lyon: Sébastien Gryphius, 1529), dedication to Fregoso, saying among other things that a pure life is expressed in pure language. *Santis Pagnini ... Isagogae ad sacras literas, Liber unicus ... Isagogae ad mysticos sacrae scripturae sensus, Libre XVIII* ... (Lyon: François Juste at expense of Thomas de Gadagne and Hugues de La Porte, 1536/37). Printed posthumously with Pagnini's dedication to Cardinal Jean du Bellay, saying he is writing against heresies on the virgin and the sacrament, and with a letter from Champier praising Pagnini. It was Gadagne, the financer of this work, whom Pagnini persuaded to subsidize additions to the plague hospital. His wife was a relative of Pagnini.

55. Centi, *op. cit.*, 26 n. 78, p. 46.

56. The dating of the speech: since we have started the aumône, the price of grain has already fallen, "pour certain ung evident miracle, attendu que nous sommes en May" (A iiii[v]). This sermon was presumably given at a meeting of consuls and notables (perhaps outdoors in the Franciscan courtyard, where large meetings were sometimes held) rather than formally from a church pulpit. That it was intended for oral delivery is strikingly clear from its style: frequent direct address, apostrophes, rhetorically repeated phrases, etc. The sermon is *not* disposed in the "modern" style of the later middle ages (theme, protheme, etc.). Rather Vauzelles seemed to be making gestures toward a Ciceronian disposition. Also, biblical events and personnages are applied directly and sometimes prophetically to events and persons in Lyon—a technique common in English pulpit oratory of the sixteenth century (see Miller Maclure, *The Paul's Cross Sermons* [Toronto, 1958], pp. 151, 173). The learned preamble on the etymology of place names in Lyon (A ii[r-v]) seems to be answering some etymological conjectures which Champier added to the 1530 edition of his *Rebeine* [cited above, n. 39], 4[v]–5[r]; and Vauzelles may have added it to the printed edition.

Lot's wife). To those who argued that it was impossible to support such a big expense and that the poor should now be chased out of the city, he said this was like sending Jesus from Anne to Caiaphas. Furthermore the new system would cost them less than handing out alms at their doors, especially since once the king had heard about it he would surely grant the city tax exemptions. To those who could think only of the danger of an uprising, he said they were washing their hands of the matter like Pilate. And besides, the only way to end the threat of riot was to end starvation. To his fellow humanists in the audience, he said that the new organization was even more important than their pet projects of a university and *parlement* for Lyon.[57] Not only would they clear the city streets of the clamorous poor, but they would also put themselves in mystic communion with the Church Triumphant. And finally, in words reminiscent of Erasmus' *Enchiridion*: "Charity is certainly much more agreeable to God than fasts, prayers, abstinence or austerity of life."[58]

A year later, with nothing permanent established, it was Pagnini's turn. The consulate was demoralized by the low pledge made by the church. Pagnini, who had acted as the consulate's go-between in the affair, told the consuls that "just because Messieurs the Archbishop and Canon-Counts won't give as much as last year is no reason to stop. Everyone must do his duty." Pagnini then did his, by putting his "splendid oratory"—the phrase is Champier's—to the service of the poor.[59]

This use of vernacular eloquence on behalf of welfare reform was an important contribution of the Christian humanists. Let us see how a scholastic would treat the subject. Brian Tierney has called attention to the astonishing lack of imagination with which canonists approached problems of poor relief at the end of the middle ages. "What was really needed by the fifteenth century was a kind of scholastic critique of employability in ablebodied vagrants." Instead the canonists repeated thirteenth-century arguments at three times the length.[60] In 1516, however, one nominalist theologian did say something new—the Scotsman John Major, a Conciliarist and distinguished professor at the University of

57. Vauzelles' brother Mathieu and his friend Claude Bellièvre were both working unsuccessfully to have a *parlement* established in Lyon.

58. Vauzelles, *Police subsidaire*, B iii[v]. Cf. Erasmus, *A Book Called in Latin Enchiridion Militis Christiani* . . . (London, 1905; based on the English translation: London, 1533), Chap. XIII, esp. pp. 171–172.

59. Arch. com., BB52, 57[r], 62[r], 77[v]; *Inventaire-sommaire des archives communales antérieures à 1790. Ville de Lyon*, ed. F. Rolle (Paris, 1865), CC849: Consulate presents Burgundy wine to Brother Santo for his "daily preaching on behalf of the poor and the hospitals." Champier to Tournon in Pagnini, *Isagogae*, C ii[r–v].

60. Tierney, *op. cit.* [above n. 8], pp. 116–119.

Paris.[61] He thought it would be a good idea for secular governments to provide for their impotent poor and prevent all begging. This view was buried in a traditional discussion of alms-giving in Major's "Fifteenth Distinction," Seventh, Eighth, and Ninth Questions on the Fourth Book of Peter Lombard's Sentences.[62] Few if any town councilors had read this. If the magistrates of Ypres referred to Major in their brief to the Sorbonne at the end of 1530, it was because some scholar had just told them how to impress that important body.[63] They were to be disappointed. Major himself had recently left the Sorbonne, and evidently he had been unable to convince even his fellow theologians of his point of view. The Sorbonne disapproved of that part of the Ypres' ordinances which forbade all public begging.

Vauzelles and Pagnini in contrast were trying to *persuade* as many people as they could to create a new social form. Furthermore Vauzelles helped shape the final organization. In his sermon he offered to write out a plan for it and gave right there some of its essentials, such as training and education for poor children, enforced work for healthy beggars, a central treasury, and administration by laymen.[64]

Administration by laymen. Let us stress that this is what these two humanist clerics wanted; for in Ypres the mendicant orders had objected to just this, as the Augustinian Lorenzo de Villavicenzo was to do years later.[65] In part, Vauzelles and Pagnini were simply being realistic:

61. John Durkan, "John Major: After 400 Years," *The Innes Review*, I (1950), 131–139; *idem*, "The Beginnings of Humanism in Scotland," *ibid.*, IV (1953), 5–24; J. H. Burns, "New Light on John Major," *ibid.*, V (1954), 83–97; Francis Oakley, "On the Road from Constance to 1688: The Political Thought of John Major and George Buchanan," *Journal of British Studies*, II (1962), 1–31; *idem*, "Almain and Major: Conciliar Theory on the Eve of the Reformation," *American Historical Review*, LXX (1965), 673–690.

62. *Joannis Maioris doctoris theologi in Quartum Sententiarum quaestiones . . .* (Paris: Josse Bade, 1516), lxx^v–lxxiiii^r.

63. Salter, *op. cit.* [above, n. 13], p. 62; Bonenfant, *op. cit.* [above, n. 14], 222.

64. Vauzelles, *Police subsidaire*, B iiii^v. No one has yet found any manuscripts or printed versions of Pagnini's poor-relief sermons, so it is at present impossible to know whether he played a creative role in suggesting new institutions. He had been interested in poor relief already in Florence and Avignon (Champier to Tournon, in Pagnini, *Isagogae*, C ii$^{r–v}$). The great preacher and humanist Johann Geiler attempted to persuade the Strasbourg authorities to set up a new system of poor relief in a series of sermons in 1497–1501, though the reform itself was not made until 1523 (F. Rapp, *op. cit.* [above, n. 9], and letter of November, 1966).

65. Nolf, *op. cit.* [above, n. 2], p. liv; Jimenez Salas, *op. cit.* [above, n. 16], p. 92 n. 11. M. Bataillon, "J. L. Vivès, réformateur de la bienfaisance," *Bibliothèque d'humanisme et renaissance*, XIV (1952), 151. Villavicenzo's book, written to attack Vives' *De subventione pauperum* and a later defense of welfare reform in Bruges by Gilles Wyt, was entitled *De oeconomia sacra circa pauperum curam a Christo instituto* (Antwerp: Plantin, 1564).

however much they hoped to reform clerical mores and motivation, it was obvious that they were the only clerics in Lyon taking initiative in regard to poor relief. In fact, the leaders of the church were rarely there at all. In 1534 the archbishop of Lyon was to hear only by letter from the consuls that "in his benign absence" (he had been living in Paris for many years), they had set up a new order for the poor, to which they hoped that he "as principal protector of the poor" and "guide for others" would contribute generously.[66] Nor had the Franciscans acted as a guide for others. They carried on their traditional distribution of free medicine to the poor, but they made no move to introduce in Lyon the low cost loans (or *mons pietatis*) which their Italian colleagues had championed some decades before and which a papal bill of 1515 had said were not usurious.[67]

Furthermore, Vauzelles and Pagnini shared with Erasmus and Vives a high evaluation of the Christian possibilities in the life of the laity. To the priest Vauzelles, lay administration of the Aumône was a potential avenue of true charity. "Follow the apostles," he said, "do not disdain to be the commissioners and agents for the poor." "*Soyez charitables vigilateurs,*" and you will appease the wrath of God, who has sent us of late so many scourges. Thus our city will be preserved and we will be pardoned in the celestial Jerusalem.[68]

The consuls and notables, of course, responded and the planning, worrying, and leg-work devolved on them. Among them were influential lawyers, with good laymen's memory for the long struggle which their commune had been carrying on against the jurisdictions of its medieval seigneurs, the archbishop and noble canon-counts of Saint John. Such a one was Mathieu de Vauzelles, Jean's brother and a doctor of laws from the University of Pavia. Already partially educated to the needs of the

66. Arch. Char., E4, 8^{r-v}. The lack of interest of the secular clergy in welfare reform is illustrated by the provincial council of the church at Lyon, March, 1527/28, which Vauzelles attended in an uninfluential capacity. There was a little discussion of suppressing Lutheran heresy and reforming clerical morals and education; much talk about whether to help pay for the king's ransom; and no talk about hospitals or the poor (J. M. Mansi (ed.), *Sacrorum conciliorum . . . collectio* (reprint; Graz, 1961) XXXII, cols. 1130 ff·

67. Allut, *op. cit.* [above, n. 39], p. 252; Lallemand, *op. cit.* [above, n. 27], IV, Part 2, 480 ff. Mansi, *op. cit.*, XXXII, cols. 905–907. The first mention that I have found of a "mont-de-piété" for Lyon is in 1571, and then it was the consulate, not the Franciscans, who made the proposal (Arch. com., BB89, 48^{r}–49^{v}). Nothing came of the project.

68. Vauzelles, *Police subsidaire,* C ii^{r-v}. On Erasmus' view of the laity, see James K. McConica, *English Humanists and Reformation Politics under Henry VIII and Edward VI* (Oxford, 1965), Chap. 2.

poor by his work reforming the Hôtel-Dieu, he was one of the few notables to urge prevention over repression even before the famine of 1531. Since he served the royal government in the Lyonnais as well as the consulate, Mathieu de Vauzelles later helped win approval from the "*gens du roi*" for the new jurisdictions that the Aumône-Générale required over vagabonds, poor inhabitants, and orphans.[69]

The contribution of lawyers to welfare reform was based on more than influence and judicial insight. They were also building up libraries of classical and humanist works (as were their colleagues in other French cities), giving each other copies of Erasmus' works[70] and frequenting the same literary milieu as Jean de Vauzelles. They may well have bought copies of the edition of Vives' *De subventione pauperum* that was printed in Lyon in 1532.[71]

Most of the notables whom Jean de Vauzelles and Pagnini harangued were merchants and industrial entrepreneurs, dealing in books, banking, textiles, and spices. With a few exceptions, these businessmen had had less exposure to humanist writings and ideas in the 1530s than the lawyers, or than their own sons were to have fifteen years later. What they did have was an understanding of accounting and of economic expansion that enabled them to see possibilities in the humanists' proposals that Vives and Vauzelles had not perceived. Some of these merchants came from well-established Lyonnais families. Others like Jean Broquin had made good marriages but had not yet reached the status of consul. Indeed Broquin might never have been elected to the consulate at all in December, 1533, if he had not distinguished himself as a treasurer for the temporary aumônes of 1531 and 1532.[72] And finally there were men—like the brilliant capitalist Etienne Turquet from the Piedmont[73]—who were

69. L. de Vauzelles, "Notice sur Matthieu de Vauzelles," *Revue du lyonnais*, 3rd ser., IX (1870), 504–529; V. L. Saulnier, *Maurice Scève* (Paris, 1948), I, 34. Arch. H.D., 1ʳ⁻ᵛ, 2ᵛ–3ᵛ. Arch. com., BB49, 215ᵛ (M. de Vauzelles suggests that a roll be made of the wealthy who can provide grain to town and that they be constrained to give). Arch. Char., E4, 5ᵛ–7ʳ, 12ʳ⁻ᵛ. Other lawyers from consular families, such as Jean du Peyrat, Claude Bellièvre and Eynard de Beaujeu, played important roles in forming the Aumône.

70. Auvray, *op. cit.* [above, n. 41], p. 358.

71. Published by Melchior and Gaspard Treschel, who also printed works by Champier and later Jean de Vauzelles' edition of Holbein's *Pictures of Death*.

72. Archives départementales du Rhône [cited hereinafter as Arch. dép.], Fonds Frécon, Dossiers Rouges, II, B. Arch. com., BB52, 1ʳ, 57ʳ⁻ᵛ, 149ʳ; Arch. Char., E138, 1ʳ.

73. Arch. Char., 1ʳ, 28ᵛ; E139, p. 24; E4, 1ʳ–13ᵛ. Turquet was not merely used as a contact for money-raising among Italian residents in Lyon, but was repeatedly present at the meetings to plan the Aumône-Générale in early 1534.

foreigners and even recent arrivals. Thus from the beginning the Aumône-Générale involved all the nations upon which the developing economy of the city was based.

What of the religion of these lawyers and businessmen? The large majority of them were Catholic at the time, and most remained so all their lives (indeed, only about a third of Lyon's inhabitants were committed Protestants at the height of the movement in 1560). For instance, Mathieu de Vauzelles was later to say that if his Holiness the Pope would just see to it that more ecclesiastical property was reallocated for the relief of the poor that "all these new and damnable sects would be easily . . . appeased and reduced."[74] In some cases, we can not categorize the notables according to religious belief. During the 1520s Jean Broquin had had for his stepfather a banker who was one of Lyon's earliest converts to the ideas of Guillaume Farel; years later Jean's own son was to become a Calvinist. Yet Broquin's mother remained a Catholic and he himself died in 1539, when religious lines were still fluid.[75] We know what this merchant thought about poor relief, but not about predestination.

Of the other welfare reformers of the 1530s, however, there are a few whose secret Protestant sympathies can be disclosed. Johann Kleberger of Nuremberg is a good example. He gave more money to the Aumône-Générale than any other individual in Lyon, including the archbishop. He could afford it, too, with the money he had amassed in commerce and banking. He had known Ulrich von Hutten, had his portrait painted by Dürer, corresponded with Erasmus, and quarreled with his former father-in-law, the humanist patrician Willibald Pirckheimer. He left Nuremberg for Lyon, but had the chance to see the new welfare organization that the German city had established in 1522. That his religious sentiments had finally settled in a Protestant mold is clear from his marriage in the mid-1530s to a woman who was a friend of Calvin and who had barely escaped the heretic's stake at which her first husband was burned in Paris in 1535. The Klebergers maintained their contacts with

74. *Traicte des Péages, Composé par M. Mathieu de Vauzelles docteur es droits . . .* (Lyon: Jean de Tournes, 1545), p. 105. Vauzelles used the chapter on privileges and exemptions of the clergy as an excuse for outlining a whole series of reforms for the Catholic clergy.

75. Sometime before 1522, Broquin's mother Pernette Andrevet became a widow and married the banker and merchant Antoine Du Blet (Arch. dép., Fonds Frécon, II, B). On this friend of Farel, see *Guillaume Farel, 1489–1565*, ed. Comité Farel (Neuchatel, 1930), pp. 120–129 and Henri Hours, "Procès d'hérésie contre Aimé Maigret," *Bibliothèque d'humanisme et renaissance*, XIX (1957), 16. After he died Pernette must have decided she had had enough of such dangerous men and married a respectable Catholic lawyer, Maurice Poculot.

Geneva, but Johann, who had no taste for martyrdom, had a quiet Catholic burial in Lyon when he died in 1546.[76]

Thus we have the coalition for welfare reform in the 1530s. It was not a "united front" of clearly defined parties, but a cooperative effort of men who came from different places and whose personal religious views covered some range; they wanted to declare, if not a war against poverty, then at least one against begging and starvation, and to make of their common city, in Vauzelles' words, "a vision of peace."

They did not have to start from scratch, of course. Despite important innovations, in some respects they were continuing medieval developments. For purposes of discussion, let us divide all efforts to relieve poverty into, first, the redistribution of wealth, and second, the creation of new sources of wealth and economic opportunity. The *forms* in which wealth was redistributed to the poor during the later middle ages—such as giving away food, money, clothes, and fuel; free medical service; price-fixing; and tax policies which favored the poor—all these *forms* persisted throughout the sixteenth century. New forms, such as subsidized housing,[77] were not tried except in a few local instances.

In both middle ages and the sixteenth century clerical and secular authorities had no intention of using welfare services to change the social order. Communal ownership of property—the extreme case of redistribution of wealth—was practiced only in such places as monasteries, Anabaptist communities, and experimental communities (started by the Spanish cleric Quiroga under the influence of More's *Utopia*) among the Indians in the New World.[78] Even as a way of life for the saintly,

76. Eugène Vial, "Jean Cleberger," *Revue d'histoire de Lyon*, XI (1912), 81–102, 273–308, 321–340; XII (1913), 146–154, 241–250, 364–386. N. Weiss, "Le réformateur Aimé Meigret. Le martyr Etienne de la Forge et Jean Kléberg," *Bulletin de la Société de l'histoire du protestantisme français*, XXXIX (1890), 245–269. Arch. Char. E150, p. 12. *Police de l'Aulmosne* [above, n. 32], p. 10. Kleberger had given 500 livres during the famine of 1531, and by mid-1539 about 2,300 livres more. The archbishop's contribution by that date was well below 2,000 livres. In Kleberger's will of August 25, 1546, he gave a further 4,000 livres to the Aumône (Arch. dép., 3E4494, 168ʳ).

77. The only example known to me of subsidized housing outside of hospitals is the Fuggerei, or cottages for elderly workers, built by Jacob Fugger in Augsburg. Professor Karl Helleiner has told me that individual Beguine houses could be "rented" by widows in the Netherlands in the late middle ages. Whether or not this constituted "subsidized low-cost housing" would depend on the amount of money given by the widows.

78. Woodrow Borah, "Social Welfare and Social Obligation in New Spain; A Tentative Assessment." Professor Borah has kindly sent me a copy of this talk, given at the Congress of Americanists in Seville, 1964, and eventually to appear as part of the acts of that meeting.

communal ownership had little appeal to the laymen of the busy city from which the Waldensians had departed three hundred years before. As one old-timer among the consuls said, "There are many poor now living [on Waldo's former street], but not voluntary ones as they were then." Rather than sharing poverty, the journeymen of Lyon were more likely to form *compagnonñages* to better their standard of living within the current framework of property ownership.[79]

If sixteenth-century poor laws did not spring from a new attitude toward property, their ambitious goal—to find practical means to eliminate all begging and death by starvation—did imply something new: now there are conditions of life that society should not and dare not tolerate *at all*, in Protestant Nuremberg and Norwich, in Catholic Ypres and Lyon. The suggestion is there, whether the urban welfare schemes succeeded or failed. And Vauzelles' sermon shows how this idea can be introduced into the old Catholic framework: "the poor are on the cross of adversity as much for the salvation of those who aid them charitably as for their own salvation," *but* they must not be so wretched that they fill the city with their complaints and their corpses.[80]

The other major difference between the medieval period and the sixteenth century in redistributing income to the poor is in administration. Medieval poor relief, though sometimes very generous, was even more fragmented and spotty than today's. At Lyon as elsewhere, there were random individual gifts in the streets and at doorways, handouts at funerals and other anniversaries, doles from monasteries and certain cathedral chapters, aid at hospitals (the Hôtel-Dieu was the only important one in Lyon), sporadic action by the consulate, and aid from confraternities to their poor members in times of hardship. Parish assistance seems to have died out, parochial revenues probably having been appropriated by patrons. Only at the cathedral of Saint John was a weekly dole adminis-

79. In 1492 Waldensian ministers from Italy were proselytising in rural villages near Lyon. When they came to Lyon, it was only for a pilgrimage to Waldo's neighborhood, not to preach. In any case, the inquisition of these men later in Dauphiné shows that they were no longer stressing apostolic poverty. (Peter Allix, *Some Remarks upon the Ecclesiastical History of the Ancient Churches of Piedmont* [Oxford, 1821], pp. 335–345.) There is no reference in any Lyonnais literary source of the sixteenth century to a continuing tradition of Waldensianism *in* Lyon. Rather Champier and other Catholics attack Lutheranism as a "rebirth" of that old heresy. The quote about Waldo's street comes from Barthelemy Bellièvre (*ca.* 1460–*ca.* 1529), in Claude Bellièvre, *Souvenirs de voyages . . . notes historiques . . .*, ed. Ch. Perrat (Geneva, 1956), p. 74. On *compagnonnages* in Lyon, see my article, "A Trade Union" [above, n. 43], 48–69.

80. Vauzelles, *Police subsidaire*, B ii^v, B iiii^v. Also see p. 229 above on the impossibility of true charity when the problem of poverty is too extreme.

tered, and the elasticity of its funds was limited by old foundations which read, for instance, "provide a supper every Holy Thursday to thirteen poor people, who will then go pray at my tomb." Whether the small group of poor who gathered at the cloister for their handout were in fact the most needy according to canon law—one would have liked to know— was anyone's guess.[81]

In the thirteenth and fourteenth centuries laymen in certain towns in Flanders and northern France (Louvain, Mons, Douai, Lille, Saint-Omer, Béthune, and others) had set up within each parish collection and distribution tables for the poor. However useful the work of these *Tables des Pauvres*, they did not centralize poor relief. The parishes' tables acted independently of each other, and ordinarily the *échevinage* had no supervision over them. Moreover many other forms of charitable relief, including the handout to individual beggars, existed side by side with the tables.[82]

Tables des Pauvres did not develop in Lyon or in most parts of Europe; but by the end of the middle ages, administrative initiative in redistributing income to the poor was already passing in one way or another into the hands of laymen—government bodies and lay confraternities. Newcomers to Lyon, such as the Germans, founded confraternities in the late fifteenth century, partly for mutual aid, and older lay confraternities expanded their activities. There were limits to what they could do, however, since some of the poor, such as the unskilled dayworker, had no confraternity to join. In any case the lay confraternities could not supply over-all administrative leadership for the city. For instance, the Confraternity of the Trinity with its 1,700 members was unable to administer the school it had founded in 1519, so much in demand were its services; and in 1527 it turned the school over to the consulate.[83]

Thus it was the lay government which was to build on its medieval activities—quarantining and other sanitary measures, taking care of the Rhône Bridge, provisioning the town with grain and wood, and fixing the weight or price of bread—and to gain control of all public welfare

81. J. Beyssac, *Les chanoines de l'église de Lyon* (Lyon, 1914), pp. xxii–xxv; J. Déniau, *La commune de Lyon et la guerre bourguignonne, 1417–1435* (Lyon, 1955), pp. 167–170; R. Fédou, *Les hommes de loi lyonnais à la fin du moyen age* (Paris, 1964), pp. 330–31.

82. Bonenfant, *op. cit.* [above, n. 14], 208–210; Marx, *op. cit.* [above, n. 27], pp. 49–59; Jean Imbert, "La Bourse des pauvres d'Aire-sur-la-Lys à la fin de l'Ancien régime," *Revue du Nord*, XXXIV (1952), 13–36; Leclère, *op. cit.* [above, n. 27], 149, 152–153. These tables were also known as the *Tables du Saint-Esprit*.

83. J. Gerig, "Le Collège de la Trinité à Lyon avant 1540," *Revue de la Renaissance*, IX (1909), 75–77.

services.[84] The consulate had already taken over administration of the Hôtel-Dieu from the church in the late fifteenth century, not long after Lyon's fairs had been instituted. The priest and the nuns were kept on, of course, along with the other personnel; but their activity was now supervised by the consuls. No doubt, the consulate's experience in the 1520s, in setting up new accounts for the Hôtel-Dieu and worrying over what to do about the foundlings lodged there, helped it for the more difficult problem of establishing the Aumône-Générale.[85]

Henceforth, all charitable distributions in Lyon and most charitable services were to be performed by a new government body, the Aumône-Générale, or by the hospitals run by the consulate. People could still give charitable bequests to their servants or acquaintances and might provide gifts of clothing and the like to poor men who carried their coffins.[86] Also the funds used by Lyonnais confraternities for mutual aid were not at this time deflected to the municipal charity, as Charles V had ordered in the Netherlands in 1531. (Perhaps this was due to the curious status of confraternities in Lyon in 1533. They had been declared illegal since the Rebeine, but in fact were being tolerated.)[87] However, all the various alms given out at Saint John and other churches and monasteries during

84. Deniau, op. cit., pp. 137–140. Kleinclausz (ed.), Histoire de Lyon [above, n. 17], I, 293–294.

85. M. C. Guigue, Recherches sur Notre-Dame de Lyon (Lyon, 1876), pp. 95–120. Arch. H. D., E1, 1ʳ–5ᵛ. Though the consulate had concerned itself with repair of buildings and financing the hospital, it had not undertaken an effective reform until 1524, when the records begin. In Paris, too, the town council had taken over the administration of the Hôtel-Dieu from the chapter of Notre Dame at the end of the fifteenth century. This process culminated in royal edicts of 1546 and 1561 placing all hospitals in France under the supervision of laymen (Roger Doucet, Les Institutions de la France au XVIe siècle [Paris, 1948], II, 808; Jean Imbert, "L'Eglise et l'Etat face au problème hospitalier au XVIe siècle," in Etudes du Droit Canonique dédiées à Gabriel Le Bras [Paris, 1965], pp. 576–592).

86. E.g., 1546 will of Florentine merchant-publisher Jacques de Giunta: 50 livres tournois to Aumône-Générale, dowries of 10 écus each for thirty poor girls (to be administered by orphanage program of Aumône-Générale), clothing for twelve poor men who carried torches at his funeral (Arch. dép., 3E4494, 190ʳ); 1558 will of potter Jean Chermet: 5 livres tournois to Aumône-Générale, 20 livres tournois for dowries for poor girls (to be administered by Aumône-Générale), 5 livres tournois for Hôtel-Dieu, 2 sous each to four poor men who will carry his coffin (Arch. dép., 3E5300, 153ᵛ–155ʳ).

87. Guigue, Bibliothèque [above, n. 39], p. 257; Allut, op. cit. [above, n. 39], p. 231; Bellièvre, Souvenirs [above, n. 79], pp. 122, 129–130. For the limitations on confraternities made in 1528–1529 by the provincial council of the church at Sens: Mansi, op. cit. [above, n. 66], XXXII, col. 1196. In 1539, a royal ordinance forbade confraternities of artisans throughout the kingdom; but they were still functioning in Lyon as elsewhere in 1561, when the Edict of Orléans ordered that all their goods and revenues be turned over to governmental authorities to be used for poor relief and education.

the year were now to be paid as a lump sum to the Aumône. No one was to give any handout of any kind in front of his house or in any public place (though no penalty was created for doing so), but contributions were to be given to an Aumône-Générale cannister or collector. All begging was prohibited[88] under pain of whipping and banishment.

For the first time in the history of Lyon a list was drawn up, based on house-to-house visits by officers of the Aumône, of all the poor inhabitants and the state of their need. Any sick people discovered in the survey were taken for free treatment to the Hôtel-Dieu. Fortunately, the consulate had recently enlarged its staff (François Rabelais was physician there at the time the Aumône was formed). Most of the others—the impotent and the working men unable to support their families—were issued tickets entitling them to relief. The ticket was neatly printed, with blank spaces left so that all the officers of the Aumône had to do was fill out the name, the amount, and length of time of the aid. The ticket-holders then went each Sunday morning to specified distribution centers and came up to receive their bread and money, "one by one."[89] Their numbers were constantly revised by further neighborhood visits and by hearings at which the poor could state their cases to the rectors.

These new arrangements, including the census,[90] were characteristic of sixteenth-century municipal charities. I suspect that the confiscation of ecclesiastical funds for the poor in Protestant areas would have made little difference to welfare services in those cities if it had not been accompanied by such administrative reform. The major economic advantage of

88. Arch. Char., E4, 12^{r-v}, E7, p. 391; *Police de l'Aulmosne* [above, n. 32], pp. 25–26; Boissieu, "L'aumône-générale de 1534 à 1562," p. 256. The institution of the Aumône as well as the prohibition of all begging was authorized by an ordinance of Jean du Peyrat, the king's lieutenant-general at Lyon (of a consular family), March 3, 1533/34. Town cries were made on the provisions of the Aumône, including urgent requests not to give alms in public.

89. Boissieu, "L'aumône-générale" [above, n. 16], p. 97, for the exact wording of the early "tillets." In the early years, parchment tickets were granted to families where the aid was evidently needed for a very long time, paper tickets to others (Arch. Char., E4, *passim*). Lead tokens had been used during the famine of 1531, but the personal ticket obviously made it easier to prevent abuses of the dole. Tickets were to be turned in if the recipient left town. *Police de l'Aulmosne* [above, n. 32], pp. 37–38.

90. Bonenfant, *op. cit.* [above, n. 14], p. 217. The Rouen census described in Salter, *op. cit* [above, n. 13], p. 115. The Lyon censuses have unfortunately disappeared, though J. F. Pound has found and described the Norwich census of 1570 (*op. cit.* [above, n. 18], 138). Brian Pullan does not report a census in Venice, but given some of the provisions of its poor law—that poor of the city be distributed among parishes so that each has its quota according to its wealth—it is clear that there must have been some sort of list prepared (Pullan, *op. cit.* [above, n. 21], pp. 173–174).

centralization was that aid could flow to many more people and more equitably than before, and that greater or lesser expenditures could be made in different times and places as needs changed (more results for each sou given). Vauzelles himself had an imprecise understanding of this, for in 1531 he had claimed merely that a "premeditated system" would cost no more than spontaneous handouts in the street.[91] It was especially the businessmen like Jean Broquin and Etienne Turquet who appreciated the economic superiority of the new system.

Welfare reform in sixteenth century towns thus extended accounting and measuring into an enlarged area of social life. If this had not happened, the premeditated systems would not have lasted a month. In the records of the chapter of Saint John, whose time and money had long been frozen into discrete blocks, the scanty date about charitable funds and their uses were scattered here and there. The records of the Hôtel-Dieu and Aumône-Générale reported in one place and in detail all income and expenditure. Admittedly, the accounting system was single not double entry, and in the early days there were some mistakes in addition. But many new or at least more precise measurements were made by the rectors. How much bread does a man eat in a day? Answer: a pound and a half[92] (see p. 271, Appendix I). How much bread and money is being given out at each distribution center each week? Is the number of people decreasing or increasing? Plans would be made accordingly.[93] How many people are entering, leaving, and dying at the Hôtel-Dieu each week, and who are they? The answers to these questions, compiled by 1529, provided the first systematic death records in Lyon. Then in 1534, the rectors of the Aumône-Générale asked the vicars in each parish to keep a list of everyone they buried, thus anticipating the king's ordinance to this effect by almost thirty years.[94] Their reason? They wanted to be sure that no family was collecting for deceased persons.

If all this came from the businessmen, humanist sensibilities did contribute something distinctive to the orderliness of the new system, particularly in the distribution of alms. In 1539 the *règlements* of the Aumône-Générale were printed by Sébastien Gryphius, the celebrated

91. Vauzelles, *Police subsidaire*, B iiii^v, C ii^{r-v}.

92. Arch. Char., E4, 1^v. As Ambrose Raftis, C.S.B., has pointed out to me, monastic institutions had made similar calculations in the medieval period as a basis for aid to the poor. The chapter of Saint John, however, was not making such observations in the sixteenth century.

93. Arch., Char., E4, 3^r.

94. Arch., H. D., E1, 3^v, F18. Arch. Char., E4, 14^v. On the development of parish records in France, see M. Fleury and L. Henry, *Des registres paroissiaux à l'histoire de la population* (Paris, 1956), pp. 17–21.

publisher of humanist texts. Possibly Vauzelles was the editor.[95] The work included a woodcut showing a Sunday distribution. (See illustration, op. p. 246.) There in the office of the Aumône are the poor of Lyon, in queues as orderly as any could have been in the sixteenth century. One beadle has his long stick just in case, but he does not need to use it. Only one crutch is in evidence, no gaping wounds, only tattered clothes show poverty. A few hands are reaching out, but no one is crying or throwing himself on the donors. And one by one, just as the ordinances said, the men, women, and children are receiving their bread and money from the beadles. The rectors are seated behind a table, one of them checking the register of the poor, another quietly handing money to a beadle. This picture is totally unlike Pieter Cornelisz' *Acts of Mercy* or Brueghel's *Caritas* or any of the other northern European works of art of the late fifteenth or sixteenth century that I have seen, which meant to depict only the virtue of charity. These are picturesque genre studies, with the importunate and pathetic poor clustered around busy donors out in the street or in a temple.[96] The Lyonnais distribution scene thus breaks with the traditional pattern to show the order and harmony that the humanist Vauzelles hoped would be achieved and that in part was being achieved in poor relief. It also illustrates what has been said earlier about the level of subsistence which welfare reformers hoped to guarantee: the poor of Lyon are shown as rather sturdy and not unattractive human beings.

In addition to redistributing wealth, a society can alleviate poverty by

95. The ordinances themselves came from the rectors of the Aumône. They are introduced by a review of the events of 1531, which uses the material from Vauzelles' *Police subsidaire*. There are also views expressed there on the merit of charity—"nous pouvons acquerir le celeste heritage avec un payement terrien"—with which Vauzelles would have agreed. On the other hand, the style of the introduction is different not only from the prophetic excitement of the May, 1531, sermon—a difference to be expected— but also from the calmer exposition of Vauzelles' commentaries to the Holbein *Pictures of Death*. Yet Vauzelles undoubtedly had something to do with the final form of the ordin- ances. He had wanted earlier to write on the subject, and was currently much concerned with the Hôtel-Dieu, which is also described in the *Police de l'Aulmosne*. Strongly interested in illustration—as shown by his work for the 1533 Entry and the Holbein *Pictures*—he could very well have programmed the woodcuts for the *Police de l'Aulmosne*. Finally, Vauzelles had Gryphius publish one of his Aretino translations the very next year.

96. I have looked through all entries in the Decimal Index to the Art of the Low Countries under Acts of Mercy and have especially benefited from the comments of W. McAllister Johnson of the Department of Fine Arts of the University of Toronto. E. Staley has reproduced a few late fifteenth-century Florentine woodcuts and drawings of the traditional acts of mercy (*The Guilds of Florence* [London, 1906], pp. 538, 545, 553). The crowds are somewhat less grotesque and less frantic than in the Netherlandish scenes but the donations occur as usual in the street. Even the *mons pietatis* is shown as a literal pile of money in the middle of the road.

creating new sources of wealth and economic opportunity. The sixteenth century was to give much greater stress to these techniques of treating poverty than the centuries before it. It took the accelerated technological innovations and the geographical discoveries of the fifteenth century to lead authorities to think in terms of "new sources of wealth," though they were still a good way from the insights of Francis Bacon, not to speak of "production possibility curves." In Lyon, it was the successful introduction of printing in the 1470s that made the consuls and notables finally aware of how employment and prosperity were connected with new industry. By 1528 the consulate was telling the king that without new manufactures in woolen cloth or silk, the populace would have a hard time supporting itself.[97]

Likewise with education and rehabilitation of the poor. In the medieval period, prisoners' debts had been paid, poor girls had been dowered by bequests, and poor boys apprenticed, but only a few individuals were helped each time. Free tuition in cathedral schools and other city schools provided for only those poor boys who were going toward a clerical career.[98] Lyon did not even have a municipal school until 1527, so strong had been the opposition of the archbishop and canon-counts to any limitation on their educational prerogative.[99]

With the Aumône-Générale, however, humanist views on education and training combined with economic interest to produce an important program for children.[100] Two hospitals were opened to receive poor orphans and foundlings leaving the Hôtel-Dieu at age seven. All the children, except those born out of wedlock, were legally adopted by the rectors—an unusual feature of the Aumône and one that symbolizes its aspirations. The boys were taught to read and write, and so was any poor

97. N. Rondot, *L'ancien régime de travail à Lyon* (Lyon, 1897), p. 34.

98. The 493 wills made in fourteenth-century Douai and examined by Françoise Leclère, *op. cit.* [above, n. 27], do not have any rehabilitative or educational bequests. J. A. F. Thomson has looked at this question carefully in wills of fifteenth-century London and found a shift in the direction of education and rehabilitation, but only a very slight one. Only 3.5 per cent of the wills studied had educational bequests and they were mostly for university studies in theology. This is in great contrast to the educational foundations of the later period, which W. K. Jordan has described in *Philanthropy in England, 1480–1660* (N.Y. and London, 1959). In the earlier period there were no foundations for apprenticeship, and only 10 per cent of the wills provided dowries for poor girls (J. A. F. Thomson, "Piety and Charity in Late Medieval London," *The Journal of Ecclesiastical History*, XVI [1965], 178–195).

99. Kleinclausz (ed.), *Histoire de Lyon* [above, n. 17], I, 136–137.

100. On this program, see Boissieu, "L'aumône-générale de 1534 à 1562" [above, n. 16], 209–222 and Paul Gonnet, *L'adoption lyonnais des orphelins légitimes* (Paris, 1935).

FRANGE ESVRIENTI PA
NEM TVVM: ET EGENOS
VAGOSQVE INDVC IN
DOMVM TVAM. CVM VI-
DERIS NVDVM, OPERI
EVM. *Esaiæ* LVIII.

PLATE I

Weekly Distribution of Bread and Money by the Aumône-Générale
(from *La Police de l'Aulmosne de Lyon*, 1539, Archives municipales de
Lyon, GG140).

La Police de l'Aulmoſne de Lyon.

IMPRIME´ CHEZ SEB.
GRYPHIVS,
1539.
Auec Priuilege pour deux ans : comme
il appert à la fin du liure.

PLATE II

The Emblem of the Aumône-Générale (from Archives municipales de Lyon, GG140).

girl with ability and inclination.[101] Bright orphan boys were sent free of charge to the municipal Collège de la Trinité, where they might mix with the sons of the well-to-do and learn from the humanist schoolmasters the college was attracting to Lyon.[102] If the orphanage educational program had limited itself to this, however, it would have gone no further than fellowships for the gifted Negro to attend Yale and Princeton go in solving the problem of the blacks in the slums of American cities. But it did go further. Most of the male orphans were apprenticed to artisans at the expense of the Aumône, sometimes in highly skilled trades— printing, smelting, painting, sword gilding, embroidering, and the like. An analysis of the apprenticeships of thirty-one boys in the first nine months of operation of the Aumône shows that the overwhelming majority of them were placed in trades more remunerative or skilled than those of their fathers (see Table 4). All the girls were dowered when they married, which was a way of helping their husbands get started. Before marriage though, some of them were put out as serving girls, and increasing numbers were trained to work in two industries new to Lyon.

The establishment of the silk industry was proposed in 1535 by the Piedmontese Etienne Turquet, who had been active in founding the municipal school as well as the Aumône-Générale. The town instantly financed him to the sum of 500 *écus*, and Mathieu de Vauzelles saw to it that various privileges were bestowed by the king.[103] The Aumône-

101. *Police de l'Aulmosne* [above, n. 32], pp. 19–20, 29–30; Paradin, *op. cit.* [above, n. 32], pp. 291–292: "Une Maistresse, pour les filles, laquelle leur apprent à filler, à couldre en divers ouvrages, à aucunes à lire, selon ce à quoy elle iuge leur esprit estre enclin, & propre." This is not as good an educational program as that recommended by Vives for girls. He wanted them all to be taught to read, and the talented ones to be allowed to go somewhat further (Vives, *op. cit.* [above, n. 1], p. 214). Luther's ordinance for Leisnig provided that the girls be taught to read. In Lille, whose poor-relief system was reformed in 1527, a burgher founded a school for poor children in 1544, where both the boys and girls would be taught to read and write. Lyon was backward in regard to female education, but see n. 163 below.

102. The admitting of qualified foundlings from the Hôtel-Dieu to the Collège de la Trinité had been anticipated by the Confraternity of the Trinity, when the school was turned over to the municipality in 1527. In 1529, however, the consulate was still discussing the question of free tuition at the college. (Gerig, *op. cit.* [above, n. 83], IX, 77–78, 83). Not until the Aumône-Générale provided elementary instruction for the foundlings and other orphan boys was there a real possibility of their going on to the college.

103. Turquet collected and distributed for the Aumône in its first year (Arch. Char., E139, p. 24; E144), as well as attending the planning meetings in early 1534. In August and September, 1536, Turquet and Mathieu de Vauzelles discussed the establishment of the silk industry with the consulate, and the need for special privileges and exemptions to encourage the industry (Arch. com., BB55., 193^r 194^v, 196^v).

TABLE 4

AN ANALYSIS OF THIRTY-ONE APPRENTICESHIPS OF ORPHAN BOYS BY THE AUMÔNE-GÉNÉRALE, APRIL–DECEMBER, 1534*

FATHER'S OCCUPATION	APPRENTICED TO
Seven Cases Where Child Apprenticed to More Skilled or More Remunerative Trade Than Father	
day laborer	dyer
day laborer	glover
joiner	locksmith
laboureur (well-off peasant, from Dauphiné)	dyer
packer	founder
packer	joiner
stocking maker (from Geneva)	grain merchant
Two Cases Where Child Apprenticed to Less Remunerative Trade Than Father	
baker	pinmaker
butcher	pinmaker
Three Difficult Cases to Determine	
dressmaker	weaver
weaver	pinmaker
weaver	pinmaker

INDICATIONS OF ORIGIN	APPRENTICED TO
Thirteen Cases Where Only Geographical Origin Given and Where Father Probably of Peasant Background	
Beaurepaire (Dauphiné)	beltmaker
Beaujeu (Beaujolais)	cutler
La Buissière (Dauphiné)	furrier
Chazelles (Forez)	furrier
"Saint" (near Bourg en Bresse)	glover
the Charolais	locksmith
St.-Symphorien-d'Ozon (Dauphiné)	locksmith
Bresse	mercer
Quincieux (Beaujolais)	merchant
"Champier" (Dauphiné)	playing-card maker
Bray-sur-Somme (Picardy)	servant to physician
"Meyssilniers"	shoemaker
Feurs (Forez)	weaver
Six Cases Where No Information Given About Father	
———	maker of pearls and scales
———	merchant
"povre orphelin"	nailmaker
———	pinmaker
"povre enfant"	sculptor
———	sculptor

* The data in this table is from Archives de la Charité, E4. There were also two boys adopted that year; one by a publisher, the other by a carpenter.

Générale, of which Turquet was now a rector, then rented several buildings in Lyon and paid the wages of Italian silk winders or spinners to teach their skill not only to the orphan girls, but also to girls in the quarter and especially to the daughters of families on the relief rolls.[104] Once trained, the girls worked for artisans whom Turquet and his partners had installed in Lyon. Thus Turquet rapidly increased his labor supply, and many poor girls learned a skill better paid than domestic service. A similar arrangement was made for the "cotton" manufacture (presumably fustian) introduced by another Italian who had had his hand in founding the Aumône.[105] Though no further training centers were set up, the rectors went out of their way in the next years to apprentice boys to Italian silk weavers, potters, gold-thread drawers, and faience makers who had recently come to Lyon. It would be interesting to know whether other European cities used their poor-relief systems to aid industrial expansion.

These features of the Aumône fulfilled quite well Jean de Vauzelles' prediction that "a great number of boys and girls would learn in their youth some art or skill which would keep them from becoming bums and beggars." Vauzelles had also promised in 1531 that the rogues and vagabonds would stop their mischief, because they would be forced to work or to leave town.[106] This is precisely what the Aumône-Générale tried to do. The work provided was digging ditches for the new fortification system and cleaning filth from the streets. It was often performed in chains and paid for only in food and drink. If the "rogues" were disobedient they were put for a while in a special "correction" tower maintained by the Aumône, and if they were caught begging they were whipped and run out of town.[107]

In evaluating this program and its relation to humanist assumptions, we must remember first of all that it could have been worse. In Rouen the healthy beggars worked in the shadow of a gallows, in Troyes under a strappado.[108] Moreover in the seventeenth century the tower in Lyon became a so-called hospital for permanently enclosing the healthy

104. Turquet elected rector Feb., 1535/36 (Arch. Char., E4, 209ʳ). "Le sire Estienne Turquet a Remonstré aud. Srs. quil est tous les jours apres Remonter sus la manufacture des veloux en ceste ville ce quil ne bonnement faire sans tousjours quelque petite aide de laulmosne" (E5, p. 271). Also, pp. 182, 272, 332, 368, 388, 398.

105. Boissieu, "L'aumône-générale" [above, n. 16], p. 222.

106. Vauzelles, *Police subsidaire*, B iiiiᵛ.

107. Arch. Char., E4, 6ʳ–7ʳ, 12ʳ, 124ʳ; Boissieu, 258.

108. *Documents concernant les pauvres de Rouen*, ed. G. Panel (Rouen, 1917), p. xxvi; M. Fosseyeux, "La taxe des pauvres au XVIe siècle," *Revue d'histoire de l'Eglise de France*, XX (1934), 418.

beggars—half prison, half workhouse. Feeling deepened against the vagabonds at the end of the sixteenth century partly because of the failure of
the enforced public works to transform these men.[109] But in the 1530s,
when the Lyonnais notables were deciding what to do about the healthy
beggars, they seemed as concerned about saving money as they were
about making the "rogues repent." While the "*maraulx*" were working
on the ditches, they were supported by tax money already allocated
for fortifications and not by the funds of the Aumône.[110]

Secondly, the widespread notion that the administrators of urban
charities were unable to distinguish between the professional beggar and
the temporarily unemployed worker is not borne out by the evidence.
Such a distinction was made in Paris in an ordinance of 1551; while in
1534 a thoughtful lawyer in Rouen told authorities there that it was hard
for a man accustomed to one craft to take just any job when he was
unemployed. If he could not find work in his craft, he should not for that
be considered "of evil nature and condition."[111] And consider this
example from Lyon: the beadles evict two unknown men for begging in
the streets; a relative comes to the rectors, explains that they are artisans
who want to find work in their craft. The rectors let them return as long as
they promise not to beg.[112] Also the families of temporarily unemployed
artisans and laborers seem to have been included in the Sunday distributions, so long as the rectors believed there was sufficient need (or "*pitié*," as
the records often put it) and that the aid was not disuading the men from
working.[113]

109. An interesting illustration of this is the change made by Paradin in the ordinances
of the Aumône-Générale which he reproduced in his *Histoire*. In the 1539 ordinances,
the tower is justified as follows: "Pour conserver et entretenir de poinct en poinct l'ordre
de l'aulmosne et affin que lesdictz Recteurs soyent bien et deument obeiz . . ." (p. 21). In
Paradin: "Pour la conservation de l'ordre & police de ceste aumosne tant generale, il a
esté besoing d'une coercion & terreur, pour tenir en cervelle & en bride aucuns des
povres qui sont turbulents: & refractaires, & qui ne veulent prester obeissance aux
recteurs . . ." (p. 292).

110. "Lors verrez vous plusieurs maraulx maris . . .," Vauzelles, *Police subsidaire*, C ii^r.
Arch. Char., E4, 6^r–7^r.

111. Paultré, *op. cit.* [above, n. 28], pp. 78–79; *Documents . . . de Rouen*, p. 50.

112. Arch. Char., E4, 98^r.

113. The rectors unfortunately did not record all their reasons in granting or denying
aumônes. Sometimes ill-health, pregnancy, age, or physical deficiency were recorded as
the occasion for the alms. In many cases, married women or men are granted aumônes,
sometimes for a specified period of time, with no explanation for the grant. The ordinances
under which the rectors operated nowhere specify that the family of a temporarily unemployed man is to be refused aid. They simply say "there are some poor householders
and craftsmen . . . heavily burdened with children and whose jobs are not sufficient to

Thirdly, in no place in Europe were the laws on healthy beggars and vagabonds much better. It is true that in Paris the men on the public works projects were paid token wages in addition to food; perhaps that city could afford this largesse more easily than Lyon. But the punishments meted out were more severe and public works as disagreeable.[114] Even in Spain, where sympathy for the deserving beggar was quite widespread, whipping and even the galleys threatened the hobo.[115]

Still when all allowances are made, we may ask why the humanist conscience, with its conviction that education can change character to some degree, did not envisage better rehabilitation for the healthy vagabond. A 1535 English proposal for poor relief offered essentially the same solution, even though the English humanist who drafted it clearly understood how a healthy working man might fall willy-nilly into permanent vagabondage.[116] The humanist could answer, of course, that education works best on the young: in Vauzelles' words, "once hooked by

nourish them." The rectors will decide whether they deserve help on the basis of number of children, what their wives do, and the character of their jobs (Arch. Char., E4, 1ᵛ). This certainly left the door open for aid for very poor families during slack seasons. Also the ordinances provided that the rectors especially scrutinize the rolls after Easter to remove any healthy persons who could find work in the summer (when employment opportunities increased), but they could readmit these same persons to distributions after Saint Martin's Day (Nov. 11) "si la pitié et necessité le requiert." This, too, suggests aid to the temporarily unemployed so long as job opportunities appeared slim to the rectors.

114. Paultré, *op. cit.*, pp. 62–63; G. Montaigne, "La police des paouvres de Paris," ed. E. Coyecque, *Bulletin de la société de l'histoire de Paris et de l'Ile-de-France*, XV (1888), 117.

115. Colmeira, *op. cit.* [above, n. 28], p. 603.

116. Elton, *op. cit.* [above, n. 15], 57–58. The English scheme involved a nationwide public works project, rather than urban projects, and the penalties for refusing to work or disobedience were prison and branding. The main improvement over the French urban projects was the suggestion of "reasonable wages." Vives proposed sending all healthy beggars who were not natives of the city back to their home town (whereas in Lyon they could remain as long as they did not beg and found a job or worked on the public projects). The remaining unemployed adults who were poor through their own fault (due to gambling, bad way of life, etc.) were to be given hard work and a small amount of food. They must not die of hunger, "but be constrained by frugality of food, hard labor and austerity to tame their passions." The forced work suggested by Vives went, however, beyond ditch-digging and construction to assigned work in textile shops. (*op. cit.* [above, n.1], pp. 200–204). In Geneva "mendiants qui peuvent travailler" from the countryside were sent to the city to work digging ditches for the fortifications (the chronicler Michel Roset, quoted by A. Biéler, *La pensée economique et sociale de Calvin* [Geneva, 1961], p. 156). Because this work was also used for refugees who came to Geneva and could not find work right away, the workers were treated with more consideration than in Lyon. Beggars and people living as vagabonds were not allowed in the city (*ibid.*, p. 153).

vile habits, one can not shake them."[117] The Aumône-Générale would eliminate the next generation of vagabonds; for now, it would stop the begging, and one might hope, as Sir Thomas More said of the unpleasant work of the bondsmen in Utopia, that the healthy beggars would "be tamed by the long hardship" of cleaning sewers and digging ditches.

I doubt that any of them were so tamed, but to have conceived a better program would have required *understanding* the beggars. It would have meant more than acquaintance with their picturesque customs and jargons, such as one finds in entertaining and satirical English rogue literature; would have meant going beyond even the wonderful sympathy and irony of Spain's *Lazarillo de Tormes* to a relativistic social examination which could serve as a basis for policy. This was conceivable in the sixteenth century: Bernardino de Sahagún and Alonso de Zorita tried to do it for the Aztecs. For some reason France produced less rogue literature than England, and few French authorities bothered to consider with Montaigne how hard it was to deflect beggars from behavior to which they were accustomed and which they found gratifying.[118]

We can see in retrospect that many professional beggars and vagabonds had skills of a kind (we certainly reward the skills of persuasion well enough today!); they traveled together and stayed together; they had partnerships for their "business"; they had initiation ceremonies and status ranks and "courts of miracles."[119] In other words they had ways to defend themselves against powerlessness and alienation. They were very poor, but no one was promising them a greater income from public works. In some ways they would be harder to "rehabilitate" than the isolated suspicious "unemployables" and semiemployed of our own

117. Vauzelles, *Police subsidaire*, B iiii.
118. On the English rogue literature, see Aydelotte, *op. cit.* [above, n. 30], Chap. VI. Bernardino de Sahagún, *General History of the Things of New Spain*, trans. A. J. O. Anderson and C. E. Dibble (Santa Fe, 1950–1961) and Alonso de Zorita, *The Brief and Summary Relation of the Lords of New Spain*, trans. B. Keen (New Brunswick, 1963). Zorita's account is slightly romanticized, while Sahagún's is often a verbatim account, without moral judgments, of what the Aztecs told him. The Franciscan Sahagún was interested in church policy toward the Indians, the judge Zorita in state policy.
Pantagruel plays all kinds of tricks, but he is not a beggar or vagabond like Lazarillo. Montaigne on beggars: in Book III, Chap. 13, of the *Essais*, "De l'experience."
119. See the testimony of an Italian vagabond in Rome, 1595 (Delumeau, *op. cit.* [above, n. 27] pp. 405–406) and the material from the ex-vagabond Pechon de Ruby's *La vie généreuse des mercelots, guez et boesmiens* (1596) described in Paultré, *op. cit.*, pp. 42 ff. Also see the excellent study by M. Gongora, "Vagabondage et société pastorale en Amérique latine," *Annales: Economies. Sociétés. Civilisations*, XXI (1966), 159–177.

cities, because they belonged to a subculture in which François Villon, for instance, had been glad to live.[120] Indeed, the professional beggars in Lyon thought the rectors of the Aumône were at fault, not themselves, and agreed with those who demonstrated the day that rector Jean Broquin was buried: "The poor can rejoice because now their enemy is dead. . . . The devils will take messeigneurs of the Aumône, and they've caught the first one now."[121]

Some of the deserving poor were also sorry to see begging outlawed, and were deterred from continuing to beg only by the threat of being striken from the relief rolls when they were caught. Others simply did not like to see beggars beaten and raised tumults among the bystanders against the beadles who did so.[122] None of this means, however, that the majority of the *menu peuple* in Lyon really respected the status of beggar, deserving or undeserving. For instance, the printers' journeymen said contemptuously of the men who refused to join their trade union, "They'll work for beggar's pay." And when, during one of their strikes, they were classified in a public cry as "vagabonds," who must go back to work or leave town within twenty-four hours, they appealed the cry to the king as "ignominous and scandalous."[123]

The poor eligible for the relief rolls had more important things to worry about than whether they could beg or not. They could object to the rectors when their weekly distribution was too little to help them live, but the rectors always had the last word. If they kept on protesting, they might be led off to the tower. They did not like surprise visits from rectors who wanted to make certain that the children they were collecting for were really theirs and still alive, any more than present-day relief recipients like midnight raids from welfare agents. They were not happy about being forbidden to spend money at taverns or on cards and dice if they wanted to receive their dole, any more than today's recipients are happy to sell some of their belongings to qualify for relief. Journeymen who were out on strike could never collect from the Aumône and simply

120. See, for instance, the study *Nineteen Negro Men* by Gertrude Zemon Gass and Aaron Rutledge (San Francisco, 1967), an evaluation of the retraining of unemployed men in Detroit as practical nurses, and A. B. Hollingshead and F. C. Redlich, *Social Class and Mental Illness: A Community Study* (N. Y., 1958), pp. 115 ff. Seventy-six per cent of the families in the lowest class in the Hollingshead-Redlich study were "completely isolated" from any community group. Family life was also disrupted, which meant further isolation.

121. Arch. Char., E5, pp. 407, 412.

122. *Ibid.*, p. 403.

123. Davis, "Trade Union" [above, n. 43], 62; Bibl. nat., *MSS*, Nouv. acq. fr. 8014, pp. 710–711.

depended on the "common purse" of their *compagnonnage* to tide them over. Such groups had to accept as a fact of life the unwillingness of all authorities to view higher real wages as a possible solution to poverty.[124]

When all is said and done though, the advantages of the Aumône for the poor outweighed its disappointments. During the years 1534 to 1561, at any one time slightly more than 5 per cent of the total population were receiving a weekly handout (see p. 273, Appendix II). It was not lavish, and the rectors do not seem to have made sufficient adjustment to inflation in granting monetary alms. But there was enough wheat bread for the week and enough money to buy, say, a few pounds of beef.[125] About three hundred children were being cared for at any one time at the new children's hospitals, while the rectors were supervising the treatment of many more of their "*adoptifs*" as apprentices or servants. The reorganized Hôtel-Dieu, which had eighty patients in early 1524, was able to cope

124. Arch. Char., E5, p. 296, E4, 149r, 112v–113r, 12v; Davis, "Trade Union," 64–65. Only at the end of the seventeenth century do a few mercantilist writers in England begin to advocate higher wages (Coleman, *op. cit.* [above, n. 10], 281). Richard A. Clowman and Richard M. Elman, "Poverty, Injustice and the Welfare State," *The Nation* (Feb. 28, 1966), 230–232.

125. The basic aumône for an adult male in the 1530s was a 12-pound loaf of wheat bread (thus somewhat more than the 10½ pounds that the rectors estimated a male ate each week) and 1 sou. Since the rectors further estimated in 1534 that the food other than bread necessary for an adult male would cost him 3 deniers per day, the basic aumône would not cover all food expenses for the week. During periods of unemployment, there would still be problems unless the aumône was raised. Two or three times the basic aumône was given to a man with wife and children, and the rectors at their discretion made adjustments upward and downward. See Arch. Char., E4, 1v, 9r; *Police de l'Aulmosne* [above, n. 32], pp. 23–24. There is no certain evidence of whether the basic aumône had been raised by 1561, though not long after that date a blind man and his wife were being given 6 pounds of bread and 5 sous (Arch. Char., E10, p. 565).

Here are the prices for a pound of beef paid by the Aumône Générale for several years up to the first religious war. Since most of them are special Lenten prices, they are probably slightly below the market price.

Date	Price in deniers
April, 1535	4½
March, 1539	5
April, 1549	6
March, 1550	6
March, 1561	6
December, 1561	8

The real effects of inflation are seen later in the century. In February, 1587, the consulate ordered butchers to sell beef to the Aumône at 23 deniers per pound (Arch. com., BB118, 24v–25r). Mutton prices were usually 2–3 deniers above beef.

with three or four times that many in later decades without a significant rise in the death rate.[126] These services relieved the worst pressures of poverty a little and may have diminished the incidence of certain infectious diseases. Though adult beggars continued to be a problem, the number of children in the streets was dramatically reduced. And during the astonishing drought in the Lyonnais in 1556, Lyon was not reduced to "a hospital of the famished."[127]

To accomplish this, the financing of the Aumône had to become better organized and more predictable than during the famine of 1531.[128] Pledges of weekly or monthly contributions were obtained from individual inhabitants, from the archbishop and all the religious establishments except the mendicants, and from the foreign "nations" residing in Lyon. If one did not come through with his pledge he might find himself being visited by a rector or even prosecuted.[129] By 1539, gifts of real estate and pensions had been made to the Aumône and they were to increase

126. In March, 1560, when there were about 215 sick people in the hospital, the ratio of deaths to entries was .20; in a four week period in late fall of 1560, when there were about 250 sick people in the hospital, the ratio was .38; in January, 1561, with about 330 people in the hospital the ratio was .30 (Arch. H. D. F21). Cf. the .30 ratio of deaths to entries in 1539–1540, when the total number of sick in the hospital was usually under 200 (see Table 2).

127. The persistence of adult begging, against which cries had to be made periodically throughout the century, was due to the tenacity of old behavior patterns and the inadequate police force of Lyon. The ordinances of 1539 specifically note the improvement in regard to child beggars, and they do not figure in later plaints by the rectors about begging. The 1539 ordinances also claim a disappearance of cases of "plague" since the institution of the Aumône. A description of the Paris welfare system in the 1550s does the same (*Police de l'Aulmosne*, p. 44; G. Montaigne, *op. cit.* [above, n. 114], 106). If true, these claims presumably reflect an increase in resistance to the plague due to the decrease in other disease and the decrease in famine. On the drought of 1556: Paradin, *op. cit.* [above, n. 32], p. 357. Crises in provisioning did not end, of course, but they were dealt with slightly more efficiently in the years after 1534.

128. *Police de l'Aulmosne*, p. 24–27; Boissieu, "L'aumône-générale" [above, n. 16], pp. 263–267. The changes from Arch. Char. E138 (1534–1535) to Arch. Char. E150 (1537–1539) already show the increase in sources of income. Simple administrative expenses for the Aumône were not high. Exemptions from the king kept the cost of certain necessities down. Rent to the Franciscan monastery for offices was low; a granary—grinding grain for the establishment—and a bakery on the large premises supplied the bread for the Aumône. The rectors and solicitors for the Aumône worked without pay; the beadles and school teachers had to be paid.

129. Arch. Char., E5, p. 215, E7, p. 470; *Police de l'Aulmosne* p. 35 (the clerk "sollicitera les particuliers donataires de l'aumosne, comme les nations estranges, & autres bienfacteurs, de porter & envoyer les dons promis. Et s'il est besoing, d'en contraindre quelcun par proces, sera tenu d'en advertir le Secretaire . . .").

enormously. Once the girls from Saint Catherine's had been trained to spin silk or fustian, their wages were paid to the Aumône until they were old enough to be dowered and leave the hospital. Finally, money came in from canisters all over town, from wills, from court fines, and even from lotteries, which were prohibited to relief recipients but permitted for donors.

All of the aid described above went to the poor people actually living in Lyon in 1534. But what about the many newcomers of the years that followed? And what about the hordes of poor who had descended upon Lyon at different times of year? Vauzelles assured his listeners during the 1531 famine that under the new plan "you will promptly see yourselves relieved of all the foreign poor with whom you are now so heavily burdened."[130] The Inquisitor Morin pounced on this statement. Hadn't the Bible said there was to be no distinction between Greek and Jew? Hadn't the early bishops of Lyon sent messengers all the way to Burgundy to invite the poor to come to the city for alms?[131] The mendicant orders of Ypres made similar objections and so did Friar Domingo de Soto of Salamanca in regard to urban relief experiments in Spain.[132] With cosmopolitanism a characteristic of both humanism and the economy of Lyon, we may well ask how the Aumône-Générale treated the foreigner.

And the answer is that a major purpose of the Aumône was to hold the city together "even though" to quote its ordinances, "its people be the most mixed with different nations of any in France."[133] As foreigners— non-Lyonnais and non-Frenchmen both—sat on the board of rectors, collected for the Aumône and contributed heavily to it, so foreign inhabitants were accepted on the relief rolls.[134] Even healthy beggars who were not natives could stay in the city if they stopped begging and went to work on the ditches. The distinctions made were between residents and nonresidents, and were never intentionally used to restrict the labor supply, a restriction which could have put some of the industrial entrepreneurs among the rectors and consuls out of business. Rather the policy

130. Vauzelles, *Police subsidaire*, B iiii^v.

131. Morin, *op. cit.* [above, n. 4], 65^r–66^v.

132. Nolf, *op. cit.* [above, n.2], p. 64. Jimenez Salas, *op. cit.* [above, n. 16], p. 90.

133. *Police de l'Aulmosne*, p. 44.

134. Non-French rectors of Aumône-Générale include: Etienne Turquet, Girardin Panse, Albisse d'Elbene, Andrea Cenami, Georges Obrecht. Among nonnatives of Lyon on weekly rolls: Jacques Perrier, shoemaker from Chambéry (Arch. Char., E4, 119^v), Mathieu du Boys, barber from Valence (177^v), widow Jane Mole from the Velay (55^v), a girl from Quirieu in Dauphiné (63^v); wife of Mathieu Vulpa, (E7, p. 237), an Italian name; Estienne Harestonny (p. 270), probably German; Jeanne de Sarragosse, "paovre femme espagnole" (E18).

was intended to protect the city from professional beggars and to prevent its treasury from being exhausted immediately. Thus all poor travelers, pilgrims, and hungry peasants were registered and given one and only one distribution, a so-called *passade*. If they were ill, they were treated and fed at the Hôtel-Dieu as long as necessary; otherwise they were ordered to leave.[135] Thus there were guards set up at the docks and bridges to keep out professional beggars and other poor, such as old women or widows with children, suspected of coming to Lyon only to get on the relief rolls. Over the years, however, thousands of unemployed artisans and young women from the country came to Lyon, found jobs, maybe left and returned again—all without being molested.

Finally, and much more serious, by 1539 there was a residence requirement, not for medical care, or for the orphanage, or for emergency aid, but for the weekly distributions. In the 1540s, it may have been as much as six years; by the end of the century it ranged from three to seven. With their limited finances and more primitive economy, of course, their law was less a violation of charity than the residence requirements (some almost as long as theirs) made for public relief today.[136]

Similar policies toward peasants, travelers, and newcomers are found in the many European cities in which welfare reform occurred, though the rapidity with which new residents were admitted to the rolls varied. Paris, for instance, had a residence requirement of three to four years (perhaps it had greater financial resources than Lyon); while Geneva, the city of refugees, had to set up a special *Bourse des Pauvres Étrangers* to deal immediately with new inhabitants.[137] At any rate no city had to feel that it was breaking completely with Christian precedent in helping residents

135. *Police de l'Aulmosne*, pp. 36–37. Almost all the *passades* were given in money. If we can assume that the standard *passade* was 1 sou, then approximately 4,100 people were thus aided from August 10, 1538, to June 30, 1539 (Arch. Char., E150), and about 4,450 people from March, 1550, through December, 1550 (E162). In case of an emergency, the funds for the *passades* were cut, and a few times these distributions stopped.

136. In March, 1537/38, the rectors refused to admit a widow to the rolls because she was not living in Lyon when the Aumône began (E5, 132ᵛ). This requirement was stated as such in the 1539 printed ordinances. From what can be seen of people who were later received at distributions, the requirement cannot have been stated as "being in Lyon in 1534" for very long after the printing of the ordinances in 1539. In 1588, the consulate speaks of a three-year residence requirement for "pauvres valides" (Arch. com., BB120, 198ʳ). Boissieu states that it was seven years, but does not give his source ("L'aumône-générale" [above, n. 16], p. 98).

137. G. Montaigne, "La police . . . de Paris" 111; Archives hospitalières de Genève, Kg 12; H. Grandjean, "La bourse française de Genève," *Etrennes genevoises* (1927), 46–60. See the valuable discussion of this problem in Pullan, *op. cit.* [above, n. 21], 165, 174–176.

ahead of nonresidents: the notion that "charity begins at home" had
been long incorporated into the canonists' analysis of how to allocate
scarce funds among numerous applicants.[138]

Moreover, the welfare reformers did not completely neglect the question
which Domingo de Soto posed: where are the people whom you turn back
going to go for help? Other towns would follow the example of reform
and the burden could then be shared.[139] Thus the Lyonnais had learned
from Vives and perhaps from Nuremberg and were to consult the Parisian
ordinances for suggestions.[140] Thus Vauzelles had rushed his sermon into
print in Lyon in 1531 and sent it to a Catholic friend in Toulouse, Jean
Barril, who had it printed there.[141] And thus the ordinances of the
Aumône-Générale were published in 1539 as "an exemplary work for
other cities and communities." The work must have been sought after,
because Gryphius made two impressions in the same year.[142] Indeed, can
we not discern an international movement for welfare reform in Europe

138. Tierney, *op. cit.* [above, n. 8], p. 57. Vives pointed out that civil law allowed such
preferences (*op. cit.* [above, n. 1], p. 201).

139. It is also possible that inhabitants of Lyon who had properties or seigniories in
rural areas aided them by direct contributions. W. K. Jordan has pointed out that Lon-
doners founded rural charities (*Philanthropy in England* [above, n. 98]); and Brian Pullan
has speculated that this might be the case for Venice (*op. cit.* [above, n. 21], 176). The
chapter of Saint John, with substantial properties in the Lyonnais, gave an annual
aumône in grain to the poor of various villages (Arch. dép., 10 G 113, 100^r, 256^{r-v}; 10 G
115, 55^v–56^r).

140. Arch. Char., E4, 4^v, 32^r.

141. The Lyon edition was purchased in 1535 in Montpellier by the Spaniard Fernand
Colomb (son of the explorer), which indicates something of the circulation of Vauzelles'
sermon (L. Galle, "Les livres lyonnais de la bibliothèque du Baron Pichon," *Revue du
lyonnais*, 5th ser., XXIII [1897], 431).

Irene Brown, who is working on sixteenth-century Toulouse, has kindly provided me
with information about Jean Barril. This wine merchant subsidized the publication of
several works in Toulouse in the 1530s, including a book of moral instruction for women
of high rank, dedicated to Marguerite of Navarre; a description of Catholic victories
by the Count Palatine Frederick; and an interesting report of Franciscan conversion and
education of Indians in Mexico.

Possibly Vauzelles' connection with Barril was through Marguerite. The Toulouse
title of Vauzelles' sermon is the same as in n. 3 above, with the following phrase added:
*Dirigee a honneste homme Jehan Barril marchant de Tholoze pour la communiquer aulx habitans
dicelle. Dung vray zelle* (Vauzelles' device).

142. *Police de l'Aulmosne* [above, n. 32], p. 17. There are several typographical differences between the title page of *La Police de l'aulmosne de Lyon*, which is call-number 355969
at the Bibliothèque municipale de Lyon, and *La Police de L'Aulmosne de Lyon*, which is
located in Arch. com., GG140; though a different woodcut was used, the emblem is
the same. At the request of the consuls and rectors of the Aumône, the Sénéchaussée
granted Gryphius a *privilège* for two years, Jan. 11, 1538/39.

during the decades after 1520, when Vives' book is published in several countries and translated into German, Italian, and Flemish; when the Ypres statutes are printed and translated by William Marshall into English; when the statutes of Nuremberg, Lyon, Paris, Chartres, and Bruges appear in print; when the Benedictine Juan de Medina describes the reform in Salamanca, Zamora, and Valladolid and pleads for others to follow?[143] These books influenced not only town councils but also kings. Urban models were behind the 1531 placard of Charles V for the Netherlands and behind Charles IX's order in 1566 that all French towns and parish organizations support their poor. For various reasons national legislation did not succeed in France, and most poor relief was to come for some time as it had in Lyon—from the cities.

The publication of Jean de Vauzelles' sermon also elicited a hostile reaction. Nicolas Morin, native of Blois and doctor of theology, had come to Lyon in 1529 as prior to the Dominicans. He received his title of Inquisitor in 1532, and his maiden effort in this capacity was *A Treatise of Catholic Erudition . . . confuting a pernicious little book which uses as a cover a zealous plea for alms for the poor of Lyon.*[144] Though never mentioning Vauzelles' name, Morin must have known he was the author. The sermon was printed anonymously because Vauzelles never put anything more than his device on any of his works,[145] but it had been given publicly and Morin could not have failed to hear of it.

143. Vives' editions given by Casanova and Caby, *De l'assistance* [above, n. 1], pp. 265–288; the Ypres editions in Salter, *op. cit.* [above, n. 13], pp. 32–33. The preface to the Latin edition of the Ypres ordinances says that many learned men are debating what to do about the multitude of paupers. The plan of Ypres is offered as a solution for others throughout the Christian republic (*Forma subventionis pauperum quae apud Hyperas Flandorum urbem viget, universae Reipublicae Christianae longe utilissima* [Antwerp: Martin Lempereur, 1531], v° of title page). Nuremberg editions: O. Winckelmann, "Die Armenordnungen von Nurnberg (1522) . . . ," *Archiv für Reformationsgeschichte*, X (1912–1913), 243–246. I know of no copy of the printed version of the Paris ordinances, but G. Montaigne says in the manuscript he sent to the Cardinal de Tournon that there was a printed edition (*op. cit.* [above, n. 114], 106). The Chartres project is described in a 1557 Latin work by the jurist Vincent de la Loupe (E. Armstrong, "Robert II Estienne à Paris," *Bibliothèque d'humanisme et renaissance*, XX [1958], 353). The Bruges system was defended by Gilles Wyts, *De continendis et alendis dome pauperibus* (Antwerp, 1562). Juan de Medina, abbot of Saint Vincent in Salamanca, dedicated his work to Prince Philip, with whom he had already discussed the project (*op. cit.* [above, n. 16], A ii^r–A iv^v).

144. On Morin, Arch. dép., 3 H 1, *passim*, and J. Beyssac, *Les prieurs de Notre-Dame de Confort* (Lyon, 1909), p. 43.

145. "Dung vray zelle," it appeared on the Toulouse edition. If Morin had had any doubts about the authorship of the work, he could easily have checked with the printer, Claude Nourry, whose name is on the title page and who lived across the street from the Dominican convent.

One would hardly know from Morin's 160-page Latin attack on Vauzelles' short piece that the subject was poor relief. Though evidently moved by the events of 1531, Morin in describing the temporary Aumône showed no awareness of its novelty or social significance. His mechanical use of biblical formulas—"And they gathered the people, sanctified the church, and assembled the elders"[146]—made the reality of reform dissolve into the distant past. Nor did his brief comments on the foreign poor—"we must turn our face from no one"—provide any guidance for the notables who argued for hours about whom precisely they could feed (just the inhabitants? peasants from nearby? sick strangers? anybody willing to dig ditches?).[147] Morin did not even take up Vauzelles' concrete proposals. As he said himself, "I have neither the vocation nor the talent for this kind of examination." When Pagnini came to see the consulate, it was to talk about poor relief; when Morin came, it was to tell the city it owed the convent some back rent.[148]

What bothered this correct doctor of theology about the exhortation was its "popular idiom," its freewheeling use of biblical examples, and especially its Erasmian sentiments. Morin is the closest one comes in Lyon to Noel Béda (whom he praised in the *Treatise*), to the hardcore Sorbonne opposition to Erasmus. He was undoubtedly unhappy about Pagnini, who continued to say, in the face of doubts from the august Faculty of Theology, that Greek and Hebrew letters helped in interpreting Scripture. As for the presumptuous Vauzelles, he would discredit him as an ignoramus whose ideas smacked of heresy.[149]

Thus Morin pedantically and humorlessly went through correcting Vauzelles' biblical metaphors. It was true that Vauzelles, carried away and composing in haste from his not very good memory, had called Hannah, Elkanah; had forgotten that Simeon had never been to Egypt; and then sent the work directly to the printer without checking his references (the printer did not check them either). For the sake of the alms given, said Vauzelles, "God had cured the sick, made the dumb to speak, the lame to walk," etc. No, said Morin, there was precisely one miracle.

146. Morin, *op. cit.* [above, n. 4], 26ʳ. The quote is from Joel 2 : 16.

147. *Ibid.*, 65ʳ–66ʳ. The discussion of the consuls and notables about obligation toward foreigners: Arch. com., BB49, 269ᵛ–273ᵛ; BB52, 56ᵛ–57ʳ.

148. Morin, *op. cit.* [above, n. 4], 31ᵛ; Arch. com., BB46, 76ᵛ.

149. Morin, *op. cit.*, 6ʳ ("ydiomate vulgari"), 77ʳ. Morin took his mandate to attack this book from the provisions of a recent provincial church council at Sens (6ʳ; Mansi, *op. cit.* [above, n. 66], XXXII, col. 1198). For the Sorbonne attack on Hebrew letters and on Erasmus: D'Argentré, *op. cit.* [above, n. 2], p. 34; M. Mann [Phillips], *Erasme et les débuts de la réforme française* (Paris, 1934), pp. 75–77, 118–120, 140.

Morin also took very literally Vauzelles' ironic reference to the Waldensians, but ignored his genuine criticism of Luther.[150]

But Vauzelles had erred most perniciously in talking of charity and ceremonies. "The experience [of the new order for giving] will bring you prompt faith," Vauzelles had said. Now this idea of "faith formed by charity" had been developed earlier by the Franciscans and, as Lucien Febvre has shown, was currently "familiar to many a devoted reader of Erasmus." It was to reappear in Lyon the next year in Rabelais' *Pantagruel*, printed by the same man who had put out Vauzelles' sermons. Calvin was to call the view a Sorbonnic lie, but our Morin blunders along telling Vauzelles that faith comes only from hearing the word of God.[151]

Morin returned to a more clearly traditional position when he defended ceremonies and masses for the dead against Vauzelles, who had cried, "It is to the living, to the living and not to the dead that are owed the alms which resurrect." Vauzelles surely knew he was sticking his neck out, for a provincial church council at Lyon, which he had attended a few years back, had prohibited anyone's speaking against masses for the dead. But the Christian humanist was not going to be deterred by people like Morin (who believed he was sneaking heretical frauds into a seemingly orthodox confession) any more than his great contemporary Erasmus was being deterred by Béda.[152]

Vauzelles won. He went about his business at the chapter of Saint John unmolested. And he made sarcastic remarks about the Pharisees and Jews who are always asking where a man had received his degree in theology.[153] Meantime one can imagine the fireworks between the two doctors, Pagnini and Morin, at the Dominican convent. Morin stayed on

150. Morin, *op. cit.*, 20^r, 31^v, 55^v, 22^r–23^v, 30^v, 6^v. Vauzelles' careful handling of biblical examples, with exact citations, in his 1538 commentaries on Holbein's *Pictures of Death* was probably a response to Morin's criticism. Vauzelles' quote on the Waldensians or Poor Men of Lyon, as they had been called: "Je me tais aussi dung aultre temps auquel Lyon fust par sa simplicite trop charitable: si grand aulmosnier que de celuy en redonda ung non petit reproche." (*Police subsidaire*, A iii^v). His criticism of Luther: *ibid.*, B iii^r, C i^v.

151. *Ibid.*, B iiii^v. A. J. Krailsheimer, *Rabelais and Franciscans* (Oxford, 1963), pp. 290–291; Lucien Febvre, *Le problème de l'incroyance au XVIe siècle* (Paris, 1947), pp. 303–306. Morin, *op. cit.*, 64^r–65^r.

152. Vauzelles, *Police subsidaire*, B iii^v; Morin, *op. cit.*, 38^v–55^r, 63^{r-v}. Mansi, *op. cit.* [above, n. 66], XXXII, cols. 1102, 1127.

153. I have looked through the registers of the chapter of Saint John for the years 1531, 1532, and 1533 and found no sign of trouble for Vauzelles, who held the judicial post of "chevalier." He came periodically to meetings to perform his regular duties (Arch. dép., 10 G 114, 37^r, 73^v; 10 G 115, 36^r, 57^r). His comment on theology degrees: *La Passion de Iesu Christ* [above, n. 50], p. 3.

as prior for a while longer, but in 1534, when some real heretics were being questioned, another religious had replaced him.[154]

And the Aumône-Générale won. Morin's attack had been too irrelevant to excite support. Most of the clergy appear to have been rather glad to be relieved of their responsibility. Chapters and Benedictine houses calmly made over all their old foundations for alms and grain distributions to the Aumône-Générale and agreed to pay a further speci-fied sum each week. The canon-counts turned over to the rectors the head-ache of administering the alms and stopping the begging at the great Pardon of Saint John—one of the special occasions when nonresident poor were allowed to flock into Lyon. The archbishopric was sued in 1537 for 250 *livres* arrears in its pledge, and when ordered by the seneschal to pay, it paid. Mendicants from outside Lyon got their *passade* along with other travelers and were forbidden to beg in the city. No one complained. The mendicant orders in Lyon itself got a modest yearly donation from the Aumône. Every Lent the rectors sent them gifts so they would remem-ber the charity in their sermons.[155]

By 1540 Jean de Vauzelles could rejoice at the extent to which the laity was involved in this great Christian work—from the would-be consuls who served as rectors free of charge, to the women who passed the cup in church and the master craftsmen who went door-to-door collecting; from the storekeepers who kept canisters on their counters, to the notaries recommending the Aumône to those about to draw up their wills. From some of the Catholic wills I have seen, it seems possible that Vauzelles' hope that money would be redirected from masses for the dead toward the Aumône was partially realized; possible, in other words, that the switch, which W. K. Jordan has so admirably documented, from religious uses to nonreligious uses in the philanthropy of Protestant England, occurred to some extent in Catholic Lyon, once a municipal charity existed. This is a problem that needs further study.[156]

154. Merle d'Aubigné, "La Réforme à Lyon. Procès inquisitionnel contre Baudichon de la Maisonneuve . . . ," *Bulletin de la société du protestantisme français*, XV (1866), 121.

155. Arch. Char., E4, 54^v–55^r, 59^v–60^r, 79^r, 128^r–129^v (the abbot of Ainay, a Bene-dictine establishment, agrees to the conversion of their annual grain distribution to the Aumône, provided that its officers prevent begging in the quarter), 139^v–140^r, 158^v–159^r, 174^r, 194^r, 203^r; E5, 133^r, pp. 215, 219 (the suit against the archbishopric for failure to pay its pledge after the death of Archbishop François de Rohan and while the see was being administered by the bishop of Autun, who had been granted the "régale" by François I); 121^r (two Poor Clares forbidden to beg publicly in town); p. 467 (a mendicant from Montpellier forbidden to beg in Lyon).

156. See W. K. Jordan, *Philanthropy in England* [above, n. 98]. Wilma Pugh, who is working on charitable bequests in seventeenth-century Lyon, says this is also her

What is clear is that, despite tactics which made many donations virtually obligatory, the Aumône still invited spontaneous action and innovation. A merchant opens a theater for religious drama; he agrees to give a percentage of the receipts from every performance to the Aumône. The printer Sébastien Gryphius turns over all the profits from sale of the ordinances to the Aumône. He also donates the profits from a sermon by Gregory Nazianzen on helping the poor[157] (the first edition in French of that Church Father, with whom Pirckheimer and Erasmus had been occupied a few years before). The Aumône-Générale also had an impact on the physicians. Champier suggests a system of licensing for physicians, surgeons, and apothecaries to raise the level of medical practice in Lyon.[158] Two other humanist physicians publish French translations of medical and surgical works for the benefit of journeymen in surgery and pharmacy. If such work was partly motivated by literary and professional considerations, the decade of welfare reform inspired its social dimension.[159]

Vauzelles and Pagnini had another success. The mendicant orders of Ypres had argued that impersonal giving to a governmental body would harden hearts and lead to indifference.[160] But the laity of Lyon had come to believe that the Aumône-Générale was a genuine expression of charity.

---

impression of Roman Catholic wills in the early seventeenth century. At the end of the seventeenth century, there is an increase in the foundation of masses and gifts to monastic orders (letter of June, 1966).

157. Boissieu, "L'aumône-générale de 1534 à 1562," 267. I have treated in an article in *Renaissance Quarterly*, XX (1967), 455–464. The translation and publication of the sermon by Gregory Nazianzen, a project which combines the interests of Christian humanism and welfare reform.

158. Allut, *op. cit.* [above, n. 39], p. 241. Champier made helpful suggestions about welfare reform at meetings of the notables in 1531 and 1532 (Arch. com., BB49, 216^v, 273^r), but he resigned his post on the consulate in December, 1533 (BB52, 168^v), and was not present at any of the meetings that planned the Aumône in early 1534. His bitterness about the Rebeine and a streak of xenophobia and nostalgia for Lyon's past ("mieulx vault ung escu entre les siens, que ung noble avec les estranges et differens de meurs et conditions," Allut, *op. cit.*, p. 226) may have made him unsuited for planning an organization which depended heavily on foreign participation. He was a personal friend of Pagnini, but was probably feuding with Vauzelles.

159. E.g., *La Chirurgie de Paulus Aegineta . . . Le Tout traduict de Latin–Francoys par Maistre Pierre Tolet Medecin de l'Hospital* (Lyon: Etienne Dolet, 1540): he has translated this for the necessity and use of surgeons' journeymen (p. 3). On the translations of Tolet and Jean Canape and on medical activities in the 1530s: V. L. Saulnier, "Lyon et la medecine aux temps de la renaissance," and H. Joly and J. Lacassagne, "Médecins et imprimeurs lyonnais au XVIe siècle," both in *Revue lyonnaise de médecine*, 1958. Though Rabelais did no translating of medical works, his public dissections in Lyon were part of this same teaching effort.

160. Nolf, *op. cit.* [above, n. 2], pp. 54–55.

For the Catholic layman, this was facilitated by certain Catholic features of the institution. For instance, every year at Easter there was an enormous Procession of the Poor—not of the donors, as one was to see much later in Paris in the Counter Reformation charitable confraternities, but of the recipients. All the orphans and the thousands of poor on the relief rolls, followed by the mendicant orders and the consuls and the rectors, paraded through town to Saint John's, singing and praying and carrying a great cross. The procession was intended partly to show the public where their money was going, as the ordinances said, and partly to arouse their good will. [161]

The emblem of the Aumône-Générale also reflects the attempt to infuse this governmental institution with charity. (See illustration, op. p. 247.) It appeared by 1539, when the règlements were printed, and characteristically was also placed on the very impersonal items—the canisters[162] and the printed tickets. A seated woman with three children pressed round her neck and body holds in her free hand a purse from which the money is pouring. On her head is perched a pelican which is striking its breast so that pelican children can drink its blood. The woman is, of course, a charity figure; the pelican, an old symbol both for Christ and for charity. And as natives and foreigners had worked together to form the Aumône, so its emblem amalgamates diverse artistic traditions. The seated charity with children was a pattern recently invented by Michelangelo (whom Pagnini had known in Italy), while the pelican on the head of a standing charity had first appeared in France toward the end of the fifteenth century.[163]

How would the Protestants have responded to the Aumône? To its Catholic trappings, unenthusiastically; but to its emblem they could respond freely from within their own doctrinal context. To quote one of the early clandestine proselytizers in Lyon, "charity is the mark by which

161. *Police de l'Aulmosne*, pp. 42–44. A similar procession was held by the Bureau des Pauvres at Paris (G. Montaigne, *op. cit.* [above, n. 114], 117), whereas at Orléans they were held four times a year (Fosseyeux, *op. cit.* [above, n. 108], 423).

162. These canisters can still be seen at the Musée des Hospices Civils de Lyon.

163. Guy de Tervarent, *Attributs et symboles dans l'art profane, 1450–1600* (Geneva, 1958–1959), cols. 302–303; V. G. Graham, "The Pelican as Image and Symbol," *Revue de litterature comparée*, XXXVI (1962), 235–243. Emile Mâle, *L'art religieux de la fin du Moyen Age en France* (Paris, 1925), pp. 317–322; R. Freyhan, "The Evolution of the Caritas Figure in the thirteenth and fourteenth Centuries," *Journal of the Warburg and Courtald Institute*, XI (1948), 68–86. Edgar Wind, "Charity. The Case History of a Pattern," *ibid.*, I (1937–1938), 322–325; *idem*, "Sante Pagnini and Michelangelo," *Gazette des Beaux Arts*, XXVI (1944), 211–235.

one knows the true disciples of Jesus . . . the truest witness we have of our faith."[164] And evidence shows that individual Protestants contributed to the Aumône, collected for it, served as rectors, and received relief, in the years up to the First Religious War.[165] Its basic institutions and policies were sufficiently acceptable to them that in 1562–1563, when the Huguenots were masters of the town, they were to change the Aumône-Générale very little. (The ward officers or *quarteniers*, who helped the rectors check on the needs and morals of the poor, were replaced by the *surveillants* of the consistory, but then they had to check on everybody's morals anyway).[166]

The Protestant support for the Aumône-Générale in the 1530s is not hard to explain. They were all living in the same growing city and knew its hazards. Some Protestants, such as Kleberger, had a humanist background and had assimilated humanist views about social rehabilitation even though they were convinced that there was no training or job by which one could rehabilitate oneself in God's eyes. And they liked the elimination of begging. As Pastor Viret was to say from Switzerland: ". . . though still detained by Anti-Christ and living in the disorder of the papists, [the Lyonnais] have so well provided for their poor that mendicity is abolished . . . . Perhaps God will have pity on them and next they'll chase out the really great hypocrites and loafers."[167]

Pastor Viret's words suggest once again the reasons why coalitions such as that which formed and sustained the Aumône-Générale did not grow into firm alliances to achieve reform of the church. Usually we talk about the breakup of alliances in terms of irreconcilable views on doctrine and the effects of persecution. Here we can see the failure in terms of

---

164. Letter of Claude Monier from prison to the conventicles of Lyon, 1551, in Jean Crespin, *Histoire des martyrs persecutez et mis a mort pour la verite de l'Evangile* . . . (Geneva, 1619), 205ᵛ.

165. Among numerous rectors who held office after they were committed to the Protestant cause were: the publisher Jean Frellon; the merchant-publisher Antoine Vincent; the important German banker and friend of Theodore Beza, Georges Obrecht.

166. The records and accounts of the Protestant regime are in Arch. Char., E10, E170, E171. The confiscation of confraternity funds for the sake of poor relief, begun in 1561, was concluded energetically by the Protestant regime. A hundred books of religious instruction were bought for the orphan girls of Saint Catherine's (E10, p. 508), which indicates either a new policy toward educating the girls or that the Aumône's policy had already turned in that direction after the 1539 ordinances were published. The mechanism of the orphanages was also used to apprentice novices from the monasteries (p. 453).

167. Pierre Viret, *Metamorphose chretienne, faite par dialogues* (Geneva: Jacques Brès, 1561), p. 229. For perceptive remarks on Calvinist reaction to poverty, see R. Stauffenegger, "Réforme, richesse et pauvreté," *Revue d'histoire de l'Eglise de France*, LII (1966), 52–58.

priorities and organizational energy. The early Protestant militants, the proselytizers risking their lives, never saw the Aumône-Générale as more than a short step in the right direction. There was no time for the militants to play a role of *leadership* in welfare reform, and, though they might use social indignation to rouse sentiment against the clergy (as Antoine de Marcourt did in his *Livre des Marchants* of 1533),[168] there were more urgent issues for sermons than poor relief. They were eager to build the new Jerusalem as soon as possible; whereas the more patient Protestants who helped create the Aumône-Générale wanted to ameliorate Lyon even before the Lord saw fit to release her from the papists. Thus in the early 1550s, Protestant pastors were urging the conventicles to set up a secret charity of their own,[169] at the same time that other Protestants were serving as rectors of the Aumône-Générale.

What is significant about the Aumône-Générale, however, is the extent to which it continued to remain "general" during the years when Catholics and Protestants were uncharitably burning and killing each other, or confiscating each other's property. In 1537, the rectors, most of them Catholic, included in their annual aid to prisoners five sous for "Francois' wife, who is a prisoner for heresy." In the tense months just before the First Religious War, some Protestants refused to give at all to the Aumône because there was discrimination against Huguenots at some distribution centers. Yet a rectorate half-Catholic and half-Protestant insisted that the *policy* of the Aumône was to give to people "indifferently, having regard only to whether there is need." The Calvinist regime of 1562–1563 let ten months of warfare go by before the rectors made a concerted effort to remove secret papists from its rolls. Then in the summer of 1563, only a few weeks after the clergy and the mass had been restored, Catholic contributions resumed to the Aumône, even though it was still administered by Protestant rectors.[170] The next twenty years, with Lyon Catholic again, were to see the same pattern. Some of the dwindling number of Protestants were discriminated against; others were received for distributions. Some Protestants gave nothing to the Aumône; others gave both to it or at least to the Hôtel-Dieu and to the Charity of

168. A biting and witty satire by a doctor of theology who had converted to Protestantism and left Lyon in 1530, though he was in close touch with the city in the next years. The work was printed in Neuchatel in 1533 by Pierre de Vingle, also a refugee from Lyon and the son-in-law of Nourry, the printer of Vauzelles' sermon.

169. Monier, in Crespin, *op. cit.* [above, n. 164], 205^v.

170. Arch. Char., E5, 147^r; E10, pp. 367, 398, 430, 584; E170, 1^r, E171, 6^v–7^v.

the Reformed Church.[171] This was not a pretty picture by any real standards of human solidarity, but that the principle of "indifferent" giving by the Aumône-Générale survived the religious wars at all is a tribute to the coalition which founded the Aumône. Unlike Nicolas Morin, they thought that misery was a greater danger than heresy to the life of Lyon.

I hope that the material in this paper will serve as a basis for further research on social and religious change during the sixteenth century. The context for welfare reform, it seems to me, was urban crisis, brought about by a conjuncture of older problems of poverty with population growth and economic expansion. Trouble was caused by country-dwellers and others from outside the city who poured in at times of famine or war (as Brian Pullan has shown so well for Venice), but also by the men, women, and children who lived in the city all the time. Protestant cities and Catholic cities and cities of mixed religious composition initiated rather similar reforms, usually learning from each other's efforts. Lyon is an example of a religious coalition for welfare reform dominated by Catholics. Is Nuremberg an example of welfare reform by a religious coalition dominated by Protestants? The fact that reform in poor relief cut across religious boundaries and that Protestants and Catholics worked together on it shows the extent to which it rested on values and insights common to both groups.[172] I have tried to show how the vocational experience of businessmen and lawyers and certain humanist concerns could provide these insights. And business men and lawyers are found throughout the town councils of Europe. Humanists or at least their writings have some impact

171. E.g., Claudine Perrussin, wife of a merchant draper, 100 livres tournois to poor of Reformed Church of Lyon, October, 1571; Charles Sartoris, Piedmontese merchant in Lyon, 4 *écus d'or soleil* to poor in the Reformed Church of Lyon who come from Piedmont, 1571 (Archives d'état de Genève, Notaires, Jovenon, II, 92^v–96^r, 89^r–92^v); Jean Chamarier, butcher and hotelkeeper of Lyon, 10 livres tournois to Aumône-Générale, 5 livres for building temples of Reformed Church, 1564 (Arch. dép., 3E 7185, August 28, 1564); Regnaud Chollet, master dyer, 25 livres tournois to the Aumône-Générale, 12 livres tournois 10 sous to the Bourse des pauvres françois étrangers at Geneva, 1567 (Archives d'état de Genève, Notaires, Rageau, IX, pp. 336–339).

172. In *Strasbourg and the Reform* (New Haven, 1967), Miriam Chrisman points out that the reform of welfare there in 1522 predated the arrival of Capito and Bucer. If some members of the town government were already drawn to Lutheran teachings, others were not. The initial reform of welfare grew out of earlier developments and was "not linked directly to the Reformation" (p. 277). Here too an examination of the welfare reformers might reveal a coalition.

on every European city. In addition, Protestant and Catholic religious sensibility and doctrine found their own paths to justify the elimination of begging and the establishment of centralized organizations to provide relief and rehabilitation. For the Catholics, I speculate that the path was ordinarily opened as it was in Lyon—by Christian humanists following an Erasmian program for reform.

There are certainly some differences between Catholic and Protestant welfare arrangements, if only in style, and they must be investigated systematically. But I am not at all sure that most of the differences in welfare systems can be explained by simple religious variables or will even break along religious lines. For instance, the poor laws of Catholic Lyon and Ypres prohibited all begging; those of the Elizabethan Poor Law allowed some licensed begging (Article X). Protestant Geneva insisted upon the principle of voluntary donation to welfare institutions; Catholic Lyon moved in the direction of obligation, whereas Catholic Paris instituted for a while a "*taxe des pauvres.*" Though controlled by the secular government, the Venetian relief organization used parish priests as well as laymen for its agents;[173] the Aumône-Générale of Lyon used church officials only when it was under Protestant control. What explains the vigor of private philanthropic institutions in Protestant England and Catholic Spain?

Also, I think we should remember how few attacks on welfare reform were based on its association with Protestant heresy. For every Nicolas Morin or Lorenzo Villavicenzo, there were ten Catholic towns that instituted the new order without opposition from the friars. The reservations of the Sorbonne about begging in Ypres do not seem to have been taken seriously by French authorities, and I cannot see that the Sorbonne pressed the issue in later years. Later on, French authorities resisted strongly the Council of Trent's canons on ecclesiastical supervision of hospitals, and even the French bishops would not accept them undiluted. Moreover the really meaningful criticism of welfare schemes, some of it made by the poor themselves, did not concern itself with heresy. The Dominican de Soto based his entire argument on principles of natural law and observations about the unequal distribution of wealth and poverty throughout Spain. Printers' journeymen in Lyon called the rectors incompetent to judge need fairly, not as laymen, but as friends or relatives of employers.[174]

173. Pullan, *op. cit.* [above, n. 21], p. 173.
174. Jean Imbert, "Les prescriptions hospitalières du Concile de Trente et leur diffusion en France," *Revue d'histoire de l'Eglise de France*, XLII (1956), 5–28. Archives

Finally, I would like to sum up the implications of this study for the current debate on the *engagement* of humanists in civic affairs.[175] Humanist circles in Lyon were interested in welfare reform partly for self-preservation like everybody else: like Champier, one might get his house pillaged. They were interested in it partly because they had relatives in the consulate or highly placed in the foreign community, or perhaps were on the consulate themselves. But their tastes and intellectual concerns as humanists gave them a distinctive approach to the problem of urban poverty. Their aesthetic commitment to classical ideals of beauty, order, and harmony made them the least able to tolerate the noise, disorder, and human ugliness on the city streets. Secondly, their interest in educational reform made them especially aware of what happened to children who were badly educated by their life as permanent or occasional beggars. They noticed the children and had the impulse to retrain them. And thirdly, their devotion to eloquence and its uses made them speak and write for reform. If one wanted a city without "clamorous complaint," one had to speak. If one wanted a "vision of peace," one could not be silent.

The Lyonnais, moved by love and fear, tried to make of their growing city a place where strangers might live as brothers. Erasmus had asked, "What else is a city but a great monastery?" And so a humanist said of Lyon in 1539 that since the poor had been so cared for, the city seemed "compared to past times, almost a true monastery and congregation of good brothers, though it be the most mixed with diverse nations of any people in this kingdom."[176] Erasmus' question is still being asked of us and we must find our way to that congregation of good brothers.

Nationales, X^{1a} 4911, 78^r. The attitude of the French church toward urban welfare schemes is suggested by its *cahier* at the Estates of 1560. The church accepts these projects, but requests that its contributions be voluntary not obligatory.

175. See, for instance, Jerrold E. Seigel, "Civic Humanism or Ciceronian Rhetoric? The Culture of Petrarch and Bruni," *Past and Present*, 34 (July, 1966), 3–48; and Hans Baron, "Leonardo Bruni: 'Professional Rhetorician' or 'Civic Humanist,'" *ibid.*, 36 (April, 1967), 21–37.

176. Erasmus, *Enchiridion*, p. 34. *Police de l'aulmosne*, p. 44, Vauzelles had used a similar image in the *Police subsidaire*—"vray cloistre de vertu" (B iiii^r).

APPENDIX I

BREAD AND ITS COST FOR THE POOR IN LYON

In 1534 the rectors of the Aumône-Générale discussed the daily diet of an adult male, and decided that it was sufficient for him to have one and a half pounds of bread plus 3 *deniers* for the rest of his food (Arch. Char., E4, 1*v*). Estimates of bread consumption in other centuries of the *Ancien Régime* have varied. M. Labrousse, for instance, has shown that from two to two and a half pounds were required in the adult diet in the mid-eighteenth century, while Pierre Goubert has wondered whether in the less pros-perous seventeenth century peasants did not consume even more than this each day.[1] G. Rudé has argued that on the eve of the French Revolution in the families of working people there was consumed an average of one pound of bread per person. A four-pound loaf would do for a husband, wife, and two children.[2]

Since the estimate of the Lyonnais rectors comes from men close to the scene who were trying to make possible a diet which would eliminate starvation and the need for begging, I think we must take their judgment seriously. Possibly the price of meat relative to bread was lower in the sixteenth century than in the seventeenth and this accounts for the difference.

In 1520, during a period of slightly below normal supply of grain, a two-pound loaf of white wheaten bread (*miche*) cost 7 deniers, whereas *pain farain* (a mixture of wheat flour and groats and husks left over from grinding wheat), which the poor ate, cost 5 deniers.[3] A week's supply of cheap bread—that is, ten and a half pounds—would cost 2 sous 2 deniers. The usual daily wage of an unskilled worker in the 1520s was 3 sous, though it might be less. This calculation does not, of course, take into account what the *gagne-denier* had to spend on bread for his wife and children. There must have been considerable strain, for around 1520 a third kind of bread was baked and illegally sold in Lyon by artisans with

1. Pierre Goubert, "The French Peasantry of the Seventeenth Century: A Regional Example," *Past and Present*, 10 (Nov., 1956), 66. The Lyonnais livre seems to have been a little lighter than the livre in Paris and northern France. This widens the difference between the estimates.

2. G. E. Rudé, "Prices, Wages and Popular Movements in Paris during the French Revolution," *Economic History Review*, 2nd ser., VI (1954), 248 n. 4.

3. Arch. com., BB39, 61ʳ.

ovens—a *gros pain* made of rye with its bran and the groats and husks left over from grinding wheat flour.[4]

This estimate for 1520 is in the same range as the much more thoroughly substantiated one made by Belgian scholars for the purchasing power of workers' salaries in Belgium in the early sixteenth century. The daily wages of a Belgian mason's journeyman in the summer would buy him about thirteen pounds of wheaten bread and twenty-five pounds of rye bread.[5] The daily wages of the *gagne-denier* in Lyon (somewhat less, presumably, than those of a mason's journeyman) would purchase fourteen pounds of the inferior wheat bread which was eaten by the poor in Lyon in 1520.

The actual amount of a poor man's budget devoted to bread depended on whether or not he was given a food-salary as well as money wages. Unskilled day laborers did not usually receive meals, whereas printers' journeymen did. This whole problem for Lyon needs further study.

In any case the fluctuations in the price of bread are suggested by the following figures for the price of grain.[6] The average price of grain in Lyon in years of normal supply and before the effects of inflation had been felt was 10 sous the *bichet*, a measure of about twenty-eight dry quarts or almost a bushel.

Date	Price in sous per bichet
1504	26–27
May, 1520	15
April, 1529	25
May 2, 1531	34
May 7, 1531	40
mid-May, 1531	55–60
June, 1546	5–6

4. *Ibid.* Paradin, *op. cit.* [above, n. 32], pp. 317–318.

5. Verlinden *et al.*, *op. cit.* [above, n. 24], 196.

6. Allut, *op. cit.* [above, n. 39], p. 353; Hauser, "Rebeine" [above, n. 39], 266–267; Arch. com., BB39, May, 1520; BB49, 268ʳ, 269ʳ, 270ᵛ; *Police de l'Aulmosne*, p. 7; A. Sachet, *Le Grand Jubilé séculaire de Saint-Jean-de-Lyon* (Lyon, 1886), p. 114.

APPENDIX II

NUMBERS OF PEOPLE RECEIVING DISTRIBUTIONS FROM THE AUMÔNE-GÉNÉRALE

The distribution rolls of the Aumône-Générale have unfortunately disappeared, as have the censuses of the poor and their needs. Records of families or individuals asking to be *added* to the rolls have been preserved in the minutes of the Sunday meetings of the rectors, but for certain periods (such as the last half of 1551, Arch. Char., E7) even this data was not given in the scanty minutes. Thus to estimate the number of inhabitants given distributions by the Aumône, we must fall back upon the weekly accounts of how much bread and how much money was given at the five distribution points. We also have guesses from witnesses in 1534 and 1558 of how many poor people "*tant grands que petitz*" (E4, 79r) marched in the annual *Procession des Pauvres*—3,000 in 1534 and more than 4,000 in 1559.[1]

From the accounts of the weekly distributions, we can at least see some trends. The weekly average of distribution to inhabitants in May, 1534, 1550, and 1561 is given in Table 5.

TABLE 5

WEEKLY AVERAGE FOR	LOAVES OF BREAD	MONEY £ s. d.
May, 1534	765	37 4 1
May, 1550	605	37 11
May, 1561	503½	55 15 6

In evaluating the amounts of the 1561 distributions, we should remember that the Charity of the Reformed Church of Lyon had been set up recently and was helping perhaps 100 to 200 families. Even allowing for this, however, it is clear that the Aumône-Générale was unable to keep pace with the population increase in Lyon in those years (roughly from 45,000 to 65,000), and that the increased stress on aid in money, whatever freedom of choice it gave the poor, did not keep pace with inflation.

In trying to extrapolate from these accounts how many people were helped—men, women, and children—we face several problems. The

1. Arch. Char., E4, 79ʳ; *La chronique lyonnais de Jean Guéraud, 1536–1562*, ed. J. Tricou (Lyon, 1929), p. 113.

273

basic aumône in the 1530s for an adult male was one twelve-pound loaf of bread and one sou. Heads of families and widows with children received in theory two or three times this much. There is no *certain* evidence that the basic aumône had been increased in 1561, despite the lower purchasing power of the sou. In fact throughout these years the rectors used their discretion in fixing the amount of aid, with a lone widow, for instance, receiving only half a loaf per week; or an old man receiving aid only in money because he could not chew bread; or a family *without* children receiving as much as 5 sous per week, or a family with seven children receiving as little as one loaf of bread and one sou. Despite all the variation in practice, it is worthwhile trying to estimate the number of inhabitants helped, if only to find the order of magnitude. Thus I am assuming that an average aumône for four people per week was one twelve-pound loaf of bread and one sou. We then arrive at the picture illustrated in Table 6.

TABLE 6

WEEKLY AVERAGE FOR	BREAD MULTIPLIED BY 4	SOUS MULTIPLIED BY 4	PEOPLE HELPED PER WEEK	ESTIMATED % OF TOTAL POPULATION
May, 1534	3060	2976	3018	7
May, 1550	2419	3004	2712	5
Mar.–Dec., 1550	2290	2965	2628	5
May, 1561	2014	4462	3238	5
Jan.–Dec., 1561	1931	4167	3049	5

On the basis of Table 6 we can say very roughly that slightly more than 5 per cent of the inhabitants were being helped by the Aumône at any one time. Since many people were aided for only a few months in the year, the percentage of the population helped at all during one year was, of course, higher.

How does this compare with poor relief in other cities? J. F. Pound tells us that Norwich in the 1570s had about 13,200 Englishmen and about 6,000 foreigners (19,200 people in all) and that approximately 5 per cent of the English population and 3.5 per cent of the total population were "permanent pensioners." [2] The town of Exeter, according to Wallace MacCaffrey's study, had about 7,687 people in the 1570s, with 160 individuals receiving help outside of almhouses in 1564–1565. [3]

2. Pound, *op. cit.* [above, n. 18], 144.
3. Wallace T. MacCaffrey, *Exeter, 1540–1640* (Cambridge, Mass., 1958) pp. 12, 113.

If we assume that 110 of these people had spouses and an average of two children (Pound's average for Norwich), we find that 5 per cent of the population was being aided there. Much comparative study needs to be done on this problem, but these estimates suggest the order of magnitude of assistance given by urban welfare organizations apart from hospitals, workhouses (or public works), and orphan training programs. Given the financial resources of sixteenth-century towns, 5 per cent is not a figure to be ashamed of.

I conclude with Table 7, which shows the details from Archives de la Charité, E138, 139, 162, 170, on distributions to inhabitants at the five distribution points in Lyon.

TABLE 7

DISTRIBUTION OF AID TO INHABITANTS BY DISTRIBUTION CENTER

CENTER	May–July, 1531 (TEMPORARY)	May, 1534 (4 WEEKS)		May, 1550 (4 WEEKS)	
	People Daily	Bread*	Money† £ s. d.	Bread	Money £ s. d.
Franciscan convent	1300–1500	1,146	53 4	990	80 15
Dominican convent	1100–1200	476	23 15	270	16 8
Carmelite convent	550	400	18	309	14 14
Church of Saint George	500	512	27 10	260	20 17
La Chanal Hospital	500–700	526	26 7 3	590	17 10
Totals	3950–4450	3,060	148 16 3	2,419	150 4

* Each bread represents a loaf of twelve pounds.
† All money is in *livres tournois*.

Mar.–Dec., 1550 (44 WEEKS)		May, 1561 (4 WEEKS)		Jan.–Dec., 1562 (52 WEEKS)	
Bread	Money £ s. d.	Bread	Money £ s. d.	Bread	Money £ s. d.
9,523	784 4 6	457	57 11	5,473	786 6
2,905	197 11	404	32 8	5,229½	436 17
3,267	196 12	520	67 13	6,504	636 18
2,813	248 8 11	331	36 13	4,189½	468 18
6,680	204 5	1,302	28 17	3,441	359 19
25,188	1,631 1 5	2,014	223 2	25,107	2,708 18